What Does Theology Do, Actually?

Matthew Ryan Robinson | Inja Inderst (Eds.)

What Does Theology Do, Actually?

Observing Theology and the Transcultural

Foreword by Grace Davie

EVANGELISCHE VERLAGSANSTALT
Leipzig

The editors wish to thank the following partners for their generous support:
The Evangelische Kirche in Deutschland
The Evangelische Kirche im Rheinland
The Ökumenisches Institut at the University of Bonn

Bibliographic Information published by the Deutsche Nationalbibliothek
The Deutsche Nationalbibliothek lists this publication in the Deutsche Nationalbibliographie; detailed bibliographic data are available on the Internet at http://dnb.dnb.de

Printed in Germany

This book is printed on aging resistant paper.

Cover: Zacharias Bähring, Leipzig
Cover Photographs: © Matthew Ryan Robinson and Andrew DeCort
Typesetting: Matthew Ryan Robinson and Inja Inderst, Bonn
Printing and binding: Hubert & Co., Göttingen

ISBN 978-3-374-06634-6 // eISBN (PDF) 978-3-374-06635-3
www.eva-leipzig.de

Note on the Cover Photographs

The cover of this book features four photographs. Positioned under the title, being the statement of the question, "What does theology do, actually?", the photographs might be seen as providing four possible answers:

Stack of Books. The first photograph is placed to meet stereotypical expectations. Theologians read and write books.

Worshippers in Mombasa, Kenya. The second photograph also meets expectations, but broadens them, drawing the imagination beyond the written word to the operations of theo-logics in religious life.

Martin Luther, Protester. The third photograph is of the statue of Martin Luther standing before the Memorial Church of the Protestation in Speyer, Germany, commemorating, not theology per se but certainly something that theology "did": The Reformation, however one marks its theological origins, gained its name from the political-theological protestation filed by six regional princes and the delegates of fourteen free imperial cities in 1529 against the emperor's silencing of Luther.

Covenant of the Neighbor Love Movement. The fourth photograph documents a social movement in Ethiopia that seeks to draw Christians, Muslims, Jews, and non-religious persons together around shared commitments to love neighbors. Over 1.000.000 people have signed the covenant.

The *What Does Theology Do, Actually?* Project

The *What Does Theology Do, Actually?* project aims not to do theology, but to observe what theologies do, around the world today, in and for the communities in which they circulate and hold meaning. How is theology understood and practiced as a semantics of global society? What kinds of problems do theologies solve and how? These questions are pursued, moreover, with specific attention given to the "transcultural". Much might be learned both about the role of Christian religion in public life and about evolving trends in theological understanding or praxis by examining comparatively the ways Christian communities encode transcultural experiences of irritation coming from the social environment (for example, climate change, protest movements, digitalization, mass migration, or global pandemics) into their self-understanding (for example, in engagement with received tradition) and self-formation (for example, in liturgy and community ethics).

This requires theoretical open mindedness and methodological agility. The project therefore follows a two-step logic. First, the project seeks to observe theological work as itself a set of social discourses or objects contingently particular to certain contexts. A focus on answering the question "What *is* theology?" privileges those who already possess the resources and power to shape what counts as being "really" theology or not. By contrast, the descriptive approach preferred by the question "What does theology do?" objectifies "theologies" as a kind of social artifact and recognizes a variety of reflected religious communications as communicating theology. Second, in this way, the project aims to disrupt dominant paradigms in academic theological research, to expand the category of theological work(s) beyond textual formats and classroom or conference situations to include a variety of spaces, symbols, practices, and artifacts that function as transmitters of reflected religious communications, and to contribute to work diversifying theological methodologies to include empirical, qualitative, and quantitative research methods.

The *What Does Theology Do, Actually?* project consists of symposia and a limited book series. An international community of theologians, sociologists, anthropologists, philosophers, scholars of religion, and practitioners, from widely differing contexts, and at all career stages are invited to disruptive dialogue with one another in the context of symposia devoted to comparative study of theological production and communication systems. The inaugural symposium called into question such basic issues as what a context is, what counts as a theological work, and what publics theologies inevitably address and how. It addressed these questions with Protestant, Pentecostal, and Roman Catholic theological interventions from Ethiopia, Nigeria, the Philippines, Argentina, Hong Kong, the USA, and Germany. Subsequent symposia and volumes in the series will continue to apply this same approach, each with a focus on a theological sub-discipline or external humanities perspective

Contents

Part 2 Which Cultures? Whose Contextuality? Determining Theological Locations

Part 3 Theology as a Social Artifact

Part 4 How Public is Theology? How is Theology Public?

Acknowledgements

This book does not represent one person's point of view, one Christian tradition's self-understanding, one historical and geographical location or just "one" of anything else. The book takes as both its method and topic a focus on the complex "inter-"s and "trans-"s that condition and construct theological research and communication today. Accordingly, behind the book's diverse contributions and group of contributing authors stand many open-ended and dynamically evolving relationships – personal, collegial, and institutional. Not only is it a product of its several contributing authors, but their authorship was in turn made possible by their own numerous personal, collegial, and institutional networks. Friends, partners, and families; colleagues, advisors, and supervisors; study programs, church communities, and travel and exchange relationships. These influences, forms of support, and, above all, the people who animate them, span multiple generations, cultures around the world, and religious and educational systems, not to mention a variety of material and embodied expressions. Collectively, and contingently, they have interrelated in a unique way to produce this particular book. And so, before turning to those complicated "inter-"s and "trans-"s of theological research and communication in the chapters that follow, I would like to thank the following persons and groups, each of whom have in various ways made indispensable contributions to the book you now hold in your hands.

I want to thank the Argelander Starter-kit PostDoc program for its generous support. This support came through the use of funds from a starter grant for the "What Does Theology Do, Actually?" symposium, out of which the present book was generated. Just as significant, however, was the opportunity this program provided to use the Old Observatory at the University of Bonn, at no charge, as a conference facility. The efforts of the first symposium reached published form thanks to the generous support of the Evangelische Kirche im Rheinland, the Evangelische Kirche in Deutschland, and the Ökumensiches Institut of the Protestant Theological Faculty in Bonn. I would also like to thank my faculty mentors, Cornelia Richter and Eberhard Hauschildt, for their unqualified encouragement and, no less, critical feedback. The kind of trust in and freedom for early career researchers that they cultivate is as important as it is rare. I will aim to honor this by acting in like manner; they set the bar high. Colleagues at the postdoctoral and doctoral level have likewise provided ever reliable and enthusiastic assistance with organization, proof-reading, and, not least, active participation. Thanks are due, in particular, to Katharina Opalka, Ann-Katrin Armbruster, and Daniel Rossa.

Saskia Held probably did not know what she was signing up for when she agreed to work with me as a research assistant during my time in the Argelander program. But she proved unassailable in response to every request: from proof-reading to indexing to conference planning to graphic design. The "What Does Theology Do, Actually?" symposium would not have come to pass, nor would the "What Does Theology Do, Actually?" project have come to life, without her creative and persistent help.

The "What Does Theology Do, Actually?" book itself is a product of the impeccable and tireless work of my co-editor, Inja Inderst. Inja always asked the right questions at the right time and gave fastidious attention to every detail, both in content and in form. My assessment of the project and framing for future efforts owe much to conversations with Inja.

Bonn, Easter 2020 Matthew Ryan Robinson

Foreword

Grace Davie (Exeter, UK)

I was introduced to the *What Does Theology Do, Actually?* project in February 2019, when Matthew Robinson contacted me about a forthcoming conference in Bonn. Might I be interested in participating as a speaker? I was not able to accept this invitation, but I was able to meet with Matthew at a conference convened by the European Society for Intercultural Theology and Interreligious Studies that took place in Sarajevo in April 2019. Both the meeting itself and the location were significant in terms of the thinking about theology that Matthew and his colleagues were keen to encourage.

I was at the Sarajevo conference as a plenary speaker, invited to introduce some of my own work on the place of religion in the understanding of Europe, both past and present, and more recently on my role in co-leading a team responsible for the chapter on religion in a multidisciplinary project entitled the International Panel on Social Progress (IPSP).[1] In talking with Matthew it became clear that our interests overlapped. The IPSP was first and foremost a social scientific endeavour, bringing together scholars from many disciplines with a view to presenting their findings to a wide variety of audiences both inside and outside the academy. Its participants had, however, to overcome their reluctance to take religion seriously, and to appreciate that researchers and policy makers whose goal is the pursuit of social progress "will benefit from careful attention to the power of religious ideas to motivate, of religious practices to shape ways of life, of religious communities to mobilize and extend the reach of social change, and of religious leaders and symbols to legitimate calls to action."[2] Theologians have a reciprocal duty and must learn to understand the situations in which they operate. No wisdom, however rarefied, exists in a vacuum, with the effect that careful attention to context is as central to theological endeavour as it is to sociological understanding.

Scholars on both sides of this disciplinary divide find themselves challenged, not least in Europe, a situation accounted for by the development of

[1] See https://www.ipsp.org for more details about the IPSP project and the publications emerging from it.

[2] Grace Davie and Nancy Ammerman, "Religions and social progress: Critical assessments and creative partnerships," in *Rethinking Society for the 21st Century: Report of the International Panel on Social Progress, Volume 3: Transformations in Values, Norms, Cultures* (Cambridge: Cambridger University Press, 2018), 641-76, here 643.

social science in the European context. Modern social-scientific thinking finds its roots in post-Enlightenment France, an intellectual milieu that saw rationality and empirical observation as the ultimate sources of knowledge. Both were underpinned by a self-consciously secular perspective, which displaced – necessarily – forms of authority which were not grounded in human reason. As a result, theological absolutism fell victim to an increasingly assertive and firmly rationalist universe. To a considerable extent, theologians reacted in similar vein, deeming any collusion with – or sensitivity to – social science to be necessarily corrupting of theology.

Clearly the stand-off took different forms in different places. In France, the dominance of secular thinking is a question of principle and has entered the public domain in the form of *laïcité* – a word impossible to translate into English since there is little in the British context that can be defined as *laïque*. In Britain, an emphasis on pragmatism and very different arrangements of church and state have engendered a rather different situation allowing for more give and take on each side. The Scottish Enlightenment, moreover, is very different from the French. Other European countries are different again and can be analysed accordingly.

As Matthew and I contemplated the situation in Sarajevo, the idea that either religion as such, or theological reflection about this, could be separated from the context in which it emerged – either past or present – was hardly credible. Religion has both formed and been formed by the history of the Balkans up to and including the present day; it is, moreover, closely linked with both ethnicity and nationalism but not coterminous with either. And as we learnt at the conference of which we were part, the consequences of these inter-relationships have at times been tragic beyond belief, but not always. Put differently: To assert that religion per se is, or is not, a source of conflict isn't helpful. It is more constructive to analyse systematically the precise circumstances in which religion is likely to be drawn into a conflict situation, recognizing that this very often compounds the problem. This, interestingly, was exactly what we argued in the IPSP chapter, which was equally concerned to stress (and to illustrate) the peace-making potential of faith leaders and faith communities, as indeed were many speakers and practitioners at the conference. Interreligious dialogue has practical outcomes at every level of society, not least that of "street-level ecumenism", by which we mean the capacities of ordinary people to get along together despite their differences.

Similar synergies are amply expressed in the chapters that follow – simply a glance at the Contents list make this point clear. The first two sections are explicitly oriented towards context, recognizing that communities and the societies of which they are part are not only different from each other, but evolve, adapt and adjust. Theology – or rather theologies – must take these developments seriously. A second theme can also be discerned: that of partners or co-workers in the theological task. If theology is to resonate effectively with the situation under review, it must find ways to link itself to the reality in which it is located. This will be done by means of what the IPSP chapter team termed "well-judged" partnerships, arguing that religious organizations of all kinds are likely to be considerably more effective in their contributions to the common good if they work alongside others, sharing the tasks – and indeed the motivating vision – whenever possible. Seeking, finding and deploying co-workers in the theological task should be seen in this light. Above all it requires imagination, beginning with the question embedded in the title of this book: *What Does Theology Do, Actually?* A string of further questions follows. Who is responsible for the theological task? Where are they working and with whom? To what extent is their work changing and for what reasons? How do they relate to each other and to the disciplines, institutions and societies of which they are part? And how do they react when the unthinkable happens?

The last question is on all our lips as I write this Foreword in the spring of 2020, self-isolating against COVID-19 in south-west England and thinking of colleagues in different parts of the world doing the same. How is theology to play its part in making sense of a global pandemic and with whom will theologians work in order to do this more adequately? A close reading of these chapters is an excellent place to start, as we think about this challenge. I recommend them very warmly.

Exeter, April 2020 Grace Davie

Introduction

"What Does Theology Do?" as a Transcultural Research Perspective: A "Model of" a "Model for" Theological Research

Matthew Ryan Robinson (Bonn, Germany)

I. Introduction

"You mean I was supposed to be doing something this whole time?" So quipped a friend on social media, picking up on a humorous echo in the question, "What does theology do, actually?", namely: that theology does not do anything. I quote that friend in particular, however, not for the wry humor, but because he embodies certain tensions strung throughout theological work, whatever it is or does. He is an American married to a German, has lived in North America, Europe and Southeast Asia, and currently resides in that most inter- and transcultural of cities, New York. He has a Ph.D. in theology from an elite North American university, with a dissertation on Augustine's understanding of divine love. He then did not fail to find a tenure track job, but that is because he did not want or look for one. He is also about as down-to-earth a person as I have known, utterly unimpressed with himself, and is currently realizing the vocation he has long cultivated, namely, of becoming a pastor. As such he embodies – embraces, actually – tensions between the local and the global, the inter- and trans-cultural, between church, state, and science, between research and practice, between the ancient and the modern, and between exegetical-, historical-, practical-, and systematic-theological approaches themselves. Friend, whether from near or afar, you have long modeled for me, in the best way, the kinds of things theology does.

Now is a good time to re-attend to Christian theological work in all of this multi-faceted conditionedness, a good time to question self-evident understandings of this work as observations on or thinking about Christian life, social evolution, geo-politics, and the unfolding of historical events as those things pertain to Christianity. One way of doing so is to expand the conversation and to pose questions from non-theological perspectives on history, science and society – for example, from the disciplines of religious studies, sociology, political science, economics, or history – to theological work itself. To make theology into an object and place it under the microscope. It may seem laughable to propose such an immense cloud of issues as a "topic" or "subject matter". I admit that it does sound slightly ridiculous even to me! And yet, people like my friend perform this interconnection in their very person on a daily basis, indeed, amazingly effectively. At the same time, the number of professional academic theologians who enjoy the luxury of the time and institutional support needed for hold all of these things distinct from one another is vanishingly small. Put another way, the vast majority of people engaged in theological reflection and communication of one kind or another around the world today find themselves doing the messy kind that tries, like all theology, to work on issues of ultimacy for a particular context, but where that context is a tangled mess of histories and biological and natural-environmental conditions rendered by globe-spanning functional social systems of politics, science, economy, religion instead of the neatly differentiated setting of a conference, a seminar, or a worship service.

How all of these things hang together in theological study and work is the subject matter of what was once called "theological encyclopedia".[1] I want to suggest that something like a renewed attention to questions of theological encyclopedia, but guided by more transdisciplinary and globally-attuned interests in the complex ways in which religious life, social evolution, geopolitics, and the unfolding of historical events interrelate with each other and structure theological work, is necessary today. This book, the symposium out of which it formed, and the project of which it is a part aim to contribute in a small way to efforts devoted, not to *doing* theology *per se* but to understanding better what theology - around the world and in its complex interactivity with nature, history, science, and society - *does*.

---

1 "Encyclopedia" stems etymologically from the Greek *ἐγκύκλιος παιδεία* (en+kyklos+paideia); "theological encyclopedia" refers, broadly, to everything that falls into the "circle of theological education". How work on theological encyclopedia is presented and where the emphasis is placed have varied significantly over the centuries: from Thomas Aquinas's efforts to give a comprehensive presentation of theological methods and knowledge in the form of a *Summa*, to Philipp Melanchthon's and John Calvin's confession-based systems of doctrine, to the Pietists' emphasis on practice, ethics, and service of the kingdom of God. In the nineteenth-century, with the formation of the modern university a university-based interest in theological encyclopedia and methodology committed to the application of modern scientific methods to theological topics became a standard feature of theological study and scholarship. The term has fallen out of use to a significant extent, and method itself receives much less attention as a question for theology generally than it once did, probably in significant part due to the differentiation and multiplication of theological subdisciplines. Although the term is used to refer to theological study and work in its entirety, it nevertheless has a Western, Latin-Church provenance and has been rather limited in its scope to theological knowledge and theological education models in the West. See for example, Gert Hummel, "Enzyklopädie, theologische," *Theologische Realenzyklopädie*, ed. by Horst Robert Balz et al, vol. 9, *Dionysius Exiguus - Episkopalismus* (Berlin andNew York: De Gruyter, 1982), 716-742. Future work on the interconnections of Christian theological work with comprehensive interests remains important; it will just need to take into consideration the globe-encircling and multi-directional nature of theological communications.

This introduction is complemented by an afterword. While the introduction outlines the theoretical and methodological roots of the What Does Theology Do, Actually? (hereafter, WDTD) project, the afterword logs the journey that led to it. In his famous essay "Religion as a Cultural System", the cultural anthropologist Clifford Geertz outlined a theory of symbols and of the communication of meaning that symbols conduct by distinguishing between "models-of" and "models-for" what is taken to be ultimately real.[2] A "model-of" is like a map: it aims to reproduce the actual landscape of the world as it is encountered, measurable, and reproducible, in order to provide a kind of guide for navigation. "The theory or chart models physical relationships in such a way – that is, by expressing their structure in synoptic form – as to render them apprehensible."[3] A "model-for", Geertz suggests, is more like a blueprint for modeling reality, for solving problems and reaching goals. In a "model-for", "the theory is a model under whose guidance physical relationships are organized."[4] Systems of symbols in human communication work in both directions, Geertz argues, and I want to suggest that theologies and theological research function in a similar way. Like symbols in Geertz's theory of religion as a cultural system, theologies "give meaning, that is, objective conceptual form, to social and psychological reality both by shaping themselves to it and by shaping it to themselves."[5] This introduction functions as a kind of "model-for": it offers a basic model for what transcultural theological research might look like and how it might be conducted. The afterword offers, instead, a "model-of": it describes the beginnings of WDTD in relation to some of my own limited wanderings through the vast landscape of theological experience, reflection, and analysis in search of exciting discoveries and good paths. In the end, of course, this introductory chapter and those following it, also have to be seen as "models-of", each surveying and charting their own maps of the landscape they have walked.

What Does Theology Do, Actually? Observing Theology and the Transcultural was the title of a symposium held at the Protestant Theological Faculty of the University of Bonn.[6] That symposium was the first in what is planned to be a series of similar symposia, each posing the same question, but with a more specific focus on the theological subdisciplines of exegesis, church history,

---

[2] Clifford Geertz, "Religion as a Cultural System," in *The Interpretation of Cultures* (New York: Basic Books, 1973), 87-125.
[3] Geertz, "Religion as a Cultural System," 93.
[4] Geertz, "Religion as a Cultural System," 93.
[5] Geertz, "Religion as a Cultural System," 93.
[6] The title of the symposium itself was *What Does Theology Do, Actually? Observing Systematic Theology and the Transcultural.* The word "Systematic" has been removed from the title of the book since the symposium itself, in the end, was not restricted to examination of the field of systematic theology specifically and had a much more interdisciplinary focus instead. It is expected that a future symposium in the series will be devoted specifically to consideration of systematic theology.

practical theology, systematic theology, and intercultural theology. Each is to be inter- and trans-disciplinary in approach (interrelating research and practice), international in scope, and drawing on the insights and questions of scholars at all career stages. The question "What does theology do, actually?" was not, actually, posed cynically, but was chosen, rather, as a practical, pragmatic way of bringing some focus to the mammoth set of questions indicated in the opening paragraphs of this chapter. At the first symposium, masters and doctoral students, postdoctoral researchers and professors, from eight different countries and five different continents, and working as teachers, pastors, or scholars in sociology, anthropology, philosophy, religious studies, and each of the traditional theological sub-disciplines were all invited to describe things that theological communications do in their diverse settings. Contributors were not expected to "represent" whole traditions, disciplines, or regions. This is just the basic framework within which WDTD operates: It is to be international and interdisciplinary and involve both first-order practitioner-partners as well as second-order inquiry, by means of mutual listening and aimed at the analysis of theological know-how.

2. From "What is theology?" to "What does theology do?"

In the run-up to the first WDTD symposium, in discussions with friends and colleagues, such a clear conversational pattern emerged that soon I could predict how the conversation would go when I talked to someone about it for the first time:

> MRR: [. . .] Yes, so we've organized a symposium around the question, "What does theology *do*, actually?"
>
> Colleague: Oh, wow. That's very interesting. It's a really good question. [. . .] So, what is the symposium going to be about, actually?

The problem that followed this exchange was also consistent and predictable: I struggled to answer. Very often, whoever I was speaking with would themselves reflect for a moment and offer something brilliantly insightful – something which I inevitably neglected to write it down, with the result that I still struggle to answer now.

Two things about that experience stand out to me as characteristic and important for the WDTD project. First, that the question of what we in theology do is so simple but that it is rarely asked. It seems like an elementary question that any theologian ought to be able to answer, or at least have an opinion about. And yet, we overlook the question, perhaps taking something like an answer to be more or less self-evident (for example, "Godtalk"). Or, related, perhaps we prefer instead to talk about what theology *is* over what theology *does*. But a subtle but significant socio-semantic shift takes place in choosing the latter question over the former. Asking what theology does directs the attention to contexts, situations, and places where "theologies" – whatever they *are* – may be observed as things that *do* things, that take on distinguishable material and symbolic forms that can be used, exchanged, acted upon and that act upon us. That is, asking what theology does results in "theology" no longer being seen as an abstract noun that is what it is everywhere; rather, it becomes plural, and theologies are seen as socio-historical artifacts – and not only those of the past, but also those of the present, including our own.

Second, the experience reminded me that theology does what it does in communication and community, and this raises questions about who participates in theological communications and theological research and about the purposes of and methods required for theological research. This point as it relates to WDTD deserves a bit of unpacking:

On one level, there are the people who participate in theological doings in the contexts, situations, and places where "theologies" may be observed as operative. These people *are* doing theology, theologies are doing things with them, and these involvements and interactions must be recognized as well as incorporated into theological research. Theologies are "lived"[7] and thus operate at the "grassroots",[8] "by the people",[9] "on the margins",[10] and in "ordinary"[11] and "local"[12] settings. Further on in this chapter, I will try to develop the point in a bit more detail, for it is deeply important for the whole WDTD project.

On another level – on the comparative and analytic level of theological research – there are those of us who are more stereotypically associated with the doing of theology, namely, theologians. Crucially, to speak of a different "level" must not be taken to imply a hierarchy of authority or superiority of insight: For, asking what theology does is a question that can be directed just as well to academic cultures, institutions, and practices, which themselves then become subjects of observation, no less than the "lived", contextual theologies "out in the field", so-to-speak. Or rather, our institutions and practices can be recognized as also being "lived" and contextual, situated in particular epistemological systems with a specific and contingent history of emergence.

---

7 Charles Marsh, Peter Slade, andn Sarah Azaransky, eds., *Lived Theology: New Perspectives on Method, Style, and Pedagogy* (Oxford: Oxford University Press, 2016).

8 Simon Chan, *Grassroots Asian Theology: Thinking the Faith from the Ground Up* (Downers Grove: Intervarsity Press, 2014).

9 Samuel Amirtham and John S. Pobee, eds., *Theology by the People: Reflections on Doing Theology in Community* (Geneva: World Council of Churches, 1986).

10 Miguel A. De La Torre and Stacey M. Floyd-Thomas, eds., *Beyond the Pale: Reading Theology from the Margins* (Louisville: Westminster John-Knox, 2011).

11 Jeff Astley, *Ordinary Theology: Looking, Listening and Learning in Theology* (Farnham: Ashgate, 2002); Jeff Astley and Leslie J. Francis, eds., *Exploring Ordinary Theology: Everyday Christian Believing and the Church* (Farnham: Ashgate Publishing, 2013).

12 Robert J. Schreiter, *Constructing Local Theologies* (New York: Orbis, 1985).

Just as at the first level, it remains important that we who are doing the theology at the second level actively participate in answering the WDTD question. But in order to understand better what we do with theology and, especially, what our theologies do with us, it is nevertheless crucial to get some other people involved: Philosophers, sociologists of knowledge and institutions, cultural anthropologists, scholars of religion and comparative religion, political scientists, psychologists, development researchers, economists. Scholars in these and other fields offer a different set of methodological tools, questions, and paradigms of measurement and evaluation: What models are available for describing the ways concepts are socially constructed and contested? What is a symbol, how do material objects come to bear them, and how do they interact with their contexts? What kinds of theological argumentation, narratives, symbols, and objects are used in the negotiation of cultural, ethnic, and political identity? How might theologies influence individual and group psychology, and open up or restrict the range of what is deemed appropriate individual and social action? The suggestion that theology can and should work interdisciplinarily is hardly unique or original to WDTD. The points, however, is that such questions are questions about what theology does and not about what theology is and that addressing them benefits from complex critical community with practictioners, community leaders, theologians, and scholars of many other academic disciplines.

Indeed, asking such questions can make a significant contribution to theological research by facilitating communication between lived theological communication and the theological analysis of lived theological communications – transdisciplinarily among academics and partners representing Christian communities and interdisciplinarily with colleagues at the university. This mediating interest is one of the core features of the WDTD project design and constitutes potentially its most important contribution. The question "What does theology do, actually?" can be helpful for overcoming artificial divisions between lived religion and academic theology, and for neutralizing unnecessary competition between confessional convictions and methodological agnosticism. Instead, the focus shifts to identification of the questions that people use theologies to ask and the problems they use theologies to solve. By gathering around the question "What does theology do, actually, in your community?", we extend to one another an invitation to present our self-understandings, practices, and claims without pressure to hedge on them, qualify them beyond recognition, or explain them away. We participate together, we include one another. For the practitioner, when all goes well, an experienced inability to explain oneself in response to the questions of another can become an opportunity for more self-examination and an occasion to cultivate deeper self-understanding. For the scholar, asking the question "What does theology do, actually?" can also be helpful for relieving academic theology of a persistent imposter syndrome, on the one hand, and for directing it away from siloed conversations, on the other.

Stanley Hauerwas once joked that "if we did not take our work [that is, as theologians] seriously, then no one would take our work seriously."[13] Many non-theologians reasonably wonder what theology does at a research university that, methodologically speaking, philosophy, history, sociology, and psychology do not already do. Taking up the question "What does theology do, actually?" as a descriptive research program might help, on the one hand, to open up lines of communication between lived theological communications and academic theological analysis while, on the other hand, providing theological inquiry with a new descriptive-analytic focus with an almost self-evident importance for the study of modern societies. In the former case, no one is required to convince another, but they are invited to try. In the latter case, the answer to the question "What does theology do?" is simply: "We produce knowledge describing what theologies are doing."

3. Reflected Religious Communications under Conditions of Transcultural Complexity: The Question "WDTD?" as a Model for Theological Research

Which raises the question of how one would go about doing that, specifically in light of the emergence of a global society and the interwovenness of the most disparate human lives with each other in what have been theorized as global "functional communication systems" such as law, economy, education, science, religion, and so on. Attention is given here to the present, but the approach might be easily adapted to historical studies as well.

Theologies are complex, and "context" might be helpfully reconceived in theology as the study of transcultural complexity.

The WDTD project attempts to dwell in webs of complexity, and in this spirit, the present volume works comparatively to foster interactions with specific attention to the complexities resulting from juxtaposition of different modes and systems of doing theological work. For this reason, the book begins with a section framed by a question adapted from J.Z. Smith: "What difference does a difference make?"[14] In this section, short impulse chapters on Filipino political theology (Hadje Sadje), the 2014 Umbrella Movement protests in Hong Kong (Che Wai), theological autobiography between East Africa and Europe (Sara Abdella Kedir), and second-generation German congregations with an

---

13 Stanley Hauerwas, *The Work of Theology* (Grand Rapids and Cambridge: W. B. Eerdmans, 2015), 21.

14 The section heading is a reference to Smith's essay: Jonathan Z. Smith, "What a Difference a Difference Makes," in *Relating Religion: Essays in the Study of Religion* (Chicago: University of Chicago Press, 2004), 251-302.

African immigration background (Elorm Nick Ahialey-Mawusi) short-circuit theological and scholarly paradigms through the presentation of particular theological perspectives that feature the kind of overlaps and mixings and matchings in theological formation, social identities, geographical locations and so on that are so characteristic of the sites of theological work being done today.

With comprehensive globalization, theologies that, from a local perspective, were once confessed as universal come to be recognized as particular to specific instances, on the one hand, which instances themselves turn out to be highly diverse internally, on the other hand. Moreover, the importance of studying the "non-religious" so-to-speak – that is, the political, economic, and philosophical-cultural – origins of theological ideas and practices is by now self-evident. This non-homogeneity and non-religiousness of theological communications might be destabilizing, both to those in "lived" settings who may worry that their beliefs and practices, their orientations toward ultimacy, are being parochialized, but also to those in academic settings who might find themselves confronted with unfamiliar non-Western knowledge forms and thus driven back to the drawing board with basic questions about how to produce knowledge in theological research.

For researchers tasked with producing knowledge about Christianity, these external and internal diversities cannot be ignored any more than the great numbers and societal significances of Christianities the world over can be ignored. Rather they must be taken up into the work of researching Christian communities' understanding of themselves. This raises methodological questions: How are diversities and differences to be reflected as accurately as possible? How can the elision of difference that takes place in the epistemological cartography of the powerful be guarded against? At the same time, internal diversities in theologies and theological research paradigms remind us that difference is no binary us-them matter because it is not absolute, not digital but analogical. As J.Z. Smith wrote, "'Otherness' is not so much a matter of separation as it is a description of interaction."[15] Overlaps and interrelations persist that join those who are far off as though they were near, with distinctions of otherness often being "found to be drawn most sharply with 'near neighbors.'"[16] Further complicating analysis is that no comprehensive catalogue of social interactions – of meetings and crossing, mixings and matchings – can be given. Their number and nature exceed researchers' observational abilities.

Sociological systems-theorist Niklas Luhmann used the term "complexity" to refer to situations of interactions exceeding the limits of connectivity: "We can say that the problem of complexity is the problem of the threshold beyond

---

[15] Smith, "What a Difference a Difference Makes," 256.
[16] Smith, "What a Difference a Difference Makes," 258.

which each element can no longer be connected with every other."[17] This becomes a problem for social researchers when a system reaches such a stage of complexity that "selection patterns become necessary and have become progressively more demanding, which is to say, more selective, more contingent, [. . .] and thus demand that a particular choice and nothing else be realized."[18] With awareness of the contingency of our theological beliefs, methods, and institutions, we in theology experience the limits of observational science and the resulting complexity of excessive interactions as particularly acute. The complexity of a globalized world society presents theological research with the challenge of finding a way to pivot around upon itself, and to observe and describe its own semantics and syntax (that is, what theologies say, how, and with what logics).

In attempting to observe the particularity of context, one quickly finds it necessary to ask "Which context?" And answers to this question – the contexts that might be considered – will look separate or overlapping, singular and multiple, depending on the perspectives from which one views the field. The kinds of complexity that appear with globalization do not map well onto distinct contexts subject to theological analysis of "inter-"actions between contexts. They rather raise anew the very question of what context even is in the first place and how contexts might be delineated. Wealthy, poor; healthy, sick; homo-, hetero-, or other sexual orientation; educated, not educated; online, offline; Western European, Eastern European, Middle Eastern, African North or Sub-Saharan, Asian, Southeast Asian, North American, Latina/o; citizen, resident (legal, not legal), refugee; immigration background or none; first, second, third generation with an immigration background; tribe, caste, class; Christian, Muslim, Jewish, Hindu, Buddhist, secular; and if Christian, then Orthodox, Catholic, Protestant, Pentecostal – the various ways of combining these variables (for example, a middle class, western European citizen with a second generation African immigration background Christian) – these yield well over 1000 possible demographic and functional combinations or "contexts" for consideration. Furthermore, particular combinations do not anymore refer to what sociologist Rudolf Stichweh has called "compact social objects" whose social aspirations, locations, or mobility are determined by the applicability of such categories (even if patterns may be observed).[19] For, precisely that applicability is in constant, dynamic, and potentially swift flux. These are, indeed, complex matters.

---

[17] Niklas Luhmann, *Introduction to Systems Theory*, ed. by Dirk Baecker, trans. by Peter Gilgen (Cambridge and Malden: Polity Press, 2013), 125.
[18] Luhmann, *Introduction to Systems Theory*, 125.
[19] Rudolf Stichweh, "Inklusion/Exklusion und die Soziologie des Fremden," in *Inklusion und Exklusion. Studien zur Gesellschaftstheorie* (Bielefeld: Transcript, 2016), 179-188, here 188.

Sorting through the syntax of these complexities as a "transcultural" semantics of a global society is what WDTD understands "contextual" theological work to entail. Attention to "context" in theology approached by focusing on "complexity", attempts to integrate into its analysis, on the one hand, the theoretical framing of a global society, that is, the societal situation of a differentiation of global functional social systems like international law, natural-scientific inquiry, sport, multi-national trade, and neo-liberal religion. Such systems transcend national, ethnic or "cultural" borders but overlap with each other in the lives of individuals and communities. In result, people often find themselves facing multiple, overlapping, and competing social participations; rarely do the duties and responsibilities of faith, work, research, and leisure coincide (except, perhaps, for individuals who are privileged enough to work for their dream sport club!). Another result is that people who are geographically distant from one another might nevertheless be close colleagues or fellow citizens, while people with the most diverse cultural or religious backgrounds are next-door neighbors. Continuing with Stichweh, social groupings and collectivities in globalized societies seem to form increasingly around inclusions in and exclusions from these functional systems of communication and exchange as measured by opportunities for participation in, contributions to, or receptions from those systems.[20] Similarly, analysis of what theologies do and how in the presence of such complexity may be helpfully described in terms of inclusions and exclusions in systems of theological communication and exchange as measured by opportunities for participation in, contributions to, or reception from those systems.

On the other hand, there is a renewed risk in such a global perspective that sites at which these powerful systemic forces intersect, namely, the lives, bodies, and communities of real human persons, might fade from view. So there is a need for another focus that can counterbalance the global by drawing attention to the ways it intersects with the local and how local forces interrupt these intersections and even exert counter-influences. It was precisely this interest that prompted Fernando Ortiz to work with the terminology of "transculturation" in his seminal study of international and local dynamics in sugar and tobacco production in Cuba in the 1940s.[21] Whether in the form of the persisting influence of cultural heritages or that of diaspora communities or local knowledges that are translated into locality-spanning or even global

---

[20] Rudolf Stichweh, "Inklusion in Funktionssysteme der modernen Gesellschaft," in *Inklusion und Exklusion. Studien zur Gesellschaftstheorie* (Bielefeld: Transcript, 2016), 17-46.

[21] Fernando Ortiz, *Cuban Counterpoint: Tobacco and Sugar* (Durham: Duke University Press, 1995 [1947]), translated from the original spanish *Contrapunteo cubano del tobacco y el azúcar* (Havana: Jesús Montero, 1940). Cf. Katja Rakow and Esther Berg, "Religious Studies and Transcultural Studies: Revealing a Cosmos Not Known Before?" *Journal of Transcultural Studies* 2 (2016): 180-203, here 185.

parlance, "a transcultural perspective tries to shed light on this polyvocality."[22] In this way, as Katja Rakow and Esther Berg argue, "a transcultural approach opens up spaces for scholars from different disciplinary backgrounds and parts of the world to engage in dialogue and make the multiplicity of voices count."[23] A transcultural lens does view essentialist and homongenous conceptions of culture critically, viewing culture instead as, ultimately, a contingent historical product. But that contingency is recognized to develop over very long periods of time and in complex, durable forms that do not change drastically from one day to the next. Focusing on the "processuality of culture"[24] can support research in theology aimed at both representative reconstructions of theological self-understandings and critical analysis of change in those self-understandings proceeding from corresponding evolutions of the groups they describe.

Now the question of context in theological research has been transformed: What might it look like in theological research to give attention to the multiple, overlapping, mutually compounding, and continuously evolving participations and expectations that characterize contemporary global society, as these things condition and are conditioned by transcultural pressures? Section two of this volume approaches these issues under the question: "Whose culture? Which Contextuality? Determining Theological Locations", riffing on the title of Alisdair MacIntyre's classic text in philosophical ethics.[25] First, analysis of complexity requires collaboration and communication; Martín Grassi, a Roman Catholic philosopher from Argentina, argues in his philosophical essay in this volume that the "con-" to any "text" is always its own "text" and that as such, con-textuality is a matter of inter-textuality. Totalizing accounts that merge standpoint with interpretive horizon falsify complexity as simplicity; at the same time, particularizing accounts must take care to recognize that the interpretive horizon is part of the standpoint's positionality as the standpoint that it is. In the terms of Jürgen Habermas's theorization of complexity in relation to social analysis, this means analysis of complexity interrelates reconstruction with self-reflection in a communicative pragmatics built around mutuality and agreement making.[26] But it cannot be said that this communica-

---

22 Rakow and Berg, "Religious Studies and Transcultural Studies," 185.

23 Rakow and Berg, "Religious Studies and Transcultural Studies", 185.

24 Rakow and Berg, "Religious Studies and Transcultural Studies", 187.

25 Alisdair MacIntyre, *Whose Justice? Which Rationality?* (Notre Dame: Notre Dame University Press, 1988).

26 See Jürgen Habermas's engagement with the problem of complexity as a dialectic between reconstruction and self-reflection in Jürgen Habermas, *Erkenntnis und Interesse* (Frankfurt am Main: Suhrkamp 1994 [1968]); English translation: Jürgen Habermas, *Knowledge and Human Interests,* trans. by Jeremy Shapiro (Cambridge: Polity Press, 1987). See also the helpful comparison of Habermas's and Niklas Luhmann's accounts of complexity by William Rasch in William Rasch, "Theories of

tive interaction reduces the complexity of comtemporary social phenomena to a preexisting anthropological foundation. Evan Kuehn, a systematic theologian and library information systems scientist, complicates the idea of reconstruction in his chapter here, preferring the terminology of "reflexivity", "observation", and "transcultural communication". Kuehn examines Ernst Troeltsch's principled approach to Christianity with a modern view of history in relation with John Mbiti's critique of the provincialization of European theology in order to call for increased self-awareness in theological research - not only of theologians' own acculturation and social positionality, but also of the duty to integrate intercultural and transcultural perspectives on theologies and theological research as risk-producing social contingency increases. Reconstruction of the conditions of self-reflection turns out to be a highly complex task. Similar to Luhmann's famous dictum that society is communication, Kuehn argues that the "is" to which theological reconstructions - for example, of culture or Christianity - refer is communication. Cornelia Richter, professor of systematic theology and hermeneutics in Bonn, then engages in an exercise in reflexive self-critique from her position in the German theological research system. Richter proposes to synthesize competing commitments felt by theological research in historically Christian Germany - on the one hand, to the scientific requirements of modern research for impartiality and critique and, on the other hand, to the training of clergy - by approaching theology generally and systematic theology specifically as social-theoretic interpretation of perceived existential concerns and social anxieties in the language and symbols of religion and, where appropriate, Christianity. She calls this a "situated dogmatics." But Richter introduces a surprising twist into her account of the interpretive task, namely, in arguing that interpretation takes the form of listening: of providing space for listening to others relating their experiences and of allowing one's own experiences to be interrupted and brought up short in so doing. In this way, both Kuehn's and Richter's chapters might be summarized by observing that, in researching complexity, theologies and theological research do not reduce but rather produces more of it.

Attention to transcultural complexity of "reflected religious communications" will inevitably push theological research through extensive methodological diversification

A certain constellation forms out of this clustering of sociological observations that offers some guidance for theological research. "Constellation" is perhaps a good metaphor, for, while I hope to draft a more robust account in the future, the individual points of a theological research model oriented by them can only be named and outlined here. Namely, I propose to understand theology as the interrelation of the ultimate with the actual in the immediate (in more

---

Complexity, Complexities of Theory: Habermas, Luhmann, and the Study of Social Systems," *German Studies Review* 14, no. 1 (1991): 65-83.

traditional terminology, the interrelation of God-world-self) and propose a corresponding approach to theological research as research on "reflected religious communications", concerning which proposals:

Before any research can be undertaken, there must always be a question. As William Rasch quipped in an essay on "complexity" in Luhmann and Habermas, "a discipline cannot be defined by what it studies, but by the constitutive question it asks."[27] The question "What Does Theology Do, Actually?" can be taken as the organizing question of a research program. Once again, the question is not asked rhetorically or cynically, but constructively. What does theology do? It researches what theologies do. Today, in a globalized and functionally differentiated world, the question must be further specified as: What is theology doing, particularly in communities intensely affected by the transcultural complexities that ramify modern life? *Whom* do theological communications serve? *What* do theological communications do for them? And *how* do theological communications function to relate those whom they serve to explicit and implicit goals or purposes? In short: how are communities processing the complexities of the transcultural (what is actual) in relation to God's design and desire (what is ultimate) in their midst (what is immediate)?

While these are very large questions, they can be made specific and rigorous through a transcultural lens focused on instances of the production of theology by concrete communities as they react to challenges of social complexity brought on by the forces of globalization and functional differentiation. Comparing Christian communities who are addressing similar constellations of challenges (for example, how religious communities draw on their theological resources to process problems of poverty, gender, ethnic conflict; migration, diaspora, identity) might enable identification of patterns in theological communication, in doctrinal and ethical understandings, and in the evolving formation of Christian identities vis-a-vis other Christian communities, non-Christian communities, and society at large. Studying the functions of theology – what theologies do in first-order, lived, and on-the-ground as well as in second-order, scientific settings – is itself an important part of what second-order, academic theology can do.

Communication and Actualization. So how would one go about observing what theologies do? First, by recalibrating theological research as "communication", all the way down. Following this sentiment, Eberhard Hauschildt, professor of Practical Theology in Bonn, begins his contribution to the present volume by referring to Paul Watzlawick's famous axiom: "One cannot not communicate." Transcultural theological research works within a theory of reality mediated by communication. The question of how to observe theologies, asked in the modern world, attends unrestrainedly to transcultural complexity, as encountered across the whole spectrum of theological communications, from the first- to the second- to the *n*th-order. The attention to

[27] Rasch, "Theories of Complexity, Complexities of Theory," 77.

complexity, *qua* the nature of complexity as a set of finite interactions exceeding comprehensive systematization, forces selection of certain phenomena and deselection of others by means of creating a distinction between things, which thereby further increases complexity. A distinction, as one selection among many possible in an actual instance, is an actualization of certain latent possibilities and one that, despite its being drawn, continues to refer to what has not been selected. As such, distinction-drawing concretizes "the unity of the difference between reality and possibility", thereby becoming "meaningful".[28] Since distinctions are drawn by observers for whom the distinction is meaningful, the resulting meaning is always a meaning-for. There is no getting "behind" the distinction, only a getting "outside" the selection. This also points to the fact that observation and distinctions function with a logic of inside-outside or inclusion-exclusion, rather than an is-is not (onto-)logic or a true-false (doxo-)logic. Distinctions are used and re-used over time in reinscriptions of the same or analogous operations, ever (re)producing new meaning. The self-reproducing process of selection and repetition of distinctions generating a body of observations is what is meant here by "communications". The process is fractal, for the structure is endlessly repeating: All first-order observations can be observed, if not by the observer making them, nevertheless by second-order observers. These latter can, in turn, also be observed as a different instance of first-order observers by yet other second-order observers, etc. But meaning, understanding, and everything that depends on these (such as decisions, agreements, plans, directives) themselves depend on making themselves "discernible as communication".[29]

Religion and Ultimacy. Communications might be regarded as "religious" when they attempt to give an exhaustive account of what is inexhaustibly complex. In religious communication, communication about the actual is set into relation to what is ultimate. Approved religious communications attempt to do this from the "inside" of the selection, in various kinds of "established settings", once again to refer to Hauschildt's chapter. These include things like rituals, holidays, and forms of care that incorporate what is unincorporatable, like the meaninglessness of death or tragedy, via communications about eternal life or an unobservable Observer's plan. The surrounding environment of a group might also be seen as an established setting, and groups' communi-

---

[28] Niklas Luhmann, *A Systems Theory of Religion*, ed. by André Kieserling, trans. by David A. Brenner with Adrian Hermann (Stanford: Stanford University Press, 2013 [2000]), 10. The characterization of communication given here adapts Luhmann's basic theory of the autopoietic communication of social systems. It is not, however, a Luhmannian theory. I say instead that it is "adapted" because it intentionally deviates from Luhmann's theory in ways that Luhmann presumably would have critiqued. Most significantly, what Luhmann theorizes as communication he understands to apply only to social systems, where I find his account also maps sufficiently well onto actual communities so as to be useful in thinking about challenges of theological method.

[29] Luhmann, *A Systems Theory of Religion*, 27.

cations are conditioned by their environments, but those communications are always communicated in terms of the meanings internal to a given group's established semantic range and having the purpose of facilitating the group's ongoing communication. Forbidden religious communications have the same goal but approach this goal by illicitly attempting to observe the unobservable observer, thereby claiming for themselves an uncontestable power of observation. Here the significance of this model starts to become clearer, for on this understanding of communication, communication includes more than written words and texts but also a variety of selection and distinction-drawing performances: More specifically focusing on religious communication, these might include things like religious law and religious offices, sacred objects that reproduce traditional meanings in situations of novel complexity, sacred spaces that reinforce boundaries of belonging, and so on. Engagement with such phenomena is of course standard in contexts of traditional religious learning and in the academic study of religion. Recognizing these, let's say, "lived" forms of religion as group-forming and -facilitating communications might be an epistemologically helpful way of rendering the systematicity and philosophical sophistication such communications contain more approachable within traditional structures of (even systematic-) theological analysis, too.

Reflection and Immediacy. Finally, religious communications are the more "reflected" the more they are characterized by finely tuned distinctions vis-à-vis the claims of other communication systems, are intentionally deployed, and are repeated or repeatable. In reflected religious communication, communication about the actual is set in relation to what is ultimate with specific reference to the concerns and self-awareness of a group in the immediacy of its current complexity. One helpful thing about this formulation is that it is attentive not only to more and less lived forms of religious communication; it is also attentive to the broader social significances and functions of religious communications in processing groups' intersections with communication systems and the competing claims those systems make on them. Jayeel Cornelio, professor of Sociology in Manila, writes in this vein about theologically-funded political nationalism in the Philippines. He examines the way that core theological concepts – including eschatology, divine sovereignty, and mission – are enlisted in asserting Philippine exceptionalism, articulating Filipino identity, shielding the Philippines against foreign threats, and in leveraging moral critique. Each case involves a precise use of religious communications or theological semantics concerning ultimacy, in a current situation, to solve immediate challenges encountered by specific churches. Offering yet a different approach, Eva Youkhana, a cultural anthropologist and acting director of the Center for Development Research in Bonn, presents a study of prehispanic dancing groups in contemporary urban landscapes in Mexico, as well as European folkish parallels. These groups display a high level of transcultural complexity, as they interrelate global (anti-)facist sympathies, environmentalist concerns, and a millenarian eschatology, while taking on Christian symbols, all expressed in the medium of cultural heritage movements that present themselves in terms of strict cultural purity. Again, this is a perfect example of reflected religious communications as the interrelation of the ultimate and the actual in the immediate. Youkhana writes that she seeks to "make a critical contribution outside of theology by analyzing religion and theologies themselves as social artifacts, which are contingent products of socio-political histories and areas of contestation." Nevertheless, through the insightful analysis of the *Conchero* dancers as a site of transcultural complexity, her transcultural analysis has as a further result that it plots a form of reflected religious communication onto the map of theological research that almost certainly would not have appeared using traditional paradigms focused on text-based religious communications and scholarly appraisals of them.

One of the most attractive qualities of the foregoing outline of reflected religious communications as a theoretical model for theological research is its orientation to socio-religious phenomena that are not traditionally interpreted as "theological" – religious, yes, but not theological. This includes things such as objects, practices, performances, and spaces. In this way, it expands the category of theological communications to less specifically academic formats. One thing that theology does may well be to look (elsewhere in space, time, geography and-or history, "outside" of the theological academy) at how certain beliefs and practices emerged in a particular context or influenced certain cultural and socio-political developments – and then to write books about it. In other words, a kind of second-order study of first-order developments. But those first-order elements can also be recognized *as theologies*, and the significance of the work first-order theologies perform in the present recommends careful consideration. At the same time, the same kind of interest once directed to first-order theological expressions can and should be directed toward second-order work, since second-order work is itself an instance of first-order work in a different register. This invites the objectification of text- and university-based formats as themselves contingent artifacts of the continuous unfoldings of cultural and socio-political (re)evolutions. The observers can be observed – by observers who, in turn, may also reasonably be observed and so on and so forth. Altogether, this should serve, not to build a hierarchy of surveillance, but precisely to flatten such hierarchies, encouraging mutuality and fairness in the asking of questions and accountability in answering them.

This model contains certain opportunities for method in theological research. On the one hand, it seems clear that theological work will continue to become more empirically driven. This trend is already reflected in the study of the ancient near east, early Judaism, and early Christianity, in study of the history of Christianity, and in practical theology. It remains an important horizon for theological research whether *systematic* theology can make it around the empirical turn and if so how it is to do so. I think that it can, I think it is important for it to do so, but I think that will mean observing systematic *theologies* in the field – something Inja Inderst, co-editor of this volume, indicates in her chapter on practical theology as well. For example, the development of systematic-theological fieldwork using qualitative research methods to collect, document, interpret, and compare the formation and functions of all manner of reflected religious communications as they operate in their communities, all in transdisciplinary co-operations with well-chosen practitioner partners, presents an exciting horizon. Here much can be learned both from classical and recent work in Intercultural Theology[30] and in Religious Studies, as well as from other disciplines - including, among others, sociology and cultural anthropology, as in the present volume.

Beyond this, referring back to the model, it seems relatively clear that selected distinctions negotiating complexity by means of interrelating ultimacy-actuality-immediacy and preserved in obdurate instances of meaning quite often concretize in objects and performances, while, on the other hand, the meanings conveyed by theological texts exceed the printed word. I think of the *Hesus Nazareno*, the Black Nazarene, which is translated every year on January 9 from the old walled city to the Minor Basilica in Manila, in a procession that attracts well over 200,000 people and can last up to 20 hours. The legends surrounding the Black Nazarene are as composite as the material object itself. Parts of the physical object originate in 17th cent. Mexico while replica replacement pieces were fashioned in the Philippines in the 1990s, but the questionability of the object's provenance and integrity leave no room for doubt among the faithful as to the excessive efficacy of its healing powers. I think also of the Kebra Negast, which Andrew DeCort examines in his chapter here. The Kebra Negast is the founding myth of Solomonic divine-right kingship that supported Ethiopian kings and emperors from at least the fall of the Zagwe dynasty in 1270 until the overthrow of Haile Selassie in 1974. It tells the story of the Queen of Sheba, who was Ethiopian, and her visit to Jerusalem to meet King Solomon. She conceived and bore a son to Solomon, and Solomon recognized this son, Menelik I, as his rightful heir. The Israelite Ark of the Covenant was spirited with Menelik back to Ethiopia, thereby theologically conferring divine election onto Ethiopian rulers and by extension, the Ethiopian Orthodox Church - and all of Ethiopia. Pictorial depictions of the story can be found displayed prominently in the halls of Addis Ababa University as well

---

[30] Though subjective and dreadfully unfair to the many other scholars doing important work in Intercultural Theology, I refer the reader simply to a few titles that have been particularly helpful to me: Ulrich Dehn, Verena Grüter et al, eds., *"Was ist Interkulturelle Theologie?"* Special Issue *Zeitschrift für Missionswissenschaft* 2-3 (2014); Judith Gruber, *Intercultural Theology: Exploring World Christianity after the Cultural Turn* (Göttingen: Vandenhoeck & Ruprecht, 2018); Klaus Hock, *Einführung in die Interkulturelle Theologie* (Darmstadt: Wbg Academic, 2011); Volker Küster, *Einführung in die Interkulturelle Theologie* (Stuttgart: UTB, 2011); Volker Küster, *The Many Faces of Jesus Christ* (Maryknoll: Orbis Books, 2001); Claudia Jahnel, *Interkulturelle Theologie und Kulturwissenschaft. Untersucht am Beispiel afrikanischer Theologie* (Stuttgart: Kohlhammer, 2016); Robert J. Schreiter, *Constructing Local Theologies.*

as in any little shop selling gifts or religious items. Protestant theologies, too, are mediated in objects, from healing waters, to the worn Sunday hymnal, to digital newsletters, to, indeed, the Bible itself: For many believers, the "Word" effects much more powerful social significances than the possible meanings of the words it comprises. Each of these examples refer to objects that might be regarded as "doing theology" on a massive scale. They exemplify the ways that the work of calibrating the world as it should be with the world as it is forms in lived encounters and re-presentations that do not, for reason of their being embodied and materially interactive, fail to possess highly nuanced theo-logics. As Alfred Gell has argued concerning the agency of artworks, such objects exhibit a remarkable capacity "for securing the acquiescence of individuals in the network of intentionalities in which they are enmeshed."[31] Skilled assistance in analysis of these sorts of theological artifacts might be found from work in the anthropology of art, subaltern studies on objects, and in work on the material turn, just to indicate a few leads that might be followed.

4. Conclusion: Possible and Plausible Futures for Theological Research

Many majority-world theologies remain invisible to Western theological research, and this might be addressed, in part by broadening of the notion of theological text, and in part by the cultivation of well-chosen transdisciplinary partnerships. Even perceiving the existence, let alone the complexity, of some of the most significant changes taking place in Christianity globally presents a profound challenge to those of us in academic European Protestant theology. Christianities of the majority world have exhibited continuous dynamic growth and striking political-economic dexterity during and since the end of the colonial period. In 1900 approximately 20% of the world's Christians lived in the Global South, whereas by 2000 that number was over 60%. Among Protestants the contrast is even more stark: Only 16% of all Protestants today live in Europe, while 41% live in sub-Saharan Africa alone. The demographic significance of emerging Protestantisms (above all, Pentecostalisms) is particularly striking: In 1900, there were no Pentecostals; in 2020, Pentecostal Christians constitute more than 25% of all Christians worldwide.[32] And yet,

---

[31] Alfred Gell, "The Technology of Enchantment and the Enchantment of Technology," in *Anthropology, Art, and Aesthetics,* ed. by Jeremy Coote and Anthony Shelton (Oxford: Clarendon Press, 1992), 40-63, here 43; see also Alfred Gell, *Art and Agency: An Anthropological Theory* (Oxford: Oxford University Press, 1998).

[32] Todd M. Johnson and Gina A. Zurlo et al, "Christianity 2017: Five Hundred Years of Protestant Christianity," *International Bulletin of Mission Research 2017* 41. no. 1 (2017): 41–52.

research on Christianities of the Global South is minimally represented within Western academic theological research. Alongside these developments (and in some ways, as part of them), one might list the *internal differentiation* of Pentecostalisms and in particular the emergence of oneness Pentecostalism; the proliferation of liberation, political, and identity-oriented theologies; and the ground-level hybrid theologies forming and sustaining life among communities with immigration backgrounds. But few actors involved in the developments just named have the academic credentials or financial independence to study in Western university settings, while scholars originating in Western countries would need decades of sharing life with people in these communities to acquire the emic knowledge necessary for fairly and accurately representing them. There are a host of factors in play, and it is not a matter of assigning blame to any institution or group. But the fact of the matter remains: These developments remain difficult to study and research well within the structures of academic theology in Europe. And it would be one thing, if we were as neatly separated into distinct "us-es" and "them-s", as contemporary populisms and resurging nationalisms that seem to be increasingly interrupting daily experience and irritating visions of life might lead us to think. But attention to the transcultural, again, highlights the ways in which we are all woven into one another's lives and communities extensively and daily *via* our common participation in functional systems of communication, trade, education, political power, and so on. The framing of the transcultural invites us to look at theology not as a *dead* artifact but as a *dynamic* and *dialogical* art of interrelating facts in community with others, as communication through which we engage – or neglect to engage – others in the negotiation of participations in shared forms of life.

However, there is a bit of tension to observe here. When the *object* of study is *subjects* – people and their values and symbols and decisions and traditions – then research in this field requires more than participant observation; it requires dialectical discernment with one another – in community – of the histories, current conditions, and possible meanings and value of the forms of life we cultivate and share with others. I want to come back to the point about doing *theologies* "in the field". My own proposal for one way of rendering visible what theology is doing in contexts currently existing off "our" radar would be to cultivate what Grace Davie in her Foreword here describes as well-chosen partnerships with practitioners at the local level and to join judiciously in the task of transcribing the theologies of local communities into forms that can be recognized and thus participate within international scientific communication systems. This is a move beyond participant observation to observant participation. The comparative analysis of communities under conditions of transcultural complexity is a work of observing what theology does at a second-order level of observation. (Stereo)typically, the scholar must remain at this level. But doing that work presupposes that the first-order level of theological communications is already visible. A combined approach of layering theological reflection and analysis might foster the production of fair and representative and good knowledge concerning what theology does.

For these reasons, the final two sections of the present volume weigh out possibility and responsibility in theological research, taking a hard look at "How public is theology? And how is theology public?" and at "Possible Futures" for work in theology. First, there is a word of caution from Constantin Plaul, systematic theologian in Halle, who in his chapter calls for nuance and critical distance in any assessment of public engagements of Christian theology today. A firm distinction needs to remain in place, he argues, between analysis of Christian heritages and theological ideas and symbols and ecclesiastical-theological efforts to stage interventions in the mode of "public theologies." On the other hand, Florian Höhne, theological ethicist in Berlin, unpacks the ways in which even non-ecclesiastical theological analysis remains nevertheless public, reflecting on the idea of theology as a form of practice and citing David Tracy's famous position that "all theology is public discourse."[33] In the end, Höhne's concern is not to make theology public so that it can speak to this or that social problem, but rather that the theological disciplines' privateness – their exclusiveness and high social barriers to entry – make theology less accessible, less participatory, and in the end cut it off from critical contributions of others. Integrating in a way the insights of Plaul and Höhne, Andrew DeCort looks to Ethiopia as a case study, where he has lived and worked in theological education and community development for fifteen years. DeCort observes that, before we even arrive at the question of whether theologies should be public and of who should be able to participate, it is simply the case that many theologies already are public, and they exercise tremendous power – ironically, however, often by requiring silence and passivity from believers in the face of injustices. DeCort dares to offer a creative interreligious public option as a public theology that is neither ecclesially driven nor exclusive to theologians, namely, practices of preferring, listening to and loving neighbors.

DeCort's proposal might be taken as an example of what Esther Reed, professor of Theological Ethics in Exeter, wants to retrieve with tropological interpretation of the Bible. The purpose of tropological interpretation is not to dictate a one-size-fits-all reading, but rather to give attention to "how crowds of people become ethical agents", specifically, Christian groups in reading the Bible. Reed's chapter dovetails nicely in this way with that of Dogara Ishaya Manomi and his program of "Exegethics". Manomi, lecturer in Bible and Theology in Jos, Nigeria and director of the Initiative for Victims' Educational and Economic Development, outlines a method of exegesis that seeks to combine historical-critical exegesis and Biblical theological hermeneutics for specific application in his sub-Saharan African, Nigerian context. The significance of

---

33 David Tracy, *The Analogical Imagination: Christian Theology and the Culture of Pluralism* (London: SCM Press, 1981), 3.

joining exegesis and ethics in the way Manomi does is that in majority-world Christianities "the skills required to do biblical exegesis are no longer historical critical methods alone, but include other skills also such as cultural analysis, contextual hermeneutics, and systematic theological skills." Offering a clear perspective on future theological sightlines, in Manomi's view, "in this enterprise lies the future of biblical exegesis." This observation of what theology is doing in African settings poses challenging questions for self-examination in European settings as well, particularly when the intercultural landscape of Europe and transcultural complexity are kept in mind. Offering an historian's eye, Gianna Zipp, church historian in Greifswald, draws attention to an important ambivalence that emerges in the transcultural approach to theological research, namely, that it would lead church historians, yes, to attend more carefully to the omnipresence of geographical and cultural bias in theological writing, but, as theological research becomes more descriptive, it becomes harder to maintain any significant difference between church history and just history. The same might perhaps be said of exegesis and early Jewish or early Christian studies. Is research on theology as reflected religious communications under conditions of the transcultural less theological? If the question is how to understand communications as theological through communication, as Inja Inderst reminds in her chapter on practical theology, then Chukwuemeka Anthony Atansi has a suggestion: Love is also a form of communication. Atansi, systematic theologian in Leuven, does not remain at the level of the descriptive in his proposal that Christology – the doctrine itself – is the transformation that takes place among a group of people, as people's encounters with the love of Christ and the love they receive from or give to other people overlap. Rather, he pushes beyond the descriptive to propose a contemplative approach to christological anaylsis. The Christology that results is less a lived theology, simply observing what other people do, and more a living theology that generously reconstructs how their theology leads them into abundant living. Atansi's powerful analysis is at once critical but from a place of deep sympathy and understanding, all of which characterize the best work in constructive theology.

It is clear from these closing summary comments that the futures of theological practice and the locations of theological communication are understood in diverse ways, and these accounts offer only a glimpse of the diversity in theological communication the world over. All of which I take to provide further recommendation of the importance of a theological research model focused on reflected religious communications that (1) attends to transcultural complexities and groups' multiple, overlapping, and mutually compounding participations in social systems; and that (2) therefore works comparatively, empirically, in creative co-operations, and close to life.

Bibliography

Amirtham, Samuel and John S. Pobee, eds. *Theology by the People: Reflections on Doing Theology in Community*. Geneva: World Council of Churches. 1986.

Astley, Jeff. *Ordinary Theology: Looking, Listening and Learning in Theology* (Farnham: Ashgate, 2002.

Astley, Jeff and Leslie J. Francis, eds. *Exploring Ordinary Theology: Everyday Christian Believing and the Church.* Farnham: Ashgate Publishing. 2013.

Chan, Simon. *Grassroots Asian Theology: Thinking the Faith from the Ground Up*. Downers Grove: Intervarsity Press. 2014.

"Christians Remain World's Largest Religious Group, but They are Declining in Europe". Pew Research Center. April 5, 2017. https://www.pewresearch.org/fact-tank/2017/04/05/christians-remain-worlds-largest-religious-group-but-they-are-declining-in-europe/ (Last accessed May 3, 2020).

Calano, Mark Joseph T. "Ginhawa as Ethic of Panatà: Body Politics and the Devotion to the Black Nazarene". *Budhi: A Journal of Ideas and Culture* 22. no. 2 (2018): 43-74.

De La Torre, Miguel A. and Stacey M. Floyd-Thomas, eds. *Beyond the Pale: Reading Theology from the Margins*. Louisville: Westminster John-Knox. 2011.

DeCort, Andrew D. "Pilgrimage: An Ancient Model for Transformative Theological Education". *The Craft of Teaching in the Academic Study of Religion.* 5 March 2018. https://craftofteachingreligion.wordpress.com/2018/03/05/pilgrimage-an-ancient-model-for-transformative-theological-education/. Last accessed: 22 May 2020.

Dehn, Ulrich and Verena Grüter et al (eds.), *"Was ist Interkulturelle Theologie?"* Special Issue *Zeitschrift für Missionswissenschaft* 2-3 (2014).

Geertz, Clifford. *The Interpretation of Cultures: Selected Essays.* New York: Basic Books. 1973.

Gell, Alfred. *Art and Agency: An Anthropological Theory.* Oxford: Oxford University Press. 1998.

Gell, Alfred. "The Technology of Enchantment and the Enchantment of Technology". In *Anthropology, Art, and Aesthetics*. Edited by Jeremy Coote and Anthony Shelton. Oxford: Clarendon Press. 1992. 40-63

Geertz, Clifford. *The Interpretation of Cultures: Selected Essays.* New York: Basic Books. 1973.

Gruber, Judith *Intercultural Theology: Exploring World Christianity after the Cultural Turn.* Göttingen: Vandenhoeck & Ruprecht. 2018.

Gutierrez, Gustavo. *A Theology of Liberation. 15th Anniversary Edition, with a New Introduction by the Author.* Maryknoll: Orbis Books. 1988 [1971].

Habermas, Jürgen. *Erkenntnis und Interesse.* Frankfurt am Main: Suhrkamp. 1994 [1968].

Habermas, Jürgen. *Knowledge and Human Interests.* Translated by Jeremy Shapiro. Cambridge: Polity Press, 1987.

Harrison, Peter. "Angels on Pinheads and Needles' Points". *Notes and Queries* 63 (2016): 45-47.

Hauerwas, Stanley *The Work of Theology*. Grand Rapids and Cambridge: W. B. Eerdmans. 2015.

Hock, Klaus. *Einführung in die Interkulturelle Theologie*. Darmstadt: Wbg Academic. 2011.

Hofheinz, Marco, Frank Mathwig and Matthias Zeindler, eds. *Freundschaft. Zur Aktualität eines traditionsreichen Begriffs*. Zürich: TVZ. 2014.

Hummel, Gert. "Enzyklopädie, theologische.eds.)" *Theologische Realenzyklopädie*. Edited by Horst Robert Balz et al. vol. 9. *Dionysius Exiguus - Episkopalismus*. Berlin and New York: De Gruyter. 1982. 716-742.

Jahnel, Claudia. *Interkulturelle Theologie und Kulturwissenschaft. Untersucht am Beispiel afrikanischer Theologie*. Stuttgart: Kohlhammer. 2016.

Johnson, Todd M., Gina A. Zurlo, et al. "Christianity 2017: Five Hundred Years of Protestant Christianity." *International Bulletin of Mission Research 2017* 41. no. 1 (2017): 41-52.

Kalu, Ogbu. *African Pentecostalism: An Introduction*. Oxford and New York: Oxford University Press. 2008.

Kim, Sebastian C. H. and Kirsteen Kim. *A History of Korean Christianity*. Cambridge: Cambridge University Press. 2015.

Küster, Volker. *Einführung in die Interkulturelle Theologie*. Stuttgart: UTB. 2011.

Küster, Volker. *The Many Faces of Jesus Christ*. Maryknoll: Orbis Books. 2001.

Luhmann, Niklas. *A Systems Theory of Religion*. Edited by André Kieserling. Translated by David A. Brenner with Adrian Hermann. Stanford: Stanford University Press. 2013 [2000].

Luhmann, Niklas. *Die Religion der Gesellschaft*. Edited by André Kieserling. Frankfurt am Main: Suhrkamp, 2000.

Luhmann, Niklas. *Introduction to Systems Theory*. Edited by Dirk Baecker. Translated by Peter Gilgen. Cambridge and Malden: Polity Press. 2013.

MacIntyre, Alisdair. *Whose Justice? Which Rationality?* Notre Dame: Notre Dame University Press. 1988.

Marsh, Charles, Peter Slade and Sarah Azaransky, eds. *Lived Theology: New Perspectives on Method, Style, and Pedagogy*. Oxford: Oxford University Press. 2016.

Nouwen, Henri. "Anton T. Boisen and Theology Through Living Human Documents". *Pastoral Psychology* 19. no. 7 (1968): 49-63.

Ortiz, Fernando. *Contrapunteo cubano del tobacco y el azúcar*. Havana: Jesús Montero. 1940.

Ortiz, Fernando. *Cuban Counterpoint: Tobacco and Sugar*. Durham: Duke University Press. 1995 [1947].

The Pew Forum on Religion and Public Life. "Global Christianity: A Report on the Size and Distribution of the World Christian Population". Pew Research Center (December 2011).

Rakow, Katja and Esther Berg. "Religious Studies and Transcultural Studies: Revealing a Cosmos Not Known Before?" *Journal of Transcultural Studies* 2 (2016): 180-203.

Rasch, William. "Theories of Complexity, Complexities of Theory: Habermas, Luhmann, and the Study of Social Systems", *German Studies Review* 14, no. 1 (1991): 65-83.

Robinson, Matthew Ryan. „Fake Friends": Zur Toleranz und Freundschaft als soziale und theologische Werte, oder wie Theologie Studierende Geflüchteten nicht Hilfe gaben, sondern mit ihnen Freundschaft fanden". *Pastoraltheologie* 107. no. 7 (2018a): 333-352.

Robinson, Matthew Ryan. *Redeeming Relationship, Relationships that Redeem: Free Sociability and the Completion of Humanity in the Thought of Friedrich Schleiermacher*. Tübingen: Mohr Siebeck. 2018.

Schreiter, Robert J. *Constructing Local Theologies*. New York: Orbis. 1985.

Stichweh, Rudolf. *Inklusion und Exklusion. Studien zur Gesellschaftstheorie*. Bielefeld: Transcript. 2016.

Tracy, David. *The Analogical Imagination: Christian Theology and the Culture of Pluralism*. London: SCM Press. 1981.

Part 1 What Difference does a Difference Make?

WHAT DOES THEOLOGY DO, ACTUALLY?

(Un)Doing Filipino Theologies

Hadje Cresencio Sadje (Leuven, Belgium; Philippines)

1. INTRODUCTION

What does theology do, actually? It is a straight forward question, but not an easy one to answer. As I interpret it, the question aims to reflect upon the significance, implications, and concrete public relevance of Christian theologies for social reality. Asking "What does theology do, actually?" invites students of theology to examine Christian theology as a public discourse.[1] Miroslav Volf has observed that "faith idles" in many spheres of life, and that many churches remain introspective with their theology.[2] He argued that it is time for churches to wake up and to address themselves to 21st century global challenges directly and to resist understandings of religion as something private. He believes that churches around the world must refuse to be silent and instead participate in policymaking. In this respect, he advocates for a removal of those artificial boundaries between "public" and "private" spheres in Christian theology. Similarly, Jürgen Moltmann has contended that Christian theology has to be public theology. Like Volf, Moltmann observed Christian theologies becoming narrow and introspective exercises and argued that the Christian theologian needs to actively engage in public debates, writing: "As the theology of God's kingdom, theology has to be public theology: public, critical and prophetic complaint to God—public, critical and prophetic hope in God."[3] He added, "Its public character is constitutive for theology, for the kingdom of God's sake."[4] In this respect, it is important to bear in mind that Christian theology, is not only propositional belief, but also behaving and

[1] Miroslav Volf, *A Public Faith: How Followers of Christ Should Serve the Common Good* (US: Brazos Press, 2011), 119-138; David Tracy, *Blessed Rage for Order: The New Pluralism in Theology* (New York: Seabury [Crossroad], 1975), 6-7; David Tracy, *The Analogical Imagination: Christian Theology and the Culture of Pluralism* (New York: Crossroad), 57.

[2] Volf, *A Public Faith*, ix-xvii.

[3] Jürgen Moltmann, *God for a Secular Society: The Public Relevance of* Theology (SCM Press, 1999), 5-6.

[4] Moltmann, *God for a Secular Society*, 5-6.

belonging.[5] Christian theology is never solely a private matter. Theologians and students of theology inevitably transform theology into values and values into involvement with public issues.[6]

In the Philippine context, the question "What does theology do, actually?" can be a tricky question. Some Filipino theologians might perceive the question as hiding certain biases behind its assumption that Christian theology has direct socio-cultural and political-economic effects, with or without a person being conscious of that fact. However, there are other Filipinos who would agree that the question is timely and relevant question – in fact, particularly so, given the current socio-political situation in the Philippines.[7] It would exceed the focus of this essay to give even a superficial summary of the complex entanglements and possibilities for Christian theologies in engaging Filipino socio-political realities. Instead, I will highlight one example each of a characteristic entanglement and a context-sensitive possibility that might be taken as representative of what Christian theology in a Filipino context does: first, the theological support for Filipino President Rodrigo Duterte and his war on drugs campaign and, second, theological critique of economic inequality as reflected in the countries persisting colonial-era style oligarchies. In both, I want to thematize the public responsiveness and relevance of Christian theologies for the social reality of a particular context. In conclusion, I propose a two-step process of, first, *un*doing theology in the Philippines in order to, second, re-form theological praxis of doing theology that pursues justice for the Philippines and Filipino people.

---

[5] Of the numerous works that could be named here, I list only a handful, drawn from different academic disciplines, that have helped me in thinking through these issues: Laura R. Olson and Adam L. Warber, "Belonging, Behaving, and Believing: Assessing the Role of Religion on Presidential Approval", *Political Research Quarterly* 61, no. 2 (June 2008): 192-204, https://www.jstor.org/stable/20299725.; Mario Weyers and Willem Saayman, "'Belonging before believing': Some Missiological Implications of Membership and Belonging in a Christian Community", *Verbum Eccles (Online)* 34, no. 1 (January 2013), http://www.scielo.org.za/scielo.php?script=sci_arttext&pid=S2074770520130001000021; Owen C. Thomas, "Theology and Experience", *The Harvard Theological Review* 78, no. 1/2 (January - April 1985): 179-201; Kevin J. Vanhoozer, *The Drama of Doctrine: A Canonical Linguistic Approach to Christian Doctrine* (Louisville: Westminster John Knox Press, 2005), 243-64.

[6] Of course, Volf and Moltmann are merely two, well-known figures. Since the dawn of the new millennium, work in public theology and political theology has grown into a vital and dynamic subfield of theological research.

[7] See Melba Padilla Maggay, *Dark Days of Authoritarianism: To Be History* (Carlisle: Langham Publishing, 2019); Nicole Curato, *A Duterte Reader: Critical Essays on Rodrigo Duterte's Early Presidency* (Quezon City: Ateneo De Manila University Press, 2017); Jonathan Miller, *Duterte Harry: Fire and Furry in the Philippines* (Victoria and London: Scribes Publications, 2018).

2. Implicit Theological Reasoning and Endorsement of Violence during Duterte's War on Drugs Campaign

Like many populist leaders,[8] President Rodrigo Roa Duterte has cultivated the image of a strongman, but also of a leader appointed by God.[9] Duterte's bloody "war on drugs" campaign has, in turn, been seen by many Filipino Evangelicals as theologically justified. For this reason, according to Filipino scholars, "Duterte's enduring popularity needs to recognise that supporting his leadership is not just a political choice. It is also religious."[10] Since Duterte was elected in 2016, his anti-narcotics campaign has been criticized[11]: Critics argue that Duterte's war on drugs is a pretense, an act of genocide, and the most violent government policy in the Philippine history.[12] Yet as Filipino evangeli-

---

[8] Vijay Prashad et al, *Strongmen: Trump-Modi -Erdoğan -Duterte -Putin* (India: LeftWorld Books, 2018).

[9] Paterno Esmaquel II, "Why Filipinos believe Duterte was 'appointed by God'", *Rappler* (June 28, 2019). https://www.rappler.com/newsbreak/in-depth/234115-why-filipinos-believe-duterte-appointed-by-god).

[10] Jayeel Cornelio and Erron Medina, "Duterte's enduring popularity is not just a political choice–it is also religious," *New Mandela: New Perspectives on Southeast Asia* (September 2018), https://www.newmandala.org/dutertes-enduring-popularity-not-just-political-choice-also-religious/. Prominent Filipino sociologist Randy David similarly contended Duterte portrayed himself as a demigod to garner public sympathy for his aggressions against the Roman Catholic Church in the Philippines. David writes: "In the age of tyranny, the absurdity of these propositions becomes immediately apparent. One would need great imagination, for example, to depict Philippine President Rodrigo Duterte as the personification of God's authority on earth, or to represent the will of the people who voted for him as the will of God. From day one of his presidential candidacy, the man has made a habit of mocking religious beliefs and observances, and of cursing and insulting bishops and priests of the Catholic faith. Since becoming President, he has increasingly sounded as though he were God's equal, if not God himself." Randy David, "Political Theology and the Rise of Tyrants," *Philippine Inquirer* (November 2018), https://opinion.inquirer.net/117537/political-theology-and-the-rise-of-tyrants.

[11] Jayeel Cornelio and Erron Medina, "Christianity and Duterte's War on Drugs in the Philippines", *Politics, Religion & Ideology* (2019): 1-40, https://doi.org/10.1080/21567689.2019.1617135; "Philippine Events of 2018" World Report 2019, *Human Rights Watch* (2019), https://www.hrw.org/world-report/2019/country-chapters/philippines. Amnesty International, "Philippines: UN Investigation Urgently Needed into Duterte Administration's Murderous 'War on Drugs'" (July 2019), https://www.amnesty.org/en/latest/news/2019/07/philippines-un-investigation-urgently-needed-duterte-war-drugs/.

[12] Leila De Lima, "President Duterte's War on Drugs Is a Pretense", *The New York Times* (July 2019), https://www.nytimes.com/2019/07/22/opinion/duterte-philippines-delima-drugs.html; Dahlia Simangan, "Is the Philippine 'War on Drugs' an Act of Genocide?" *Journal of Genocide Research* 20, no. 1, (2001): 68–89,

cal theologian Nestor Ravillas observes, many Filipino evangelicals have been supporters, defenders and apologists of Duterte's war on drugs campaign. Ravillas writes:

> The May 2016 Philippine national elections are an interesting example. A man who allegedly engineered a series of summary killings in the town where he reigned as mayor for twenty years won the presidential race. This phenomenon was coupled with the surprising participation of evangelical Christians in the said elections through attending campaign rallies, engaging in public debates, sifting through social media to vent their opinions, and even more so, openly endorsing their own candidates; thus things that were invisible in many past elections became more visible. But the most astounding thing that happened in this awakened interest of many evangelicals in politics is the open support they accorded to the presidential candidate, Rodrigo Roa Duterte, despite all the killings and acts of violence attributed to him, not to mention his usual badmouthing.[13]

Jayeel Cornelio and Erron Medina, conducted empirical research to understand how various Filipino religious groups respond with Duterte's bloody war on drugs campaign. The data were drawn from the Payatas district, which is one of the poorest villages in Quezon City Metro Manila, Philippines and, since 2016, a hotspot of the Duterte government's anti-drugs campaign.[14] Cornelio and Medina documented people's self-affiliations to various religious groups, and asked the following questions: How do different Christian groups understand the "war on drugs" in Payatas? How have they responded? What accounts for the differences in their responses?[15] After processing the data, Cornelio and Medina concluded:

> Our conjecture is this: There is an implicit theological reasoning that underlies the wide support for the War on Drugs. This conjecture needs to be validated in future research that involves everyday believers. However, for now, we take it based on our findings that the silence of religious groups on the War on Drugs is not just a chilling effect of Duterte's systematic attack on them. It may be the result of the absence of participatory deliberation about the common good even among religious individuals. Our research suggests that within religious groups themselves,

---

https://doi.org/10.1080/14623528.2017.1379939; Steffen Jensen and Karl Hapal, "Police Violence and Corruption in the Philippines: Violent Exchange and the War on Drugs", *Journal of Current Southeast Asian Affairs* 2 (2018): 39–62, http://nbn-resolving.org/urn:nbn:de:gbv:18-4-11264.

[13] Nestor M. Ravillas, "Embedded Violence: The Evangelical Violent Formation and the Rise to Power of President Rodrigo Roa Duterte," *Asia Journal of Theology* 32, no. 1 (April 2018): 51.

[14] Cornelio and Medina, "Christianity and Duterte's War on Drugs in the Philippines," *Politics, Religion & Ideology* (2019): 153-54.

[15] For example, the Catholic parishes, Baptists, Evangelicals, Charismatics, Iglesia ni Cristo (INC), and Ang Dating Daan (ADD). Cornelio and Medina, "Christianity", 3.

> theological opportunities to reflect on the complexity of governance, human rights and public accountability is absent.[16]

The implicit nature of theological reasoning that underlies the wide support for Duterte's war on drugs is one of the greatest challenges facing Filipino theologians today. It makes Christian theology difficult to confront and, at the same time, potentially dangerous especially many Filipino evangelical Christians see violence as a normal part of Christian theology and their everyday life.[17] I would suggest, that, in the case of Evangelical support for Duterte's war on drugs, this "implicit theological reasoning" has enabled a lack of self-awareness and even blind fanaticism that, further, support abuses of power, racism, sexism, and other forms of human sufferings.[18]

3. (Colonial) Theologies in the Philippines and Theology for the Philippines Illustrated by the Persistence of Oligarchy

Christian theologies shape individual thoughts, actions, and interactions by interweaving believing, behaving, and belonging. In these ways, they influence what happens in society at large. Although its forms vary, Christian theologies cannot be reduced to propositions or thinking, in which form doctrine is often separated from social life, but refer to complex ways of life. So a praxiological quality is integral to the work of theology - to what theology does - in which reflection and action combine and relate reciprocally to one another for a particular situation.[19] From my personal point of view, the potential for theologies to function at an implicit level and in unrecognized ways, illustrated by ongoing Christian support for Duterte's violent war on drugs, makes it crucial that contemporary Filipino theologians - whether Evangelical, Pentecostal, Catholic, or Charismatic - devote fresh, focused attention on the complex effectivity of theological discursive practices for the particular situation of the Philippines today.

For several decades now, there has been significant concern in Philippine theological discourse to challenge Western ways of doing theology.[20] Filipino

---

[16] Cornelio and Medina, "Christianity", 18-19.

[17] Ravillas, "Embedded", 51.

[18] Esmaquel II, "Why Filipinos". See also Omer Bartov and Phyllis Mack, eds., *In God's Name: Genocide and Religion in the Twentieth Century* (New York and Oxford: Berghahn Books, 2010 [2001]), 1-78, http://www.jstor.org/stable/j.ctt9qcq8t.

[19] Charles Davis, "Theology and Praxis", *CrossCurrents* 23, no. 2 (Summer 1973): 154-68.

[20] Agnes M. Brazal, *A Theology of Southeast Asia: Liberation-Postcolonial Ethics in the Philippines* (Maryknoll: Orbis 2019), xv-xxxiii; Daniel Franklin Pilario, "Mapping Postcolonial Theory: Appropriations in Contemporary Theology," *Hapag* 3, no.1-2

Catholic theologians Daniel Franklin Pilario and Catalino Arevalo, for example, classifies contemporary efforts with reference to three models or trends in theological focus: *first,* mainstream theology; *second,* contextual theologies; and *lastly,* praxis (also, liberation) theologies.[21] According to Pilario:

> The first area is [. . .] "mainstream theology" - one which uses the discourse of the magisterium as its base for reflection. The second sphere of theological interest is "culture" in general. Part of the conscious attempt to construct a distinctly "Filipino" theology, this theological trend delves into the complexity of the Filipino traditional culture, its popular religions, its language and cultural structures, in order to discern the Good News already embedded in it. And the third trend directly engages Marxist analysis and praxis towards the economic, political, social and cultural transformation of society.[22]

Among the three approaches, Pilario finds the third, praxis-oriented or liberationist most appealing since theological work done in this vein tends to articulate theological-moral response to the colonial legacies of poverty, inequality, and injustice in the Philippines. Many Filipino scholars share this orientation, contending that modern Philippine society is a product of colonial matrices of power, and this is also true of contemporary Filipino theologians doing theology in concrete historical situations dealing with the reverberations of Western colonial domination: massive poverty, homelessness, unemployment, corruption, tyrannical governance, and now climate change.[23] A similar observation was made by a Filipino protestant theologian Eleazar S. Fernandez.[24] Though inspired by Filipino Catholic theologians like Karl Gaspar and Ed de la Torre, Fernandez popularized a "theology of struggle" among mainline Protestant groups in the Philippines.[25] According to him, Philippine history is a history of colonial rule and of political and especially economic exploitation. He writes:

(2006): 9-51. Dindo Rei M. Tesoro and Joselito Alviar Jose, *The Rise of Filipino Theology* (Pasay City: Paulines Publishing House, 2004), 15-198; Edicio De La Torre, *Touching Ground, Taking Root: Theological and Political Reflections on the Philippine Struggle* (Manila: Socio-Pastoral Institute, 1986), 184.

[21] Daniel Franklin Pilario, "The Craft of Contextual Theology: Toward a Conversation on Theological method in the Philippine Context," *Hapag* 1, no. 1 (2004): 5-39.

[22] Pilario, "The Craft of Contextual Theology", 5-6.

[23] Julio Labayen, "Asian Suffering and the Christian Hope", *Testimony Amid Asian Suffering,* ed. T.K. Thomas, (Singapore: CCA, 1977), 9.

[24] Rev. Dr. Eleazar Fernandez is an incumbent president of the Union Theological Seminary Philippines. See, for example, his *Teaching for a Culturally Diverse and Racially Just World* (Eugene: Wipf and Stock, 2014); *Burning Center, Porous Borders: The Church in a Globalized World* (Eugene: Wipf and Stock, 2011); *Reimagining the Human: Theological Anthropology in Response to Systemic Evil* (St. Louis: Chalice Press, 2004).

[25] Eleazar S. Fernandez, *Toward A Theology of Struggle* (Maryknoll: Orbis Books, 1994), 19-32.

> The history of the Filipino people is a history of struggle: a struggle to form a nation that truly embodies the sentiments and aspirations of the people, and a struggle against the negative forces, both within and without, that continue to abort the people's cherished dreams. Caught up in the vortex of the rise and fall of global empires, the Filipinos found their dreams always nipped in the bud by their supposed liberators.[26]

Despite extensive modernization in the post-colonial Philippine context, Philippine society continues to struggle with and reproduce its colonial legacies. This struggle is illustrated by the "rule of the few" that structures economic functioning and social participation opportunities to a profound extent.[27] On May 18, 2017, business columnist of *The Philippine Star* newspaper Boo Chanco, commenting on oligarchic economics in the Philippines, wrote:

> ...Indeed, the two wealthiest people in the Philippines, according to the Forbes 2012 annual rich list, Henry Sy and Lucio Tan, were worth a combined $13.6 billion or six percent of the entire Philippine economy. In contrast, about 25 million people, or one quarter of the population, lived on $1 a day or less in 2009, which was little changed from a decade earlier. The oligarchs have been sucking the blood out of our economy for a very long time. Many of the elite families have dominated since the Spanish colonial era. The Ayalas and Aboitizes control large chunks of the economy to this day and it seems, forever. They essentially got their capital from ridiculously large land grants given by the Spanish colonizers and accumulated profits from businesses through generations. These gave them a big head start to control major industries from property development to banking and telecommunications.[28]

The 2019 Forbes Philippines report shows that under Duterte's economic policies, Henry Sy, Lucio Tan, Ayala, Aboitizes, are still included on top 20 Filipino billionaires.[29] Aside from these, according to IBON Foundation:

---

[26] Fernandez, *Toward,* 8-9.

[27] Specifying this critique of oligarchy, Nathan Gilbert Quimpo diagnoses a cluster of interrelated problems including: bossism, electoral clientelism, and cacique democracy. See Nathan Gilbert Quimpo, "Review Article: Oligarchie Patrimonialism, Bossism, Electoral Clientelism, and Contested Democracy in the Philippines," *Comparative Politics* 37, no. 2 (January 2005): 229-50; cf. Paul Hutchcroft, *Booty Capitalism: The Politics of Banking in the Philippines* (Ithaca: Cornell University Press, 1998); John Sidel, *Capital, Coercion, and Crime: Bossism in the Philippines* (Stanford: Stanford University Press, 1999).

[28] Boo Chanco, "Duterte and Oligarchs," The Philippine Star (May 18, 2017), https://www.philstar.com/ business/2017/05/18/1701283/duterte-and-oligarchs. See also Michael Johnston, Syndromes of Corruption: Wealth, Power, and Democracy (Cambridge: Cambridge University Press, 2005), 137-44;

[29] "Philippines' 50 Richest," Forbes Philippines' 50 Richest 2019 Ranking (2019), https://www.forbes.com/philippines-billionaires/list/#tab:overall.

> The Duterte administration's economic policies increased the net worth of the country's richest Filipino and the profits of the largest corporations. The 40 richest Filipino's net worth grew from Php3.69 trillion in 2016 to Php3.81 trillion in 2018. The net income of the top PSE-listed firms grew from Php683 billion to Php769 billion in the same period. On the other hand, the average daily basic pay of wage and salary workers nationwide was virtually stagnant in the last 17 years. Adjusted for inflation, this grew by only 1.7% to Php364 in January 2018 since 2001.[30]

Simply put, the already huge gap between how much the majority of ordinary Filipino households earn monthly, and that of the country's top earners is widening. Using the Philippine legislature, the rich, powerful, and famous protect their interest.[31] Consequently, the Philippine economic disparity has led to billionaires get richer and richer, the Filipino poor get poorer.[32]

Massive wealth inequality is not unique to the Philippines. My claim, however, is that because of the extent to which massive wealth inequality conjugates into social class structures, the existential context of the Philippines is experienced at the level of lived social reality as economically determined. This issues a call to Filipino Christian theologies seeking to attend to lived experience to engage in socio-economic critique and to articulate practical, problem-focused alternatives for life in community.[33] In many ways, the situation in Philippines now resembles the situations in Latin/South America in which liberation theology emerged. This is one of the main reasons why theologies of liberation remain popular and important to Filipinos. Dominador Bombongan Jr., following John Sobrino, noted that "responding to poverty related issues is usually the bread and butter of liberation theologians if not

---

[30] "Richest getting richer," *IBON Foundation* (August 1, 2019), https://www.ibon.org /richest-getting-richer/.

[31] See Shiela S. Coronel, Yvonne T. Chua, Boomba B. Cruz, and Luz Rimban, *The Rulemakers: How the wealthy and well-born dominate the Congress* (Quezon City: Philippine Center for Investigative Journalism, 2004).

[32] Ralf Rivas, "In Charts: Rich Philippine regions get richer, poor ones barely improve," *Rappler* (May 30, 2019), https://www.rappler.com/business/231871-charts-regions-get-richer-poor-ones-barely-improve-philippines; "PH economy growing but poverty still high – World Bank," *Rappler* (May 30, 2018), https://www.rappler.com/business/ 203680-economy-poverty-rate-philippines-world-bank-report-2018; "The World Bank in the Philippines," *World Bank* (April 4, 2019), https://www.worldbank.org/en/country/ philippines/overview; "Poor Filipino families worst hit by rising July 2018 inflation," *IBON Foundation* (August 8, 2018), https://www.ibon.org/ poor-filipino-families-worst-hit-by-rising-july-2018-inflation/.

[33] Robert B. Fox, "The Study of Filipino Society and its Significance to Programs of Economic and Social Development," *Philippine Sociological Review* 7, no. 1/2 (January - April, 1959): 2-11;

their *raison d'être*."[34] He argues further, "liberation theologians take the cause of the poor not because it is a fashionable thing to do but because it is what they are called to do as a source of engagement."[35] For Bombongan, while each theology of liberation focuses on different social issues, they share the common principle that the central Christian message is to proclaim the Kingdom of God and liberation of the poor and oppressed to an unjust society.

Even if Filipino theologies of liberation have also been misinterpreted and criticized by many conservative Filipino Christians for overreliance on Marxist ideologies,[36] theologies of liberation or praxis theologies continue to be fruitful in the Philippines precisely because of the ways they speak to the lived experiences of Filipino Christians struggling with economic oppression and politically sanctioned violence.[37] Filipino liberation theologies have, in fact, produced new fruit in the form of more recent Filipino contextual and postcolonial theologies.[38]

---

[34] Dominador Bombongan, Jr., "Social Exclusion: The New Name of Poverty," *Hapag* 5, no. 1-2 (2008): 9-34.

[35] Bombongan, Jr., "Social Exclusion",9.

[36] One of the best examples of this was the publication of James Whelchel entitled, *The Path of Liberation: Theology of Struggle in the Philippines* (Quezon City: New Day Publishers, 1995). Another interesting piece written by American anthropologist Kathleen M. Nadeau entitled, *Liberation Theology in the Philippines: Faith in a Revolution* (2001), discusses the ways theologies of liberation have been variously applied in the Philippines by Catholic priests and laity according to context, for example, in rural and urban settings, but with a shared set of economic and political concerns. See Kathleen M. Nadeau, *Liberation Theology in the Philippines: Faith in a Revolution* (Westport and London: Praeger, 2002), 73-92.

[37] Agnes M. Brazal and Danny Franklin Pilario, "Disciplines, Interdisciplinarity and Theology," *Hapag* 4, nos. 1-2, (2007): 5-25; Danny Franklin Pilario, "The Craft of Contextual Theology: Towards A Conversation on Theological Method in the Philippine Context," *Hapag* I, no. 1 (2004): 5-39.

[38] Brazal, *A Theology*. Jose De Mesa, *Why Theology is Never Far From Home* (Manila: Dela Salle Unniversity Press, 2003), 5-12; Lawrence S. Pedregosa, "Theoretical Propositions in Doing A Filipino Postcolonial Theology," *Justitia* 16, (2011): 19-49; Daniel Franklin Pilario, "Mapping Postcolonial Theory: Appropriations in Contemporary Theology," *Hapag* 3, no. 1-2 (2006): 9-51. Bernie Mabalay, "Reshaping Theology of Struggle in the Context of Globalization," *Christian Conference of Asia: Congress of Asian Theologians CATS III (*April 18-22, 2016), 1-40; Melba Padilla Maggay, *The Gospel and Culture: Contextualization Issues Through Asian Eyes* (Mandaluyong City: OMF Literature Publishers, 2013), 5-179; Wonsuk Ma, "Doing Theology in the Philippines: A Case of Pentecostal Christianity," *Asian Journal of Pentecostal Studies* 8, no. 2, (2005): 215-233; E. Acoba et al, *Doing Theology in the Philippines* (Mandaluyong City: OMF Literature Publishers, 2007), 3-50; Antonio B. Lambino et al, *Towards "doing theology" in the Philippine context* (Manila: Cardinal Bea Institute for Ecumenical Studies, 1986).

4. A "PROPHETIC MINISTRY"? UNDOING THEOLOGY IN THE PHILIPPINES TO DO THEOLOGY FOR THE PHILIPPINES

The analysis offered here is prompted by the observation that Filipino society generally and certain Filipino Christian theologies in particular remain to a significant extent products of Western colonialization and that recognition and diagnosis of this reality is crucial for any corrective efforts seeking improvement in areas of poverty, racism, or unjust governance among others. I want to suggest that any forms of theology in the Philippines that remain detached from the contextuality specificity of Filipino lived experience in relation to such issues will not only fail to make improvements but will continue to function as implicitly theologies that tolerate or even support injustice. Much Filipino theology currently lacks this attention to local context and therefore struggles to find relevance in the broader society. As Filipina social anthropologist and activist Melba Padilla Maggay writes:

> It is precisely because the Church has retreated from the world that the Gospel now lacks a context. We have allowed the world to become secularized, and the Church's influence to be narrowed within the four paltry walls of the local church. In the process, the Word has become ghostly, a pale shadow of the Logos who, as John describes it, has been seen with the eye, has been looked upon and touched with the hands.[39]

For Maggay, finding contextual relevance in Philippine society is a key challenge for Filipino Christian communities.

As a closing word, I see the kind of contextual relevance that Ravillas, Bombonan, Maggay and others have called for as the meaning of the "prophetic ministry" of Christian community and a prophetic *un*doing of theology as a key aspect of what theology must at times do. Christian communities and their theologies need to articulate and to exercise both aspects of this prophetic task. Under Duterte's political regime, Christian theologians in the Philippines need to engage first not in doing but in *un*doing theology. By this I mean the work of making implicit theological reasoning visible and critiquing complicities in violence and injustice. I have attempted to engage in this kind of undoing in this chapter. Second and in coordination with that, Christian theologies in the Philippines need to be re-formed in ways that attend to and cultivate justice in particular contexts of specific problems facing Philippine society. The prophetic task is to offer social-cultural and political-economic critique and to provide realistic, fair, and problem-oriented solutions to threats to human well-being. In the Philippines, these problems are systemic and require systemic change. Filipino theologians need to conduct critical analyses of all social systems, and the intentional or unintentional functioning of implicit

---

[39] Melba Padilla Maggay, *Transforming Society: Reflections on the Kingdom and Politics* (Quezon City: Institute for Studies in Asian Church and Culture, 2004), 28.

theological reasoning in them that maintain structural evil, justify forms of violence, and protect the few powerful at the expense of the many weak.

BIBLIOGRAPHY

"PH economy growing but poverty still high - World Bank." *Rappler* (May 30, 2018). https://www.rappler.com/business/203680-economy-poverty-rate-philippines-world-bank-report-2018. (accessed October 15, 2019).

"Poor Filipino families worst hit by rising July 2018 inflation." *IBON Foundation* (August 8, 2018). https://www.ibon.org/poor-filipino-families-worst-hit-by-rising-july-2018-inflation/. (accessed October 15, 2019).

"Richest getting richer." *IBON Foundation* (August 1, 2019). https://www.ibon.org/richest-getting-richer/. (accessed October 14, 2019).

"Philippines' 50 Richest." *Forbes Philippines' 50 richest 2019 Ranking* (2019). https://www.forbes.com/philippines-billionaires/list/#tab:overall. (accessed October 14, 2019).

"Philippines: UN investigation urgently needed into Duterte administration's murderous 'war on drugs'." *Amnesty International* (July 8, 2019). https://www.amnesty.org/en/latest/news/2019/07/philippines-un-investigation-urgently-needed-duterte-war-drugs/. (accessed September 29, 2019).

"Philippine Events of 2018." *World Report 2019, Human Rights Watch* (2019). https://www.hrw.org/world-report/2019/country-chapters/philippines. (accessed September 29, 2019).

"The World Bank in the Philippines." *World Bank* (April 4, 2019). https://www.worldbank.org/en/country/philippines/overview. (accessed October 15, 2019).

Abinales, Patricio, and Donna Amoroso. *State and Society in the Philippines*. Lanham: Rowman and Littlefield Publishers, 2005.

Abinales, Patricio. "The Philippines: Weak State, Resilient President." *Southeast Asian Affairs* (2008): 293-312.

Abinales, Patricio. "Progressive-machine politics in early iwentieth-century U.S. politics and colonial state-building in the Philippines." In *The American Colonial State in the Philippines: Global Perspectives,* edited by Julian Go and Anne L. Forster, 148-81. Durham: Duke University Press, 2003.

Acoba, Emo. et al, *Doing Theology in the Philippines*. Mandaluyong City: OMF Literature Publishers, 2007.

Aldridge, Alan. *Religion in the Contemporary World.* Cambridge: Polity Press, 2000.

Asad, Talal. *Formations of the Secular: Christianity, Islam, Modernity*. Stanford: Stanford University Press, 2003.

Berger, Peter L. *The Sacred Canopy*. New York: Anchor Books, 1967.

Bombongan, Jr., Dominador. "Social Exclusion: The New Name of Poverty." *Hapag,* 5, no. 1-2 (2008): 9-34.

Brazal, Agnes M. and Danny Franklin Pilario. "Disciplines, Interdisciplinarity and Theology." *Hapag* 4, nos. 1-2, (2007): 5-25.

Brazal, Agnes M. *A Theology of Southeast Asia: Liberation-Postcolonial Ethics in the Philippines.* Maryknoll: Orbis, 2019.

Bruce, Steve. *Religion and Modernization.* Oxford: Oxford University Press, 1992.

Casanova, José. *Public Religions in the Modern World.* USA: The University of Chicago Press, 2012.

Chanco, Boo. "Duterte and Oligarchs." *The Philippine Star* (May 18, 2017). https://www.philstar.com/business/2017/05/18/1701283/duterte-and-oligarchs. (accessed October 13, 2019).

Cornelio, Jayeel and Erron Medina. "Christianity and Duterte's War on Drugs in the Philippines." *Politics, Religion & Ideology* (2019): 1-40. https://doi.org/10.1080/21567689.2019.1617135. (accessed October 9, 2019).

Cornelio, Jayeel and Erron Medina. "Duterte's enduring popularity is not just a political choice–it is also religious." *New Mandela: New Perspectives on Southeast Asia* (September 3, 2018). https://www.newmandala.org/dutertes-enduring-popularity-not-just-political-choice-also-religious/. (accessed October 16, 2019).

Coronel, Shiela S., Yvonne T Chua, Boomba B. Cruz and Rimban Luz. *The Rulemakers: How the wealthy and well-born dominate the Congress.* Quezon City: Philippine Center for Investigative Journalism, 2004.

Curato, Nicole. *A Duterte Reader: Critical Essays on Rodrigo Duterte's Early Presidency.* Quezon City: Ateneo De Manila University Press, 2017.

Davis, Charles. "Theology and Praxis." *CrossCurrents* 23, no. 2, (SUMMER 1973): 154-68.

De La Torre, Edicio. *Touching Ground, Taking Root: Theological and Political Reflections on the Philippine Struggle.* Manila: Socio-Pastoral Institute, 1986.

De Lima, Leila. "President Duterte's War on Drugs Is a Pretense." *The New York Times* (July 22, 2019). https://www.nytimes.com/2019/07/22/opinion/duterte-philippines-delima-drugs.html. (accessed October 7, 2019).

De Mesa, Jose. *Why Theology is Never Far From Home.* Manila: Dela Salle University Press, 2003.

Esmaquel II, Paterno. "Why Filipinos believe Duterte was 'appointed by God'" *Rappler* (June 28, 2019). https://www.rappler.com/newsbreak/in-depth/234115-why-filipinos-believe- duterte-appointed-by-god. (accessed September 7, 2019).

Fernandez, Eleazar S. *Toward A Theology of Struggle.* Maryknoll: Orbis Books, 1994.

Fox, Robert B. "The Study Of Filipino Society And Its Significance To Programs Of Economic And Social Development." *Philippine Sociological Review* 7, no. 1/2 (January - April, 1959): 2-11.

Franco, Jennifer. *Elections and Democratization in the Philippines.* New York, Routledge, 2001.

Hoogendoorn, Brigitte, Cornelius A. Rietveld, and André van Stel. "Belonging, believing, bonding, and behaving: the relationship between religion and business ownership at the country level." *Journal of Evolutionary Economics* 26, no. 3, (July 2016): 519–50. https://link.springer.com/article/10.1007/s00191-016-0447-7. (accessed July 28, 2019).

Hutchcroft, Paul. *Booty Capitalism: The Politics of Banking in the Philippines.* Ithaca: Cornell University Press, 1998.

Jensen, Steffen and Karl Hapal. "Police Violence and Corruption in the Philippines: Violent Exchange and the War on Drugs." *Journal of Current Southeast Asian Affairs* 2 (2018): 39–62. http://nbn-resolving.org/urn:nbn:de:gbv:18-4-11264. (accessed October 7, 2019).

Joaquin, Nick. *The Aquinos of Tarlac An Essay On History As Three Generations* 3rd ed. Manila: Solar Publishing Corporation, 1986.

Johnston, Michael. *Syndromes of Corruption: Wealth, Power, and Democracy.* Cambridge: Cambridge University Press, 2005.

Labayen, Julio. "Asian Suffering and the Christian Hope." *Testimony Amid Asian Suffering,* edited T.K. Thomas. Singapore: CCA, 1977.

Lambino, Antonio B. et al. *Towards "Doing Theology" in the Philippine Context.* Manila: Cardinal Bea Institute for Ecumenical Studies, 1986.

Lara, Jr. Francisco J. *Insurgents, Clans, and States Political Legitimacy and Resurgent Conflict in Muslim Mindanao, Philippines.* Quezon: Ateneo De Manila University Press, 2014.

Ma, Wonsuk. "Doing Theology in the Philippines: A Case of Pentecostal Christianity." *Asian Journal of Pentecostal Studies* 8, no. 2 (2005): 215-33.

Mabalay, Bernie. "Reshaping Theology of Struggle in the Context of Globalization." *Christian Conference of Asia: Congress of Asian Theologians CATS III* (April 18-22, 2016), 1-40.

Maggay, Melba Padilla. *Dark Days of Authoritarianism: To Be History.* Carlisle: Langham Publishing, 2019.

Maggay, Melba Padilla. *The Gospel and Culture: Contextualization Issues Through Asian Eyes.* Mandaluyong City: OMF Literature Publishers, 2013.

Maggay, Melba Padilla. *Transforming Society: Reflections on the Kingdom and Politics.* Quezon City: Institute for Studies in Asian Church and Culture, 2004.

Miller, Jonathan. *Duterte Harry: Fire and Furry in the Philippines.* Victoria and London: Scribes Publications, 2018.

Moltmann, Jürgen. *God for a Secular Society: The Public Relevance of Theology.* London: SCM Press, 1999.

Nadeau, Kathleen M. *Liberation Theology in the Philippines: Faith in a Revolution.* Westport and London: Praeger Publishers, 2002.

Olson, Laura R. and Adam L Warber. "Belonging, Behaving, and Believing: Assessing the Role of Religion on Presidential Approval." *Political Research Quarterly* 61, no. 2 (June 2008): 192-204. https://www.jstor.org/stable/20299725. (accessed July 22, 2019).

Omer, Bartov, and Phyllis Mack, eds. *In God's Name: Genocide and Religion in the Twentieth Century.* New York and Oxford: Berghahn Books, 2010. http://www.jstor.org/stable/j.ctt9qcq8t. (accessed October 8, 2019).

Pedregosa, Lawrence S. "Theoretical Propositions in Doing A Filipino Postcolonial Theology." *Justitia* 16, (2011): 19-49;

Pilario, Daniel Franklin. "Mapping Postcolonial Theory: Appropriations in Contemporary Theology." *Hapag* 3, no.1-2 (2006): 9-51.

Pilario, Daniel Franklin. "Mapping Postcolonial Theory: Appropriations in Contemporary Theology." *Hapag* 3, no. 1-2 (2006): 9-51.

Pilario, Daniel Franklin. "The Craft of Contextual Theology: Towards A Conversation on Theological Method in the Philippine Contex." *Hapag* 1, no. 1 (2004): 5-39.

Prashad, Vijay et al. *Strongmen: Trump-Modi -Erdoğan -Duterte -Putin*. India: LeftWorld Books, 2018.

Quimpo, Nathan Gilbert. "Review Article: Oligarchie Patrimonialism, Bossism, Electoral Clientelism, and Contested Democracy in the Philippines," *Comparative Politics* 37, no. 2 (January 2005): 229-50.

Ravillas, Nestor M. "Embedded Violence: The Evangelical Violent Formation and the Rise to Power of President Rodrigo Roa Duterte." *Asia Journal of Theology* 32, no. 1 (April 2018): 44-59.

Rivas, Ralf. "In Charts: Rich Philippine regions get richer, poor ones barely improve." *Rappler* (May 30, 2019). https://www.rappler.com/business/ 231871-charts-regions-get-richer-poor-ones-barely-improve-philippines. (accessed October 15, 2019.

Saroglou, Vassil. "Believing, Bonding, Behaving, and Belonging: The Big Four Religious Dimensions and Cultural Variation." *Journal of Cross-Cultural Psychology* 42, no. 8 (2018): 1320–40. http://citeseerx.ist.psu.edu/viewdoc/ download?doi=10.1.1.922.7296 &rep=rep1&type=pdf. (accessed July 8, 2019).

Sidel, John. *Capital, Coercion, and Crime: Bossism in the Philippines*. Stanford: Stanford University Press, 1999.

Simangan, Dahila. "Is the Philippine 'War on Drugs' an Act of Genocide?" *Journal of Genocide Research* 20, no. 1 (201): 68–89. https://doi.org/10.1080/ 14623528.2017. 1379939. (accessed October 7, 2019).

Tesoro, Dindo Rei M. and Joselito Alviar Jose. *The Rise of Filipino Theology*. Philippines: Paulines Publishing House, 2004.

Thomas, Owen C. "Theology and Experience." *The Harvard Theological Review* 78, no. 1-2 (Jan. - Apr., 1985): 179-201.

Taylor, Charles. *A Secular Age*. Cambridge: Harvard University Press, 2007.

Tracy, David. *The Analogical Imagination: Christian Theology and the Culture of Pluralism*. New York: Crossroad, 1982.

Tracy, David. *Blessed Rage for Order: The New Pluralism in Theology*. New York: Seabury. New York: Crossroad, 1975.

Vanhoozer, Kevin J. *The Drama of Doctrine: A Canonical Linguistic Approach to Christian Doctrine*. USA: Westminster John Knox Press, 2005.

Volf, Miroslav. *A Public Faith: How Followers of Christ Should Serve the Common Good*. Grand Rapids: Brazos Press, 2011.

Weekley, Kathleen. *The Communist Party of the Philippines 1968-1993: A Story of Its Theory and Practice*. Quezon City, University of the Philippines, 2001.

Weyers, Mario and Saayman, Wilem. "Belonging before believing': Some missiological implications of membership and belonging in a Christian community." *Verbum Eccles. (Online)* 34, no.1 (Jan. 2013). http://www.scielo.org.za/scielo.php?script=sci_arttext &pid=S2074-77052013000100021. (accessed September 29, 2019).

Whelchel, James. *The Path of Liberation: Theology of Struggle in the Philippines*. Quezon City: New Day Publishers, 1995.

Transformations of African Christianity

From the First- to the Second-Generation of African Churches in Germany

Elorm Nick Ahialey-Mawusi (Hamburg, Germany; Togo)

1. Introduction

An increase in migration over the past two decades from the "Global South" to Germany has contributed enormously to the diversification of the German population. Among those who have migrated to Germany and other European countries are many West Africans, who bring along with them, among many other assets, their "social, cultural and spiritual capital"[1]. This has, in turn, facilitated the establishment of African Diaspora churches. For the past twenty years, Germany has recorded a significant increase in the establishment of these churches. According to Werner Kahl, reasons for the appearance and growth of such churches include: An increase in the number of African Christians in Europe; racism in Europe, which can be felt even in the European churches, and a significant Christian and cultural self-confidence of Africans.[2]

Churches attended largely by individuals with a migration background serve many purposes, including offering a spiritual home for many Africans, preservation of African identity, and social networking in overcoming different challenges faced in the host lands.[3] The very first Christian church of African origin in Germany was the Celestial Church of Christ, founded in 1974 in Munich[4]. Other African churches were founded later from the 1980 onwards.

At present there are more than three hundred registered migrant churches with an African origin in Hamburg alone. For the whole of Germany, the

[1] Afe Adogame, *The African Christian Diaspora* (New York: Bloomsbury Publishing, 2013), 101-122.

[2] Werner Kahl, *Vom Verweben des Eigenen mit dem Fremden: Impulse zu einer transkulturellen Neuformierung des evangelischen Gemeindelebens* (Hamburg: Missionshilfe Verlag, 2016), 55.

[3] Kahl, *Vom Verweben*, 55.

[4] Benjamin Simon, *From Migrants to Missionaries: Christians of African Origin in Germany* (Frankfurt am Main: Peter Lang: 2010), 20. The congregation is, in fact, less representative of African churches in Germany today, which are more Pentecostal and charismatic in nature.

estimate is about two thousand such congregations. The membership varies from a dozen to a few hundred active participants. The majority of these churches in Hamburg have West African leadership and membership, predominantly Ghanaian. This is due to the fact that Hamburg, the harbor city in Germany, has become the center of Ghanaian presence in Germany. Therefore, the majority of the churches have Ghanaian leadership and membership. This is followed by Nigerian congregations and other (French speaking) West African countries such as Togo.[5]

2. African Churches in Germany: Classification, Ecclesiology and Theologies

In his book *Sent Forth: African Missionary Work in the West*, Kwiyani Harvey dealt extensively with the theme of African migrant churches in the West. He identified four streams of African immigrant Christianity, the largest being the Pentecostal/Charismatic group. In the context of Germany, most of these are what is often referred to as "one-man-churches". However, the presence of the Church of Pentecost – the biggest Pentecostal church in Ghana and having a national leadership and that has overtaken the Roman Catholic Church in membership numbers last year (2018-2019) for the first time – is equally significant. The other categories are mainline African Christians who have joined mainline western Christians or form an ethnic-specific congregation with a mainline church. The two primary groups are the Ghanaian Methodist Church and the Presbyterian Church of Ghana. The third and the fourth stream are the Roman Catholic tradition and finally the African Initiated Churches (AICs).[6] This classification is essential for the discourse on African Christianity in Europe. Many classify African migrant churches under the general umbrella of Pentecostal/Charismatic churches due to an expected mirroring of the pentecostalization of Christianity in Africa. Contrary to expectation, however, Kwiyani's categorization highlights the blurring that occurs already by the time of the second generation.

The language of communication in these churches is often a West-African language: In the case of Ghanaian-led churches this is especially Twi, but also Ewe. If the congregations have an international West-African membership, the language might be English or French. At times, when German visitors are present, German translations will be provided. But the language of communication is never solely or even mostly German. Services are celebrated more or less in an identical way as compared to those "back home". The acting found-

---

[5] Information obtained from the internal data of the African Christian Council, Hamburg (unofficial).

[6] Harvey C. Kwiyani, *Sent Forth: African Missionary Work in the West* (Maryknoll: Orbis Books, 2014), 25.

ers and pastors are mostly male. Regularly, visiting preachers are invited from West-Africa to run programs. Sermons and prayers are often centered around such interconnected topics as: casting away (out) evil spirits, breaking ancestral curses, declarations of supernatural healing and success in life through divine intervention, the power of the man-of-God, the giving of offerings. The Church of Pentecost, the Methodist church of Ghana, the Presbyterian Church and the Ghana Catholic Mission, have also occasionally received their pastors sent from Ghana.

African Diaspora churches have developed their own theologies which are not significantly different from those of home. These theologies are informed by some factors such as: tradition and culture, worldviews, diaspora identity, low level of education and theological formation, and low level of socio-economic opportunities. In the churches, these theological orientations are often intersected by difficulties related to (lack of) proper documentation or visas, (absence of) residency permits, and the '3D' jobs that often constitute their occupation (Dirty, Dangerous and De-humanizing).

3. Reverse Mission or Mission Impossible? The Second Generation

From early in the 1980s until present day, these pastors felt called by God to "reach out and win the Germans for Christ". They felt "called" by God and "sent" to Germany as "missionaries" in order to re-evangelize or "rechristianize" Germans, who according to them, have abandoned the very faith they once sent missionaries to Africa to proclaim. Hence the notion of "reverse mission". This vision, however, has not materialized. Germans (more specifically, Germans with no immigration background) can rarely be found in these congregations. They serve the needs of West-African migrants in their own languages and cultures, and they function as a "home-away-from-home" and as networks of spiritual, psychological, and social assistance in times of need and crises. Gradually, this awareness is redefining the mission statements of the churches. For instance, the African Christian Council, Hamburg (an umbrella organization that regroups over 60 African-led churches in Hamburg) defines its mission with the following statement: "Reaching the Africans through the Africans". They explain further: "More than twenty-thousand immigrants of the African descents live in Hamburg. These are the people that we reach with our goals. [sic]"[7]

Kwiyani identified two factors that contribute to the survival of African churches in the West, namely: The current flow of African migration to the West and the explosion of Christianity in Africa. He cautioned, however, that

---

[7] African Christian Council Hamburg, http://www.africanchristiancouncil.de/ (accessed on 15.08.2019).

new immigration policies in the West that are aimed at stopping Africans migration to the West will gradually be a threat to the continuous existence of African churches in the coming years. Besides, he predicted that the growth of Christianity in Africa could reach its peak in the next decades and that the majority of Africans coming to the West might not necessarily be Christians any longer. That may contribute to the decline of African Churches. With a great deal of skepticism, he observed that "the immigrant congregation is a convenient survival tactic that would not be necessary under different circumstances."[8] Considering the threats identified, one can infer that the "next generation" of Africans in the West may well be the source of continuity for these churches.

The experience of the second generation of African Christians in Germany, nevertheless, takes a different course. In the second decade of the new century, a new development is taking place in the context of the presence of West-African inhabitants in Germany. The younger "up-and-coming" generation – those who have grown up in Germany, but whose parents hail from West-Africa – is increasingly breaking away from their parental churches. For these Christians, their mother tongue is German even though most know English or French quite well. But often they can only understand some of the mother-tongue of their parents without being able to communicate in it fluently. Many of them do not have a personal migration history. They are not migrants, but German citizens. They are challenged to negotiate their identity in between the cultures and traditions of both Germany and the countries of origin of their parents. This constellation has necessitated and, in fact, now generated new modes and forms of communal life. The recent creation of Christian faith communities by the second-generation of African migrants in Germany is a case in point. In what follows, I will describe the experience of the congregation I pastor with a special focus on "doing theology", transculturality, and identity.

4. THE CASE OF LIVING GENERATION CHURCH

I come originally from Togo, and I lead the *Living Generation Church* (LGC) formed in 2014 in Hamburg. I came to Germany a decade ago in my early 20s. I had completed a first degree in literature at the University of Education in Winneba (Ghana). My father served as minister of the United Pentecostal Church International in Togo. In Germany, I joined a number of West-African Pentecostal churches. While studying theology at the Missionsakademie at the University of Hamburg and then at Hermannsburg in conjunction with Göttingen University, I became increasingly dissatisfied especially with the leader-

---

[8] African Christian Council Hamburg, http://www.africanchristiancouncil.de/ (Accessed on 15.08.2019).

ship role of some African migrant pastors. I tried to process some of this in my seminar papers, as I reflected on, for example, human rights abuses in migrant churches. At present, I am preparing a doctoral research project on African churches of the second generation in the diaspora.

LGC is a juridical entity with the status of "e.V." (*eingetragener Verein*, that is, "registered association") that celebrates its services in the youth center of the St. Georg Church in Hamburg, a Protestant congregation of the main German Protestant church body, located adjacent to the main train station. At present, LGC has a regular church attendance of about 100 to 120 young people, roughly ranging between the ages of 15 and 35. The vast majority of the members grew up as children in African migrant churches. Upon reaching adolescence, they left their parents' churches. A larger number came from the Methodist Church of Ghana due to unresolved conflicts between the youth group in a church that wanted to organize themselves independently from the leadership and the minister sent from Ghana. In 2018-2019, LGC has welcomed the membership of many first-generation adults as well. Reasons given for joining LGC by the members include the following:

- Interest in a faith community that provides them with a safe space where they can feel free and at home, where they can express their faith in their own way and in their own language - that is, in German - and where their concerns are addressed in a meaningful and productive manner;
- The experience of a support group of like-minded people with similar experiences and a similar spiritual orientation;
- Problems in accepting the authority claims of pastors in the parental churches where it is - in line with traditional cultural values - deemed inappropriate to question statements or positions of the pastor or the elders;
- Lack of resonance with the subject of Satan and demons as found in their parents' churches;
- A critique of the emphasis on money-giving as precondition of divine intervention in the parents' churches;

In LGC, they appreciate the leadership's commitment to being approachable, which is not the experience they have had in their parents' churches. The LGC mission statement states that our mission consists in "communicating the Gospel in a meaningful way to our generation", [9] while the motto of LGC is:

- Transformation - of lives of individuals and communities
- Reconciliation - among people and between people and God
- Empowerment - for good and better living

The leadership group of about 12 members consists of 10 women and two men who are mainly youth. There is also a "committee of elders" the role of which

[9] Living Generation Church, "This is a Living Generation," http://living-gen.com/about/our-mission/. (Accessed on 07.11.2019).

role is mainly to "advise" or offer pastoral care especially in the area of marriage and in times of bereavement.

At LGC, the language of communication is German throughout. Contrary to the churches of the first generation, the question has always been whether there is a need for translation from German to English. I do sometimes preach in English, but it is always translated live into German. About 100-120 people attend church services every Sunday; of these, approximately fifteen are young people with German/European parents ("bio-Deutsch") or an American, English or Turkish background. The gender ratio is approximately 60% woman, 40% men. The service lasts three hours (11:30 - 14:30).

The liturgy, service, and the sermon of LGC are appealing and relevant to its members, and the service is participatory throughout and not pastor centered. There are times, such as times for study of the Bible, during which many members express their own views and insights, often on a highly reflected level. The time of testimony and sharing is another time during which members share their personal experiences. The liturgy is a blend of West-African and German traditions. In many neo-Pentecostal African migrant churches, the Lord's prayer is usually not included. LGC, however, has learned to appreciate its value in the German ecclesial context. At the end of the service, there is always a dinner served for the whole congregation.

In LGC, the issue of identity and *Heimat* ("home") is addressed directly and indirectly a number of times. Some of the young people still at times visit their parental churches whenever they feel the need to visit "Africa". At the same time, they would feel embarrassed to have their German friends with no African background join them to the African migrant churches. The young people at LGC would also not join German churches. One of the reasons, among others, is that when one goes into a typical Protestant church, one looks at the congregation and the leadership, and these churches do not represent the diversity present in the society, even though the message they communicate values it. At LGC, diversity is a defining characteristic and is celebrated in an embodied way every week.

As I just mentioned, LGC also appeals to some non-African Germans as well, including young people. This is all the more remarkable in a context where a great number of young people have turned away from the established Protestant and Catholic churches, both of which continue to experience significant decrease in membership. Many younger people feel those churches are not able to connect with them and their spiritual needs in meaningful ways. In LGC, a relevant theology is in the process of developing which might have the potential to become meaningful to other Germans of the younger generation, many of whom have a spiritual longing that is often not met in the established Protestant churches. For these reasons, non-African young Germans consistently visit LGC.

LGC so far has been successful in translating the Christian gospel message in meaningful and relevant ways to young people, especially those with an African family background. It bridges a large cultural gap between the churches of their parents with their African traditions and values, on the one hand, and the German establishment churches and society, on the other hand. LGC flourishes and makes sense "in-between" these options, as one creative and productive forum for the children of West-African migrants in negotiating their identity as Christians between the culture of family origin and the culture of residence.

In a way, LGC offers not so much an "in-between" but a space for interrelating these experiences. The idea of an integrated reality is of high importance to the members of LGC. They want to see the impact of faith and identity apart from a Sunday morning experience. They want to see how their faith speaks life into the places where they work, where they study, where they play, where they worship, and every aspect of their humanity. Their Christian identity is present(ed) consciously or unconsciously in everyday life. They do not divide interests depending on where they are.

The apparent break in ecclesiology from the churches of the first generation is identifiable in the ways the services are conducted, the languages used, the form of music, the liturgies, the notion of power and authority in the church, questions of hierarchy, church polity, church order and structures, and church leadership. The break in theology addresses the issues of worldviews, quite different to those of the first generation which are highly informed by the realities of African cultures. The hermeneutical keys for explaining and understanding the scriptures are very much informed by lived realities and experiences that are significantly different from those of the first generation – for example, in terms of social circles and opportunities, socio-economic status, cultural milieu, political situation and orientation and so on. And these lived realities form the basis of their theologies. This requires "doing theology" in meaningful, efficient and relevant ways.

5. CHALLENGES

Along with the unique profile of these new church initiatives of the second-generation of African migrants come certain challenges. Among them are adequate and relevant theological formation, places of worship or meeting, and financial instability.

In order to ensure the sustainability of this new development, it is imperative that the leaders of these developments acquire relevant theological training that will equip them for the work. The theological education offered in German universities is inadequate to the current situation at hand for various reason – not least, because it is not accessible to most pastors with an immigration background. The various theological *Fortbildungen* ("continuing education" programs) designed to offer introductions to formal theological education for migrant pastors leading migrant congregations and to expose them to the cultural and historical underpinnings of the European societies in order to facilitate a dialogue and ecumenical activities between the migrant churches and the European churches – these have struggled to appeal to first- or second-generation pastors as they approach the task ahead. New forms of theological training and education are therefore required that will blend together practices from German traditions as well as Pentecostal/Charismatic traditions. And for leaders and pastors of churches with an African migration background, this must be a biblically oriented theology and a theology of formation that takes "spiritual" formation seriously.

Another serious concern and challenge that is faced by these churches remains affordable and readily accessible places of meeting. Usually, they use church rooms and halls of other churches, sometimes mainline German churches and sometimes migrant churches. In the case of the Living Generation Church, the youth center of a German church is used. In many cases, they have limited, allocated time to use the space. Due to insufficient space and time allocation, many activities and projects remain incomplete or potential and aspirations for growth and development are left unfulfilled.

Finally, finances are a major challenge for these developments. They do not receive any external financial support for the most part. Income is generated internally through offerings and tithes. This makes it difficult to undertake projects and to plan activities. Besides, many of the people – from the leaders and pastors to other workers – work on voluntary basis. Consequently, the pastor and the workers cannot be fully committed to their duties and responsibilities (which I do not say in a criticizing way).

6. Conclusion

Looking closely at the transformation that occurs from the first- to the second-generation, the break-away in ecclesiology, the development of a suitable new theology that best addresses the realities of the second generation, the new challenges that arise, and the continual effort to find meaningful and appropriate solution to the challenges, one can observe that the functionalities of religious communications transcend theology or religious studies as discipline, and that they are just as much sociological concerns. "What does theology do?" Taking the church experience of the second-generation of Germans with an African migration background, in this chapter, I have sought to highlight the ways theology becomes effective and meaningful by engaging context and content, generation and location, in the lived realities and experiences of particular communities' socio-cultural situation.

BIBLIOGRAPHY

Adogame, Afe. *The African Christian Diaspora.* New York: Bloomsbury Publishing, 2013.

Living Generation church. *This is a Living Generation.* http://living-gen.com/about/our-mission/ (Accessed 11. 07 2019).

African Christian Council Hamburg. *ACCH.* http://www.africanchristiancouncil.de/ (Accessed 15. 08. 2019).

Kahl, Werner. *Vom Verweben des Eigenen mit dem Fremden: Impulse zu einer transkulturellen Neuformierung des evangelischen Gemeindelebens.* Hamburg: Missionsverlag, 2016.

Kwiyani, Harvey C. *Sent Forth: African Missionary Work in the West.* Maryknoll: Orbis books, 2014.

Simon, Benjamin. *From Migrants to Missionaries: Christians of African Origin in Germany.* Frankfurt am Main: Peter Lang, 2010.

Going Westward to Do Theology

The "Crisis of Care" and Theological Practice

Sara Abdella-Kedir (Addis Ababa, Ethiopia)

I. Introduction

In September 2018, I boarded an airplane from Addis Ababa, Ethiopia – heading to Scotland to study theology in the University of St Andrews. Little did I know that I would experience a personal crisis during this time. As a person who had multiple times worked with foreigners who came to Ethiopia and who had struggled with "culture shock", I was aware that it would be inevitable for me, too. I also knew its external signs and was waiting for them to occur. Most of these happened during my first three months as expected. I felt lonely, hated the weather, had to train my brain to forget the Ethiopian clock which starts at dawn instead of midnight, and I was so tired of speaking English all the time. I derided people's enthusiasm and optimism, and I often felt like their smiles were plastic. None of these were surprises, even if being able to anticipate did not save me from suffering the anticipated. However, I did not expect that cultural dislocation could become a crisis in my theological practice. At those times, I began to feel like the reason I wanted to do theology was lost. It was not something I could quite articulate, but it felt like the heart was ripped out of my theological practice most of the time. It was really hard to care the way I used to care about what I was doing - it felt meaningless. In response, I felt so melancholic at times. At other times, though, I was frantically trying to fight this loss of meaning, feeling stretched between an idealized past and a hazy future. This hurled me into an existential abyss, leading to cycles of depression and anxiety.

This short essay is part of my attempt to articulate this experience of crisis. Part of what difference the difference of contexts in which one studies and practices theology makes, I will argue, is the fact that what a learner cares about is embedded in the narratives of the self which have deep relationships with the socio-historical realities – including the bodily and material conditions – in which one is positioned. As such, I want to go beyond the common notion of "cultural dislocation" seen as something independent of the nature and task of theological practice and hence as something an international student, in this case myself, might likewise experience independently of her theological practice. I went westward as a student to study theology, but it was I, a person with a body and a particular experience and certain hopes for the future. What could it mean to study theology then as the whole person I was and am?

2. Care at the Root of Theological Practice

As I just mentioned, I am originally from Ethiopia. If my reader is not very familiar with Ethiopia, it is an Eastern African country and one of the poorest countries in the world. I have a deep desire, as most Ethiopians would, to balance out that shameful self-understanding with certain facts: Ethiopia is a home of one of the earliest civilizations, of one of the earliest forms of Christianity, of one of the earliest forms of Islam, and perhaps even of the earliest *homo sapiens*. I would continue: Ethiopia earned the tag, "the African country never colonized!" by stopping colonial invasion before it took root. These are some of the defensive drums we Ethiopians beat when our country is labelled as one of the world's poorest!

Despite my desire to do this I am not going to beat that drum of a glorious past, in this essay. (Or maybe I already did!) I would rather do the other thing: name some of the saddening realities of contemporary Ethiopia. Ethiopia is an economically poor and politically unstable country where millions suffer from hunger and millions more still are displaced due to ethnic and tribal based violence.[1] Ethiopia has been a home for tyranny. It is home for the worst types of dehumanization aimed at undercutting political dissidence, often including long-term imprisonments, killings and mutilations.[2] It is a country where women suffer from cultural atrocities like female genital mutilation,[3] abduction to be forced into early age marriage which often includes rape, and multiple forms of domestic abuse. It is a country where the vulnerability of the child is exploited through child labor and molestation.[4] I come from a country that has too high a view of itself, yet has suffered from uncoordinated and frustrated collective agencies, hijacked revolutions, and deflated hopes!

It was very normal for me, as a town girl, to see beggars on the street. My parents have taught me to be thoughtful whenever I had extra-cash, and so I give some money sometimes. Sometimes I spend a week or two thinking and

---

[1] To see a report on the number of internally displaced people (2 million) and the recent rate of displacement, see Human Rights Watch, "World Report 2019: Rights Trends in Ethiopia," Human Rights Watch, 2019, https://www.hrw.org/world-report/2019/country-chapters/ethiopia.

[2] Human Rights Watch.

[3] 28 Too Many, "Country Profile: FGM in Ethiopia" (28 Too Many, October 2013), 35–46, https://www.28toomany.org/static/media/uploads/Country%20Research%20and%20Resources/Ethiopia/ethiopia_country_profile_v1_(october_2013).pdf.

[4] ILO, "Ethiopia: Overview of Child Labor Situations in Ethiopia," International Labor Organization, 2008/2007, https://www.ilo.org/ipec/Regionsandcountries/Africa/WCMS_101160/lang–en/index.htm.

talking about how depressing it is to know that we live in a country where many people cannot afford one meal a day. But it quickly recedes into the unconscious, and life goes on as usual. The banality of poverty normalizes the suffering caused by it. This normalization, for me, was disrupted in the rainy season of 2008 (which is summer in the western hemisphere). This was the year when I was recruited as one of the Evangelical Christian students to participate in a summer mission camping called "Global Project 2008: Ethiopia," a mission trip in which mostly American Evangelical college students from InterVarsity USA were accompanied by Ethiopian Evangelical college students from Evangelical Students and Graduates Union of Ethiopia (EvaSUE). Each Ethiopian student had a counterpart from Intervarsity.

As my camping friends and I treaded the streets of Addis, the beggars no longer sat on the corners of sidewalks like they used to. As soon as they saw that my Ethiopian friends and myself are walking with our white American friends, they clung to us, saying "Money! Money!" and sometimes "No food! Money!" The presence, gaze and shock of my American friends disrupted the normalization of suffering. Every day that we walked the streets of Addis, we, the Ethiopian students, had to see and name poverty and suffering that we had normalized for years.

After these shocking encounters, we often had to go back to our guesthouse and have bible study and prayer meetings. It simply meant that we had to think and speak about God and pray to God after being awake to the suffering that surrounds us. Speaking simply, we had to name God in the midst of suffering. This brought up a number of questions: how do we name God within the reality of banal suffering, *this* suffering of *these* people? How do we even name *this* suffering which is so pervasive?

These questions in 2008 led me to realize that faith is interwoven with the material realities of existence. This is no mere realization, however. As I am beginning to understand it now, this was a mark of a quasi-conscious orientation of my life towards a life of faith awake to the above-mentioned realities. Perhaps this was the beginning of what Harry Frankfurt calls "care", irreducible neither to the epistemological question of "What should I believe?" nor to the moral question of "What should I do to (for) others?"[5] The question related to care is rather a nagging interrogation of the (quasi-) conscious orientation of the self: "What should I do with myself?"[6] Marlène Jouan helpfully defines Frankfurtian notion of care as follows: "To care about something is to guide oneself, both in particular courses of action and in life generally, in light of something which is important to us, to such a point that the object of our care

---

[5] Harry G. Frankfurt, T*he Importance of What We Care about: Philosophical Essays* (Cambridge and New York: Cambridge University Press, 1988), 79–81.

[6] Frankfurt, *Importance,* 83.

is constitutive of what we are."[7] Jouan, once more helpfully, treating this Frankfurtian notion of care as very similar to the Heideggerian notion of care (*Sorge*), makes explicit what is implicit in Frankfurt's work: care as an existential and ontological category that underpins and orients even the questions of what to do or believe.

If Frankfurt's care is comparable to Heideggerian *Sorge*, it is also similar to Paul Ricoeur's notion of "solicitude" as developed in his *Oneself as Another* since the Ricoeurian "solicitude," like the Heideggerian *Sorge*, is concerned with a question of the constitution of subjectivity. An explicit development on the Heideggerian *Sorge*, Ricoeurian solicitude is a mode of the self's constitution in its reciprocal and dialectical relation with the world.[8] Solicitude is even richer (and, at the very least, stood the test of my personal story) than *Sorge* because, without disdaining *Sorge* as an ontological category, Ricoeur overcomes the relegation of narrative in Heidegger. The ontological nature of solicitude is narratival. Our solicitudes, if we follow Ricoeur, are therefore located in the stories of the selves that we *become* as we relate to the world in which we are located. As such, solicitude is the category in which "the self perceives itself as another among others,"[9] within a story that has temporalized spatial dimensions. Thus, the cares that arise from the geographical and social locations of the self are constitutive of the self.

When I joined the Ethiopian Graduate School of Theology (EGST) in 2015 to do postgraduate studies in theology, there was a further solidification in my life's orientation towards a desire to name God within, and never regardless of, the banality of *this* suffering of *these* people. Theological study was slowly unfolding in my experience as a way of being in solicitude: Why and how is God named in Ethiopia in the midst of *this* suffering of *these* people and *this* country? What is the role of theological education in the naming of *this* suffering, and of God in the midst of *this* suffering? As I have come to understand it now, what underpins my care to study theology is tightly related to my grappling with these questions. I was eventually being orientated to do theology with this particular care which required of me a sort of particularity in theological practice that resists any short-circuited universalization in naming and

---

[7] Marlène Jouan, "Harry Frankfurt's Metaphysics of Care: Towards an Ethics without Reason," *Philosophy & Social Criticism* 34, no. 7 (September 2008): 761–62.

[8] Paul Ricœur, *Oneself as Another* (Chicago: University of Chicago Press, 1992), 309–10.

[9] Ricœur, *Oneself*, 192. One should note that Frankfurt also distinguishes care as a narrativized, or storied fundamental category. We can observe Frankfurt's attempt to narrativize care by noting how he differentiates it from categories of desire and belief, which according to Frankfurt, do not necessarily have to be storied. I am not here necessarily agreeing with Frankfurt with the non-necessity of narrative for desire and belief. I just want to show that his contrast between care and desire and belief can be used to show the essential narrative structure of care.

studying the naming of God. I was in the middle of this process of solidification of care when I went to the university of St Andrews to do theology.

3. Going Westward: A Crisis of Care

As I mentioned in the introduction, the heart of this essay lies in my personal attempt to understand the crisis that loomed over the period of my theological study at the University of St Andrews. Of course, the cycles of depression and anxiety that I went through during these months can be understood as parts both of the academic life which is fraught with the evaluative gaze of the academic community and of "culture-shock." My attempt to thematize what I call in this section "a crisis of care" does not necessarily mean the negation of these two explanations. The claim is rather that the explanation cannot be reduced to these two, especially if these two are to be treated as categories independent of "a crisis of care." Therefore, I am rather complexifying the problem of "going westward" and the kinds of differences that differences of context make (or at least made, in my particular story) by adding to the equation the notion of care as a category of quasi-conscious and quasi-reflexive orientation of one's life.

Given my understanding of the solidification of my refusal to name God regardless of the profound human suffering I witnessed, of course it is now less surprising to me that I had multiple moments of crises. In St Andrews, I was doing Analytic Theology. Given the contestability of its disciplinary boundaries and the limited space I have here, I am not going to try to define Analytic Theology. What played a larger role in my crisis has to do not as much with the definition of disciplinary boundaries as with what happened inside and outside the class room. So, what did I do when I studied Analytic theology? With my professors and the colleagues in my cohort, I spent most of my time thinking about the relationship between God's self-revelation in history and what that might mean for our understanding of both God and history; learning and working on the various theories of atonement; finessing our definitions of forgiveness and personhood; and debating over the dogmatic and logical plausibility of this or that doctrine, for example, that of social trinity. These activities indicate the nature of the courses in general.

I do not wish to imply general disapproval or even personal distaste of these, and to the contrary, the history of theology attests to their deep importance to the Christian tradition. However, it was rather difficult for me to find meaning in them and somehow fit them in the larger picture of my life's orientation. A student from a poor, unstable country who made it to Scotland to study in a prestigious university, thinking about big, "universal" topics. Some (these "some" can be imaginary!) might say that I should have nothing to complain about. I also told myself that there should be no substantial problem. But problems do not always occur where we are waiting for them to happen!

In this case, the theological practice that started growing out of the "care" (in its Frankfurtian and Ricoeurian sense) that has been orienting my life, dissonated with the kind of practice Analytic Theology offered. Perhaps, at a more profound level, this dissonance in practice is a dissonance of orientation of theological practices due to their differing "cares" rooted in different contexts. A crisis resulted at the site of the self from this, in effect, displacement of the self as the primary site of care or solicitude. This is what I call the crisis of care. If care or solicitude in the Ricoeurian sense is narrativized and constitutive of the self, then moving into a social or geographical location in which the object of care appears, at least from the perspective of the subject who cares, absent or invisible causes a kind of crisis in the self. In this sense, stabilizing the orientation of the self requires a community of care. When I say "community of care," I have in mind a kind of community that has both systems of meaning in which the object of care is recognizable and meaningful as well as having social practices in which the self can participate to be orientated towards the object of its care.

As such, the loss of a "community of care" can cause a serious crisis in care. This crisis in care raised questions that *I* had to answer, questions that were, as such, *personal* questions: "How is *this* suffering of *these* people rendered cognizable in a place where almost none have beheld it? And how can I continue my theological education in a setting where my object of care does not seem cognizable?" This very personal, very particular question sounds self-absorbed and hence scandalous, especially in the context of something as public as an academic conference or a scholarly publication. This scandal of particularity is meant to be what Emmanuel Katongole calls "an interruption of dialogues."[10] My hope is that this particular story will participate in different attempts to interrupt theological dialogues which go on as if these cares which are rooted in contexts across borders do not matter to theological practice.

4. Conclusion: Hopeful Interruption

This interruption began within myself, in a form of yet another interrogation: "Why did I board on a plane to come to Scotland to study theology?" The answer to that opening question bespeaks an uncomfortable truth: In "the west" and back "home" as well, you are a "legitimate" theologian only if you are educated in a "western" university. Contemporary theological practice has a global nature, which has centers of symbolic power that can validate or invalidate practitioners and forms of practices. If I was to keep doing the things that I care about in a socially recognizable manner, I had to sooner or later get on that

---

[10] Emmanuel Katongole, "A Tale of Many Stories," in *Shaping a Global Theological Mind*, ed. by Darren C. Marks (Aldershot, Burlington: Ashgate, 2008), 90.

plane and find myself in a strange context doing theology - or so I thought. Theology offers a collection of historical, theoretical and practical resources that I use to help me orient my life towards my object of care, and to do it I have to move to a strange context that fails to provide "community of care." But without a community of care, my object of care seems to be meaningless and to lack social practices that allow me to keep orienting my life towards what I care about. This has the power of undercutting theological practice and invalidating cares germane to particular contexts. There is a tension here that may well be intrinsic to "global theology" or "transcultural theology." The "globalization" of theological practice and the erection of its centers of symbolic power in certain parts of the globe results in contradictions, and the recognition of these contradictions calls for reflexive interruptions of theological dialogue. The interruption I am proposing is meant to call the dialogue to holds in view not only individual particularity but more specifically the ways theology interacts dynamically with the solicitudes and cares of theologians. Like me.

Bibliography

28 Too Many. "Country Profile: FGM in Ethiopia." 28 Too Many, October 2013. https://www.28toomany.org/static/media/uploads/Country%20Research%20and%20Resources/Ethiopia/ethiopia_country_profile_v1_(october_2013).pdf.

Frankfurt, Harry G. *The Importance of What We Care about: Philosophical Essays.* Cambridge [England] ; New York: Cambridge University Press, 1988.

Human Rights Watch. "World Report 2019: Rights Trends in Ethiopia." Human Rights Watch, 2019. https://www.hrw.org/world-report/2019/country-chapters/ethiopia.

ILO. "Ethiopia: Overview of Child Labor Situations in Ethiopia." International Labor Organization (ILO), 2008 2007. https://www.ilo.org/ipec/Regionsandcountries/Africa/WCMS_101160/lang--en/index.htm.

Jouan, Marlène. "Harry Frankfurt's Metaphysics of Care: Towards an Ethics without Reason." *Philosophy & Social Criticism* 34, no. 7 (September 2008): 759–97.

Katongole, Emmanuel. "A Tale of Many Stories." In *Shaping a Global Theological Mind,* edited by Darren C. Marks, 89–93. Aldershot: Ashgate, 2008.

Ricœur, Paul. *Oneself as Another.* Chicago: University of Chicago Press, 1992.

Umbrella Movement 2014

Theology in the Street Searching for Identity

Chan Che-wai (Hong Kong, China)

1. Introduction

The people of Hong Kong have long been searching for an "identity" of their own both before and since the colonial era. However, for the people of Hong Kong, returning to their "mother country" is not what retrieving their "identity" means. "Identity," to Hong Kong people, requires autonomy.[1] Individuals exercising autonomy in making their own choices means that what one person or group regards as a good life may not be the same as what another person or group thinks. But each should have the opportunity to pursue a "new life" - one which they consider to be a better life. This is what it means to "identify" with one's own life. In Hong Kong in 2014 the relationship between identity and the right to political self-determination came into sharp focus in what became known as the Umbrella Movement. The movement catalyzed sharply divergent theological responses with immediate reverberations in the responses of Christian groups. The following reflection illustrates some of the differences in social action that these differences in doing theology can make.

2. Why did the Umbrella Movement Come About?

After many, long years struggling, but in vain, for true democracy with universal suffrage, a massive movement broke out in Hong Kong in 2014 which led to a 79 days' occupation of part of the city's business and transportation hubs such as Admiralty, Causeway Bay, Tsimshatsui and Mongkok in protest to the Chief Executive and all the Legislative Councillors for a true democratic and universal suffrage, electing Chief Executive and all the Legislative Councillors. The so entitled "Umbrella Movement" highlighted just how many people in Hong Kong had been struggling to maintain a sense of identity of as citizens of

[1] A slave has no autonomy. An autonomous individual is the master of his own life and in this sense experiences dignity. A life with choice is a life of dignity as Eric Stoddart has argued in his discussion of "coming to oneself." Eric Stoddart, "Spiritualty and Citizenship: Sacramentality in a Parable," *Theological Studies* 68, no. 4 (2007): 761-79, here 765.

Hong Kong and to achieve political autonomy. The Umbrella Movement also led to – or maybe it is better to say – "revealed" a Hong Kong theology that works out on the street.

To recognize and understand the functions of theology in the Hong Kong setting, as revealed by the movement, it is important to observe the situation of the youth. Before the Umbrella Movement, Archbishop Paul Kwong of the Hong Kong Sheng Kung Hui had addressed certain challenges facing young people in Hong Kong when he wrote:

> Politically, Hong Kong is a "Special Administration Area" [. . .] under the "One Country, Two Systems" formula. [However], [i]n the years leading up to 1997 and Hong Kong's return to Chinese sovereignty, there [was] a general sense in which Hong Kong people felt that we were left out of the decision-making process about our own future. [. . .] Economically, [Hong Kong] is a wealthy city [. . .]; however, there is a growing gap between rich and poor, a higher level of unemployment, [. . .] Not all Hong Kong people have benefited from [their] city's prosperity.[2]

During the Occupation, on 6 October 2014, a young female protester, Gemma Yim, being interviewed by the New York Times, said,

> There is no space for dreams in Hong Kong. We just have money, we just have the titles, we just have the middle class [. . .] We have the right to have a good life. We have the right to be protected by a government that is represented by the people [. . .] I feel more and more depressed because I feel like the government can do whatever they want, because they have the backing of the Chinese government.[3]

A sense of social powerlessness and political estrangement drove the younger generation to join the Umbrella Movement. Paul Kwong and Gemma Yim, each in their own ways, were drawing attention to the reality that the younger generation, though educated, saw themselves as on the losing side of a growing wealth disparity, with little chance of climbing up the social ladder while also increasingly being left out of the process of decision making concerning their own political futures. They felt that both rather self-identity and social identity were being exploited by the autocratic Hong Kong Special Administrative Region (HKSAR) government as well as the Chinese government. Hoping against hope, they believed that if they were granted the right, through a universal suffrage, to choose their own Chief Executive (the highest official who rules Hong Kong) and a government truly representative of the people, elected by the people and serving the people, they could express their political ideals for

---

[2] Paul Kwong, "Hong Kong Sheng Kung Hui," in *The Blackwell Companion to Political Theology*, ed. by Peter Scott and William T. Cavanaugh (Oxford: Blackwell, 2013), 253-62, here 257.

[3] Michael Forsythe and Alan Wong, "Protest Organizers Claim Progress for Hong Kong," *The New York Times*, October 6, 2014, <https://www.nytimes.com/2014/10/07/world/asia/hong-kong-protests.html?module=inline>.

the city. With a democratic government, Hong Kong could be developed to be an equal and fair society. Their humble petition was that they be able to pursue their own will for a good life in this manner.

3. Occupy Central with Love and Peace

It was in response to this situation, and based on the intention of the citizens of Hong Kong to fight for autonomy and the right to 'true', 'democratic' and 'universal' suffrage for the Chief Executive in 2017 and the Legislative Councilors in 2020, that Assistant Professor of Hong Kong University Faculty of Law Benny Tai Yiu-ting initiated a movement of 'Occupy Central with Love and Peace' (OCLP) in 2013. He was joined in this effort by Professor of Sociology at Chinese University of Hong Kong Chan Kin-man and Reverend Chu Yiu-ming of Chai Wan Baptist Church. Benny Tai believed this action was a "most destructive weapon of civil disobedience."[4] The occupation began in September 2014. Its purpose was to urge the then Chief Executive C.Y. Leung and his government to submit a proposition for real, equal, and universal suffrage on the elections of the Chief Executive and all the Legislative Councilors. Already much earlier, in 2013, in an open forum, I had a face-to-face discussion with Benny Tai concerning his idea of "Occupation." On that occasion he explained that he hoped universal suffrage might enable the citizens of Hong Kong to vote to create a democratic Hong Kong. More specifically, the fight for a democratic local government was not to challenge the China's government, but to help solve the economic, social and wealth disparity problems.

The three "occupation initiators" Benny Tai Yiu-ting, Chan Kin-man, and Chu Yiu-ming expected a democratically formed government would create a good and just Hong Kong, to deal with the growing gap between rich and poor by providing the equitable distribution of resources and equal opportunities to everyone in all walks of life.

The state party in China, however, was insistent on guaranteeing its autocratic rule over Hong Kong. To make sure the elected Chief Executive fit the profile desired by the Standing Committee of the National People's Congress (SCNPC) of Mainland China, the SCNPC interpreted the election method on 31 August 2014 to mean that the only one candidate who had an endorsement from more than half of the Election Committee members could be eligible for being voted directly by all the voters. The move proved controversial, howev-

---

[4] Benny Tai, "Most Destructive Weapon of Civil Disobedience," *Hong Kong Economic Journal*, January 16, 2013, <http://oclp.hk/index.php?route=occupy/article_detail&article_id=23>. Cf. Justin K. H. Tse, "The Umbrella Movement and the Political Apparatus: Understanding 'One Country, Two Systems'," in *Theological Reflections on the Hong Kong Umbrella Movement*, ed. by Justin K.H. Tse and Jonathan Y. Tan, (New York: Palgrave Macmillan, 2016) at 50.

er, since this election committee did not reflect the popular will of the people of Hong Kong.

Young people showed anger in response to what was widely viewed as a fake election. To protest, student organizations called for a class boycott or school strike for a week from 22-26 September 2014.[5] Without having received a positive answer, and wanting to further pressure the HKSAR government, on the last day of the class boycott, hundreds of "radical" students gathered before and then occupied what is known as "Civic Square."[6] To respond to the occupation, the then Chief Executive, C.Y. Leung ordered the police to fire tear gas bombs among the student protesters on Sunday evening, 28 September 2014. But this served only to motivate more and more students and young people to flock to Central in support of the student protesters. On 29 September 2014, in the morning, Benny Tai and the student leaders announced the kick-off of the OCLP.

It was the 87 tear gas bombs in particular that continued to provoke the Occupation Movement, which then lasted for 79 days until 15 December 2014. The police forces harshly suppressed the demonstrations and attacked the occupants, also using pepper spray and batons. The occupants' "weapons" consisted simply of umbrellas used for protecting themselves from tear gas and pepper spray. It was for this reason that the movement was called "Umbrella Movement." It is estimated that altogether over 1,300,000 people participated the occupation, among them 300,000 students who regularly stationed themselves at the occupied areas including Admiralty, Wanchai, and Mongkok.

4. What did Churches, Theologians, and Theology do in the Context of the Umbrella Movement in Hong Kong?

During the Umbrella Movement, only a few churches, faith groups and a small number of what might be called "parachurches" openly supported the movement. These included creative innovations like the St. Francis Chapel found in the streets of Hong Kong and the digitally located Umbrella City-Cyber Church, both of which formed during the occupation.

Most of the Christian churches remained silent or claimed neutrality in political dispute. Some of the established churches like the Evangelical Free Church of China (EFCC), and Hong Kong Sheng Kung Hui (HKSKH, Anglican), not only showed apathy, but their leaders even acrimoniously criticized the

---

[5] The two biggest student organizations were the "Hong Kong Federation of Students" (HKFS) and "Scholarism." The former was a university student organization, while the latter was secondary school student organization.

[6] That is, the East Wing Forecourt of the Central Government Offices.

people, in particular the Christians, who were involved in the Occupation. The Revd. Daniel Ng of the EFCC openly opposed OCLP and threatened that church members who participated in the Umbrella Movement might possibly be excommunicated. He said, "Christians should pray for authority, respect the governor, and assist the government or the ruling party in achieving the designated goals."[7] The Rt. Revd. Paul Kwong, the Archbishop of the Hong Kong Sheng Kung Hui, expressed his doubts about the occupation, saying that "universal suffrage is not a panacea" for solving the problem of the livelihood of the people and other political and economic issues.[8] On 6 July 2014, when he delivered a sermon for Theology Sunday at St. Paul's Church, he observed that Jesus remained silent in the face of Pilate, like a lamb awaiting slaughter. Silence is better than saying anything, the Archbishop argued, and, with this invoking of the crucifixion of Jesus, he sought to persuade his congregants to keep silent about social and political issues.[9]

However, other theological perspectives came to the fore that sat at odds with Kwong's. In particular, a Liberation-theological emphasis stood out. As fellow Anglican, the Revd. Dr. John Corrie, Chaplain of the Church of the Good Shepherd in Lima, once wrote, "the conviction that the Christian faith is relevant to politics." He added:

> Eschatology speaks of a transformation of this world through the Kingdom of God, which calls for change, social and political, in the hope of the fulfilment of God's purposes. [. . .] Trinitarian political theology therefore will seek ways of combining order with justice, power with love, authority with service, triumph with suffering, grace with action, law with freedom and so on.[10]

In this vein, Hong Kong Public Theologian, Dr. Lap-yan Kung, Associate Professor in the Department of Cultural and Religious Studies at the Chinese University of Hong Kong, argued that a Liberation-theological model was applicable to the context of the Umbrella Movement. Building on Jon Sobrino's atonement model,[11] Dr. Kung outlined a Liberation Theology for the situation in Hong Kong. He suggested that, (1) liberation must be pursued, first and

---

[7] Shun-hing Chan, "The Protestant Community and the Umbrella Movement in Hong Kong," *Inter-Asia Cultural Studies* 16, no. 3 (2015): 380-95, here 382.

[8] Paul Kwong, "Universal Suffrage is not a Panacea," *Provincial Echo*, 1 September, 2013. Issue 1956. http://echo.hkskh.org/issue.aspx?lang=2&id=131.

[9] Tony Cheung and Lai Ying-kit, "Reverend Paul Kwong tells congregation that pro-democracy advocates should keep quiet," *South China Morning Post*, July 8, 2014, https://www.scmp.com/news/hong-kong/article/1549485/reverend-paul-kwong-tells-congregation-pro-democracy-advocates-should.

[10] John Corrie, "Towards a Trinitarian Political Theology," *Anvil* 6, no. 1 (1989): 33-44, https://biblicalstudies.org.uk/pdf/anvil/06-1_033.pdf.

[11] According to Jon Sobrino, "Jesus is for some, the oppressed, and against others, the oppressors," in *Jesus the Liberator: A Historical-Theological Reading of Jesus the Nazareth*, ed. by Jon Sobrino, Paul Burns, and Francis McDonagh, trans. by Orbis Books (Maryknoll: Orbis Books, 1993), 13.

foremost, from and for the oppressed people rather than from the reference point of political power; (2) a church should live among the poor if it is to be a church for the poor; (3) Hong Kong must construct its very own liberation theological framework. The primary concern in Kung's framework was to ask the core question – "Who is my neighbor?"[12]

5. Conclusion

Christian faith attunes believers and non-believers to experience God and God's direction in their lives, especially in moments of special significance or importance. In those moments, theological guidance can be seen as a "cry for life." Evangeline Anderson-Rajkumar insists that theology must be done in the context. She argues that,

If theology is understood as a critical reflection of one's faith in God, of one's God-experience, then it is self-implied that every human being who is uniquely different from another has varied God-experiences, varied ways to understand and to express the same. Every theology is an articulation of faith and is contextual too [. . .] Contextualizing theology therefore is an act of faith, responding to the groans that come from different corners due to life-diminishing, life-denying powerful systems, unjust judicial structures, social orders etc.[13]

The path ahead for the citizens of Hong Kong struggling to find and preserve a sense of "identity" that endows them with the autonomy to pursue "new life" is rugged. But as the political situation in Hong Kong has been worsening, and the HKSAR government has been strengthening its effort to suppress democracy in Hong Kong, the strength of the will to seek liberation also has increased, as the recent protests in summer 2019 have shown. Likewise, it is to be expected that public action toward liberation will continue to stimulate and draw upon conflicting theological arguments. Thus, the 2014 Umbrella Movement and the Hong Kong liberation theology it prompted are no (religious) relics of a political past but vectors for interpreting a possible future.

---

[12] Sam Tsang, "Exegeting the Occupation of Hong Kong: The Umbrella Movement as a Battleground for Liberation Hermeneutics," in *Theological Reflections on the Hong Kong Umbrella Movement Tsang,* ed. by Justin K.H. Tse and Jonathan Y. Tan (New York: Palgrave Macmillan, 2016), 131-62, here 132.

[13] Evangeline Anderson-Rajkumar, "Towards Theologizing in Context: Our Vision and Goal," *Indian Journal of Theology* 36, no. 1 (1994): 109-19, here 109-10, https://biblicalstudies.org.uk/pdf/ijt/36-1_109.pdf.

BIBLIOGRAPHY

Anderson-Rajkumar, Evangeline. "Towards Theologising in Context: Our Vision and Goal", *Indian Journal of Theology* 36, no. 1 (1994): 109-19.

Chan, Shun-hing. "The Protestant community and the Umbrella Movement in Hong Kong." *Inter-Asia Cultural Studies* 16, no. 3 (2015): 380-95.

Cheung, Tony, and Ying-kit Lai. "Reverend Paul Kwong tells congregation that pro-democracy advocates should keep quiet." *South China Morning Post*, Published 8th July, 2014. https://www.scmp.com/news/hong-kong/article/1549485/reverend-paul-kwong-tells-congregation-pro-democracy-advocates-should.

Corrie, John. "Towards a Trinitarian Political Theology." *Anvil* 6, no. 1 (1989): 33-44. https://biblicalstudies.org.uk/pdf/anvil/06-1_033.pdf..

de Gruchy, John W. "Democracy." In *The Blackwell Companion to Political Theology*, edited by Peter Scott, and William T. Cavanaugh, 439-54. Oxford: Blackwell Publishing, 2004.

Forsythe, Michael, and Wong, Alan. "Protest Organizers Claim Progress for Hong Kong." The New York Times, 6th October, 2014. https://www.nytimes.com/2014/10/07/world/asia/hong-kong-protests.html?module=inline.

Kwong, Paul. "Hong Kong Sheng Kung Hui." In *The Blackwell Companion to Political Theology*, edited by Peter Scott, and William T. Cavanaugh, 253-62. Oxford: Blackwell, 2013.

Sobrino, Jon, Paul Burns, and Francis McDonagh, eds. *Jesus the Liberator: A Historical-Theological Reading of Jesus the Nazareth*. Translated by Orbis Books. Maryknoll: Orbis Books, 1993.

Stoddart, Eric. "Spiritualty and Citizenship: Sacramentality in a Parable." *Theological Studies* 68, no. 4 (2007): 761-79.

Tai, Benny. "Most Destructive Weapon of Civil Disobedience." Hong Kong Economic Journal, 16th January, 2013. http://oclp.hk/index.php?route=occupy/article_detail&article_id=23.

Tsang, Sam. "Exegeting the Occupation of Hong Kong: The Umbrella Movement as a Battleground for Liberation Hermeneutics." In *Theological Reflections on the Hong Kong Umbrella Movement*, edited by K.H. Justin Tse and Jonathan Y. Tan, 131-62. New York: Palgrave Macmillan, 2016.

Part 2 Which Cultures? Whose Contextuality? Determining Theological Locations

Theology, in-between Texts

An Essay on Context and Intertextuality

Martín Grassi (Buenos Ares, Argentina)

1. Introduction: Theology, in-between Particularity and Universality

Theology is a very peculiar discipline, no doubt about it. In its writing, in its being performed, theology is not an objective science that examines particular natural or social phenomena, but neither is it merely a subjective or cultural expression of religious belief addressing the Divine. Theology seems to be, somehow, in the middle: It performs a hybrid discourse that takes a historical religious practice and turns it into a universal and timeless set of claims about God, the world and the human. In this chimeric nature of Theology, in-between the particular and the universal, a decision is *not* to be taken: Theology cannot be a *particular* discourse without losing its *normative* essence, that is, it cannot be simply the description of a certain ritual; nor can theology be an absolute language about a universal and abstract God, for it belongs to a historical religious expression. *In this tension, theology is traditionally based, but with a universal drive.* Due to this inner paradox, questions about context in theology have arisen especially in the past two centuries after the historical turn in the 19th and the linguistic and hermeneutical turns in the 20th century. If theology is rooted in religious expressions coming from particular communities, how can theology not be contextual? But, if theological claims pretend to be universal and normative, how could theology still remain contextual? It seems that theologians must sail in between Scylla and Charybdis, avoiding both the imminent crush into particularity and being swept away into universality, navigating an impossible middle-way towards an unknown Ithaca. The danger of universalism in theology is that, in speaking from nowhere, it speaks to nobody: Theology should address the particular believing communities in their own language, in their own conceptual frames, pointing to their particular problems and dramas. The danger of particularism in theology is that, in resting in the particularity of a certain historical community, theology stops pushing the whole of history towards a unique divine kingdom. In political terms, either each city has its own god, or every city is already under the one God's sovereignty.[1] This *aporetic* nature of theological discourse is, however, absolutely central to the religious communities that address God as the lord of history, for God should be meaningful in their present situation but also extend its lordship to the entirety of history as such. Therefore, it seems to be necessary to examine in depth how theology faces contextuality. However, one should first examine what does the very notion of "context" mean.

2. The Dialectic of Text and Context

Since human phenomena are *meaningful*, they can be considered metaphorically as *texts*: They are *organized* in some manner, under certain rules or criteria, that renders them *intelligible* or readable. Although we do not refer to human actions as "texts" in daily conversations, it is interesting to notice that we do speak commonly about the "context" of our actions. Ironically, this word, "context," coming from linguistics or literature, was given a kind of universal value to describe any phenomenon in its relation to a broader situation, while hiding, in some way, its very essence of being just a metaphor. Perhaps for that same reason, the concept of "context" has not been yet rigorously defined: It is a word that seems to have already a clear meaning (which is what usually happens with a "dead metaphor"). However, a proper understanding of the context as a concept is needed, and one should then examine its dialectic relationship with the concept of "text" from which stems, taking a close look to the Latin prefix "con-" (with). I will start, then, establishing some orienting remarks.

First, the dialectical relationship between text and con-text depends on what is considered a text, for it is not at all clear when or where a certain text starts and when or where it ends. It is only when a text is already defined, when a text has certain limits, that one could relate it to what surrounds it and clarify that which goes "with the text" (*con-text*). One could ask, nevertheless, how does a text become a text. The question is not capricious, for there are no instructions or universally valid rules to determine the limits of a single text: It is only by a *decision* that one can state the limits of a text and identify it as being a particular text. Therefore, if defining a text depends on a decision, so does its context. Because a text is something to be understood – and thus to be interpreted – and because interpretation entails considering what surrounds the text, the dialectical relationship of text and context is a matter of herme-

[1] It is important to notice that I am going to stick in my analysis to the Christian tradition, although this problem could also be traced using a history of religions approach. However, the issues of contextuality and universality are quite different in religious traditions that have a more cosmological nature, and these deserve their own proper examination.

neutics (the art of interpreting), and this understanding requires a previously made decision concerning what to consider a text and what to consider its context. Let us take a simple example: Reading a book. One could say that it is not possible to understand all of a given work from one author without relating it to the whole of that author's writings; one could similarly say that the understanding of a single paragraph in that book requires relating it to the whole of the book; or even that each word in a single sentence must be read in relation to the whole sentence. Thus, the question becomes, what is the simple, *atomic* (non-divisible) unit of text in what I am reading? Is there any? Interpreting something as a text depends on the *decision* one makes, a decision that will, of course, also partially determine what is its con-text. And yet, a first difference between text and con-text appears here: Whereas a text is always something defined, limited, identified, the con-text is only defined by its being around a certain text, and as such, it is both unlimited and unidentifiable: therefore, whereas we answer the question of what a text is by means of a decision, we cannot say what its context is in absolute terms because, in an analogy with the notion of *horizon*, what surrounds a particular position is only determined in its being related to a center, whereas its contours are, by definition, infinite and undeterminable.

Second, a text (both the text that one writes, and the text that one reads) is something that one *knits*[2] and, in doing so, one gives shape to the whole by defining its knot. My understanding of a text, therefore, depends on my decision over the starting point (or "starting text") from which I engage the whole – and its surroundings: Should I interpret the whole book from *this* certain chapter, the chapter from *this* sentence, the work of an author from *this* certain book, *et cetera*. My decision on the "starting-text" will define both the text and the context; if my decision was different, that would surely arrange the whole otherwise, and my understanding would also be different.

Third, texts (both those read and those written) are being re-arranged all the time, but especially when something really *happens*, when there is an *event* that cannot be just included in the existent composition or interpretation, but that somehow forces re-arrangement of the composition as a whole. This is the case when one says that an event "makes history": An historical narrative is written/understood with reference to this event, from the meaning we give to this event. Somehow, from the very moment we acknowledge an event "as such", we already define it as the "starting-text" that will give a certain meaning to the text and that will, thus, influence arrangement of its context. However, once again, the relationship is dialectical, for one can only consider an event to be meaningful if it is already happening in a certain context that provides meaning for it.

---

[2] Etymologically, "text" comes from the Latin *textus*, which stems from the verb *textere*: to weave, to fabricate.

Every writing process – and writing is the general name for "giving meaning" – entails, therefore, a dialectical relationship of text and the context. One possible way to think about the text and the context is by pointing to the difference between what is being written (or what is being understood) and what has already been written (or what that has already been understood, as when one refers to a *canonical* interpretation of a text): This dialectical relationship is often referred in terms of the tension between *tradition and innovation*. On the one hand, every act of writing re-shapes what has been written/understood, and every new trace is somehow producing a new meaning; on the other hand, every act of writing/understanding is, also, repeating what has been written/understood before, for writing/understanding cannot produce meaning from nowhere. The text is always being written/understood from and toward meaning: There is no beginning of writing/understanding, nor there is an end; there is no capitol letter that started the great text of meaning, nor final punctuation that closes it. *Meaning and text happen in the mean-time*, between the first and the last, in-between the *alpha* and the *omega*, already in writing/understanding and always *typo-graphically*. Meaning happens within the traces of writing/understanding, in the realm of *túpos*: prints, seals, and stamps. There is no meaning before the alpha nor after the omega. Thus, every text is in con-text because it is with other text, and no writing/understanding will set meaning up or shut it down: The horizon comes from behind and ahead of us, and the blurring line that seems to be the end of the world and of our journey is just a matter of perspective. In short, every text (or read) has a context because every text happens in this world, in space and time, in history and in language.

The questions remain: What does *con-text* actually mean? What or which is the text around which there is a con-text? And what is this "con" (with) around that text all about? Where or when does "it" begin, and when or where does "it" end. Here in Bonn, for instance, we are within a certain political, social and cultural situation (a "context"); the German we speak, the democratic political order, etc., are the "con" of the "texts" we perform (and text in this usage, of course, has very broad connotations, including the actions we make). But one could also say that the German language, democracy, etc., are the "texts" that are performed within a broader context, that is, Roman-Christian civilization or even the history of evolution. Therefore, where does the context of my actions really starts, and where does it end? Evidently, both text and context are constructions we build *arbitrarily* (with the echo of the latin *arbitrio* being intended): A text and its "con-" are always built as a holistic structure, defined and particularized in some manner, and the building of these structures knows no rules. It seems that the notion of con-text as being infinite turned into a definable notion, just as the one of text: both text and context are the product of a decision over what must be taken as the semantical unit of our understanding. However, if the con-text as such is also the product of a decision, because it must have some kind of unity to be referred to, then how can we distinguish between the product of a decision over what is considered to be a text, and what is considered to be its con-text? What is the difference between them?

3. "Out of Context", or the Demand for Intertextuality

Let us now turn to the case of theology and examine the dialectical relationship between text and context in relation to it. To start with, one could ask why the question of context is even important to theology. Here we must be careful. Viewed from one angle, the question of contextualization is important when there are practical issues at stake, whether ethical-political problems or problems related to communication. Viewed from another angle, the question of contextualization also has a "critical" motivation that comes from a hermeneutical, sociological and historical analysis of human cultural productions. If we consider research in physics, for instance, we are not going to find physicists worrying about whether their work is "out of context"; in 2019, no physicist will wonder whether he should stick to an Aristotelian cosmology or, perhaps, to a Newtonian framework. But it is often the case that a physicist wonders about the context of his or her research when practical issues come to the table: Is this research interesting for the Academy, today? Is this research going to have a (good or bad) political or ethical use (as in the case of quantum physics and the making of the atomic bomb)? Should I retain the language that I use in scholarly publications when I teach 15 years-old students? Does my research entail causing any damage to someone or to the environment when making the experiments? All of these questions aim at contexts or situations in which scientific work is done, and then questions concerning contextualization become relevant. Of course, a historian of the sciences could very well point out how the physical theories depend on the political and cultural situation of their time, but this is a question that is relevant *a posteriori*, that is, once the text has been already written. Moreover, it is relevant to the historian looking from the future, not to the scientist researching in the present.

However, in the case of theology, the question of contextualization seems to be relevant *a priori*: Theology *in its doing* entails reflection on its belonging to a context. Theology is by nature hermeneutical, and thus a discipline that is (or at least ought to be) first of all aware of its historicity. Let us take a look at the case of a Christian theologian and his/her *doing* (that is, *writing*) theology. Let us imagine that she/he is a theologian from South America in the 1970's, so that his/her con-text (that which surrounds *making* theology) could be described by elements such as: the use of Spanish language, social inequality in the region, communist revolutions and military dictatorships and the deep religiosity of the people. Granting that he/she lives within that situation, does this mean that his theoretical discourse on God will be shaped by the idea of

Jesus born poor, politically engaged to free humankind from oppression? In other words, ought all theologians working in South America in the 1970's to have built *liberation theologies*. The answer, I would suggest, is no: There were many kinds of theology in South America in those years. Should we say that, if she/he was not a liberation theologian (or a reactionary theologian, as a counterpart), she/he was theologizing "out of context"? At this point, the dialectical relationship of text and context gets more complicated, but, in a way, also more clear: One could say, contrary to the description I just gave, that it is not text that defines context, and rather, the other way around, that it is context which is defining text. However, this is not possible, because the very notion of con-text is absolutely infinite and, therefore, not de-finitive: The horizon as such cannot define my position, although clearly it is *given* in my position. Only text defines a context, not the other way around. And this is clear also in the expression of being "out of context": If con-text is what surrounds a text, then there is no such a thing as an out-of-context. It is as impossible to have a text without a con-text as it is to be in a position without horizon. The reason is simple: The concept of con-text is a relative concept, only meaningful in its reference to a text, and once we introduce the idea of "context", we cannot get rid of it, for context will always be that which belongs necessarily to a text.

Does the expression "out of context" have any meaning at all, then? Yes it does, and it is absolutely important to discern the way this expression is used. For this expression is a controversial and polemic claim, addressed *against* someone *in the name* of something. One criticizes someone for speaking or writing "out of context" because what he/she writes or what she/he does, leaves aside important aspects which she/he should address somehow. But this objection is only possible *in the name* of that which has been left aside. Therefore, if one takes a close look at this problem, it is clear that the "context" in the expression "out of context" is no longer a con-text, but it is itself already a text: If the context of a Latin American theologian is defined as the particular historical situation of social inequality built by a capitalist oppressive system in Third-World and colonial regions, then of course not addressing these issues is sufficient reason to say that his/her work is "out of context". However, this so called "context" is a "text" defined by someone – in this case, for instance, a liberation theologian. This context is but a broader text in which the text in question could and perhaps should be integrated; in other words, the description of the particular situation is one possible historical narrative, constructed itself as a "normative" text by which every text is judged to be (or not to be) "out of context". However, since the idea of context is now the result of a decision, one could find one certain context just as suitable as other contexts in the making of one's texts. In other words, a certain context is just one possible narrative amongst others. A Christian theologian could well refer to the whole Christian theological tradition as his/her context, and someone could by the same token claim that his/her work is "out of context" *in the name* of the history of dogma, for example.

The question of con-textuality is, therefore, a question of inter-textuality, that is, of how a certain text refers itself to other texts, to broader and normative narratives. The writing of a certain context is but the writing of a broader and normative text which all texts should somehow address. A Latin American theologian in the 70's will be "out of context" if his/her text does not refer to the social responsibility of the Christian kerygma, but it will also be "out of context" if it does not refer to the former Councils, or even to the Sacred writings, *et cetera*: its being "out of context" just depends on which texts this particular text addresses. The relationship between the text and what "surrounds" it is, then, a question of inter-textuality, for what surrounds texts are also texts, and the concept of context alone is not sufficient enough to clarify how a text is "out of context". The question of being "out of context", thus, can only refer to the way in which a certain text meets certain other broader and normative texts. In other words, whereas the concept of con-text is, in itself, by its very etymological composition, an undetermined and infinite one, we need to think the concept of con-text as being already a text, and, therefore, turn the question on con-textuality into a question of inter-textuality. This seems to be the only way to better understand the issue of context in theology.

However, the dialectics of text and context (understanding now contextuality as intertextuality) are even more complicated still, for one could also examine how – in the text of a certain theologian – a certain "context" (Christian theological tradition) meets another certain "context" (Latin American political situation in the 1970s). Because we are dealing with relative constructions such as narratives and texts, one could always find broader narratives in which another narrative should be integrated. As essentially historical, all narratives and texts will always belong or refer to other narratives and texts, all of them being contingent and, therefore, made normative only by the authoritative claim of some power (that is, a claim made in the name of a sovereign principle, whether God, the church, or the people). The question that follows, of course, is "*cui bono*": Whom does this claim actually benefit? But this question is not an objective or disinterested one: No one should be able to claim that someone is just "out of context", hiding the arbitrary and interested construction of what is being called "context". Again, the polemical dimension of theology (and of every discipline whatsoever) is negotiated in-between texts: A context as such (in its very etymological sense), due to its infinity and indeterminacy, can never enter into a struggle or a debate.

4. THE CLASH OF THE TEXTS IN LITURGY

One possible way to face the question of con-textuality as inter-textuality in theology is by examining the work of theology in relation to role of liturgy. The Greek word *leitourgía* means, etymologically, the "work of the community/people", and its theological importance resides in the understanding that every religious belief is shaped by the way a certain community address what it considers to be sacred. In other words, religion is never a private matter, but a communitarian action, a certain form of shared life in relation to the sacred towards the sacred. As communitarian action, religion becomes itself a text, a meaningful and shared set of behaviors and discourses: meaningful because they are shared, shared because they are meaningful. However, "liturgy", understood as a "work of the people" (from *leito-ergos*), expresses already the way in which people live their lives: The way they speak, the way they move, the way they relate to each other, the way in which they understand relations of power and subjection, the way they treat nature, *et cetera*. In liturgy, the peculiar kind of living of a certain community comes forth and shapes the expressions of their relationships to what they hold sacred. Theology, as a "scientific" or "rational" reflection on faith, is, thus, built in close conversation with liturgy. Although it may be tempting to understand dogma and doctrine as mere (abstract) rational constructions that stem from an (likewise abstract) revelation; but in so doing, we lose sight of the historical dynamics of revelation, which, certain orthodox and neo-orthodox Protestant theologies of revelation notwithstanding, does not "happen" in a particular point in time, but develops in history, that is on political, social and cultural ground. Theology, as the building of rational paradigms for understanding the relationships obtaining between people and what they hold sacred, is shaped from the very beginning by the "forms of life" of the worshiping community. However, although liturgy shapes theology, theology also shapes liturgy, in a dialectic that takes place in history mainly by the institution of rules and rituals according to both the understanding of the former practices and the new formulas which structure the faith as such. The Nicene Creed for example, arises out of the liturgy of the early Christian community, but it is also the product of critical debates and decisions of the Council of Nicea, which in turn influenced subsequent liturgy. We can say, on the one hand, *lex orandi, lex credenda,* but only because we also say, *lex credenda, lex orandi.*

When understanding the work of theology itself in relation to liturgy, one cannot avoid highlighting the importance of con-textuality – a connection which is particularly important when examining the ways in which Christianity has migrated and developed around the globe. The interrelation of highly divergent communal ways of life or "liturgies" has been a constitutive feature of the movement of Christianity from its very beginnings, and this quite naturally has produced challenges in mutual understanding and new forms of common life. As the *ergos* of one people was confronted and engaged by that of another people, questions concerning how to relate both *ergoi* in a meaningful way to each other but also to "similar" sacred objects. In this synergetic (*synergos*, work together) encounter, a new "liturgy" is born. The work of peoples that understand themselves to be *called out* by the sacred (*ekklesía*) becomes a *calling to* the other people to join in (*ekklesiastós*, preacher). Furthermore, this calling to others is filled with a *calling for* God's universal kingdom to come by the power of the Spirit (*epí-klesis*). To the extent that all parties do this and a new liturgy forms, liturgy might be seen as an *eclectic* choosing of the significant elements of the encounter. In like manner to eclectic liturgy, then, theological work might be seen as chosen and established forms of life built up other-wise.[3]

The case of liturgy also help to redefine *con-text* in terms of *inter-textuality*. On the one hand, it shows that the "con-" ("with") of the text is not just what surrounds the text, but the active *inter-vention* (the coming in between) of *other* "textual" elements (that is, meaningful elements that can be organized in a text) in the making of the text: Specifically with reference to theology, a certain theological text meets *alter-native* texts (those "born in another place)" to join a conversation (or debate or argument) - a certain *commerce* or "interchange".[4] On the other hand, by the same token, liturgy also redefines contextuality as inter-textuality, for theology acknowledges the contexts in which it works as other texts that it must engage. Liturgical theology, then, stresses the fact that the oft-discussed "fusion of horizons" is done in terms of intertextuality, for the horizon (as the metaphor for context) is itself already a text, as discussed above. Liturgy expresses, in short, how a certain text is activated and operationalized by its encounter with *another text*. Therefore, *contextuality* (as *intertexuality*) *is not a thing, but an operation*: It is the operation by which a certain text (the theological text) engages with other texts (such as cultural, historical, political texts that shapes the worldview of an "other" community). And, as an *inter-textual* operation, theology is both able to regulate its connections with other texts, but incapable of completely controlling the coming and going of signs and meanings. As with any other text, theological work is not fully governed by authors. This could be a cause for some concern regarding faithfulness and truth, but it remains nevertheless the very possibility for any theology at all.

---

[3] However, the meeting of different peoples in the context of missionary work will always show (as the very word *mission* indicates) that the relationship among the peoples is a hierarchical one, where the missionaries bring the pagans the word of truth, and in this way it reveals itself to be problematic. Acknowledging the new context for an already defined liturgy is not *per se* neutralizing the violent elements: It could also be a strategic move to achieve dominance just as easily as a form of mutual exchange where both cultures are enriched. As it is a very complex question to address, and this essay is not aiming at that particular situation, I must leave it to the side for now, but it was necessary at least to point this problem out.

[4] Whereas in Latin and romantic languages one could say "*inter-cambium*", the usual English word for describing commercial trades is "*ex*-change", stressing the movement that goes from someone to another one that the prefix "ex" refers to, letting aside, however, the "in-between" that the prefix "inter" denotes. Although the word (coming from Old French) "*inter*-change" also exists in English, it is rarely used.

5. Theology's Universal Drive: The Work of [All] People or the Work of Mone?

However, despite their intimate connection, liturgy and theology are essentially different: Whereas liturgy expresses the work of a certain community and, in this way, remains in the realm of particularity, the theology that community produces aims at a universally true value for its claims. Both theology and liturgy are essentially normative, insofar as they organize a way of speaking and of acting towards the sacred. The very space of the sacred is defined by this normative prescription: The sacred is defined by its difference from the profane, and this is a prescriptive difference regarding how to behave towards different kind of objects. So the claim that liturgy and theology are essentially different is not a matter of normativity *per se*. Rather, it is a matter of the extension of this normativity beyond a particular community, as theology does in making claims about all of reality.

This universal dimension of theology is particularly troublesome in relation to the question of context and intertextuality. If context is the concept that aims at the infinite horizon surrounding a certain text, as the broader text to which every text is subjected or is related to, theological text seems to break down these dialectics. As discussed, texts are meaningful *because* of their belonging to and with a broader set of texts. That is, texts are meaningful only by way of their belonging to a tradition, to a history; in this way, texts happen both in the middle of time and "in the mean(ing)-time". Theology, however, grasps at the very origin of meaning. Theology, as a discourse that speaks about the origins of all things in the name of God, is *archaeological* (from *arché-lógos*; that is, a discourse about sovereignty over beginnings). Theology is the only discourse that, even though all discourse takes place in time, nevertheless attempts to speak beyond time. If context was understood as the broader text to which a certain text relates, then theological text may be understood to reject, or exceed all context: Theology is the ultimate context, or the text of the Ultimate, that text which can no longer be subjected to any other. In other words, theology is the *sovereign text* because it shapes the ground of every text to come. And, in this way, theology is but the articulated discourse of a worldview (*Weltanschaung*), with the important difference that it does not see itself as a particular worldview, but as the *true view of the world*. If theology considers itself as a narrative *amongst-others*, then, it would not be theology any longer, but just another kind of literature. This absolute normativity is due to the essential duty of theology, for it speaks about its only master or sovereign: God. Science could be also considered universal, but it will always depend on a broader text, for no particular science aims at the origin of the world and of meaning as such. Theological *un-con-textuality* is fundamentally found in its narratives on creation and eschatology, for both aim at the "outside of history": Both aim to the *beginning before the beginning* and to the *end after the end*. Language is already playing the fool with us, of course, for there cannot be any clear meaning when speaking of something beyond or before meaning. The beginning and the end are just as illusory as the line dividing earth and heaven. The end and the beginning of the world are but the expression of a certain decision, namely, the decision to establish the world and history as a whole, as a singular text. Therefore, by aiming at these "events", theology becomes meaningless, for its texts lack any context: Theology establishes the very origin of text or meaning as such, and by doing so, it establishes the whole outside which there is nothing, some kind of "absolute text", a text with no ties to anything else.

Theology surpasses the dialectics between text and context in the name of an *ultimate text*, a text that does not know any further horizon. However, this move to establish an ultimate, timeless narrative is as impossible as speaking without language. Theology is doomed to failure, for, despite its patently historical nature, it wishes to speak of what is beyond history. Theology struggles with the *fact* that it is historical and culturally situated, because it places itself beyond any *fact* as such. Facts are what has been already produced, performed and signified, whereas theology wills to speak about producing the conditions for the possibility of any signification as such. If theology should stop struggling with its timeless and universal nature, and simply claim that it is one expression of a context situated alongside other expressions – as any other human language and discourse – then it would cease to be theological. In other words, theology will forever be normative, for it aims to write the meaning of the cause, origin, and coming of meaning. Sociology, anthropology, physics, chemistry, history, literature, economics, political science, can content themselves with description (or at least set this as their aim): For they are texts in contexts, and they do not know nor try to know what is beyond this great text of history and tradition. Theology, by contrast, wills to see the whole of history from its outside, whatever the sight-post is (ethical, metaphysical, political), and defines the whole of history as a single text. At this very point we can find again the idea that every con-text is but a text, is defined as such and, therefore, turned into a (broader) text that gives meaning to the texts that depend on it: In the case of theology, one could say that the context for every text (the context to which every text is subjected) is defined and, thus, turned into text. In other words, the theological text marks the territorial boundaries within which any and all intertextuality takes place; there is no other broader text (context) to which a text could be referred.

Now, this tension within theology, this drive towards ultimacy or principality, produces further tensions between liturgy and theology. Now, the "work of the people" meets the idea of the "universal people". On the one hand, the work of a worshiping community ceases to be the work of a particular people, and becomes the work of "the people of God" understood not as one particular religious community but the church universal. On the other hand, the work of the church is not just the work of a particular kind of people, but represents the work of the entire humanity, for God is now the father of us all, and the lord of every nation (*pantokrator*). And, just as there is no place for two sovereigns, the one God shall prevail over anything or anyone who stands in front of Him. The plural world of "civic religions", where sovereignty was to be defined in battle, leads to a monarchical monotheism where victory of the one God is just *a matter of time*. And, of course, this also changes radically the very nature of liturgy and theology: In a way, liturgy is not about a particular people, but about people universally (humankind) as represented in the one universal church. The work of the church is no longer a particular work, but a universal one: The work of the people is the work of everyone – that is, of none. Theology, therefore, does not speak any particular language, but the language of all persons. If God is the Lord of everything (*pantokrator*), and his Word (*logos*) is for everyone (*kata holos*), then as representatives of the one God, Christians speak a universal language. That is, a language without language. Here, the epistemological question regarding a transcendental and an empirical subject meets the theological question concerning the universal people of God and its instantiation in particular communities. It's the myth of the tower of Babel meets Pentecostal *glossolalia*. So, does theology speak every language, for they speak none?

6. The Failure of Theology and the Ongoing Making of History

Being historical and, at the same time, aiming at the un-historical seems to belong to the nature of theological work. But why is this failure not considered a sufficient reason to leave theology behind, once and for all? Because we just cannot. The great text of history, the great text of tradition is composed as a certain whole: We call this a worldview. This world-view entails arranging everything that happens in the world within a structure that gives meaning to it. Theology is the discourse about that structure, about the principles with which the whole building of the world is built. Theology is archeological and architectural, for it gives meaning to the *arché*, to the origin, and in so doing puts the other elements in place that hold the building up. Of course, like all texts, theology can only give meaning to what explains meaning in a "negative way", refraining itself from attempting to speak in an absolutist language, that is, in a language that is no longer a language, no longer attached to anything – a text without a context. Thus, theology cannot be "out of context", as it is itself a text already. However, theology is somehow always "out of context", because theology is structuring the context itself by referring it to the very origins of meaning: It constructs the ultimate context (the end and the beginning of the horizons) as the absolute text to which every other text is subjected. But it does build this absolute text by means of language, that is, by already belonging to a broader text which shapes its enterprise. Theological text is, then, essentially *mis-taken*, for it wills to be what it cannot be. But there is no theology outside this paradox.

Theology, thus, makes history out of history, and in so doing shows its unique capability of producing whole-world narratives. Theology speaks in the name of God, and God (or its name) is, ultimately, what holds the world together. Theology, as *archetypical* as it is, is within typography. And, as long as it speaks/writes, theology will have to face context. Nevertheless, I would prefer to think that doing theology is not about being "out *of* context", but "out *for* context". Whereas the universal God could be "analphabetic", as it were, theology can only write with letters. And, as far as it *writes*, theology enters into an ongoing text that has been already written. However, theology shapes as deeply as any writing could – or even would – the text in which it comes to be. Revelation, let us say, occurs within an existing tradition: On the one hand, this tradition (context) makes it possible to recognize revelation as an event and give it meaning, define it as a text. On the other hand, because the event of revelation is considered to be the most meaningful one in history, the theologian must re-arrange the context for which it holds meaning in such a way that the event becomes the heart of the ongoing story ~~(*innovation*)~~. In other words, to make the event of revelation meaningful, theology goes "out for a context", searches the elements in the context that will make the new event meaningful, and, at the same time, transfigures the context to be redefined by the new "text-point" around which it gravitates. For instance, when the first Christian communities started writing theology, many of them found in the Latin and Greek context – with its art, philosophy and political system – the appropriate words, concepts, images, metaphors, to write their own text. Of course, the new text was no longer Greek, but Christian, and yet Christian theology would be meaningless without its Greek context. The same could be claimed of every theology that is written by different communities, each of which find in their own situation the proper context to write their theological text, and by doing so, rearranging the very context they first met. Missionary experiences have well shown not only how theology cannot happen "out of context", but also how theology is an active discourse that writes its text by going "out *for* context", giving a whole new meaning to the world in which it develops by organizing the context around the name of God. This expression *"out for context"* is another way to say that theology is about engaging a dialogue between texts, jumping into a never ending inter-textual operation.

In sum, theology is the operation of turning a certain context into an ultimate text, that is, the operation of breaking down the very idea of context by shaping the very edges of our horizons of meaning. By doing so, it makes possible all intertextual operations, for it offers the grounding text to which all texts are related. By the same token, by establishing the limits of history, theology renders indistinguishable the difference between text and context, for the theological text does not have anything outside itself. This is the very reason why theology can become fundamentalist, for it aims at establishing a definite text, a definite history, a definite meaning to the world. Alternatively, by reflecting on the historical and perspectival nature of all human discourses, theology can also acknowledge its limits and open the position of the fundament to other texts that seek to build a worldview. But, again, work at "fundamental" levels is unavoidable in theology, for reasons already discussed. Although "Great Narratives", as Lyotard called them, must be viewed with reasonable suspicion, at the same time the world itself only becomes meaningful in an archaeological discourse. Karl Jaspers suggested that among the different cyphers that open the way to transcendence, *failure* is the ultimate and most meaningful of them all: Using con-texts – texts in community, intertextuality – to refer to the pre-textual conditions for the possibility of any text having meaning is an impossible task. To know, however, requires that we meet and communicate – that is, produce theological texts – with one another. Paradoxically, theology, as an archaeological discourse, both wills to be beyond history and in so doing keeps history – thinkable, communicable wholeness – going. Theology holds the key (*cypher*) to the future, not to disclose it (*de-cyphered*), but to open it as becoming (*un-cyphered*). Theological discourse constructs, deconstructs and reconstructs the world anew. By establishing grounding text, theology calls all fellow texts, con-texts, to come and contextualize each other in endless conversation, including other grounding texts (that is, other theologies). Once the world was turned into Word (*logos*), a dialogue (*dia-logos*) could begin.

On Theological Reflexivity

and the Ambiguities of Transcultural Communication

Evan Kuehn (Chicago, USA)

1. Introduction

The social scientific concept of reflexivity has been employed in different ways and produced an immense literature that peaked two or three decades ago; this essay, then, only claims to follow after some selective insights that have been established more thoroughly. I will demonstrate that theology understood as reflexive inquiry has a long history even when it isn't recognized, that this history is ambiguous and sometimes problematic, and finally that these problems should not prevent us from pursuing a reflexive stance concerning the social conditions of theological functions, because reflexivity is also productive of new social forms and discourses that are fundamental to transcultural communication.

I will discuss two versions of reflexivity: reflexivity as a self-consciousness about the position of the researcher in relation to their inquiry (following Bourdieu and many others), and reflexivity as a concept defining a sociological theory of modernity (following Ulrich Beck, Anthony Giddens, and others).

In sociological and anthropological research, reflexivity usually amounts to some brief remarks in preface about the background, biases, and pre-understanding of the researcher. These situating remarks are offered as a recognition, in the midst of ethnographic study, that the researcher has their own perspective. Put differently, that which is represented in research is not simply the objective truth, but rather it is also determined by the subjective stance of the anthropologist.

As a theory of modernity, reflexivity is more complex, and we will discuss it further later, but in general we can define reflexive modernity as "self-confrontation with the effects of risk society [I.e., a society that forms itself on the basis of unknown future contingencies created by industrial modernity] that cannot be dealt with and assimilated in the system of industrial society."[1] Reflexive modernity, like social scientific reflexivity, seeks to make the determining conditions of a situation explicit.

---

[1] Ulrich Beck, Anthony Giddens, and Scott Lash, *Reflexive Modernization* (Stanford: Stanford University Press, 1994), 6.

Another way of stating the distinction between these two theories of reflexivity is that the first sort of reflexivity, as pursued in ethnographic research, is a methodological stance, or a posture of the researcher. The second sort of reflexivity, that of reflexive modernity, operates at the level of metanarrative. It is a grand theory that seeks to explain how basic conditions of modern European culture serve to destabilize global society's institutions and assumptions in the process of its natural development. One is reflexivity at the micro-level, and the other at the macro-level.

It seems that, with a few notable exceptions,[2] reflexivity as a consideration of theological methodology has been overlooked. Why is this the case? It is not obvious to me that theologians are simply being negligent. In many cases systematic theological inquiry performs different tasks than ethnographic research, and some of these tasks may not require reflexivity in the same way that ethnography does. On the other hand, it may be that reflexivity has been underexamined in theology because it is always present, and has become a background assumption that is never made explicit. The social systems theorist Niklas Luhmann defines the task of theology as self-observation of the subsystem of religion.[3] If theology plays such an observing role within a social system, then it is inherently reflexive, even when it is not "observing" religion in any empirical sense. Such an understanding of theology as Christian self-observation is reflected within theologians' self-understanding as well, at least within modern Protestantism. Reflexivity might be said to be first acknowledged as theology's primary function in Friedrich Schleiermacher's understanding of theology as *Glaubenslehre*. Reflexivity in theological method is a distinctive aspect of its modernism, then.

For Schleiermacher, *dogmatic theology* is the systematic representation of beliefs prevalent in the churches at any given time, and is understood as a subset of *historical theology*. As such it verifies other branches of theological study.[4] Ernst Troeltsch developed this Schleiermacherean insight in his own presentation of systematic theology a century later, defining the theological task as "a participant in the never-ending process of religious production. It is a formation of religious faith, corresponding to a particular set of circum-

---

[2] See Kieran Flanagan, *Sociology in Theology: Reflexivity and Belief* (New York: Palgrave Macmillan, 2007); Natalie Wigg-Stevenson, *Ethnographic Theology: An Inquiry into the Production of Theological Knowledge* (New York: Palgrave Macmillan, 2014); Christian Scharen and Aana Marie Vigen, *Ethnography as Christian Theology and Ethics* (New York: Continuum, 2011).

[3] Niklas Luhmann, *Introduction to Systems Theory* (Malden: Polity, 2013), 108.

[4] Friedrich Schleiermacher, *Brief Outline of Theology as a Field of Study: Revised Translation of the 1811 and 1830 Editions*, ed. and trans. Terrence Tice (Louisville: Westminster John Knox Press, 2011), 13 (§27); Friedrich Schleiermacher, *The Christian Faith*, trans. Terrence Tice, Catherine Kelsey, and Edwina Lawler (Louisville: Westminster John Knox, 2016), 131 (§19).

stances."[5] It is in Troeltsch that we can identify some of the greatest promise, and ambiguities, of reflexivity in theology.

2. Ernst Troeltsch's Europeanism

Ernst Troeltsch's critique of the claims to absoluteness made by Christian theologians presents a double-edged sword for intercultural and transcultural theology. On the one hand, Troeltsch's critique of absoluteness is *the* major force that opened European theological discourse to new transcultural possibilities in the twentieth century. On the other hand, Troeltsch's critique of absoluteness also reinscribed a problematic Europeanism that works against transcultural communication. This particular history of reflexivity in theology and its ambiguities mirrors the wider concern, also expressed by social scientists, about the potentially self-sabotaging effects of reflexive methodologies.

In order to think about this problem, I want to call what Troeltsch did an attempt at *reflexive theology*. Troeltsch's theology can be characterized as reflexive insofar as it established historical consciousness as essential for methodology and employed this stance in his critique of religious claims to universal validity. [6]

Troeltsch was not the only scholar of religion to open up the field to interreligious and intercultural research, but he was notably the most prominent *theologian* who worked towards these goals at the beginning of the 20th century. Because of this, I propose that Troeltsch offers a helpful place to begin a genealogy of intercultural theology. For the most part the theological work that we call intercultural has been standing on the shoulders of non-theologians: historians, psychologists, and especially sociologists and anthropologists of religion. Troeltsch, the "systematic theologian of the History of Religions school," wrote as a theologian (though he engaged in extensive interdisciplinary research on religion, especially sociological, as a matter of course). For this reason alone, Troeltsch should be of interest to those who ask the question, "What does theology do?" with an eye to its potential transcultural functions.

In Ernst Troeltsch's late essay, "The Place of Christianity Among the World Religions," he offered a retrospective assessment of his understanding

---

[5] Ernst Troeltsch, *The Christian Faith*, trans. Garret Paul (Minneapolis: Fortress Press, 1991), 12.

[6] See especially Ernst Troeltsch, "Historical and Dogmatic Method in Theology," in Ernst Troeltsch, *Religion in History*, ed. by Ernst Troeltsch and trans. by J.L. Adams and W.F. Bense (Minneapolis: Fortress, 2007), 11-32; "Religion and the Science of Religion," in *Ernst Troeltsch: Writings on Theology and Religion*, trans. and ed. by Robert Morgan and Michael Pye (Louisville: Westminster John Knox, 1990), 82-123; and Ernst Troeltsch, *The Absoluteness of Christianity and the History of Religions*, trans. David Reid (Louisville: Westminster John Knox Press, 2005).

of the place of Christianity in history, from his 1901 *Absoluteness of Christianity and the History of Religions,* to his historical study of Christian social teachings, and finally to the first half-part of his magnum opus, *Historicism and Its Problems,* which was left incomplete upon his death in 1923. Earlier in his career, Troeltsch had raised important criticisms of the absolute claims to Christianity's validity made by systematic theologians. Two decades later, he sets the theological question of validity "considerably into the background":

All our thoughts and feelings are impregnated with Christian motives and Christian presuppositions; and, conversely, our whole Christianity is indissolubly bound up with elements of the ancient and modern civilizations of Europe. From being a Jewish sect, Christianity has become the religion of all Europe. It stands or falls with European civilization; whilst, on its own part, it has entirely lost its Oriental character and has become Hellenized and westernized.[7]

Troeltsch goes on to argue that this understanding of the intertwining histories of Christianity and Europe has important implications for missionary activity:

> The great religions might indeed be described as crystallizations of the thought of great races, as these races are themselves crystallizations of the various biological and anthropological forms. There can be no conversion or transformation of one into the other, but only a measure of agreement and mutual understanding.[8]

There are numerous problems with this statement, most blatant among them being a racialist understanding of religion and culture. Even setting aside his biological determinist theory of culture, though, Troeltsch offers a dubiously closed conception of human cultures, where mutual understanding might be achieved, but "no conversion or transformation." This is problematic for a number of reasons. First and foremost, it has been roundly falsified by the history of global Christianity in the twentieth and twenty-first centuries. While certain institutional forms and norms of Christianity might be plausibly said to be bound up with European civilization, for the most part it is patently obvious that Christianity is no longer, if it ever was, an exclusively occidental or Euro-American religion.[9]

---

[7] Ernst Troeltsch, *Christian Thought: Its History and Application,* ed. and with an introduction by Baron F, von Hügel, trans. by various hands (London: University of London Press, 1923), 24.

[8] Troeltsch, *Christian Thought,* 29-30.

[9] The tendency to circumscribe religions along national or state boundaries, which is not unique to Troeltsch among classical social theorists, has also served to perpetuate an assumption among some theorists of globalization that religion does not play an important role in the emergence of global societies. For a critique of Ulrich Beck, Anthony Gibbens, and others on this, see Bryan S. Turner, "Reflexive Traditionalism and Emergent Cosmopolitanism: Some Reflections on the Religious Imagination," *Soziale Welt* 61, no. 3/4 (2010): 313–18.

The second problem with Troeltsch's conclusion here comes in his closed model of culture. Culture is a "crystallization" for him, and does not transform with reference to other cultures. Troeltsch does not recognize what Peter Burke calls "cultural hybridity," or what in the present volume we are referring to as the "transcultural functions" of religion. This is an oddly essentializing impulse even by Troeltsch's own lights, because he does recognize that the Christian religion went through a long historical process of Europeanization in the first place - that is, he recognizes fluidity within the history of Christianity between non-European and European social forms. Also, he elsewhere critiqued the idea of an unchanging essence of Christianity.[10] Nonetheless, Troeltsch seems to believe that the various tracks of cultural development have solidified in modernity, and that a strong path dependency determines European religiosity from this point forward. "We cannot live without a religion," he writes, "yet the only religion that we can endure is Christianity, for Christianity has grown up with us and has become a part of our very being."[11] Even within the boundaries of European identity, then, there is no transcultural possibility: no opportunity of conversion or self-differentiation.

Troeltsch's historical methodology, and his critique of Christian theological claims to absoluteness, shifted theological discourse away from earlier dogmatic forms and toward a public theology, or historical theology - that is, toward theology that seeks greater humility about the scope of its claims through limiting their application by referring to the contextual nature of theological claims in general. This model helpfully allows theology to negotiate public situations where not all parties agree, for instance, where one person has experienced a miracle that another hasn't. At the same time, Troeltsch's theology is clearly an instance of self-consciousness that is not fully self-conscious about its own shortcomings. Reflexivity always bears traces of the context that it foregrounds, even as it attempts to move beyond the blind spots of unrecognized contexts. For Troeltsch, this amounted to a Eurocentrist Europeanism that was present despite the important work that he had initiated in moving beyond absoluteness claims on behalf of early dogmatic forms of theology. At times it is not clear that these late lectures are in line with more general trajectories notable in Troeltsch's thought toward a greater pluralism and an account of modern individualism and mysticism that is not so constrained by asymmetrical structures of cultural and societal power. It may also be that Troeltsch's intentions in these statements were to reunify a recently war-torn European culture, and so his emphasis falls on Christianity as a European phenomenon out of geopolitical considerations. In this case, what he

---

[10] Ernst Troeltsch, "What Does 'Essence of Christianity' Mean?" in *Ernst Troeltsch: Writings on Theology and Religion*; see also Lori Pearson, *Beyond Essence: Ernst Troeltsch as Historian and Theorist of Christianity* (Cambridge: Harvard University Press, 2008), 124-81.

[11] Troeltsch, *Christian Thought*, 25.

offers should not be read as a culturally bound Euro-Christianity, but rather as a transcultural Christianity that can speak across the chasm then preset between postwar England and Germany. Whatever explanation might be provided, Troeltsch nonetheless draws normative conclusions from self-reflexive methods that end up working against the basic values of reflexivity, at least as we read him from our twenty-first century vantage point.

3. John Mbiti on Theological Provincialism

In 1974, the Kenyan philosopher of religion John Mbiti published an important essay on "Theological Impotency and the Universality of the Church," where he criticized theological research in developed countries for being ignorant of the theological problems and questions present on the ground:

> Half of today's Christendom lies outside the fenced cloisters of traditional theology. This theology is largely ignorant of, and often embarrassingly impotent in the face of, human questions in the churches of Africa, Latin America, parts of Asia, and the Islands. Thus the Church has become kerygmatically universal, but is still theologically provincial, in spite of the great giants of theology.[12]

Mbiti's critique of Western, developed world theology turns the tables on the reflexivity that we have gained from a historical consciousness about faith. The theologians he critiques work in "the fenced cloisters" of elite universities, and although this sort of theology has supposedly opened up a more critical understanding of Christianity among the world religions, it also has had the unintended effect of provincializing itself. The theological impotence Mbiti identifies is viscerally present in a fictional story he tells about a doctoral student in theology, recently graduated from university and returning to his home. Amidst the celebration of the student's arrival, a crisis occurs. His sister falls to the ground suddenly, possessed by the spirit of her great aunt. The crowd calls upon the student, who after all must be an expert on spiritual matters because of his theological training, and asks him what to do. Mbiti writes:

> He looks around. Slowly he goes to get Bultmann, looks at the index, finds what he wants, reads again about spirit possession in the New Testament. Of course he gets the answer: Bultmann has demythologized it. He insists that his sister is not possessed.[13]

How should we read this story?

---

[12] John Mbiti, "Theological Impotence and the Universality of the Church," *Lutheran World* 8 (1974): 251-60, 253.
[13] Mbiti, "Theological Impotence and the Universality of the Church," 253.

First, we can call this vulgar Bultmannian response to the possessed sister a reflexivity of sorts: the student is historicizing religious experience and attempting, however awkwardly, to contextualize a univocal, or absolute assertion of demon possession in light of modern psychiatric, medical, and critical-biblical scholarship. At the same time, we can say that he is anything but reflexive: A recognition of his own critical epistemological position has paralyzed him, created distance and distrust between him and the community, and has not helped anyone to understand the situation any better. The sister remains unexorcised and indeed, undiagnosed.

The prodigal theologian is self-conscious of a non-mythological worldview that distinguishes his own stance from that of the early Christian communities. As a Christian theologian, he has historicized those normative texts which serve to define his faith. At the same time, Mbiti argues that this reflexivity ill suites him to the needs of his home community, which is, at least in this situation, more at home in what Bultmann would call the "mythical world picture" of the New Testament. Mbiti helpfully turns the tables for us here: A full 26 years before Dipesh Chakrabarty's influential book of the same name, Mbiti is, very explicitly, *Provincializing Europe* with regard to its theological discourse.[14]

I do not think we need to endorse everything about Mbiti's account of the situation. A number of unasked questions are left with merely assumed answers. First and foremost, is it really the job of the theologian to be an exorcist, even if we were to grant that the woman is actually possessed? But the illustration does show the ambiguities created by European forms of reflexivity, especially those that are historically and culturally determined.

Nor are these problem encounters simply a phenomenon of communication between colonial and subaltern, or developed and developing, societal milieus. Another classic example of a similar critique of theological reflexivity is Helmut Thielicke's *Little Exercise for Young Theologians*, where a seminarian returns to his congregation, without crossing any significant societal boundaries, and still encounters significant problems moving between the subsystems of the religious community and the university in communicating effectively.[15]

Critical self-reference is necessary for establishing a context-rich field of study and discourse where one's own faith commitments or cultural condition is separated from one's interpretation of the Other. These examples, however, demonstrate that inadequate forms of reflexivity can create context-sensitive perspective while still trapping the researcher within various limiting self-perceptions. We can derive at least three ambiguities from this fact:

---

[14] Dipesh Chakrabarty, *Provincializing Europe* (Princeton: Princeton University Press, 2000).

[15] Helmut Thielicke, *A Little Exercise for Young Theologians* (Grand Rapids: Eerdmans, 1962).

1. Reflexivity can become an obstacle to recognizing oneself in another or another in oneself.

We can think of methodologically adequate reflexivity in terms of the Aristotelian mean of bravery, standing between timidity on the one hand, and rashness on the other. Rashness with regard to transcultural communication would be an assumption that all cultures should be judged by the standards of one's own, that there is no necessity to bracket the context that conditions one's view of reality. Timidity, on the other hand, would look like a strong cultural relativism that is so cognizant of one's own context-conditioned reality that one is unable to take the risk of finding oneself in another, or finding the other in oneself. Reflexivity that is adequate for transcultural communication recognizes the risk in identifying universalizable aspects of human being within the social conditions of one's context and across contextual differences, but also recognizes that some point of connection and commonality must be present, otherwise transcultural communication could never succeed.

Another ambiguity created by context-consciousness arises from the fact that:

2. Reflexivity seeks to foreground the very traditions that it claims to transcend.

Troeltsch, for instance, sought to move beyond an absolutist understanding of Christianity that unduly universalized the ever-changing conditions that were a function of European forms of social life, and not an immutable or apostolic deposit of faith. Despite these efforts, he ended up defining Christianity as an explicitly European cultural synthesis. That is, he avoided the universalization of Europeanism not by identifying a plurality of Christian identities in and outside of Europe, but rather by foregrounding the European tradition as definitive of the faith, at least as it exists in global modernity.

A final ambiguity of reflexivity is not actually a potential problem or challenge that reflexivity introduces to theological reflection, but rather a fact that raises doubts about how viable reflexivity really is as a methodological stance in theology. Namely:

3. Some of the most promising transcultural forms of religiosity today are decidedly non-reflexive in their theological discourse. This fact should give us pause.

Think of global religious movements that are currently growing in numbers or influence. These include violent and non-violent fundamentalisms of various religious traditions, as well as charismatic and conversionist evangelical religious movements. Such traditions appeal to the witness of the Holy Spirit or the perspicuity (though not always the literal interpretation) of sacred texts without significant reference to the cultural conditions that mediate these particular manifestations of divine revelation, or to the claims of revelation that are present and equally well (or equally poorly) substantiated in other religious traditions. If the vitality and development of religious life is occurring, even within the globalizing and increasingly cosmopolitan context of modern social life, largely without reference to reflexive stances, what values attract us as theological researchers to reflexivity? And to what extent do these values conflict with the lived religious faith that we intend to study?

None of this is meant to be a complete critique of reflexivity as a methodological principle or an explanation of the emergence of social complexity. Indeed, we cannot even begin to engage with transculturality without at least a nascent reflexive stance, and a reflexive theory of social systems. But transcultural functions of religious communication and globalizing modernity are always subject to feedback loops that question their own grounds, and reflexive analyses are no exception to this fact. Being explicit about how reflexivity creates problems for understanding the transcultural forms of theology is important, then. This explicitness also helps the theological researcher to form better questions to ask about how we should proceed: What do we hope to achieve in understanding religious life as responding to transcultural pressures? What assumptions do we make about our own identity in relation to this process? How does theological communication work to integrate itself within the life of religious communities, or perhaps disrupt the normal function of religious life? How does social theory succeed or fail in understanding modern religion as a transcultural phenomenon, and in what ways can theology contribute to more adequate social-theoretical models of religion with regard to this transculturality?

4. What does Reflexivity Produce?

Reflexivity is not simply epistemological or perspectival in nature. It doesn't simply create more awareness on the part of the researcher. This awareness itself is actually produced by social conditions, and in turn can produce new social realities. The reciprocity between social conditions and our consciousness of them makes it important to talk about the reflexivity of an individual researcher in the same sentence that we talk about reflexivity in social structures, for instance in the idea of "reflexive modernity." Even the rarefied social systems theory of Niklas Luhmann, which completely banishes persons and consciousness from its understanding of communication systems, grounds itself in the inherent reflexivity of social theory. This is the main characteristic that Luhmann identifies as distinguishing his social systems theory from previous sociological theories of society: "Cognition of social systems depends on social conditions, not only on account of its object, but also as cognition; indeed, the cognition (or definition or analysis) of actions are themselves actions."[16] What do these reflexive cognitive actions do, on a systemic level?

---

[16] Niklas Luhmann, *Theory of Society, vol.1*, trans. by Rhodes Barrett (Stanford: Stanford University Press, 2012), 4.

A reflexive theological position says that my understanding is mediated by my own context, and does not constitute a straightforwardly objective view of reality. Maybe one can arrive at this position by pure strength of self-understanding, but this is unlikely. In most cases, a process of recognition forms the basis of the reflexive stance. We see that an Other makes sense of reality in a way that contradicts our own sense-making, and we notice, qua armchair anthropologist, that this other way of sense-making is grounded in certain aspects of others' forms of life. We then recognize that our own view of reality is similarly traceable to how we have been raised, our cultural and socio-economic context, etc., and learn to constrain our appraisal of the validity of this viewpoint (at least when we are being reflexive), because we see that it is pointless to argue for it as universalizable when the conditions for its existence are not universalizable.

For example, I may speak with a colleague in Bonn about the social work of the Evangelischer Kirchenkreis. I am not surprised by the fact that congregations here do social work, because my own church community in Chicago has also hosted refugee families, regularly brings meals to a local homeless shelter, and offers its building space for Russian language classes. What may surprise me, however, is the extent to which the financing of German religious communities is mediated by state tax structures, rather than simply through voluntary giving in a collection basket. Additionally, I may quickly surmise that the social welfare work and religious education done by churches in Germany is much more extensive than in the United States, and functions in much closer relationship with the state than is the case in the United States.

I easily recognize the socially conditioned nature of religious ministry in Germany, because the operative social conditions are readily apparent to me as a non-resident. They stand out as different from those conditions to which I'm accustomed. From this encounter with difference, I am also in a much better position to recognize that what is just natural to me in the American religious context actually has non-universal social conditions of its own. As I develop a reflexive stance about my own religious context, then, I can better articulate the social conditions of American denominationalism and non-denominationalism, the strongly voluntary and sectarian nature of American Protestant religiosity, and the conflicting xenophobic and cosmopolitan impulses in American life that lead some churches to host refugees while other churches preach Islamophobic rhetoric from the pulpit.

This reflexivity can form the basis of a sociological theology of the church, which doesn't cease to be theological in its inquiry on account of its being concerned not simply with the phenomenology of religious community, nor with the material conditions of religious association, but rather with social conditions insofar as they contribute to religious practices and interpretations, which themselves are also always producing social conditions for future formations of religious life. [17]

This recognitive and reflexive process allows us to see ourselves and others better, but it also defines the Other in terms of a complex field of sometimes conflicting, and always revisable, views of life. One question we should ask ourselves is: What is lost in the perspectivalism that reflexivity produces? The naïve perspective that what I am used to is "natural" will certainly be lost. In addition, what we can call the "absolute voice" is lost. By the absolute voice, I mean any self-expression that seeks to speak about how things are without reference to context. The absolute voice can simply be the sort of pre-reflective first-person stance that most of us find ourselves in most of the time, or it can be a more robust stance of faith: that the woman experiencing seizures on the ground is possessed by a spirit, or that God is working in one's life to guide circumstances toward a particular end. The absolute voice explains reality by reference to the transcendent, but these explanations themselves do not simply transcend the social conditions of the person voicing them. Reflexivity limits these voices insofar as they claim validity beyond their particular context, and they often do claim such validity simply because they are rarely voiced with reference to their context.[18]

5. What does Theological Reflexivity Produce?

For an ethnographer in the field, reflexivity is simply subjectivity in the service of objectivity: Reflexivity produces an interpretation of other cultures that is not distorted by unrecognized assumptions about oneself. By making explicit one's own context, the hope is that this context will not surreptitiously affect the ethnographer's observations. Further, it may provide helpful triangulation whereby the perspective of the ethnographer isn't simply presented on its own, but rather is anchored to a concrete life context.

For a theologian, reflexivity serves the task of making descriptive and normative claims about the world. Reflexivity produces theological interpretations that are not distorted by unrecognized universalist assumptions that fail to take into account socio-cultural and other conditions for the actuality of religious faith.

Although we have discussed some problematic aspects of Ernst Troeltsch's contributions to reflexivity in theology and the history of religions, we can

---

[17] For more on theology as social-theoretical reflection on the conditions of religious communication in society, see Matthew Ryan Robinson and Evan F. Kuehn, *Theology Compromised: Schleiermacher, Troeltsch, and the Possibility of a Sociological Theology* (Minneapolis: Lexington Books/Fortress Academic, 2019).

[18] Troeltsch calls these two forms of the absolute voice "natural absoluteness of naive perception" and "naive absoluteness in the religious realm." See Troeltsch, *The Absoluteness of Christianity*, 138-9.

also point out more constructive aspects of his work. In a number of shorter essays throughout his career,[19] Troeltsch addressed the effect that modern historical consciousness and the Christian encounter with world religions would have on Christianity's self-understanding of its missional vocation. Troeltsch speaks helpfully - and out of a reflexive position - of a "spiritual and scientific mediation" between religious traditions that goes beyond a mission of "world conquest by propagandistic churches." The goal of this mediation is *Verständigung*, or agreement, and Troeltsch says that this comes "out of tolerance, and not out of mission."[20]

More recently theologians have called our attention to the importance of going beyond tolerance and pursuing thicker virtues of sociability such as friendship,[21] but we can discern such steps in Troeltsch's own appeal to tolerance as well. What Troeltsch calls agreement we often discuss in terms of friendship, conviviality, empathy, or other similar concepts. The main point is that in a context-conscious environment of overlapping and conflicting deep formations of belief, (1) totalizing descriptions are no longer compelling, (2) competitive relationships must be sharply curtailed and limited to non-coercive forms of dialogue, and (3) common humanity should be affirmed in certain concrete ways as a result of these new religious conditions.

Moving beyond systematic theology, we can ask what does reflexivity produce at the level of religious social systems? Or perhaps a better way to ask the question is, what does reflexivity produce at the societal level, whether religious or non-religious, that is theologically significant? Answering these questions is more difficult because of the level of complexity involved. Ulrich Beck and Niklas Luhmann both see reflexivity functioning at the societal level in response to *risk*. Modern society is defined by its development in response to future contingencies that are never fully known.[22]

For Luhmann, the basis of risk society is the differentiation of societal subsystems (for example, of law, religion, art, education) such that there is no single account of the contingencies produced by societal development. As a result, risks must be taken, and these risks are determined by reflexive re-

---

[19] See Ernst Troeltsch, "Missionsmotiv, Missionsaufgabe und neuzeitliches Humanitätschristentum," in *Schriften zur Religionswissenschaft und Ethik 1903-1912*, Kritische Gesamtausgabe 6.1 (Berlin: De Gruyter, 2014), 483-516; Ernst Troeltsch, "Die Mission in der modernen Welt," in Ernst Troeltsch, *Gesammelte Schriften* II (Aalen: Scientia Verlag, 1962), 779-804; Ernst Troeltsch, "Konservativ und Liberal III," *Die Christliche Welt* 30, no. 35, (August 1916): 678-83.

[20] Troeltsch, "Konservativ und Liberal III," 682.

[21] See Matthew Ryan Robinson and Kevin M. Vander Schel, eds., *Beyond Tolerance: Schleiermacher on Friendship, Sociability, and Lived Religion* (Berlin: De Gruyter, 2019).

[22] See Ulrich Beck. *Risk Society: Towards a New Modernity* (London: Sage, 1992); Niklas Luhmann, *Risk: A Sociological Theory*, trans. Rhodes Barrett (New York: Aldine de Gruyter, 1993).

sponsiveness to society's contingencies.[23] Luhmann thinks that older sociological theories of religion erred in identifying religion's basic social function as one of societal integration in the face of various contingencies. In fact, all social systems, and not just religious systems, serve this integrative function if they are functioning at all. Religion in particular can instead be distinguished by its function of explaining various social contingencies in reference to transcendence. While the risk-taking operations that are constantly constructing modern society operate in the immanent realm of contingencies, religion "juxtapose[es] every distinction that can be used in observation (recognition, imagination, action, etc.) with its countervalue of transcendence."[24] Religion, that is, looks at an immanent field of contingencies and makes statements like: "all things happen according to God's judgment." Luhmann describes this as a preservation of meaning through the symbolization of what is indeterminate:

> Religion guarantees the determinability of all meaning against the accompanying experience of constantly referring to the indeterminable. In older societies, the irreversibility of the past could be used in this way, allowing religion to be comprehended as memory. This situation, however, changes if theological reflection is involved. It allows paradoxes to enter into communication precisely because a unity (which could not be formulated differently) can then be symbolized.[25]

This idea of religion offering a reflexive stance, or as Luhmann might call it, a "second-order observation," of societal negotiations of contingencies by reference to something that transcends these contingencies, is helpful. In this way, reflexivity becomes a common project that can speak to the various contingencies of transcultural and intercultural negotiations of difference. Theological reflexivity at the societal level could take any number of forms, and I will offer only a few examples here.

First, we can consider the multiple refugee crises that are immediately relevant to societies around the world. One can ask from the position of a receiving state like Germany or the United States: What risks are present in welcoming refugees from a conflict zone, and on the other hand what risks are present if hospitality is not extended to these people? If the state actively discourages the hospitality of the churches, how do these reasons of state infiltrate the self-understanding of national churches as pseudo-theological expla-

---

[23] As a side note, the concept of risk becomes important for Troeltsch's later writings about the task of compromise that leads to a constantly developing cultural synthesis. It would be worthwhile to investigate the relationship between risk and Troeltsch's theory of cultural synthesis as anticipating important social theoretical research in the 1980s-1990s on risk theory as a way of explaining post-industrial modernity.
[24] Niklas Luhmann, *A Systems Theory of Religion,* trans. by André Keyserling (Stanford: Stanford University Press, 2013), 89.
[25] Niklas Luhmann, *A Systems Theory of Religion,* 90.

nations for our responsibility toward our neighbor? On the other hand, if the state encourages policies of hospitality, how are these political reasons adapted within theological discourse, and to what extent are theological reasons distinguished from non-theological reasons? And all of these questions can be turned the other way around as well: How do theological observations and operations of hospitality and friendship act reflexively within the wider society in a way that constructs new forms of discourse and structures of reception of the Other? These are not merely questions of curiosity. A process of communicative rationality aiming for mutual understanding means that context-specific reasons are constantly being incorporated in unexpected ways within traditions of discourse, and go on to affect future terms of engagement between persons, institutions, and society at large.

Another theologically relevant theme of modern self-understanding and reflexivity that has received significant attention is that of *human rights* discourse. Human rights are grounded in earlier theories of human being and political right, but the immediate postwar experience has indelibly shaped our understanding of ourselves as fundamental rights bearers, and has done so by self-critical observation of the life and dignity of victims of atrocity and instabilities created within postcolonial contexts. At the same time, human rights scholars and activists have more recently recognized that the European context from which our understanding of human rights arose in the 1940s is often ill-equipped to meet the needs of multilateral and global human rights abuses in cultural contexts with potentially different understandings of human being and societal function. This moment of reflexivity in the study of human rights is an opportunity for creative new solutions, but also a point of risk, where future contingencies remain unstable. We should not be surprised to find opportunities for theological work in this area of acute indeterminacy.

6. Conclusion

As we consider what systematic theology has done, is doing, and might do within the scope of transcultural communication, it is important that we establish at least some conditions for the possibility of these operations. I have argued that reflexivity is one such condition, and not one that is unambiguous in its effects. Reflexivity, either through poor application or through functions perfectly natural to it, can create problematic, or at least unpredictable, outcomes not only for theological research, but also for the social structures that are constantly being formed and reformed in theological discourse. At the same time, we should not try to avoid reflexivity in our theological research. It stands at the heart of every significant development of post-industrial modern societies, and cannot be avoided in any case. It *can*, however, and *should*, be pursued with wisdom gained from past mistakes and present theoretical models of society, in order to better define what transcultural functions systematic theology can pursue in its research.

Bibliography

Beck, Ulrich, Anthony Giddens, and Scott Lash. *Reflexive Modernization.* Stanford CA: Stanford University Press, 1994.

Beck, Ulrich. *Risk Society: Towards a New Modernity.* London: Sage, 1992.

Chakrabarty, Dipesh. *Provincializing Europe.* Princeton: Princeton University Press, 2000.

Flanagan, Kieran. *Sociology in Theology: Reflexivity and Belief.* New York: Palgrave Macmillan, 2007.

Luhmann, Niklas. *Introduction to Systems Theory.* Malden: Polity, 2013.

Luhmann, Niklas. *Risk: A Sociological Theory.* Translated by Rhodes Barrett. New York: Aldine de Gruyter, 1993.

Luhmann, Niklas. *A Systems Theory of Religion.* Translated by André Keyserling. Stanford: Stanford University Press, 2013.

Luhmann, Niklas. *Theory of Society, Vol.1.* Translated by Rhodes Barrett. Stanford: Stanford University Press, 2012.

Mbiti, John. "Theological Impotence and the Universality of the Church." *Lutheran World* 8 (1974): 251-60.

Pearson, Lori. *Beyond Essence: Ernst Troeltsch as Historian and Theorist of Christianity.* Cambridge: Harvard University Press, 2008.

Robinson, Matthew Ryan and Evan F. Kuehn. *Theology Compromised: Schleiermacher, Troeltsch, and the Possibility of a Sociological Theology.* Lexington/Fortress, 2019.

Robinson, Matthew Ryan and Kevin M. Vander Schel, eds. *Beyond Tolerance: Schleiermacher on Friendship, Sociability, and Lived Religion.* Berlin: De Gruyter, 2019.

Scharen, Christian B. and Aana Marie Vigen, eds. *Ethnography as Christian Theology and Ethics.* New York: Continuum, 2011.

Schleiermacher, Friedrich. *Brief Outline of Theology as a Field of Study: Revised Translation of the 1811 and 1830 Editions*, edited and translated by Terrence Tice. Louisville: Westminster John Knox Press, 2011.

Schleiermacher, Friedrich. *The Christian Faith.* Translated by Terrence Tice, Catherine Kelsey, and Edwina Lawler. Louisville: Westminster John Knox, 2016.

Thielicke, Helmut. *A Little Exercise for Young Theologians.* Grand Rapids: Eerdmans, 1962.

Troeltsch, Ernst. *The Absoluteness of Christianity and the History of Religions.* Translated by David Reid. Louisville: Westminster John Knox, 2005.

Troeltsch, Ernst. *The Christian Faith.* Translated by Garret Paul. Minneapolis: Fortress Press, 1991.

Troeltsch, Ernst. *Christian Thought: Its History and Application*, edited and with an introduction by Baron F. von Hügel. Translated by various hands. University of London Press, 1923.

Troeltsch, Ernst. "Religion and the Science of Religion," in *Ernst Troeltsch: Writings on Theology and Religion*, translated and edited by Robert Morgan and Michael Pye, 82-123. Louisville: Westminster John Knox, 1990.

Troeltsch, Ernst. "Historical and Dogmatic Method in Theology." In *Religion in History.* Translated by J.L. Adams and W.F. Bense, 11-32. Minneapolis: Fortress, 2007.

Troeltsch, Ernst. "Konservativ und Liberal III" in *Die Christliche Welt* 30, no. 35, 31 August (1916): 678-83.

Troeltsch, Ernst. "Die Mission in der modernen Welt." In *Gesammelte Schriften* II, 779-804. Scientia Verlag, 1962.

Troeltsch, Ernst. "Missionsmotiv, Missionsaufgabe und neuzeitliches Humanitätschristentum." In *Schriften zur Religionswissenschaft und Ethik 1903-1912. Kritische Gesamtausgabe 6.1*, edited by Trutz Rendtorff and Katja Thörner, 483-516. Berlin: De Gruyter, 2014.

Troeltsch, Ernst. "What Does 'Essence of Christianity' Mean?" In *Ernst Troeltsch: Writings on Theology and Religion*, translated and edited by Robert Morgan and Michael Pye, 124-81. Atlanta: John Knox Press, 1976.

Turner, Bryan S. "Reflexive Traditionalism and Emergent Cosmopolitanism: Some Reflections on the Religious Imagination." *Soziale Welt* 61, no. 3/4 (2010): 313–18.

Wigg-Stevenson, Natalie. *Ethnographic Theology: An Inquiry into the Production of Theological Knowledge*. New York: Palgrave Macmillan, 2014.

What Systematic Theology Does

Reflecting on the Christian Faith in its Polyvalent Situatedness

Cornelia Richter (Bonn, Germany)

1. Introduction

Systematic Theology as a subdiscipline of German Protestant Theology is currently facing at least three challenges which at first sight seem to be disparate, or maybe even antagonistic to one another, namely, discerning: (a) theology's role within the scientific community of universities, (b) theology as closely connected to the Protestant Churches, and (c) theology's task to critically reflect on and clarify both society's religious and spiritual demands. As I will show in the *first part* of the chapter, all three fields of engagement demand methodologically different approaches and manifold interactions with, for example, sociology of religion, religious studies, or spiritual care, to name but a few. As all of these tasks have developed within the very specific cultural heritage of not only European but specifically German-speaking Protestant theology, they are most directly relevant for this cultural context; in this sense this chapter on dogmatic theology in Germany is clearly a work in contextual theology of a kind.

Yet, as will be explored in the *second part* of the chapter, there seems to be an inherent commonality in all three challenges as all three of them seem to find their core points in basic existential needs expressed in religious or spiritual experiences and, in turn, in theological reflection on those experiences. As an example, I will concentrate on the Eucharist or (Holy) Communion and shortly describe its dogmatic, confessional, and denominational differences in the variations characteristic across the German-speaking Churches. As different as they are, they do share a common root in the Biblical sources, on the one hand, and as an expression of the fundamental and existential human need for nourishment, on the other. In Systematic Theology, it is of utmost importance to understand that dogmatic essentials are not only and not primarily a question of cognition and learnedness, but that they also relate to fundamental anthropological issues which address mental as well as bodily, individual as well as collective experiences. Even more, it may well be that it is the presupposition of such a fundamental anthropological dimension of existential needs that might allow or even call for a global perspective on what it is that we do in systematic theology.

Now, the problem here is of course, that whatever we define as a basic or existential need from our German perspective might not at all meet basic needs in other places of the world. For even if such existential dimensions might be linked to indisputably universal anthropological constants, their global dimension must be defined carefully: All human beings are born in some way or another, for example, but what it means to be born or to give birth varies widely across different perspectives around the world. Similarly, it is true that all human beings ultimately die, but we know all too well that there is a difference between the violent deaths of adults and children because of war, terror, hunger, a car crash, etc. and the peaceful passing of a comparatively wealthy, socially secure elderly person. There is also tremendous diversity to be found in the ways the meaning of death is interpreted: In the interpretations of some cultural and religious contexts, human beings "pass", in those of other contexts they simply "stop living", in yet others they "change their mode of existence" and so on. Similar observations can be made of love and hate, grief and sorrow. All of them are bound to our diverse cultural contexts and the character of their specific social, political, economic, and educational forms and institutions.

What does this mean for our understanding of the Christian Eucharist or (Holy) Communion? This will be discussed in the *third part* of the chapter. For the sharing of bread and wine in, with, and under Jesus Christ offers a symbolic space of remembrance, expression, and participation worldwide. Yet, even though the eating of bread and drinking wine refer both to the fundamental anthropological and existential need of being nourished as well as to a core feature of Christian faith and practice around the globe, they also demonstrate the incommensurability of our religious contexts and experiences.[1] The Eucharistic elements of bread and wine might be offered worldwide, but that

---

[1] For an approach to the Eucharist that takes in account this aspect of anthropological commonalities by understanding the Eucharist via the perspective of anthropological meal and cultural memory theories cf. Thomas O'Loughlin, *The Eucharist. Origins and Contemporary Understandings* (London et al: T&T Clark, 2015), esp. 61-121; see also Thomas O'Loughlin, "The Grammar of Meals," in *Eating Together Becoming One. Taking Up Pope Francis's Call to Theologians*, ed. Thomas O'Loughlin (Collegeville: Liturgical Press Academic, 2019), 21-32. O'Loughlin's approach is interesting because he searches for a middle way between ontology and empiricism: He tries to avoid the hard ontological claim of anthropological commonalities (he calls it "universally valid statements") by taking in account socio-cultural variety and personal preferences, as well as everyday experience. Further, he combines this with a comparative-historical social analysis ranging from early human communities to contemporary society. In this comparison, he finds evidence for seeing in bread and wine a practical-spiritual orientation that is constant across a wide range of settings or situations of human life. O'Loughlin's stands somewhere in between the hard universal-generalizing claim of anthropological commonalities and the relativization of such universal claims that comes with attention to variety in experiences and perspectives. The present essay seeks to explore a similar middle way with attention to meals and Holy Communion.

does not mean they are perceived, received, shared, and valued in the same way: not globally, not collectively and not individually. And we must take this variety of experiences in receiving the Eucharist into account in our dogmatic reflections on bread and wine as a core element of the Christian faith. In the third part of the chapter, therefore, I will present five examples which might help us to better understand the complex relation of our task as theologians to listening to peoples' experiences, relating relate them to our Christian traditions, and critically reflecting on their implications for what we currently do in Systematic Theology.

2. Systematic Theology as an academic and constructive discipline

Doing systematic theology at a faculty for Protestant Theology in the heart of Europe, especially in the German speaking countries, first of all, means being part of a research university, with all the challenges and demands that system of science brings with it, from the employment of multiple forms of epistemological and methodological inquiry to the maintenance of structures of difference and consensus. Within this scientific community, theology has lost the position of privilege it held in previous centuries when it defined what should and would be researched within the academy. All other academic disciplines have long since differentiated themselves internally, demonstrated their independence, and in this way been completely emancipated within what used to be a hegemonic system lead by theology and philosophy.[2] Yet, at the same time, theology is still highly respected within the scientific community in Germany. There is a clear demand for theological reflection as long as it does not claim any uncritically normative power, as long as it does not simply refer to dogmatic presuppositions or norms of faith for which no sufficient epistemological reasons could be given. The interest in theology at European research universities generally and German universities in particular reflects (a) an awareness of the significances of the cultural heritage of Christianity and need for research on society that examine these significances. It is expected that this research (b) will be conducted in a learned, methodologically self-reflexive and of course self-critical way and that it (c) effectively investigate situated human experience.

At the same time, though, second, the majority of our students will work within the Protestant Churches of Germany, Austria, or Switzerland, or they will teach religion in elementary and secondary schools, both of which require an official qualification for doing so (*Kirchliches Examen* or Master of Educa-

[2] The documentation of this overall tendency can be found in many of the contributions to the, so far, thirty-three volumes of the *History of Universities* series (Oxford: Oxford University Press, 1981-2020 [ongoing]), currently edited by Mordechai Feingold.

tion (M.Ed.), respectively) and a call – a "*vocation*", that is, being hired – from the Churches. Hence, premises of methodological agnosticism and the needs and demands of ecclesial practice are both part of our daily routine – a context unique to the German-speaking countries of Europe. The societal context of our theology is still to a very great extent determined by Western European Christianity, even though the degree of feeling attached to the church as a particular community is currently fading in intensity. The latter is, of course, part of the modern process of secularization, and it is easy enough to demonstrate its dynamics in an institution like the church due to their extremely high symbolic influence. Yet, the problem is not unique to the churches, and similar processes of declining affiliation and involvement can be observed at the site of many other instances of institutional bonding (for example, in the case of the Red Cross, fire brigades, political parties, labor unions, music schools and sport clubs). In the German context, there is evidence that people tend to engage more in temporary projects meeting basic needs (for example, Bread for the World, Terres des Femmes, support for migrants), and that they are more than willing to donate for special dramatic events (for example, the 2019 fire Notre Dame de Paris), but that many hesitate to invest in life-long memberships, especially if they are – as with the German church's "tax"-like system (*Kirchensteuer*) – linked to annual fees.[3] Sociologist Andreas Reckwitz has thus called our society a "society of singularities" (instead of society as a collective body).[4] So one of our most important challenges as a society as a whole is to better understand what it is that makes people alert to common aims and goods of society and to participate in them.

Taking both the research and professional fields of theological work together helps to form a picture for our tasks within Systematic Theology as one of the theological subdisciplines. The picture comes into even clearer focus if we, third, consider an increasing interest not only in religious needs, but also in explicit forms of spirituality – with the latter becoming more and more relevant within the German speaking context. Even though, as observed above, Christianity in its institutionalized forms and measured by membership numbers continues to experience decline in Europe, forms of spirituality and spiritual practice like belief in natural healing powers or various sorts of transcendental beliefs become quite widespread. The same is true for what we call implicit forms of spirituality which are even less articulated in distinct

---

[3] The logic behind these processes of a more project- and event-like decision-making in voluntary/honorary, social, and/or financial engagement in current German society can be seen in a complex interaction between psychological, social, and cultural factors and fictions (that is, narratives), for the German context of society and scholarship latest described by Andreas Reckwitz, *Die Gesellschaft der Singularitäten. Zum Strukturwandel der Moderne* (Berlin: Suhrkamp Verlag, 2019), esp. 119-79.

[4] Cf. The title and concept of Reckwitz, *Gesellschaft*. An English translation is planned for May 2020, cf. Andreas Reckwitz, *The Society of Singularities. On the Structural Transformation of Modernity* (Cambridge, Oxford, and Boston: Polity Press, 2020).

expressions of faith or belief systems, but remain rather below the surface of expression: a sense of belonging to a greater whole, feelings of acceptance, feeling connected to something holy or processes of transcending oneself. Even though these various forms of spirituality quite often develop outside the churches and possibly even at a critical distance from them, more often than one might expect, people remain surprisingly open, expecting, and trusting/trustful towards the churches' symbolic presentation of and resonance for transcendence. This can clearly be seen in the increase of church attendance on special events like Christmas Eve when families, who usually would not even come near any Church service at all, still somehow do want to share the "holy night"; or in the increasing demand for traditional and new *rites de passage* in which people express a need for affirmation and accompaniment at critical moments of transition in life; or in the almost exclusive ability of the church to gather people from across all political parties and social groups in case of a national catastrophe for a spontaneous memorial service.

The task for Systematic Theology, especially for doing dogmatic theology, hidden in all three of these points is to better understand the complex positionality of theology as it becomes marginalized in the society but still sensitive to the manifold explicit and implicit expressions of religion and spirituality in society, all while remaining a highly estimated member of the academia. In all three respects, it is our task as systematic theologians to articulate the comforting, orienting, and existential meanings of Christian faith as present and experienced in society by means of dogmatic and ethical analysis as well as to carefully observe and critique doctrinal, moral, and practical assumptions: What does the Christian faith have to say about life being given and taken, about nourishing body and soul, about losing one's way, about fear, anxiety and hope, about aggression, violence and peace? Even though existential meanings might be considered to be anthropologically universal, they differ greatly not only by specific context and surrounding but also depending on the various situated experiences which shape perceptions of life and God.

The art of doing dogmatic theology is, then, twofold:

On the one hand, dogmatic theology must understand itself as an academic discipline, arguing in methodological distance from religious practice and putting all our traditions, ideas and imaginations to the test in as critical a way as possible. Otherwise we will lose credibility in our role providing critical historically and philosophically grounded correctives to developments in Christianity and what the Christian churches are doing, actually. Such a loss would be significant, for religions are always at risk of yielding to fundamentalist and violent movements due to the complex ways they interweave eternal truths, identity as a community, emotional transcendence of the self and, hence, an existential orientation toward life.

On the other hand, dogmatic theology can only be performed if it understands itself as *self*-reflexion on what it actually means to be Christian: Hence, we turn to the Scriptures; we are acquainted with the manifold transformations of the Christian faith and belief throughout the history of the Jewish-Christian tradition; we reflect on central themes of the Christian faith along with their premises, values, and consequences; and we sort through the various ways Christian faith and praxis interrelate in our own time. So we try to understand, for example, perception of and belief in the presence of God and why God's perceived absence is so disastrous for humans; what it means to perceive God himself in the face of Christ; or what it might mean to gather in the Spirit of life. Dogmatic theology thus has to find words and offer meaning to the symbolic language of the Christian traditions.

This includes, of course, reflection of liturgical traditions as well. In this connection, my former Bonn colleague Günter Bader understood the sermon to provide understanding and guidance for a current situation, while the liturgy is based on understandings that have been handed on for decades, meanings with which we have become familiar, and practices in which we feel at home.[5] In a similar way, by interpreting current transformations both within churches and society, dogmatic theology considers new visible, audible, and expressive subjects that are being or might be filled with meaning and offers new perspectives on them from within the Christian traditions. This is not at all a trivial issue which could be reduced to reclaiming and reformulating our tradition. Instead, we have to be aware of the fact that, in the ways we phrase and rephrase the Christian faith, we help people to feel at home in its language or not, making the Christian faith understandable and accessible or not. Hence, dogmatic statements are not themselves religious confessions, much less are they to be taken as the Word of God. Rather, dogmatic theology is better understood in a constructive sense as a kind of intermediary work, facilitating the intersections of the experiential and the existential by helping to shape language, to give wording, to offer meaning, and in so doing to open up space for religious perception and experience of God.

3. Bread and Wine: Reflecting Our Cultural Heritage

In the first part of this article, I described how the demand for theology in the German and European context stems in part from the significance of and interest in the cultural heritage of Christianity for Europe, though not only for Europe of course. I explained that it is expected that academic study of this heritage be conducted in a learned, methodologically self-reflexive and of course self-critical way. At the same time, I argued that the ability to show the ongoing significance of Christianity for contemporary society and individual

[5] One could see "Predigt als rezentes Sich-Einspielen, Zuspielen von Sinn, dagegen Liturgie als Längst-Eingespieltsein, Sich-Eingespielthaben." Günter Bader, *Die Abendmahlsfeier. Liturgik - Ökonomik - Symbolik* (Mohr: Tübingen 1993), 11.

forms of life requires that work in theology also attend to situated experiences and the existential orientations they yield. I now want to illustrate the interrelation of these three points by means of reflection on a representative example: namely, the Supper. The Eucharist, [Holy] Communion, or Lord's Supper – the sharing of bread and wine – is one of the most fundamental practices in Christianity.[6] As a cultural heritage, it dates back to early Jewish traditions in which it was common for the father of the house or the eldest to break bread and share it around the table and to take a cup of wine and say words of blessing before sharing. For all those who know how Pita bread is baked and served in Israel up to this day, this does not at all come as a surprise. Another Jewish tradition in the background of Christian observance of the Supper is the Pessach. Held on the fifteenth day of the month of Nisan and lasting for seven days, with the Seder-meal on the last evening as its highlight, Pessach is celebrated in remembrance of the Exodus, remembering liberation and autonomy (Chag ha-Cherut). We do not know exactly whether Jesus' last supper was actually held as a Pessach meal or not, but nevertheless the Seder-meal on the last evening of Pessach might have served as an example. Taking both strands of the tradition together – the more daily routine of sharing bread and wine with some blessing, on the one hand, and Pessach, on the other hand – it is most probable that Jesus and his disciples would have enjoyed a meal in their last evenings together in Jerusalem similar to what we today term the "Lord's Supper" (Κυριακὸν δεῖπνον).

In the ritual Christian celebration of the Supper, the most important statements are repetitions of what it is assumed that Jesus himself might have said. The problem here is that we do not know exactly what Jesus said, for Paul and the Gospels vary in the wording they attribute to Jesus. In Protestant churches we usually cite Paul's version:

> [T]he Lord Jesus in the night when he was betrayed took bread, and when he had given thanks (εὐχαριστήσας), he broke it, and said: "This is my body which is for you. Do this in remembrance of me." In the same way he took the cup also, after supper, saying: "This cup is the new covenant in my blood. Do this, as often as you drink it, in remembrance of me." (1 Cor 11, 23-25).

The Synoptic Gospels of Matthew and Mark kept almost similar versions, while some manuscripts of Luke kept a shorter version without the "given for

---

[6] The Orthodox, Catholic, and Lutheran traditions often refer to the meal as the "Eucharist" or "Holy Communion", while the Reformed Protestant tradition and Evangelical groups have often preferred "Communion" or the "Lord's Supper". In German-speaking Protestant churches, the term most commonly used is "Abendmahl", which combines German words for "evening" (Abend) and "meal" (Mahl) and so, very literally translated into English, means "evening meal". Thus, in order both to maintain a distinction from any particular tradition while at the same time acknowledging and owning the particularity of my own context, I will refer throughout the follow to "the Supper."

you [. . .] poured out for you". In John we do not find the same scene of the Lord's Supper, but in John 6 there are several themes, which are most likely drawn from and-or meant to be associated with it: Jesus presents himself as the "living bread" (John 6, 51), and Jesus explains in his speech in the Synagogue in Capernaum that the eating of the Son of Man's flesh and the drinking of his blood equals eating his flesh and drinking his blood (John 6, 53-55). In one version or another, the words of Paul or the Synoptic Gospels are cited whenever the Supper is celebrated, with this being followed in Lutheran services by the blessing using words taken from John (esp. John 6, 51).

The Christian denominations in the German-speaking countries differ, however, in the understanding of what exactly happens in the Supper. Roughly speaking: The Roman-Catholic and [Eastern] Orthodox traditions take the transubstantiation of bread and wine into flesh and blood as the very core moment of the Supper; it is the mysterium which can only be performed by the priest due to his sacramental ordination. The Protestant Lutheran churches do not believe in the transubstantiation of the elements, but do affirm the real presence of Christ in the bread and wine of the Supper. The core moment lies in the words of institution and the blessing of the bread and wine as well as in the moment of sharing it among the believers, the minister being but one of those believers. The Protestant Reformed churches do not link bread and wine to any sort of transubstantiation or real presence, but set the accent on the act of remembrance facilitated by repentance. The Supper is not shared very often, but when it does take place, the bread and wine are shared as symbolic elements providing common focus for the whole community of the faithful, the minister being in no way authoritatively higher than any member of the parish. Even though these three of these models vary in the level in intensity between mysterium, real presence and symbolic remembrance, all of them preserve the link between a basic anthropological need and its cosmological frame. The Supper symbolizes the basic human need for food and drink for survival and, in this way, witnesses to our bodily needs. Already prenatally we depend on being given nourishment, we have to rely on what is given to us by others who themselves are nourished from other things beyond themselves. In other words, further, bread and wine not only symbolize everyday human needs, but also our belonging in Creation.

It does not come as a surprise that the Judeo-Christian traditions knows so many narrations of people being fed by God, of receiving bread and water or wine from God, that we might even speak of a narrative of bread and wine. The concept of the narrative refers to typical fundamental structures underlying our narrations.7 In their widest possible sense they give meaning to while

---

[7] On this understanding of narrative, see the work of Normann Ächtler in Normann Ächtler, "Was ist ein Narrativ? Begriffsgeschichtliche Überlegungen anlässlich der aktuellen Europa-Debatte," *Kultur-Poetik* 14, no. 2 (2014): 244-68, here 247: "Narrative sind sinnstiftende und die Erfahrung systematisierende Erzählmotive bzw.

structuring or systematizing the experiences we narrate as subject matters, while simultaneously providing as intersubjectively relevant schematizations, for example, as restitutive or as transformative narratives. Operative at such a deep level, they prefigure our dogmatic thinking as well as our liturgical and symbolic language, and it is critical to bear this in mind in all our theological expressions. Concerning narrations of bread and wine, there is, for example, the relation to another prominent narrative within the biblical texts, namely the narrative of creation, just hinted at above. The creation stories are brought to mind when, for example, we refer to the narrative relating a miraculous provision of food in the Hebrew Bible as well as in the New Testament: Israel who found itself nourished by manna in the deepest deserts; Jesus who regularly gathered people to eat and drink together, sharing meals and inviting people to share their food with others. By doing so, he not only taught basic principles of social integration and the moral cultivation of friendship. He also showed was able to nourish thousands with five pieces of bread and two fish only. The narratives relating such miraculous provision link feeding and nourishment to a fundamental narrative of continuing creation. God is believed to offer water and manna in midst of the desert because God is seen as the Creator of all things. Jesus is found capable of feeding thousands of people with only a few small portions because he is believed to transcend all quantitative limitations. (The same logic that explains his ability to command the forces of stormy weather and seas.) So these narratives confess Jesus, as the beloved Son of God, driven by the divine spirit, as one who is uniquely able to provide for and to nourish the whole of creation – especially those who experience an existential need for being nourished. So, in the end, it does not come as a surprise that he is presented as giving himself in bread and wine and showing himself able to transgress the borderlines of life and death.

As a methodological consideration, such a reading of biblical narratives with and through one another requires of course a kind of synchronic reading of the texts. In order to really understand the richness of the biblical sources, this should of course be accompanied by diachronic readings and careful application of exegetical methods. Doing all of that exceeds the scope of the present chapter. The point however, is that what we "actually do" in the field of Systematic Theology always also includes at least relating human experience and Christian practice (for example, the Supper) not only with one another but also with the resonance and heritage of both in the biblical sources – not to mention in the Creed(s) of the Early Church and their interpretation in the dogmatic traditions, leading to the various confessional and denominational groups.

Textschemata, die sich in Texten im weitesten Sinne zum Ausdruck bringen und als intersubjektiv orientierende Schemata rezipiert werden."

4. Bread and Wine as a Complex Task for Situated Dogmatics

I have described (a) the need for academic systematic theology as stemming from the felt significance of and interest in the cultural heritage of Christianity for Europe. As I further noted, (b) academic study of this heritage be conducted in a learned, methodologically self-reflexive and self-critical way. And I have been arguing (c) that the ability to show the ongoing significance of Christianity for contemporary society and individual forms of life - that is, meeting the demand expressed in (a) - requires that work in systematic theology attend to situated experiences and the existential orientations they yield.

Systematic theology is for good reasons expected to formulate some kind of guidelines of the Christian faith; it is expected to articulate the essential contents of the Christian faith, that is, to define what it is that those who share in Christian faith hold in common. That task must be taken seriously, for the power of the Christian faith to nurture common identity through symbolic remembrance is a function of its ability to communicate this common faith clearly and compellingly. Yet, different from (earlier) approaches to systematic theology that sought to lay out the core features of the Christian faith as a normative first step from which followed a series of demands concerning believers' experiences and behaviors, the situated dogmatics approach I am describing is to be understood from within the whole set of the theological disciplines: It is closely related not only to biblical studies and the historical development of the Christian faith in its denominational differentiations, but is also responsive to core elements of pastoral care, of liturgy and questions of church leadership: Theology not only reflects hermeneutically on texts and the cognitive features of the Christian faith but it also recognizes and considers the influence of the circumstances in which human beings encounter the Gospel: How the Gospel is read and heard, how it is perceived in singing, praying, speaking and in being silent. It is about light and darkness displayed in cathedrals or small chapels; it is about the clear order of high liturgy or the more fluid communicative dynamics found in evangelical parishes; it is about the time allowed for the Gospel, be it the early morning, be it in midst of a busy day, be it in an evening song. In all of these, the context and the individual situatedness of how and when a human being is met by the Gospel can make a difference. Yet, even though all of this is self-evident, for example, in all branches of practical theology, it is unfortunately less reflected in dogmatic theology. The following examples demonstrate how very different the meaning of bread and wine can be perceived and lived, in which way the intimacy of eating and drinking as well as of coming together can be experienced, and how closely that is linked to the specific situations people find themselves in.

Example 1: In Protestant Churches in Germany, sharing bread and wine is not part of every Sunday service, but is performed on special Sundays or in other special services only: In some parishes such Sundays would be the major ecclesiastical Sundays like Maundy Thursday, Easter, and Pentecost to name but a few; in other parishes the Supper might also be received, for example, each first Sunday of the month. Especially during high holidays, many people Sunday services and other special services, so the services can last quite a long time: The Supper is usually celebrated by having the believers gather around the altar in a circle in groups of approximately thirty to forty people, and if two or three consecutive rounds are required in order to welcome all, the whole observance might take twenty minutes. Since the Supper is placed in the third of fourth liturgical part of the worship service, this unfortunately gives people a chance to leave after the sermon and before the Supper. Though uncommon, as many as half of the parishioners might choose that option if they feel the service is taking too long. They obviously do not consider the Supper to be the most important and central part of the service, but take it rather as a sort of add-on – nice to have but not necessary. One gets the impression that it is enough for them to listen to the Word of God, for they do not seem to long for sharing the intimacy of bread and wine. But what does this mean in dogmatic respects? Is it possible to live on the Word alone? Are those believers literally "fed" and satisfied, or, to phrase it more provocatively, are they even "fed up" already? Is this a phenomenon typical of our rich, satisfied and content mid-European, German-speaking societies? If that were the case, this would raise further dogmatic questions: What then, if not the sharing of bread and wine, would and could be the essential feature of our Sunday services? Is there be another ecclesial setting, form, or medium in which we might share community with and in Christ?

Example 2: In German parishes, it has become quite popular not to take the cup into one's own hands and drink the wine, but to keep the bread and dip it into the wine (*intinctio*). The bread sometimes barely touches the wine, as if it were a liquid to be avoided. And, indeed, that is the reason in the background: People practice the *intinctio* because they consider it unhygienic to share the cup together. In times of (globally) increasing virus infections like the flu or the Covid-19 coronavirus of 2020, this practice, on the one hand, seems to be more than reasonable. Yet, from a dogmatic-theological perspective, the questions at hand are quite different: What does this indicate about people's participation in the intimacy of the community sharing bread and wine? What is it that their attention is drawn to in the first place? Participation or caution and distance?

Example 3: Some time ago, I attended a large, early morning ecumenical service, bringing together believers from all parts of the world. In approaching the service, a woman from a Latin American country joined me. She almost seemed to rush towards the church and, full of joyful expectancy, repeated over and over: "Oh how I need to be nourished, how I need to be fed!" If I am perfectly honest, I have to admit that my first thought was that it was, indeed, early enough not to have had breakfast yet. Giving it a second thought, it occurred to me that bread and especially wine would perhaps not be best to replace proper breakfast. So might she really be hungry in a physical sense? Would we not be better off stopping by a bakery? She did not look like she might be homeless or otherwise in direct physical need. So it was only in the third approach that I finally grasped the meaning of her sentence: Whether she had breakfast or not was not at all in question. Instead she was referring to the both very existential as well as highly dogmatic dimension of being nourished by the divine, of not only consuming the divine but of being consumed at the same time. How very ashamed I felt that that dimension of Holy Communion until that very moment had never even occurred to me.

Example 4: In pastoral care in hospitals people suffering severe, terminal illness need not only literal bread and wine, but they often ask for the Supper in the sense of "last rites". Taking bread and wine for these believers is often difficult for very bodily reasons: They may need to be fed, they may struggle to chew and swallow, they may not be able to take the cup themselves - yet they long for this very last nourishment. So again, we have to ask in both existential and dogmatic respects: What kind of nourishment is this? Sharing the remembrance of the suffering of Christ? Final demonstration of being physically able to eat and drink? A farewell to the human need of being nourished? Ultimate statement that there is nothing more to be said but only to be perceived? Bodily anticipation of the coming new life? Symbolic unification with the eternal dynamics of Creation?

Example 5: In the German Protestant Churches, participation in the Supper is open to everyone in praxis, even though Church law restricts participation to the baptized, regardless of a person's tradition, confession, or denomination. For, sharing bread and wine is a matter, indeed, of sharing. In the Roman-Catholic Church this is different:[8] Participation in the Supper is limited to members of the Roman Catholic Church, for it presupposes belief in the ordination of the priest in apostolic succession and in the transubstantiation of bread and wine consecrated by nobody else but the priest. Both of these aspects are essential for the full acknowledgement of the doctrine of the Roman-Catholic Church. Those who do not subscribe to these and-or who do not hold to its moral standards are not to participate in the Supper in the Roman Catholic Church and, hence, are to be excluded from it. A Roman Catholic Christian who would like to attend the Supper in a Protestant Church would not be right to do so and would not be fulfilling his/her Sunday duties. So sharing bread and wine here is obviously not so much a question of sharing but of belonging, following the logics of inclusion and exclusion. Exceptions from the rule will only be valid in case of danger of death and/or in case of

---

[8] I hasten to add that the dimension of sharing is seen as crucial for the constitution of community in some Roman-Catholic theological approaches, though with differing emphases. Cf. O'Loughlin, *Eucharist*, esp. 112-118, 159-178, 197-201.

extreme spiritual need.[9] Even though many Roman-Catholic priests are no longer willing to control who is about to receive the Supper, this logic of inclusion and exclusion can be most disappointing if not offensive. How much more so, if this logic of inclusion and exclusion is not only a confessional division but a division of colour, ethnicity, or social belonging, if not as a matter of policy then a reality of practice? Does this not completely counteract with the whole idea of sharing bread and wine? And even more so: Does this not completely contradict the dogmatic idea of ecclesia in its most existential dimension?[10]

5. Conclusion: Systematic Theology as Reflection on Polyvalent Situatedness

What I find so intriguing in all five examples is that they only vaguely reflect the Christian faith as it is tidily summarized, for example, in the Creed or elegantly outline in the theology of the Reformation. Instead, they show the high influence, even the determining power, of the situated differences we encounter in our religious practice. All of them vary, for example, in the degree and character of the existential urgency attributed to commemorating Jesus and his disciples and their sharing in a final supper together, much less the integrative idea of the Supper, the sharing of bread and wine and the anticipation of redemption. The examples display a wide range, from no urgency at all to the most intense of experiences imaginable. Most of them relate to situations which we did not choose but to which we must nevertheless respond. In such situations, we can only decide where to direct our focus and what to do next: What is the most pressing problem we have at hand? Is it some form of injustice? Is it hunger? And who is to decide which topic is most urgent? What are we to do if the problems do not arise from our own contexts but from global dynamics? What would global dynamics mean for the outline of our own context? To put it simply: Where does our context start, where does it end? Could there even be something like "the" context we live in?

If all of these questions could and should be posed, however, then what dogmatic theology has to do, actually, is to open spheres of resonance for this variety of situated experiences, spheres of resonance in which situated experiences are not only heard and taken seriously but in which they become re-

[9] Cf. the Code of Canon Law of the Catholic Church, canons 844 §§ 1-5; 913 §2; 916; 921 §§ 1-3; 922. Catholic Church, Code of Canon Law: New English Translation (Washington, DC: Canon Law Society of America, 1999).

[10] Of this opinion is again O'Loughlin, Eucharist, XV. This is why he recently took up the challenge to discuss the question of intercommunion from the perspective of an open-minded participant close but nevertheless sophisticated Catholic theology, cf. Thomas O'Loughlin, *Eating Together Becoming One. Taking Up Pope Francis's Call to Theologians* (Collegeville: Liturgical Press Academic, 2019).

lated to the ongoing transforming process of dogmatic conceptual reflection. This implies, however, that systematic theology is no longer to be understood as dogmatic theology in the classical sense of stating correct doctrine. Instead, it is closely linked to work in the hermeneutics of religion, to the various forms of critique of religion, and to the hermeneutics of lived experience. Dogmatic theology in this sense seeks to understand the basic elements of the Christian faith in how they emerged within their historical contexts, why and how they were transformed in such manifold ways, how they can be understood for our own context at present, in which way they might need to be corrected, and in which way they might again be transformed in the future. In all of this, systematic theology has to follow the epistemological and methodological state of the art of its own time and in this respect has to remain distinct from religious practice – but remaining distinct does not mean to remain indifferent or distanced. Instead, being aware of the difference between religious speech and systematic theological reflection means that the latter is interested in, observing, and listening to a wide polyvalence of religious imaginations, convictions, feelings, symbolic, and metaphorical expressions: Systematic theology has to listen to and has to take seriously what people experience and which stories they tell, what they despise and what they strive for, what they are afraid of and what they hope for. In doing so, systematic theology becomes constructive theology in that it critically reflects on and seeks to connect these current religious expressions to what has been said and thought, told and written throughout the Christian traditions – because it is only in the continuous communicative exchange with biblical texts, the historically developed dogmatic traditions, and contemporary questions that we are able to understand the performative power of Christian faith for our own time and that we are able to adapt our approaches in a critical way for a hermeneutics of embodied and lived experience.

Bibliography

Ächtler, Normann. "Was ist ein Narrativ? Begriffsgeschichtliche Überlegungen anlässlich der aktuellen Europa-Debatte." *Kultur-Poetik* 14, no. 2 (2014): 244-68.

Bader, Günter. *Die Abendmahlsfeier. Liturgik – Ökonomik – Symbolik*. Mohr: Tübingen 1993.

Catholic Church. *Code of Canon Law: New English Translation*. Washington, DC: Canon Law Society of America, 1999.

History of Universities. Edited by Mordechai Feingold. Oxford: Oxford University Press, 1981-2020 [ongoing].

O'Loughlin, Thomas. *Eating Together Becoming One. Taking Up Pope Francis's Call to Theologians*. Collegeville: Liturgical Press Academic, 2019.

O'Loughlin, Thomas. *The Eucharist. Origins and Contemporary Understandings*. London et al: T&T Clark:, 2015.

O'Loughlin, Thomas. "The Grammar of Meals." In *Eating Together Becoming One. Taking Up Pope Francis's Call to Theologians*, edited by Thomas O'Loughlin, 21-32. Collegeville: Liturgical Press Academic, 2019.

Reckwitz, Andreas. *Die Gesellschaft der Singularitäten. Zum Strukturwandel der Moderne.* Berlin: Suhrkamp Verlag, 2019.

Reckwitz, Andreas. *The Society of Singularities. On the Structural Transformation of Modernity.* Cambridge, Oxford, and Boston: Polity Press, 2020.

Part 3 Theology as a Social Artifact

Viewing and Dancing Nature

Environmental Conceptions and the Politics of Belonging of the *danzantes prehispánicos*

Eva Youkhana (Bonn, Germany)

1. Introduction

Pre-Hispanic dancing groups are increasingly visible in urban settings in Mexico as well as in European and North-American cities. Participants live and experience a spirituality that is grounded in the myths and the cosmic visons of Mesoamerican cultures, their environmental conceptions, and their sociocultural and political practices. Esoteric interpretations of the world, the value added to indigenous cultures, the rejection of modern societies, their rationalism and individualism, and the belief that the present world is close to its end (*millenarism*) place them into the sphere of the New Age movement.

The article discusses the extent to which the environmental ideas of pre-Hispanic and so-called *Conchero* dancers are the result of developments in postmodern societies from which the New Age movement emerged.[1] By looking at transcultural religious spaces and the diverse and overlapping ontologies between human beings and nature, it will be shown how nature is commodified and included into the dancers' esoteric worldview in order to draw attention to the evils of postmodernism. It will be examined how the practice of dancing and the construction of countercultural identities (Aztec-nationalist and pre-modern, *hispaneca* and post-modern) influence the senses of belonging of the movement in different (Latin American, European) settings. In addition, the question will be approached concerning how the expression and enactment of ontological differences in New Age movements also provoke right wing and (eco)fascist worldviews.

All the thoughts and ideas presented here are result of research conducted during my employment as a PostDoc in the Research Network on Latin America "Ethnicity, Citizenship, Belonging" in the wake of which I studied forms of conviviality and contestation of Latin American migrants living in Madrid /

---

1 Cf. Eva Youkhana, "Spirituelle Migration und urbaner Lifestyle: Die danzantes prehispánicos in der CSA La Tabacalera in Madrid," In *Urbane (T)Räume. Städte zwischen Kultur, Kommerz und Konflikt,* ed. by Hans-Jürgen Burchardt/Olaf Kaltmeier/Rainer Ölschläger (Baden-Baden: Nomos, 2015), 197–211.

Spain. I had the chance not only to observe but also to dance with a *Conchero* dancing group on a weekly basis, which allowed me to interview the affiliated dancers and get to know their collective spirituality as well as the underlying, partly different cosmic visions of the dancers. Together with my interest in anti-fascist topics and the study of right-wing extremist movements, which are increasingly socially embedded and amalgamated with ecological movements, I identified symbolic features (mainly published in their internet representations) that allows for a comparison of the different New Age movement groups. As a researcher and citizen interested in religious practices and their political manifestations, I deal with the global symbolic entanglements and underlying theoretical underpinnings, images of nature and myths of these movements.

The essay serves the purpose to make a critical contribution outside of theology by analyzing religion and theologies themselves as social artifacts, which are contingent products of socio-political histories and areas of contestation. These religious products and practices embody colonial and post-colonial trajectories of increasingly intertwined localities. By looking at different forms of cultural expression, beyond the study of texts and institutions, we can expand our understanding of diverse forms of (human and non-human) agency that theo-logics might exert and corresponding possibilities for creative contestation and re-coding.

2. Pre-Hispanic Dancing Groups: Origins

The tradition of the Pre-Hispanic or *Conchero* dancers has its origin in the ancient culture of the Nahua speaking people, the Oltecs, Chichimecs, Zapotecs, and Aztecs. They were people from the region of the Mesa Central who had settled in the valley of México since the 4th century BC. Their economy was based on agriculture and they had a strongly hierarchical social order. With the colonization of Mesoamerican cultures and habitants by the Spanish, the new Christian doctrine, supported by military and administrative expansion of the conquerors, had an enormous impact on these traditions. Their religious and cultural practices never totally disappeared, but a syncretism formed in which the values and experiences of the native population were integrated.[2]

The starting point of the *danza conchera* (dance of the shells) is seen according to the legend as a form of resistance by the Chichimecs, a semi-nomad Aztec population, against the occupation of contemporary Querétaro.[3] As their militant resistance was quickly broken, the people developed a dancing practice, accompanied by musical instruments and the shell as an alternative way

---

[2] cf. http://danzantesconcheroshispanos.es/historia/.

[3] Yolotl Gonzalez Torres, *Danza tu Palabra - La Danza de los Concheros* (Mexico: INAHCONACULTA, 2005), 113.

to resist. The complex and powerful movements together with the burning of resin (copal) and its rising smoke connected the dancers with the four Aztec deities Quetzalcoatl, Huitzilopochtli, Tóxcatl and Tezcatlipoca, with which they asked for their support against the destructive and displacing power of the Spanish.

The peaceful but energetic and identity-giving dances were a thorn in the side of the colonizers, as they maintained the native cosmic vision and the resistance of the oppressed despite their religious fusion with Christianity.[4] The combination of Christian elements imported by the colonizers, such as clothes, and musical instruments with pre-Spanish ceremonial images, led to an integrated spiritual dancing practice with popular religious character which shaped the life of the *métis*, the increasingly mixed Mexican population.[5] Nonetheless, the dance and the dancers disappeared from the spotlight in the succeeding centuries and again gained public attention only after the Mexican revolution.

3. Pre-Hispanic Dancing Groups as Part of a Nationalist Project

Immediately after the revolution, the *Concheros* gained attention once more in the Christero War (1926-1929), when the post-revolutionary government introduced anticlerical measures to undermine the power of the rather conservative Catholic Church.[6] Ironically, the *Concheros* became defenders of the Catholic Church and therefore had to suffer prosecution by the newly established government.

In post-revolutionary Mexico and in the context of national identity formation (*Mexicanidad* and *Indigenismo*), the dances gained in significance beginning in the 1930s. On the modern stage, in theatre spectacles, and with the emergence of an increasingly artistic middle class indebted to the memory of the precolonial era, the "heritage of the Aztec empire"[7] was evoked and folklorized. Likewise, pre-Hispanic musical instruments such as the *huéhuetl*

---

[4] Gonzalez Torres, *Danza tu Palabra*, 114. See also: Maya Nadig, "Körper, Performanz und Spiritualität als Instrumente der Konfliktbewältigung bei Danzantes Aztecas in Mexiko," in *Migration und religiöse Dynamik*, ed. by Andrea Lauser, Cordula Weissköppel, and Cordula (Bielefeld: Transcript, 2008); Francisco de la Peña, "Milenarismo, nativismo y neotradicionalismo en el México actual," *Ciencias Sociales y Religión. Asociación de cientistas sociales de la religión en el Mercosur* 3 (2001): 95-113.

[5] de la Peña, "Milenarismo," 99.

[6] Maria Concepción Marquéz Sandoval, "The Cristero War (1926-1929)," in *The Great Events in Religion: An Encyclopedia of Pivotal Events in Religious History*, ed. Florin Curta and Andrew Holt (Santa Barbara, California: ABC CLIO, 2016), 894-99.

[7] Renée de la Torre, "Tensiones entre el esencialismo azteca y el universalismo New Age apartir del estudio de las danzas 'conchero-aztecas'," *Trace*, 54 (2008): 61-76.

(Mexican percussion instrument) and the *teponaxtle* (Mexican slit drum) were readopted into the repertory of popular music. The dance was primarily reanimated in states with a Nahua speaking population. In the 1950s, a new urban middle-class movement, *Movimiento confederado restaurador de la cultura de Anáhuac,* even claimed the retrieval of a kind of "purity" which allegedly predominated the indigenous past.[8] The Aztec deities with *Ometéotl (El es diós),* the Dual God spearheading them, were revived for the popular religious beliefs.

As de la Torre describes, pictorial representations of Mexican natives often show how the movement interpreted the Aztec race in earlier times: a man with a perfect body, in a superior position and always looking up - a victorious warrior.[9] The glorification of natives in the 1940s and 1950s was part of a national project promoted by post-revolutionary artists in Mexico to idealize the Mexican past and to use cultural productions, artifacts, and art to include the indigenous population into the overall project of Mexicanity. Through the political penetration of culture, it became a strong actor, a powerful ally, which the post-revolutionary class gladly used for their political project.

Today, the *Movimiento confederado restaurador de la cultura de Anáhuac,* whose members for example get publicity through spectacles on the Plaza Mayor in Mexico D.F., distinguish two cultures in their home country: (1) The culture of their illustrious ancestors and (2) the hispano-Europeans, who, according to one of the masterminds of the movement, Lic. Rodolfo Fernando Nieva López Zenkizka Kuauhtli, represent the rule of the Europeans.[10] According to the movement's homepage, "*Mexikayotl* (mexicanity) is the reintroduction of the *kalpulli,* the industrialization of the country, the creation of Mexican capital, the training of Mexican technicians, the exclusion from our private and public life of all those strange ideas, customs or doctrines, which distort or weaken the purity and vigor of the Mexican nationality."[11] This strong statements shows, according to Nadig[12] that the aztec dancing groups in Mexico deny their Catholic heritage and its doctrine that should be excluded from the process of becoming a real Mexican. The practitioners instead ascribe to themselves the role of a guardian of pre-Hispanic culture whose main task is to "re-indianize" and "aztequizise" Mexican society and recon-

---

[8] de la Peña, "Milenarismo," 96.

[9] Renée de la Torre, "Alcances translocales de cultos ancestrales. El caso de las danzas rituales aztecas," *Cultura y Religión* 1, no. 1 (2007): 1-19; Enrique Florescano, *Quetzalcóatl y los mitos fundadores de Mesoamérica* (México: Taurus, 2004).

[10] http://movimientoconfederado.com/Inicio.html.

[11] "La Mexikayotl es la reimplantación del kalpulli, la industrialización de país, la creación de capitales mexicanos, la formación de técnicos mexicanos, la exclusión de nuestra vida privada y pública, de todas aquellas ideas, costumbres o doctrinas extrañas, que desvirtúan o debilitan la pureza y vigor de la nacionalidad mexicana." (http://movimientoconfederado.com/Mexicayotl.html).

[12] Nadig, "Körper," 257.

struct precolonial society. In order to leave the dark side of modernity, coloniality, and of 500 years of sociocultural and political sinking, the movement retrieves a vivid culture consisting of dance, language, poetry, mathematics, traditional medicine, meditation, agriculture and reading *Nahuatl* texts *(Amoxtli, Teotlamatiliztli)* in order to recuperate the past. [13] For the practitioners, the dance is an important act to de-colonize the bodies and to create a continuous internal harmony.[14]

4. PRE-HISPANIC DANCING GROUPS AS A POSTMODERN PHENOMENON

Since the 1970s, the dancing groups, as Nadig describes,[15] have grown within urban centers as well as among Hippie movements worldwide, fueled in part by the onset of the Age of Aquarius in 1948.[16] According to Francisco de la Peña the appearance of the "new Mexicanism" and the New Age Movement there, coincided with the publication of the book *La mujer dormida debe dar a luz* (English: "the sleeping woman should give birth"), written in the 1970s by an unknown author with the pseudonym Ayocuan. "In this work, Ayocuan, a student of history at the University of Mexico during the 1950s, tells of his initiation into the sacred traditions of Mexico and Tibet thanks to the help of a German character, the 'colonel'."[17] The story of the initiation of Ayocuan, the author of the book, to the Aquarian Age, is, according to him, closely related to his encounter with a German Nazi, the "coronel", who was involved in Adolf Hitler's effort to find and make use of the cosmic energies that were, or still are, assigned to Tibetan lamas. After the war and his trip to Tibet, the German travelled to Mexico, as one of the most important places for the awakening of a new sacred culture. Here, he is reported to have met Ayocuan with whom he shared his "knowledge" and esoteric prophecy that the laying *volcán Itzac-*

---

13 de la Peña, "Milenarismo," 95-113; de la Torre, "Tensiones," 61-76.

14 Nadig, "Körper," 245-272.

15 Nadig, "Körper," 245-272.

16 The Age of Aquarius is an astrological age referring to the advent of the New Age movement in the 1960s and 1970s. There are different calculations about the onset of the Age of Aquarius. In Mexico the era started in 1948, probably drawing on the calculations of Dr. Serge Reynaud de la Ferrière who posited the year 1948 as the starting point (de la Peña, "Milenarismo," 104, Albert Amao, *The Dawning of the Golden Age of Aquarius: Redefining the Concepts of God, Man and the Universe* (Bloomington: Author House, 2012).

17 My translation from the original Spanish: "En este trabajo, Ayocuan, estudiante de Historia en la Universidad de México durante los años cincuenta, relata su iniciación en las tradiciones sagradas de México y de Tibet gracias a la ayuda de un personaje alemán, el 'coronel'." From de la Peña, "Milenarismo," 103.

cíhuatl, the "sleeping woman", would wake up and cause the Pre-Hispanic cultures to rise up again.[18]

The story of Ayocuan and the "coronel" shows that many different influences, even the omnipotent ideas of the "Drittes Reich", come together in the Mexican New Age movement, which assists in comparison of their worldviews and the notions of superiority of the native populations. Because of their magical-esoteric interpretations of the world, the defense of the higher valence of the indigenous culture within which *ratio,* body, and mind are considered as entangled entities, the refusal of western civilized paradigms such as rationalism, individualism, democracy), and their Millenarism, the *Conchero* dancers can be assigned to the New Age movement.[19] By following a spiritual eclecticism of European esotericism, Tibetan orientalism and Indianist instauration, they pursue a unification of these spiritual traditions at a planetary level.[20] Nonetheless, dancing is part of decolonial[21] liberation and mobilization of the Aztec roots, myths and cosmovisions. At the same time, the dancers reflect processes of individualization of society and the de-institutionalization of the religious beliefs that is based on the mobility of the believers and that is expressed in social fragmentations, interferences, political renovations and identifications.[22] Studies on *Conchero* dancing groups worldwide assume that the practitioners are recruited from the middle classes, the social group which is mainly affected by so-called post-modernity and who most fear economic and institutional upheavals.[23]

The concept of post-modernity was used by Marc Augé in order to explain how society is becoming more transitive and relations more individualized against the backdrop of new information-, communication- and transport-media.[24] Augé argues that travelers move within different isolated spaces that he calls non-spaces and within which any relations to belongings bound to history and territory are lost. This de-territorialization of individuals manifests itself in the formation of new religious relationships in which traditional institutions of the world religions lose their importance and followers. Instead, new spiritual practices, customs, and skills develop through spiritual migrants whose beliefs are maintained without belonging to a religious institution, such

---

18 de la Peña, "Milenarismo," 103.

19 de la Torre, "Tensiones," 61-76; Nadig, "Körper," 245-272.

20 de la Peña, "Milenarismo," 104.

21 The concept of de-colonization of the body is used mainly in emancipatory art and public theatre in Latin America order to illustrate the physical perceived oppression by colonial history and colonization.

22 Nadig, "Körper," 252.

23 de la Peña, "Milenarismo," 100, argues that the dancing groups were recruited for a long time from migrants of rural areas to the urban Centers where they primarily belonged to the poorest section of the working class.

24 Marc Augé, *Los no lugares. Espacios del anonimato* (Barcelona: Gedisa, 1992); Marc Augé, *Por una antropología de la movilidad* (Barcelona: Gedisa, 2007).

as the Catholic Church.[25] The *Conchero* dancers as subjects of post-modernity have turned away from world religions and their institutions in search for new theo-logical horizons. According to Bochinger *et al*,[26] these spiritual pilgrims or migrants are part of a religious plurality that contests ecclesiastical control and new religious orientation in order to liberalize from world religious rules. Not only the divine, but, just as much, a greater universality are expressed and found in their everyday (dancing) practices.[27] With the re-localization of global references within the New Age movement and the trans-localization of Aztec mysticism and traditionalism, the *Conchero* dancers gain power over their own spirituality, as de la Torre emphasizes.[28]

In this way, the *Conchero* dancers are not part of an ethnic or indigenous movement, but a spiritual movement and the cultural expression of an increasingly urban and middle class *mestizo*,[29] affected most strongly by the collectivization processes ascribed to post-modern conditions.

5. TRANSNATIONALIZATION AND THE POLITICS OF BELONGING

As Renée de la Torre describes, global processes and the transnationalization of the dance practices have caused a shift in identity constructions that were previously borne up by the symbolism of the Aztecs.[30] She argues, giving the examples of dancing practices of different dancing groups in diasporic communities, that processes of transnational de-territorialization and re-territorialization have different impacts on the senses of belonging of the dancers and the modalities of interpreting Mexicanity. On the one hand, the cultural globalization leads to a radicalization of the notion of Mexicanity, an essentialization of the Aztecs, and the adoption of an identity of the elected Mexican race realized by the Chicano population in the United States. On the other hand, there is a movement called "Neo-Mexicanity" that has been captured by a network of New Age practitioners. They are looking for a "Mexican" spirituality by interacting with an alternative faith community in Spain that has created a new identity called *"hispaneca"*. The latter enjoy influences of hybrid cultural roots and construe "Mexicanity" as "a kind of pollination, able to fly without limits, to pass through the flows of the new winds of the new

---

25 Grace Davie, "Believing without Belonging: Is this the Future of Religion in Britain?" *Social Compass* 34, no. 4 (1990): 455-469.

26 Christoph Bochinger et al, *Die unsichtbare Religion in der sichtbaren Religion. Formen spiritueller Orientierung in der religiösen Gegenwartskultur* (Stuttgart: Kohlhammer, 2009).

27 Bochinger et al, "Die unsichtbare Religion," 66.

28 de la Torre, "Alcances," 1-19.

29 de la Peña, "Milenarismo," 96.

30 de la Torre, "Tensiones," 61-76.

era, and with its contacts, to create new hybrids in conjunction with other cultures, in other races, in other nations, and even in other continents (Europe)."[31] While both streams originate from the same phenomenon of "aztequization" of the *Conchero* dancers and the reinvention of nativist aesthetics within a world of spectacles in post-revolutionary Mexico,[32] they indicate the different political projects, senses of belonging and conceptions of nature.

6. Conceptions of Nature and Society in the New Age Movement and "Postmodern" Pre-Hispánic Dancing Groups

One important aspect of the dancers' conviction is increasing environmental degradation worldwide. The exploitation and domestication of nature and natural resources together with the displacement and the oppression of indigenous populations and the destruction of their cultural expressions form one of their main concerns. To give an answer to the environmental and thus civilizational crisis, and to solve related problems, they seek a transformation of their internal vision outward toward nature and society. Again, a Mesoamerican cosmic vision and conceptions of nature model the way of integrating the biophysical environment into a universal spirituality.

> In this sense, there are a good number of testimonies that make it clear that among various Mesoamerican groups, plants and animals are considered "living" beings, with a "heart", capable of "speaking", endowed with a consciousness and capable of manifesting the sacred. In other words, flora and fauna are incorporated into an imaginary world that serves precisely to explain the real world, this is what I called elsewhere, expanding on Westheim's term, a mythical biology, considering that the term alludes to an essential aspect of the Mesoamerican worldview. [33]

---

[31] My translation from: "[. . .] de la mexicanidad una especie de polinización, capaz de volar sin límites, de transitar por los flujos de los nuevos vientos de la nueva era, y con sus contactos, crear novedosos híbridos en conjunción con otras culturas, en otras razas, en otras naciones, e incluso en otros continentes (Europa)." See de la Torre, "Tensiones," 74.

[32] de la Torre, "Tensiones," 74.

[33] My translation from: "En este sentido, existe un buen número de testimonios que hacen patente que entre diversos grupos mesoamericanos a las plantas y animales se les considera seres "vivos", con "corazón", capaces de "hablar", dotados de una "conciencia" y susceptibles de manifestar lo sagrado, en otras palabras, la flora y la fauna están incorporadas a un mundo imaginario que sirve justamente para explicarse el mundo real, a esto es a lo que llamé en otro lugar, ampliando el término de Westheim, una biología mítica, considerando que el término alude a un aspecto esencial de la cosmovisión mesoamericana." Manuel Alberto Morales Damián,

The mythic understanding of biology places plants and animals into the center of a sacred world. Flora and fauna, as Damián puts it, are incorporated into an imagined world and are therefore needed to explain the real world. Agrarian products such as maize and maguey were reported to be acts, whether tribulations or triumphs, of the deities. In this conviction, all beings have divine spirits or are homes for a deity.

Living consistent with Pre-Hispanic conceptions of nature is part of a "deep ecology" within the New Age movement of today, in which ideas, feelings, spirituality and action are to be combined. As Krieger and Jaggi write:

> Deep ecology - like most New Age currents - basically takes a biocentric view. It is not man and his needs that are at the center of this world view, but the integrity of the whole biosphere, that is, nature, animals, plants and humans, and their relationships to each other. [34]

Within this perspective, human beings and the rapid growth in human population are considered to be problematic because the perdurability of nature is subordinated to the interests and survival of the human species. According to Arne Naess, one founder of the concept of "deep ecology", society has the "goal not only of stabilizing human population but also of reducing it to a sustainable minimum without revolution or dictatorship. . ."[35]

The idea of deep ecology is recently gaining prominence through the diverse climate action movements (Fridays for Future, Extinction Rebellion) that rightly combat the modern conditions of production and consumption which appropriate nature and thus, endanger the globe and all forms of existence therein through the belief in progress, uncontrolled economic growth and liberalization of markets. In the so-called Anthropocene, which has been proposed as a geological epoch characterized by the greatest human impact on earth, we favor industrial and technological solutions for development and have established environmental conditions that destroy and displace alternative forms of human-nature relationships.

While the climate action movements provide political solutions to the human-caused destruction of the environment, the deep ecology movements

---

"Hombre y medio ambiente en el pensamiento prehispánico," in *Patrimonio, identidad y complejidad social. Enfoques interdisciplinarios*, ed. By Patricia Fournier and Fernando López (México City: Instituto Nacional de Antropología e Historia, 2010), 71-80.

[34] My translation from: "Deep Ecology - wie auch die meisten New Age Strömungen - vertreten im Grunde eine biozentrische Sichtweise. Nicht der Mensch und seine Bedürfnisse stehen im Zentrum dieses Weltbildes, sondern die Unversehrtheit der ganzen Biosphäre, also der Natur, der Tiere, der Pflanzen und Menschen, und deren Beziehungen zueinander." In David Krieger and Christian Jäggi, *Natur als Kulturprodukt: Kulturökologie und Umweltethik* (Basel, Boston, and Berlin: Birkhäuser, 1997): 259.

[35] Krieger and Jäggi, *Natur als Kulturprodukt*, 259.

understand human-nature relationships and all natural phenomena in a rather spiritual way. So-called cosmic elements of life, for example, are thought to be expressed within multiple symbolic relations - relations which, rather than biophysical processes, better explain the operations of the universe. Within this cosmic vision, all is spiritual. According to Damián, "...it's not just the plant and animal kingdoms, but also the topographical elements (mountains, valleys, rivers, lakes), atmospheric phenomena (wind, rain, rainbows, etc.), and the heavenly bodies (the moon, the sun, Venus, Mars, etc.) possess the same characteristics that we have pointed out for the flora and fauna: life, heart, speech, consciousness, sacredness."[36]

The deep and sacralized alliance with nature is practiced by the New Age movement as much as by *Conchero* dancing groups of *hispaneca* origin through the designation and ritualization of so-called "power places". These power places serve as sites for pilgrimage and sensorial interaction with nature. Ivakhiv distinguishes between natural and cultural sites, with the latter being "believed to have been constructed in coordination with natural energies represented by the former."[37] It is believed that ancient cultures all over the world, for example Mesoamerican temples, "constructed their own monuments on powerful 'energy points'."[38] Thus, natural sites of power are seen as the source of cosmic energies where "the power, vitality or sheer otherness of non-human nature seems obviously present, places where the Earth seems to speak, relatively obscured by the din of modern civilization."[39] According to Damián, these qualifications can be assigned to different landscapes such as mountains, unusual rock formations, spectacular lakes and canyons, falls and hot springs, and others sites characterized by some outstanding quality. Such natural sites are of utmost importance for pilgrimages of the believers from all over the world due to their power to initiate personal transformation for those interacting with them, in turn provoking different forms of tourist practices and consumerist desires among the pilgrims.

The spiritually-charged nature and biosphere-centered belief, often connected to lifestyles with "Naturromantik", in the New Age language also known as Gaianism, are points of contact for many groups among popular movements that also show racist and anti-Semitic tenors. These groups consolidate their blood and soil ideologies by moving into small village communities in order to follow the principles of organic farming, with handicrafts enter-

36 My translation from: "[. . .]no se trata sólo de los reinos vegetal y animal, también los elementos topográficos (montañas, valles, ríos, lagos), los fenómenos atmosféricos (viento, lluvia, arco iris, etc.) y los cuerpos celestes (la luna, el sol, Venus, Marte, etc.) poseen las mismas características que hemos señalado para la flora y la fauna: vida, corazón, habla, conciencia, sacralidad." Morales Damián, "Hombre y medio ambiente".

37 Adrian Ivakhiv, "Nature and Self in New Age Pilgrimage," *Culture and Religion* 4, no. 1 (2003): 93-118, here 98.

38 Ivakhiv, "Nature and Self in New Age Pilgrimage," 98.

39 Ivakhiv, "Nature and Self in New Age Pilgrimage," 97.

prises adapted to conservationist principles. In Germany, for example, right-wing national settlers have taken over agricultural farms in the East in order to live out Nordic traditions. They refer to the movement of the 'Artamanen', a young and folkish-minded people who formed, in the 1920s to reconquer once-Prussian ground with their close-to-nature and pagan lifestyle.[40] Today, these right-wing farmers are close to the German Identitarian movement and several activist, folkish-oriented groups, which, according to their self-perception, represent the ideology of "ethnopluralism".[41] The folkish settlers, or Bio-Nazis, as Podjavorsek named them in his Podcast from 2017,[42] perform as agro-ecologists, they partly take up some aspects of esotericism, the ecological movement, and animal protection, while they are at the middle of modern trends opposing anthropocentrism and rejecting the achievements of the Enlightenment for humanity and western rationalism. The construction of natural and cultural sites and power places materialize in stone steles and other artefacts and symbolize their relatedness to nature.[43] In the framework of spiritually-induced nature protection, migration is regarded as an environmental stress factor, constituting a point of overlap with conservative and reactionary groups in immigration societies. Against the wake of increasing migration and refugee movements, the idea of ethnopluralism, coined by emancipative indigenous movements in Latin America, takes on a different, rather reactionary meaning.

These folkish settlers as much as the pre-Hispanic dancing groups belong to a diffusely acting ecological movement within New Age activism that assembles different political streams – from left wing activists to apolitical groups and the political right. These groups have a comparable reference to nature and jointly idealize the supposed harmony of human-nature relations in "close-to-nature" societies worldwide.

7. Conclusion: Environmental Conceptions and the Politics of Belonging within the New Age Movements

Beginning with the example of *Conchero* dancers, it was shown how the nativism, neo-traditionalism and anti-anthropocentrism of the New Age movement seek to transcend religious anthropocentrisms and related human-nature divide, as seen for example in some Christian theology. The revitalization of pre-

[40] Andreas Förster, "Siedler auf befreiter Scholle," *Der Freitag* 33 (2015): 3.

[41] And their right-wing extremist acts and expressions are protected by the German protection of the constitution.

[42] https://www.deutschlandfunkkultur.de/voelkische-siedler-im-laendlichen-raum-der-bio-nazi-von.976.de.html?dram:article_id=379541.

[43] Förster, "Siedler," 3.

Hispanic culture and related cosmic visions together with ritualized spiritual practices elevates nature and associates religious beliefs and "close-to-nature" ideologies with environmental responsibility. The practices of dancing often realized on sacred sites, or assumed power places values the ecosystem through interactive spiritual practices in order to overcome a human-nature divide and perceived ontological differences connected to western binary and rational paradigms of thought.[44] By referring to an idealized past, the *Conchero* dancers and renovators of the culture of the *Anahuac,* as much as the folkish settlers who appeal to the pagan *Artamans* in Germany pursue nationalistic and racist projects that praise an idealized origin in resistance to or rejection of others. Although a comparison of these two examples of New Age movements requires a much closer look at their practices and theo-logics, a certain coherence of environmental concepts and related political projects can be identified. Their worldviews, on the one hand, are grounded in holism and radical human-nature relationality, with a strong commitment to ecology and sustainability. On the other hand, both movements profess an ideology of blood and soil within which their own line of cultural descent may appear superior to others. By espousing esotericism and in this way connecting other movements holding comparable ontological convictions, they found an epistemic bond with other groups within the New Age movement, from left-wing eco-villagers to right-wing folkish settlers. The nevertheless persisting, inherent differences unfold in various socio-political projects, politics of belonging, and areas of contestation, all of which together inhibit clear political positions and positioning. The danger of infiltration of alternative environmental programs by racist streams can be observed in strains of the so-called eco-fascist movement, which promotes a radical anti-human discourse that devalues (at least part of) the human population in relation to nature and promotes social control and engineering.

With their decolonial practices and performances that draw attention to the coloniality of the Americas, the *Conchero* dancers or *hispaneca* must also be interpreted as part of a worldwide movement that opposes the destruction of the foundations of life. The measurement of their contribution to environmental protection, indigenous empowerment, and decolonization is highly context specific and certainly depends on the resoluteness to set themselves apart from reactionary currents within these trans-local movements. The examination of their cultural expressions and sociopolitical practices that may transform dominant religious codes is still open for scrutiny and should become subject to more multi-sited ethnographies as well as theological case-studies.

---

44 Graeme Nicholson. "Ontological Differences," *American Philosophical Quarterly* 33, no. 4 (1996): 357-74.

BIBLIOGRAPHY

http://danzantesconcheroshispanos.es/historia/ (Accessed: 13.02.2020)

http://movimientoconfederado.com/Inicio.html (Accessed: 13.02.2020)

Amao, Albert. *The Dawning of the Golden Age of Aquarius: Redefining the Concepts of God, Man and the Universe.* Bloomington: Author House, 2012.

Augé, Marc. *Los no lugares. Espacios del anonimato.* Barcelona: Gedisa, 1992.

Agué, Marc. *Por una antropología de la movilidad.* Barcelona: Gedisa, 2007.

Bochinger, Christoph, Martin Engelbrecht, and Winfried Gebhardt. *Die unsichtbare*

Religion in der sichtbaren Religion. Formen spiritueller Orientierung in der religiösen

Gegenwartskultur. Religionswissenschaften heute, vol 3. Stuttgart: W. Kohlhammer, 2009.

Davie, Grace. "Believing without Belonging: Is this the Future of Religion in Britain?" Social Compass 34, no. 4 (1990): 455 - 469.

De la Peña, Francisco. "Milenarismo, nativismo y neotradicionalismo en el México actual." Ciencias Sociales y Religión. Asociación de cientistas sociales de la religión en el Mercosur 3 (2001): 95-113.

De la Torre, Renée. "Alcances translocales de cultos ancestrales. El caso de las danzasrituales aztecas." Cultura y Religión 1, no. 1 (2007): 1-19.

De la Torre, Renée. "Tensiones entre el esencialismo azteca y el universalismo New Age a partir del estudio de las danzas 'conchero-aztecas'." Trace 54 (2008): 61-76.

Florescano, Enrique. *Quetzalcóatl y los mitos fundadores de Mesoamérica.* México: Taurus, 2004.

Förster, Andreas. "Siedler auf befreiter Scholle." Der Freitag 33 (2015): 1-3.

Gonzalez Torres, Yolotl. *Danza tu Palabra - La Danza de los Concheros.* Mexico: INAHCO-NACULTA, 2005.

Ivakhiv, Adrian. "Nature and Self in New Age Pilgrimage." *Culture and Religion* 4, no. 1 (2003): 93-118.

Krieger, David and Christian Jäggi. *Natur als Kulturprodukt: Kulturökologie und Umweltethik.* Basel, Boston, and Berlin: Birkhäuser, 1997.

Lauser, Andrea and Cordula Weissköppel. *Migration und religiöse Dynamik: ethnologische Religionsforschung im transnationalen Kontext.* Bielefeld: Transcript, 2008.

Marquéz, Sandoval and Maria Concepción. "The Cristero War (1926-1929)". *In The Great Events in Religion: An Encyclopedia of Pivotal Events in Religious History,* edited by Florin Curta and Andrew Holt, 894-899. Santa Barbara, California: ABC CLIO, 2016.

Morales, Damián and Manuel Alberto. "Hombre y medio ambiente en el pensamiento prehispánico." In *Patrimonio, identidad y complejidad social. Enfoques interdisciplinarios,* edited by Patricia Fournier and Fernando López, 71-80. Mexico City: Instituto Nacional de Antropología e Historia, 2010.

Nadig, Maya. "Körper, Performanz und Spiritualität als Instrumente der Konfliktbewältigung bei Danzantes Aztecas in Mexiko." *In Migration und religiöse Dynamik,* edited by Andrea Lauser and Cordula Weissköppel, 245-272. Bielefeld: Transcript, 2008.

Nicholson, Graeme. "Ontological Differences." *American Philosophical Quarterly* 33, no. 4 (1996): 357-374.

Youkhana, Eva. "Spirituelle Migration und urbaner Lifestyle: Die danzantes prehispánicos in der CSA La Tabacalera in Madrid." In Urbane (T)Räume. Städte zwischen Kultur, Kommerz und Konflikt, edited by Hans-Jürgen Burchardt, Olaf Kaltmeier and Rainer Ölschläger, 197-211. Baden-Baden: Nomos, 2015.

Claiming the Nation

Theological Nationalism in the Philippines

Jayeel Cornelio (Manila, Philippines)

1. Introduction

The Philippines is the only Christian nation in Asia, a claim widely rehearsed in Philippine society. It is, for one, often found in media commentaries about Filipinos and their spectacular religiosity.[1] Even state agencies resort to this characterization.[2] For many religious leaders, the assumption is even taken for granted. This is why they support legislative moves to teach "biblical literacy" and "Christian principles" in public schools.[3] So deep-seated is the idea that it becomes a problem whenever one accounts for corruption, poverty, and other social ills in the Philippines. The question often asked is, "Why do we rank as a corrupt country despite being the only Christian nation in Asia?"[4]

The claim is a mistake for two reasons. The first is that the state, based on the constitution, is secular. The practice of religion in public space, such as religious processions, is generally allowed in the spirit of benevolent neutrality. In this manner, the Supreme Court recognizes the contribution of religion to public life.[5] The second reason is demographic. Proportionally speaking, Timor Leste, the youngest nation-state in Southeast Asia, has by far more Catholics than the Philippines.

Alongside "showcase of democracy", the label was applied to the Philippines when the country gained its independence from the US in 1946. Although these labels asserted the uniqueness of the country in post-war Asia,

---

1 Jack Miller, "Religion in the Philippines," (n.d.), <https://asiasociety.org/education/religion-philippines> (accessed March 26, 2020).

2 Embassy of the Philippines, "About the Philippines," (n.d.), <https://londonpe.dfa.gov.ph/115-abtphl> (accessed March 26, 2020).

3 Agenzia Fides, "Study of the Catholic Religion and the Bible in Public Schools: The Bishops Say 'Yes'," (2019), <http://www.fides.org/en/news/66789-ASIA_PHILIPPINES_Study_of_the_Catholic_religion_and_the_Bible_in_public_schools_the_Bishops_say_Yes> (accessed March 30, 2020).

4 Shaun Silagan, "Something Is Wrong with Filipino Faith," (2019), <https://www.rappler.com/views/imho/244618-opinion-something-wrong-filipino-faith> (accessed March 26, 2020).

5 Jayeel Cornelio, "Religious Freedom in the Philippines: From Legalities to Lived Experience," *The Review of Faith and International Affairs* 11, no. 2 (2013): 36-45.

they "denoted a condescending attitude that had alienated the Philippines from her neighbors."[6] Thus the country's Foreign Secretary wanted them abandoned as early as the 1960s. And yet the idea that the Philippines is the only Christian nation in Asia persists.

The point of this chapter is to show that in spite of its geopolitical undertone, the claim gained traction over time because it became a powerful religious assertion. The official documents of the Catholic Church were initially instrumental in this regard.[7] But as I will show in this chapter, the religious landscape in the Philippines has become far more diverse. Many Christian groups now assert their claim to the nation in their own ways.[8]

I frame these assertions in terms of theological nationalism, which refers to discursive claims made by religious groups about the Christian identity of the Philippines. They do so using theologically inspired justifications, which invoke religious resources (like Scriptures and spiritual encounters) to argue for the divine destiny of the country as the only Christian nation in Asia. To this end, I will highlight discourses emanating not just from the Catholic Church but also other religious groups. Jose Mario Francisco has written important works analyzing official statements of the Catholic Church on the nation and nationalism.[9] This chapter builds on his by also drawing on other emerging groups such as megachurches like *Victory* (Every Nation), evangelical churches like *Jesus is Lord* (JIL), and indigenous and Restorationist churches like *Iglesia ni Cristo* (Church of Christ) and the *Kingdom of Jesus Christ* (KJC).

Towards the end, the chapter reflects on the consequences of theological nationalism for social and political life in the country. It is by reflecting on the consequences of theological nationalism that I critically address the question, "What does theology do, actually?"[10] Specifically, by claiming that the Philip-

---

[6] The New York Times, "Filipino Explains New Nationalism; Lopez Says Country Feels 'Accepted' in Asia," (1964), <https://www.nytimes.com/1964/04/12/archives/filipino-explains-new-nationalism-lopez-says-country-feels-accepted.html> (accessed March 27, 2020).

[7] Jose Mario Francisco, "People of God, People of the Nation: Official Catholic Discourse on Nation and Nationalism," *Philippine Studies: Historical and Ethnographic Viewpoints* 62, no. 3-4 (2014): 341-76.

[8] Tom W. Smith, "Beliefs About God across Time and Space," (2012), <http://www.norc.org/PDFs/Beliefs_about_God_Report.pdf> [accessed April 20, 2019]; Jayeel Cornelio, "The Philippines," in Kenneth Ross, Todd Johnson, and Francis Alvarez, eds., *Edinburgh Companions to Global Christianity: Christianity in East and South-East Asia* (Edinburgh: Edinburgh University Press, 2020), 242-253.

[9] Jose Mario Francisco, "'In but not of the World': Filipino Catholicism and Its Powers," in Stephen Bullivant et al, eds., *Theology and Power: International Perspectives* (Mahwah: Paulist Press, 2016).

[10] This chapter's critical focus on claiming the nation does not deny the extensive work on the impact of theological reflections on community life around the Philippines. Basic ecclesial communities, for example, have been instrumental in

pines is a Christian nation, theological nationalism fails to effectively confront religious diversity and the changing dispositions towards moral concerns such as divorce, same-sex marriage, and gender equality. Equally worth noting is that theological nationalism parallels the rise of strongman politics.[11]

2. WHAT IS THEOLOGICAL NATIONALISM?

Theological nationalism must be situated in wider debates about religion and nationalism. In the course of their development, theories about nationalism, especially those that derive from the experience of Western Europe and North America, were primarily secular and teleological.[12] As a result, religion was framed as a backward institution, and the formation of the modern nation-state as devoid of any religious influence. In classical sociology, legal-rational authority accompanied the rise of the state and its bureaucracy, whose assumption was that leadership and decision-making could not be based on tradition or charisma. Instead they ought to rely on rules and democratic principles. In other words, loyalties were based on "the idea that the legitimacy of the state was rooted in the will of the people, divorced from any religious sanction."[13] Discussions about nationalism have therefore focused on political independence, economic autonomy, and citizenship rights.

In his landmark text, van der Veer reintroduces religion to conversations about nationalism, given the experience of competing religious claims over national identity in India.[14] This much has been true in India as it has elsewhere around the world. With religious nationalism, the nationalist project

protesting the presence of large-scale mining. Important reflections have also been written about the Second Plenary Council's call for the Philippine Church to be a Church of the Poor. William Norman Holden, "Ecclesial Opposition to Large-Scale Mining on Samar: Neoliberalism Meets the Church of the Poor in a Wounded Land," *Religions*, 3:3 (2012): 833-61; Eleanor Dionisio, ed., *Becoming a Church of the Poor: Philippine Catholicism after the Second Plenary Council* (Quezon City: John J. Carroll Institute on Church and Social Issues, 2011).

[11] Karen Bray, "Ungrounded Innocence: Confronting Christian Culpability in White Nationalism," in Jeffrey Robbins and Clayton Crockett, eds., *Doing Theology in the Age of Trump: A Critical Report on Christian Nationalism* (Eugene: Cascade Books, 2018), 45-52.

[12] Talal Asad, "Religion, Nation-State, Secularism," in Peter van der Veer and Hartmut Lehmann, ed, *Nation and Religion: Perspectives on Europe and Asia* (Princeton: Princeton University Press, 1999), 178-96.

[13] Mark Juergensmeyer, *The New Cold War?: Religious Nationalism Confronts the Secular State* (Berkeley and Los Angeles: University of California Press, 1993), 11.

[14] Peter van der Veer, *Religious Nationalism: Hindus and Muslims in India* (Berkeley and Los Angeles: University of California Press, 1994).

and accompanying political action are grounded in a religious confession.[15] For its actors, the confession informs the law, ethics, business, and cultural projects of the nation-state. But the way it takes shape is not the same everywhere. In varying degrees, religious nationalists have claimed territory, prescribed a standard historical narrative, and asserted sovereignty. Buddhist nationalism in Southeast Asia and Christian nationalism in the US are some examples.[16] Violence, in some cases, has accompanied actions against religious minorities. In India, for example, religious nationalism was largely targeted at Muslims.

For some scholars, the rise of religious nationalism is a reaction to the imposition of a Western European model of state secularism in religious societies.[17] In Iran, religious nationalism was a rejection of Western culture and values. Other scholars find in religious nationalisms ideologies that have reflected only the interests of "a small, educated, and privileged few within non-Western societies" themselves.[18] Sri Lanka and several Latin American countries are examples of this. The paradox is that while secular nationalism itself offered a *telos* in terms of rights and progress, religious nationalism countered by also grounding its eschatology in a divine vision of the future. Interestingly, the failure of secular nationalism to bring about progress in these societies coincides with the religious vision becoming more persuasive. In this sense, the ability of religious nationalism to bring people together is a collective resistance to ontological insecurity, which, some observers would argue, is felt at the global level.[19]

My interest in this chapter narrows down to the theological content of these visions. By "theological nationalism", I refer to the discursive act to assert the religious identity of a nation-state by drawing on theological justifications. Put differently, it is a theology that claims the nation. The discursive act has two aspects. The first is the content of the religious claim itself over the identity of the nation-state: *What exactly is being claimed?* The second is the theological basis of the claim: *What are the religious worldviews, beliefs, or convictions that inform the claim to the religious identity of a nation-state?* This choice to be narrow recognizes that inasmuch as religious nationalism takes shape in varying degrees around the world, its manifestations all rely on a

---

[15] Troy Robert Mack, "Religious Nationalism," in Timothy Demy and Jeffrey Shaw, eds., *Religion and Contemporary Politics: A Global Encyclopedia* (Santa Barbara: ABC-CLIO, 2019), 22-26.

[16] Charles Keyes, "Theravada Buddhism and Buddhist Nationalism: Sri Lanka, Myanmar, Cambodia, and Thailand," *The Review of Faith & International Affairs*, 14:4 (2016): 41-52.

[17] Willfried Spohn, "Multiple Modernity, Nationalism and Religion: A Global Perspective," *Current Sociology*, 51:3-4 (2003): 265-86.

[18] Juergensmeyer, *The New Cold War?*, 24

[19] Catarina Kinnvall, "Globalization and Religious Nationalism: Self, Identity, and the Search for Ontological Security," *Political Psychology* 25, no. 5 (2004): 741-67.

religious vision and basis. Thus, the theological content and its underpinnings demand a closer look.

This emphasis on the theological content of religious nationalism draws inspiration from recent scholarship. The first is the influential work on Christian nationalism in the US, which argues that it cannot be reduced to ethnocentrism, political ideologies, or other worldviews.[20] Christian nationalism must be assessed on its own as a set of beliefs about such matters as the Christian identity of the country, Christian values in policy making, religious symbols in public spaces, and prayer in public schools. These variables are religious convictions that have been influential in leading religious believers to vote for Donald Trump even though he was not known for his religiosity.

The second is the work of historian Joel Cabrita on Isaiah Shembe's theological nationalism, Shembe was the founder of the Nazaretha Church in South Africa.[21] Analyzing Shembe's statements and prayers in the early 20th century, Cabrita demonstrates that the religious leader believed that it was his influential church, and not the Zulu monarchy, that would reestablish the embattled nation. His prayers, for example, were in effect commentaries on the sins of the monarchy, which was being judged by Jehovah. Its only redemption lay in being part of the Nazaretha church, whose leader claimed himself to be the evidence of divine forgiveness. The religious vision was in the social order Shembe promised: peace, health, and unity as the Zulu people submitted to the will of Jehovah. To him, validating the church's divine calling was the conversion of important chieftains. In effect, Shembe's nationalism articulated a theology of his church that had the divine mandate to critique the existing monarchy and offer national redemption through membership.

This chapter builds on these works by analyzing theological nationalism in the context of democracy and religious diversity. Indeed, following Talal Asad, doing so is particularly important because of the "moral heterogeneity of modern society."[22] Also, Asad's work interrogates the complex relationship between religion and the secular. While the secular, in the form of the state, limits the power of religion, theological nationalism in effect rejects this compartmentalization. Paying attention to the theological content and basis of religious nationalism is analytically useful in recognizing the religious dimensions of contemporary politics. In the context of the Philippines, doing so is

---

20 Andrew Whitehead, Samuel Perry, and Joseph Baker, "Make America Christian Again: Christian Nationalism and Voting for Donald Trump in the 2016 Presidential Election," *Sociology of Religion* 79, no. 2 (2018): 147-71.

21 Joel Cabrita, "Isaiah Shembe's Theological Nationalism, 1920s–1935," *Journal of Southern African Studies* 35, no. 3 (2009): 609-25.

22 Talal Asad, *Formations of the Secular: Christianity, Islam, Modernity* (Stanford: Standford University Press, 2003), 187.

more important given its religious diversity and the rise of a populist strongman that challenges liberal democracy.[23]

Finally, who articulates theological nationalism? As a discursive act, its sources are necessarily diverse. In fact, this is an important lesson derived from recent work on polydox theology.[24] Although institutional theology and everyday theology are two different strands in theological development, they can end up reinforcing each other. Indeed, religious nationalism in secular politics plays out in a similar manner. Religious leaders (like Isaiah Shembe) provide the "institutional theology" backing the divine identity of the nation and the role of the church in its fulfillment. But politicians and their followers are instrumental as well. When he ran for President, Donald Trump was widely supported by conservative religious leaders even though he was not known to be pious himself. His strategy of invoking the Bible worked for him during the campaign. Politicians and religious entities characterized Trump as the last hope to preserve the Christian future of the US.[25] But even the voting preferences of people themselves had a theological dimension. Beliefs about such issues as Christian values and symbols, prayer in public schools, and the nation's divine destiny are positively and significantly correlated with voting for Donald Trump.[26]

3. Claiming the Nation

In this section, I want to explain how theological nationalism has taken shape in Philippine society. Because of its history and predominance, the Catholic Church, through its bishops, has produced many statements. Jose Mario Francisco has written about these statements.[27] But as a contribution to the literature, I wish to emphasize that the religious landscape in the Philippines has become far more diverse now. Many Christian groups, including megachurches, independent evangelical churches, and indigenous churches, have become influential in terms of membership, finances, and even political presence. Around the country, they are visible as congregations that gather in malls on a given Sunday or television programs that spotlight their preachers. Some of their religious leaders are now elected officials. And yet, in spite of this diver-

---

23 Mark Thompson, "Bloodied Democracy: Duterte and the Death of Liberal Reformism in the Philippines," *Journal of Current Southeast Asian Affairs* 35, no. 3 (2016): 39-68.

24 Christine Tind Johannessen-Henry, "Polydox Eschatology," *Studia Theologica - Nordic Journal of Theology* 66, no. 2 (2012): 107-29.

25 Philip Gorski, "Why Evangelicals Voted for Trump: A Critical Cultural Sociology," *American Journal of Cultural Sociology*, 5 (2017): 338-54.

26 Whitehead, Perry, and Baker, "Make America Christian Again," 164-165.

27 Francisco, "People of God, People of the Nation: Official Catholic Discourse on Nation and Nationalism"; Francisco, "'In but Not of the World': Filipino Catholicism and Its Powers," 91.

sity, these religious organizations find a common interest in claiming the nation.[28] I will be drawing from the official statements of these churches to discern the contours of their theological nationalism.

The Catholic Church

At the onset, I recounted how the idea that the Philippines is the only Christian nation in Asia was a geopolitical claim that asserted the uniqueness of the country in the region.[29] But eventually it became thoroughly religious. During the National Eucharistic Congress in 1954, no less a figure than President Ramon Magsaysay himself dedicated the Filipino people to the Sacred Heart of Jesus: "We are especially grateful for the light of faith, which we uniquely among the nations of the Far East enjoy, and for the air of freedom in which, shielded by our Constitution, we may live and act with the liberty and dignity befitting men who have been created in the image and likeness of God."[30] For Coeli Barry, given the rise of Communism in Asia, it was unmistakable that the consecration was at once religious and political.[31] The move was heavily criticized in the media for various reasons including as a violation of the principle of church-state separation.[32]

Through the writings of its bishops, the Catholic Church played a significant role in galvanizing this claim. Relying on bishops' statements from the 1940s, Francisco narrates the trajectory of this imaginary. [33] In the 1940s, nationalist sentiments that rejected the role of the Church engendered a defensive disposition on the part of the bishops. Specifically, in the wake of Philippine independence, public education became a battleground for the Catholic Church over the elimination of religious instruction and the introduction of nationalist publications. In 1950, the Catholic Welfare Organization (CWO), the predecessor of today's Catholic Bishops Conference of the Philippines (CBCP), condemned the teaching of Rafael Palma's biography of Jose Rizal:

---

[28] Cornelio, "The Philippines."

[29] This is not to deny the longer genealogical history of the formation of the Christian identity of the Philippines. The Spanish project of organizing settlements around a church and civil buildings was both religious and political. So were the religious practices and devotional materials that "provided the metanarrative that functioned as the Christian epic for native society". Francisco, "People of God, People of the Nation: Official Catholic Discourse on Nation and Nationalism," 346.

[30] Leo Cullum, "President Magsaysay's Consecration of the Philippines to the Sacred Heart," *Philippine Studies* 5, no. 1 (1957): 45-70, here 47.

[31] Coeli Barry, "Polyglot Catholicism: Genealogies and Reinterpretions of the Philippine Catholic Church," *Pilipinas* 32, Spring (1999): 59-81.

[32] Cullum, "President Magsaysay's Consecration of the Philippines to the Sacred Heart," 45

[33] Francisco, "People of God, People of the Nation: Official Catholic Discourse on Nation and Nationalism; Francisco, "'In but Not of the World': Filipino Catholicism and Its Powers," 91.

> We believe that we would seriously fail in our duty if we did not raise our voice of warning and protest against the attempt by the enemies of the Catholic name to impose on the young people in our public schools the reading of a book written by a well-known anti-Catholic, which is highly offensive to the religious sentiment of over 80 per cent of the population of the Philippines.[34]

From the 1960s onwards, a shift took place in which the Catholic Church began seeing its role as to side with the Filipino people, particularly the marginalized. The shift coincided with the Second Vatican Council. For Francisco, statements released by the CBCP from then on viewed the Philippines as a Catholic nation "at work in the task of national development."[35] This was a major turn for the Catholic Church, which beforehand was accused of elitism. In 1970, the CBCP declared "the Philippines is a Christian and a democratic country."[36] In the spirit of this conviction, the clergy made commentaries on social and political concerns. In fact, in the Pastoral Exhortation on Philippine Politics, the CBCP claims that "our faith in God has played a key role in major events of our history–even in a decidedly political matter like the People Power Revolution of EDSA."[37] Indeed, social justice as an ideal has underpinned Catholic movements around the country in the struggle for democracy and human rights especially after 1986.[38]

To this day, the Catholic Church, through its Catechism for Filipino Catholics, continues to frame the Philippines as "the only Christian nation among our Asian brethren. There are deep affinities between Christ's message and the Filipino's inmost ways of thinking and acting."[39] In recent years, the CBCP has also approved the annual consecration of the Filipino people to the Immaculate of Heart of Mary: "Behold, as we gather before your Immaculate Heart, we desire, the Church of the Lord in our land, joined in heart and mind with all our people, *isang bayang Filipino [one Filipino nation]* – to unite

---

[34] Joint Statement of the Catholic Hierarchy of the Philippines on the Book, "The Pride of the Malay Race," 6 January 1950 cited in Francisco, "People of God, People of the Nation: Official Catholic Discourse on Nation and Nationalism," 352.

[35] Joint Statement of the Catholic Hierarchy of the Philippines on the Book, "The Pride," 356.

[36] Statement on Civic Responsibility, 9 July 1970 cited in Francisco, "People of God, People of the Nation: Official Catholic Discourse on Nation and Nationalism," 352.

[37] Francisco, "People of God," 352.

[38] Antonio F. Moreno, *Church, State, and Civil Society in Postauthoritarian Philippines: Narratives of Engaged Citizenship* (Quezon City: Ateneo de Manila University Press, 2006).

[39] Catholic Bishops Conference of the Philippines, *Catechism for Filipino Catholics: Special Subsidized Edition for Filipino Catechists* (Manila: Episcopal Commission on Catechesis and Catholic Education, 2008), 1.

ourselves with the consecration which, for love of us, your Son made of himself to the Father."[40]

Emerging Churches

The religious landscape in the Philippines is now diverse.[41] Even if Catholicism remains the dominant church in the population, religious diversity is evident in the rise of independent Christian organizations, many of which have also gone global to cater to the needs of Filipino migrant workers. Megachurches like *Victory* (Every Nation), evangelical churches like *Jesus is Lord* (JIL), and indigenous and Restorationist churches like *Iglesia ni Cristo* (Church of Christ) and the *Kingdom of Jesus Christ* (KJC) already represent millions of members around the country. Their convictions differ on such matters as soteriology, ecclesiology, worship, and the divinity of Christ. Their prominence is evident in several respects. For example, their buildings are unmistakable architectural feats, which I have elsewhere described as "religious worlding".[42] They are also known for their many television programs. Finally, they are involved in local and national politics in ways that shape electoral outcomes. There are of course other religious groups that might be mentioned here, but I highlight these groups as the most visible and fastest growing. Put differently, these Christian churches constitute the minority, but their visibility is no longer deniable.

Analysis of their theological claims to the nation requires some nuance. The claims are made on the basis of (a) the divine calling of the nation and (b) the need to uphold values God wants for the Philippines in order for it to progress. In my view, these logics differ from the theological nationalism of the Catholic Church. Many of the official statements of the Catholic Church about the Philippines are deployed in defense against ideologies inimical to its religious heritage, which ultimately defines Filipinoness. In other words, there is a strong link between being Catholic and being Filipino. This is not the claim of the emerging churches. By appealing to the divine calling of the nation and to biblical values, they are in effect asking for spiritual conversion for the sake of the nation. Implicitly, this appeal is a critique of the failure of the Catholic Church to inspire moral and national renewal.

---

40 RCAM, "Consecration to the Immaculate Heart of Mary," (2019), <https://www.rcam.org/index.php/component/k2/item/443-consecration-to-the-immaculate-heart-of-mary> (accessed April 5, 2020).

41 Jayeel Cornelio, "Global and Religious: Urban Aspirations and the Govenance of Religions in Metro Manila," in *Handbook of Religion and the Asian City: Aspiration and Urbanization in the Twenty-First Century,* ed. by Peter van der Veer (Berkeley: University of California Press, 2015), 69-88.

42 Jayeel Cornelio, "Religious Worlding: Christianity and the New Production of Space in the Philippines," in Juliette Koning and Gwenaël Njoto-Feillard, eds., *New Religiosities, Modern Capitalism and Moral Complexities in Southeast Asia* (New York: Palgrave Macmillan, 2017), 169-97.

To inspire renewal was indeed the hope of Brother Eddie Villanueva who ran for the presidency in the Philippines in 2004 and then again in 2010. The founder and head pastor of *Jesus is Lord*, the biggest Evangelical church in the Philippines, Villanueva formed a party believing that the country needed to be governed by righteous leaders. The party was called *Bangon Pilipinas* (Philippines Arise), and Villanueva's campaign was run by the *Intercessors for the Philippines* and the *Philippines for Jesus Movement*, two organizations Villanueva himself founded in the 1980s. Launched as initiatives for God and country, they "pray for a transformation" on the premise that "only the gospel can change the course of history."[43] *Victory*, a church that targets students, espouses the same principle. The church is not politically involved in a strict sense, but their belief is that "as we reach out to students in the campuses, we help them grow in their character and faith, which translates to their ability to not only transform their campuses, but also their communities for the better."[44] The principle is that converting students while in universities can make them values-driven influencers of society. Established in the 1980s, *Victory* now has more than 90 outreach churches and 400 missionaries in 700 campuses around the country.

Evident in the theological nationalism of emerging churches is the divine calling of the Philippines. This divine calling is most of the time linked to global missions. This much is true in the case of *JIL* and *Victory*, churches that have outreaches around the world. For them to send missionaries is the divine destiny of the Philippines, which explains why they have established training centers in the country. At the same time, missionary work is tied to their "discipleship". *Victory*, for example, has developed "Ten Days" - a short-term missions program that deploys members around Asia. For *Victory*, "our role in our larger global movement is to reach every nation in Asia. Quite simply, Asia is our mission field [. . .] However, if we are to 'make disciples of all nations' (Matthew 28:18-20), it is imperative that we identify and plant churches in key cities of the region [. . .] This is how we honor God and make disciples in Asia."[45]

---

43 Villanueva lost in both attempts, but in 2018 he won when he ran as the representative of the Citizens' Battle Against Corruption, a party-list member of the House of Representatives. Giovanni Maltese, "Reproductive Politics and Populism: Pentecostal Religion and Hegemony in the Philippines," *Journal of Law and Religion* 34, no. 1 (2019): 64-84, here 75; Jayeel Cornelio, "Jesus Is Lord: The Indigenization of Megachurch Christianity in the Philippines," in *Pentecostal Megachurches in Southeast Asia: Negotiating Class, Consumption and the Nation*, ed. by Terence Chong (Singapore: ISEAS, 2018), 127-55.

44 Every Nation Philippines, "A Message from Pastor Joseph Bonifacio," (2020), <https://www.everynation.org.ph/campus-ministry/> (accessed April 7, 2020).

45 Every Nation Philippines, "A Message from Pastor Michael Paderes," (2020), <https://www.everynation.org.ph/world-missions/> (accessed April 7, 2020).

In other cases, theological nationalism is rooted in the prophetic calling of churches and their founders. *Iglesia ni Cristo* (INC), for example, declares itself to be the one true church in the last days, whose founder, Felix Manalo, was prophesied in the Bible itself. INC, which was established in 1914, believes that Manalo was the Filipino "Angel of the East" who fulfilled "ancient prophecies set forth in Isaiah (41:9-14, 43:5-6, and 46:11-13), Revelation (7:1-3) and other biblical texts."[46] Today INC has more than 2 million members around the world. Its worldwide expansion has been made possible by its global media, philanthropic work, and its aggressive training of missionaries who speak local languages.[47] Similarly, the Kingdom of Jesus Christ claims that its founder, Apollo Quiboloy, is the "Appointed Son of God". Quiboloy himself had a mystical encounter at the foot of Mt. Apo in Davao City, which convinced him that the place was destined to be the New Jerusalem. He has transformed the area into the *Prayer Mountain and Paradise Garden of Eden Restored.*[48] The church claims 7 million followers around the world, with the Philippines playing a central role in the last days. Alluding to Scriptural references, his life story recounts the encounter with God as follows: "'The standard I used in this mountain for salvation is the standard I will use all over the world, the Father had said. 'I will send you to them. I have many children in the cities of the world. They don't know you and you don't them, but when they hear your voice, they will follow you because My sheep know My voice.'"[49]

4. What Does Theological Nationalism Do, Actually?

I now return to the two questions I posed at the onset concerning theological nationalism as a discursive act: What exactly is being claimed? And what are the religious worldviews, beliefs, or convictions that inform the claim to the religious identity of a nation-state? Theological nationalism claims the Christian identity of the Philippines, but, as I have discussed above, what this entails differs depending on who makes the assertion. For the Catholic Church, it has been about education, politics, and social justice. For the emerging churches, it has been about divine calling, global missions, and national renewal. The justifications also differ. For the Catholic Church, the country's

---

[46] Robert Reed, "The Iglesia Ni Cristo, 1914-2000. From Obscure Philippine Faith to Global Belief System', *Bijdragen tot de taal-, land- en volkenkunde / Journal of the Humanities and Social Sciences of Southeast Asia* 157, no. 3 (2001): 561-608, here 569.
[47] Jayeel Cornelio, "Religion and Civic Engagement: The Case of Iglesia Ni Cristo in the Philippines," *Religion, state and society* 45, no. 1 (2017): 23-38.
[48] Cornelio, "Religious Worlding: Christianity and the New Production of Space in the Philippines," in Koning and Njoto-Feillard, eds., *New Religiosities, Modern Capitalism and Moral Complexities in Southeast Asia*, 169-97.
[49] Apollo Quiboloy, "Life and Calling," (2019), <https://www.apolloquiboloy.com/life-calling-apollo-quiboloy/> (accessed April 7, 2020).

long history with the faith and its consecration to God are powerful ontological statements. For the emerging churches, by contrast, the basis is found in encounters with God, the centrality of spiritual conversion, and even the Great Commission.

But what does theological nationalism do, actually? I end this chapter by reflecting on this question in view of its social and political consequences. It is a double-edged sword that can be used either for the common good or as a weapon against proponents of a different moral or religious worldview.[50] This tension is to be expected, given the discussed churches' religious diversity and competing truth claims about divine authority, morality, and the common good. For example, social justice and national renewal through converted "disciples" are two principles that operate with different assumptions and end goals. Clearly, at the core of these differences lie competing visions of what it means to be a Christian nation. Such identity is normative, but not homogeneous. This is because the religious claim to the nation is no longer the monopoly of just one institution. As a result, the Catholic Church might hold on to this conviction, but it is not above criticism. As I have mentioned above, Asad asserts this point in terms of modern society's moral heterogeneity.[51] The success of emerging churches in the Philippines has validated much of their foundational narratives about their divine calling to transform the nation and evangelize Asia. In my view, paying attention to the theology of these nationalisms is a novel way to approach understanding religious diversity in the Philippines today.

Indeed, a case can be made that theological nationalism has engendered compelling visions of the common good. Over the years, the Catholic Church has worked for human rights, progress, and democracy around the country. These efforts have been inspired by renewed calls for the Filipino Church to be a Church for the Poor.[52] This is of course not unique to the Catholic Church. Iglesia ni Cristo's religious philanthropy around the country is also arguably derived from their theological nationalism.[53]

But the contemporary theological claim to the nation poses its own problems as well. Inasmuch as it has served the common good, theological nationalism has also been weaponized against policies inimical to Catholic doctrine.[54] In the name of national holiness, Catholic clergy and lay have resisted progressive policies involving artificial contraceptives, divorce, same-sex

---

[50] Francisco, "'In but Not of the World': Filipino Catholicism and Its Powers," 95.

[51] Asad, "Religion, Nation-State, Secularism," 182.

[52] Dionisio, *Becoming a Church of the Poor,* 5.

[53] Cornelio, "Religion and Civic Engagement: The Case of Iglesia Ni Cristo in the Philippines," 23.

[54] Francisco, "'In but Not of the World': Filipino Catholicism and Its Powers," 95.

marriage, and gender equality.[55] When Pope Francis visited the Philippines in 2015, he urged the faithful to resist what he called "ideological colonization" through contraception and same-sex marriage.[56] In fact, the Catholic Church has relied on intellectuals and lawyers to lobby its case in Congress.[57] Interestingly, some religious leaders themselves or members of their religiously inspired parties have become politicians. In this capacity, they have used the Bible to argue that Duterte's bloody war on drugs is necessary to cleanse society and that Filipinos are called to obey the authorities.[58] They have also used theological insights to argue against moves to legalize same-sex marriage and gender equality in the country.[59]

These recent developments raise important concerns about the contributions of religion to public life in the Philippines. It is important for both observers and religious actors themselves to think about these contributions, not just because of its implications for church-state separation, but because the majority of Filipinos do not agree with religious influence on policymaking.[60] One issue is religious diversity and the pursuit of the common good. Theological nationalism has embraced a very narrow understanding of Christianity and citizenship, which has overlooked legitimate calls for divorce and gender equality, for example. Advocacy in support of such initiatives has been drowned out by theological nationalism. In this sense, theological nationalism contradicts the principles of dialogue, openness, and diversity

---

[55] Jayeel Cornelio and Robbin Dagle, "Weaponising Religious Freedom: Same-Sex Marriage and Gender Equality in the Philippines," *Religion & Human Rights* 14, no. 2 (2019): 65-94; Julius Bautista, "Church and State in the Philippines: Tackling Life Issues in a 'Culture of Death'," *SOJOURN: Journal of Social Issues in Southeast Asia* 25, no. 1 (2010): 29-53; Anne Raffin and Jayeel Serrano Cornelio, "The Catholic Church and Education as Sources of Institutional Panic in the Philippines, *Asian Journal of Social Science* 37, no. 5 (2009): 778-98.

[56] Francis Rocca, "Pope Urges Filipino Families: Dream, Resist 'Ideological Colonization'," (2015), <https://www.catholicnews.com/services/englishnews/2015/pope-urges-filipino-families-dream-resist-ideological-colonization.cfm> (accessed March 02, 2020).

[57] Enrique Niño Leviste, "In the Name of Fathers, in Defense of Mothers: Hegemony, Resistance, and the Catholic Church on the Philippine Population Policy," *Philippine Sociological Review* 64, no. 1 (2016): 5-44.

[58] Jayeel Cornelio and Erron Medina, "Christianity and Duterte's War on Drugs in the Philippines," *Politics, Religion & Ideology*, 20:2 (2019): 151-69; Jayeel Cornelio and Ia Marañon, "A 'Righteous Intervention': Megachurch Christianity and Duterte's War on Drugs in the Philippines," *International Journal of Asian Christianity* 2, no. 2 (2019): 211-30.

[59] Cornelio and Dagle, "Weaponising Religious Freedom"; Cornelio, "The Philippines."

[60] Gerald Nicolas, Loila Batomalaque, and Gladys Rabacal, "Qualified Confidence: Church, State, and Public Opinion," in *Becoming a Church of the Poor: Philippine Catholicism after the Second Plenary Council*, ed. by Eleanor Dionisio (Quezon City: John J. Carroll Institute on Church and Social Issues, 2011), 90-101.

embraced by public theology (a theme discussed by other contributors in this volume).[61] The other issue is related to theological nationalism and the rise of populist leaders like Duterte who threatens he "will kill anybody [who will] destroy my country."[62] Theological nationalism and populism parallel each other in upholding the nation and defending it against its enemies, many of whom are imagined in the name of national holiness and renewal. Much has been said about the politics of illiberal reform and the rise of populist strongmen. It is only now that the religious dimension of support for populist regimes is receiving scholarly attention. Following the empirical questions raised in this chapter, succeeding work should focus on everyday theological nationalism.

Bibliography

Agenzia Fides. "Study of the Catholic Religion and the Bible in Public Schools: The Bishops Say Yes." Last modified 2019. Accessed March 30, 2020. http://www.fides.org/en/news/66789-ASIA_PHILIPPINES_Study_of_the_Catholic_religion_and_the_Bible_in_public_schools_the_Bishops_say_Yes.

Asad, Talal. "Religion, Nation-State, Secularism." In *Nation and Religion: Perspectives on Europe and Asia*, edited by van der Veer, Peter and Hartmut Lehmann, (Princeton: Princeton University Press, 1999), 178-96.

Barry, Coeli. "Polyglot Catholicism: Genealogies and Reinterpretions of the Philippine Catholic Church." *Pilipinas* 32, (Spring) (1999): 59-81.

Bautista, Julius. "Church and State in the Philippines: Tackling Life Issues in a 'Culture of Death'." *SOJOURN: Journal of Social Issues in Southeast Asia* 25, no. 1 (2010): 29-53.

Bray, Karen. "Ungrounded Innocence: Confronting Christian Culpability in White Nationalism." In *Doing Theolgoy in the Age of Trump: A Critical Report on Christian Nationalism*, edited by Robbins, Jeffrey and Clayton Crockett, (Eugene: Cascade Books, 2018), 45-52.

Cabrita, Joel. "Isaiah Shembe's Theological Nationalism, 1920s-1935." *Journal of Southern African Studies* 35, no. 3 (2009): 609-25.

Catholic Bishops Conference of the Philippines. *Catechism for Filipino Catholics: Special Subsidized Edition for Filipino Catechists.* (Manila: Episcopal Commission on Catechesis and Catholic Education, 2008).

---

[61] Stephen van Erp, "God Becoming Present in the World: Sacramental Foundations of a Theology of Public Life', in *Grace, Governance and Globalization*, ed. by Stephen van Erp, Martin Poulsom, and Lieven Boeve (London: Bloomsbury Academic, 2017), 13-27; Joseph Rivera, *Political Theology and Pluralism: Renewing Public Dialogue* (New York et al: Palgrave Macmillan, 2018), 82.

[62] Sofia Tomacruz, "Duterte: Don't Be President If You Can't Kill', (2020), <https://www.rappler.com/nation/253338-duterte-do-not-be-president-cannot-kill> (accessed April 7, 2020).

Cornelio, Jayeel. “Religious Freedom in the Philippines: From Legalities to Lived Experience.” *The Review of Faith and International Affairs* 11, no. 2 (2013): 36 - 45.

Cornelio, Jayeel. “Global and Religious: Urban Aspirations and the Govenance of Religions in Metro Manila.” In *Handbook of Religion and the Asian City: Aspiration and Urbanization in the Twenty-First Century*, edited by Peter van der Veer. Berkeley: University of California Press, 2015), 69-88.

Cornelio, Jayeel. “Religion and Civic Engagement: The Case of Iglesia Ni Cristo in the Philippines.” *Religion, state and society* 45, no. 1 (2017): 23-38.

Cornelio, Jayeel. “Religious Worlding: Christianity and the New Production of Space in the Philippines. ,” In *New Religiosities, Modern Capitalism and Moral Complexities in Southeast Asia*, edited by Juliette Koning and Gwenaël Njoto-Feillard. New York: Palgrave Macmillan, 2017), 169-97.

Cornelio, Jayeel. “Jesus Is Lord: The Indigenization of Megachurch Christianity in the Philippines.” In *Pentecostal Megachurches in Southeast Asia: Negotiating Class, Consumption and the Nation*, edited by Terence Chong. Singapore: ISEAS, 2018, 127-55.

Cornelio, Jayeel. “The Philippines.” In *Edinburgh Companions to Global Christianity: Christianity in East and South-East Asia*, edited by Ross, Kenneth, Todd Johnson, and Francis Alvarez. 242-253. Edinburgh: Edinburgh University Press, 2020.

Cornelio, Jayeel and Robbin Dagle. “Weaponising Religious Freedom: Same-Sex Marriage and Gender Equality in the Philippines.” *Religion & Human Rights* 14, no. 2 (2019): 65-94.

Cornelio, Jayeel and Ia Marañon. “A ‘Righteous Intervention’: Megachurch Christianity and Duterte’s War on Drugs in the Philippines.” *International Journal of Asian Christianity* 2, no. 2 (2019): 211-30.

Cornelio, Jayeel and Erron Medina. “Christianity and Duterte’s War on Drugs in the Philippines.” *Politics, Religion & Ideology* 20, no. 2 (2019): 151-69.

Cullum, Leo. “President Magsaysay's Consecration of the Philippines to the Sacred Heart.” *Philippine Studies* 5, no. 1 (1957): 45-70.

Dionisio, Eleanor, ed. *Becoming a Church of the Poor: Philippine Catholicism after the Second Plenary Council.* Quezon City: John J. Carroll Institute on Church and Social Issues, 2011.

Embassy of the Philippines. “About the Philippines.” Last modified n.d. Accessed March 26, 2020. https://londonpe.dfa.gov.ph/115-abtphl.

Every Nation Philippines. “A Message from Pastor Joseph Bonifacio.” Last modified 2020. Accessed April 7, 2020. https://www.everynation.org.ph/campus-ministry/.

Every Nation Philippines. “A Message from Pastor Michael Paderes.” Last modified 2020. Accessed April 7, 2020. https://www.everynation.org.ph/world-missions/.

Francisco, Jose Mario. “People of God, People of the Nation: Official Catholic Discourse on Nation and Nationalism.” *Philippine Studies: Historical and Ethnographic Viewpoints* 62, no. 3-4 (2014): 341-76.

Francisco, Jose Mario. “‘In but Not of the World’: Filipino Catholicism and Its Powers.” In *Theology and Power: International Perspectives*, edited by Stephen Bullivant et al. Mahwah: Paulist Press, 2016.

Gorski, Philip. “Why Evangelicals Voted for Trump: A Critical Cultural Sociology.” *American Journal of Cultural Sociology* 5 (2017): 338-54.

Holden, William Norman. "Ecclesial Opposition to Large-Scale Mining on Samar: Neoliberalism Meets the Church of the Poor in a Wounded Land." *Religions* 3, no. 3 (2012): 833-61.

Johannessen-Henry, Christine Tind. "Polydox Eschatology." *Studia Theologica - Nordic Journal of Theology* 66, no. 2 (2012): 107-29.

Juergensmeyer, Mark. *The New Cold War?: Religious Nationalism Confronts the Secular State.* Berkeley and Los Angeles: University of California Press, 1993.

Keyes, Charles. "Theravada Buddhism and Buddhist Nationalism: Sri Lanka, Myanmar, Cambodia, and Thailand." *The Review of Faith & International Affairs* 14, no. 4 (2016): 41-52.

Kinnvall, Catarina. "Globalization and Religious Nationalism: Self, Identity, and the Search for Ontological Security." *Political Psychology* 25, no. 5 (2004): 741-67.

Leviste, Enrique Niño. "In the Name of Fathers, in Defense of Mothers: Hegemony, Resistance, and the Catholic Church on the Philippine Population Policy." *Philippine Sociological Review* 64, no. 1 (2016): 5-44.

Mack, Troy Robert. "Religious Nationalism." In *Religion and Contemporary Politics: A Global Encyclopedia*, edited by Demy, Timothy and Jeffrey Shaw. 22-26. Santa Barbara: ABC-CLIO, 2019.

Maltese, Giovanni. "Reproductive Politics and Populism: Pentecostal Religion and Hegemony in the Philippines." *Journal of Law and Religion* 34, no. 1 (2019): 64-84.

Miller, Jack. "Religion in the Philippines." Last modified n.d. Accessed March 26, 2020. https://asiasociety.org/education/religion-philippines.

Moreno, Antonio F. *Church, State, and Civil Society in Postauthoritarian Philippines: Narratives of Engaged Citizenship.* Quezon City: Ateneo de Manila University Press, 2006.

Nicolas, Gerald, Loila Batomalaque, and Gladys Rabacal. "Qualified Confidence: Church, State, and Public Opinion." In *Becoming a Church of the Poor: Philippine Catholicism after the Second Plenary Council*, edited by Eleanor Dionisio. 90-101. Quezon City: John J. Carroll Institute on Church and Social Issues, 2011.

Quiboloy, Apollo. "Life and Calling." Last modified 2019. Accessed April 7, 2020. https://www.apolloquiboloy.com/life-calling-apollo-quiboloy/.

Raffin, Anne and Jayeel Serrano Cornelio. "The Catholic Church and Education as Sources of Institutional Panic in the Philippines." *Asian Journal of Social Science* 37, no. 5 (2009): 778-98.

RCAM. "Consecration to the Immaculate Heart of Mary." Last modified 2019. Accessed April 5, 2020. https://www.rcam.org/index.php/component/k2/item/443-consecration-to-the-immaculate-heart-of-mary.

Reed, Robert. "The Iglesia Ni Cristo, 1914-2000. From Obscure Philippine Faith to Global Belief System." *Bijdragen tot de taal-, land- en volkenkunde / Journal of the Humanities and Social Sciences of Southeast Asia* 157, no. 3 (2001): 561 - 608.

Rivera, Joseph. *Political Theology and Pluralism: Renewing Public Dialogue.* New York: Palgrave Macmillan, 2018.

Rocca, Francis. "Pope Urges Filipino Families: Dream, Resist 'Ideological Colonization'." Last modified 2015. Accessed March 02, 2020. https://www.catholicnews.com/

services/englishnews/2015/pope-urges-filipino-families-dream-resist-ideological-colonization.cfm.

Silagan, Shaun. "Something Is Wrong with Filipino Faith." Last modified 2019. Accessed March 26, 2020. https://www.rappler.com/views/imho/244618-opinion-something-wrong-filipino-faith.

Smith, Tom W. "Belies About God across Time and Space." NORC, University of Chicago. Last modified March 09, 2013, 2012. Accessed April 20, 2019. http://www.norc.org/PDFs/Beliefs_about_God_Report.pdf.

Spohn, Willfried. "Multiple Modernity, Nationalism and Religion: A Global Perspective." *Current Sociology* 51, no. 3-4 (2003): 265-86.

The New York Times. "Filipino Explains New Nationalism; Lopez Says Country Feels 'Accepted' in Asia." Last modified 1964. Accessed March 27, 2020. https://www.nytimes.com/1964/04/12/archives/filipino-explains-new-nationalism-lopez-says-country-feels-accepted.html.

Thompson, Mark. "Bloodied Democracy: Duterte and the Death of Liberal Reformism in the Philippines." *Journal of Current Southeast Asian Affairs* 35, (3) (2016): 39-68.

Tomacruz, Sofia. "Duterte: Don't Be President If You Can't Kill." Last modified 2020. Accessed April 7, 2020. https://www.rappler.com/nation/253338-duterte-do-not-be-president-cannot-kill.

van der Veer, Peter. *Religious Nationalism: Hindus and Muslims in India*. Berkeley and Los Angeles: University of California Press, 1994.

van Erp, Stephen. "God Becoming Present in the World: Sacramental Foundations of a Theology of Public Life." In *Grace, Governance and Globalization*, edited by Stephen van Erp, Martin Poulsom, and Lieven Boeve. 13-27.London: Bloomsbury Academic, 2017.

Whitehead, Andrew, Samuel Perry, and Joseph Baker. "Make America Christian Again: Christian Nationalism and Voting for Donald Trump in the 2016 Presidential Election." *Sociology of Religion* 79, no. 2 (2018): 147-71.

Religious Communications in Transcultural Contexts

Theological Developments in Changing Societies

Eberhard Hauschildt (Bonn, Germany)

1. Introduction: On the Complexity of (Religious) Communication

"One cannot not communicate" – this is the first of Paul Watzlawick's five famous basic axioms about communication.[1] Whenever one human is aware of another human, this axiom applies. Whatever is observed by one person about another – be it talking or not talking, ways of moving in a given space, or even the perception of odors – a human person who is aware of another person will find herself or himself in a communicative link, even if that link consists in a decision to ignore the other person completely.

So, communications take place all the time. In view of this, it is reasonable to give attention to possible logics and patterns of communication. For example, psychological theory, which focuses on the relation to the self in processes of communication. Or sociological theory, which focuses on the interrelation among the partners, small groups, and wider groups up to society in general. Here we have two different theories with differing starting points, conceptual frameworks, and epistemological interests, which enable the identification of distinctive patterns in communication – the one sociological, the other psychological. *Communication itself*, however, is neither social nor psychic. We merely find social and psychic *dimensions* intertwined in the communicative act.

Similarly, theology and other religious sciences develop theories in the interest of understanding how ideas, imagination and experiences of the transcendent are communicated. That is to say, in such communications there is a further dimension involved, but one nevertheless still intertwined with the social and the psychic dimension. So, when we reflect on *religious communication* we take on a perspective looking at *a very complex communicative phenomenon*. In theory, it might make sense – for example, for analytical purpos-

[1] Cf. Paul Watzlawick, Janet H. Beavin, Don D. Jackson, *Menschliche Kommunikation: Formen, Störungen, Paradoxien* (Bern: Hogrefe AG, 2017 [1969]).

es – to isolate the psychic, the social, and the religious dimensions from each other. But only in theory; for this does not work in practice. And it also does not make sense when sociologists claim that something is not religious, but "in reality" is social or when theologians claim that something is not social, but "in reality" it is religious. Neither reducing observed religion to an exclusively sociological perspective nor reducing it to an exclusively theological perspective will produce results which are mindful enough. A reasonable, balanced interrelation of what you can see and understand when you work with a sociological perspective with what you see and understand when you work with a theological perspective, however, is helpful, as are similar co-operations between sociological perspectives and psychological perspectives. When reflecting on doing theology, I will try to do both, look at social general patterns in religious communication as well as at the specifics of practice in doing theology.

2. Situatedness in Contexts of Religious Communication

Looking at phenomena of religious communication, we can also observe the situatedness of such communication. Religious communications take place in situations, are influenced by them, react to them.

In the case of religion and theology, in any given situation you often find concepts of eternity present and active, for example, when religions and theologies talk about transcendence and about God. And religious communications may also seek to make such eternity "observable", for example, with rituals that seem not to change and symbols that seem to be always the same. Nevertheless, it is clear that contexts play a role even here, including not only contexts of time and place, but many other contextual factors.

To take just one example from a few years ago: It was my job to give a Christmas Eve sermon in the "university church" (a large room designed as a church, but situated within the main building of the university). I had prepared my sermon a week in advance. The sermon I wrote focused on the angels' announcement or declaration of "peace of earth", according to Luke chapter 2 – following the lectionary for Christmas 2016. Then, just five days before Christmas Eve, a terrorist intentionally drove a stolen truck right into a Berlin Christmas market, killing several visitors. It was, of course, the top story in the news for days. Even if I had given my sermon exactly as I had originally planned it and had ignored the attack: it would not have stayed the same sermon – due to its changed context.

Contextual situatedness is inevitable all the time – not only when national disasters happen. One result of this is that religious communications are different in different contexts, and what they are "actually doing" changes to a significant degree. Jayeel Cornelio and Eva

Youkhana show shown impressive examples for this in this book. What the religious communications of Roman Catholics and Evangelicals or of other religious movements do is not always the same thing that you might expect, based on knowledge of their Christian traditions and what is written about them in the textbooks. It is more complicated, it reacts to local contexts and situations, and thus it may change.

Therefore, one of the jobs of theory in scholarship – and this is no less true within academic theology than in other disciplines in the humanities and cultural studies – is to observe those changes, to analyze what has changed, in which way and what made it change like that. Unfortunately, we have to admit: theory always comes a bit too late, "after the fact". Practical theology, my own academic field, in a way always comes too late. Innovations of practitioners always come first, have always already happened when I and my colleagues arrive on the scene.

So at its best, academic practical theology may only be able to detect current trends. And these trends – and how much more our observations of them – will be valid for only so long. For further situational changes are always rendering our predictions obsolete, or at least making it necessary to revise them continuously.

3. Religious Communication in Established Settings

Having said all of this, however, I would like to draw attention to another characteristic of religious communications beyond their situatedness. And this I will call the "established settings" in which religious communications often take place. Implicit in what I have said thus far is that religious communications are much more flexible than some critical perspectives on religion might think and than some traditional perspectives might like. But now I want to show that, for all their *flexibility*, we should not ignore the *fixed and established* nature of much religious communication. So: What do I mean by "established settings"? As a theorist, I am interested in what produces the relative persistence of particular communicative situations.

(And before I continue let me already lay open right here why I am interested in this. One reason is that I am not only a researcher, but also a *teacher*. I teach students of theology in my field of practical theology. I want to teach them in such a way that they will be better prepared for their future practice when they are called to "do" theology in their congregations, in those future situations and contexts which I myself am unable to predict. A second reason why I am interested in established settings is that, not only as a researcher and a teacher, but also as a human being who participates in various local and global communities, I am interested in the improvement of common life in pluralized societies that are home to the most diverse religious groups and that therefore serve as the spaces in which their situated communications develop and circulate.)

But back to the question: What produces the relative persistence of particular communicative situations or "established settings"? I want to discuss three factors.

"Larger Climate"

This first factor follows directly from the observations just made concerning contextuality and situatedness. Obviously direct contexts and momentary situations play a big role and require flexibility in religious communications. But since all contexts and situations have neighboring contexts with which they more or less interact, it also makes sense not merely to observe the local momentary situation, but to look at the wider context and in a broader time frame. For this broader environment, let me choose the term "larger climate". It forms an integral part of contexts and situatedness. The larger climate does not change as rapidly as more immediate levels of context, but nevertheless it has quite an impact even if we don't notice it or even when we want to ignore it.

It is the task of theory to inform and reflect about such larger climate for religious communication. So that we don't overlook the big and global trends. They seem to be ignorable at the moment, but will not be in the long run. Modernization and globalization factors, majority and minority figures and trends on the global level are of such kind. For example: In 1910, roughly 66% of all Christians lived in Europe; 100 years later only 25% percent do.2 Such large-scale climate changes are relevant even when you live in Germany.

So both the local and the global climate must be taken into account. A new word appeared in the 1990s, namely, the term "glocal", accompanied by the slogan: "think global and act local". Since the 1990s, it has become necessary to act global while thinking local – because while important concepts and future ideas are being communicated on a global level, the bodies and lived well-being of real people still unfold in forms of local community.

Anthropological Patterns

Now we come to the second factor involved in the production of established settings: I call it "anthropological patterns of communicative actions". There are many things common to humans in general. One of them is a set of "codes of communication" and from that follow typical practices which en-code communications. Let me point just to a few of them:

- There is a type of *"religious speech communication":* the practice of giving a monologue on religious topics in front of a larger group of listeners.
- There is also a type of *"festive group communications":* religious celebrations in a larger or smaller group. Here a variety of communication codes, words, music, objects, smells etc. are employed. It goes without

[2] http://www.globalreligiousfutures.org/religions/christians (Accessed Feb 25,2020).

saying that cultural concepts play a role here. Celebration styles vary across contexts and traditions, and concepts of celebration will likewise vary accordingly.

So, to continue by listing further examples, this time of culture-saturated settings:

- There is a type of communicative *"care interaction":* Someone supporting someone else by handing out resources like food, or doing things like providing medical treatment, or listening and providing emotional and psychological assistance.
- There is a type of more or less formal learning and *"educational communication"*.

And of course new settings may also develop, for example connected with the role of media in communication. In the 16th century, the invention of printing changed the status of reading in religion. In our times, digital communications have begun to change religious practice to, what by all indications, will be an equally profound extent. So we could add to the list:

- There is a developing type of digital religious communication settings.

So, settings also are not completely stable. The type of care interaction, which I mentioned before, also changes when you go beyond the practice of merely handing out alms in the form of food or money, for many societies also have systematized care through state organized forms of solidarity and empowerment led by care professionals.

Traditional Settings

The third factor involved in producing established settings is tradition. Culturally saturated religious traditions as they have developed in a certain denomination or religion. This factor works in two directions. At first sight, traditions seem to provide well-established boundary markers. They serve to create internal identity and distinction from others. For example male Jews are circumcised, Catholics celebrate in Latin, Protestants read the Bible, Pentecostals speak in tongues, and Muslims do not eat pork. However, even stable traditions may change – and do change in their meaning: for example when Catholics do not celebrate mass in Latin any more. And taking such markers for granted can lead to real confusion, for example, when you meet Ethiopian Orthodox Christians: For, like Jews, they practice male circumcision and, like Jews and Muslims, they do not eat pork. Further, new boundary markers may appear, as we are seeing in various churches' teachings and practices regarding homosexuality.

Yet, traditions deal not only with identity and boundary markers. It is also very interesting to note that the ways established settings participate in trend toward a growth in *morphological conformity between different religious traditions*. The presence of plurality in, through, and under changes in the global and local climate often involves traditions in processes that lead them to become more similar to one another. So you have a global growth of awareness of plurality and more pluralization within local societies, on the one hand, and, on the other hand, at the same time a process of homogenization including its local variations. Examples are observable in the German context: "Preaching" communications are no longer only important for Protestants; what used to be called pastoral care has become of interest as well for Muslims; Protestants come up with their ways of fasting by not eating sweets in the weeks before Easter. So you see new conformities alongside typical varieties according to contexts and religious traditions, in how those adaptions exactly take place.

Summed up in one - seemingly paradoxical - sentence: Religious traditions become more similar the more plural they become!

4. Doing Reflected and Scholarly Theory

The transformational processes I tried to describe *are* the contexts of our time. And they produce an increase in transcultural interaction - interactions of individuals and localities which are in themselves already a complex mixture. Religious communication today takes place not simply among pure Protestants, Catholics etc., neither only in the form of a dialogue between *the* Catholics and *the* Protestants or between *the* Christians and *the* Jews, Muslims, Hindus, Buddhists, but rather between mixtures and varieties of all of the above. To paraphrase William James: it's *the varieties of religious communication* [. . .]

[. . .] And in pluralized and globalized societies, no less. Just to mention, as an example, one no longer uncommon experience of one of my children in the city of Bonn: being the child of a liberal protestant German Father and an Ethiopian Orthodox mother who participated in a church graduation ceremony of the Catholic primary school where he was enrolled and received the blessings of the Catholic priest, accompanied moreover by his best friend whose mother is a Marokkian Muslim and father an Italian. The contexts of contemporary religious communication are no more simply intercultural and interreligious and interconfessional constellations, but *transcultural, transconfessional, and transreligious* ones. Such "trans-" communications do not take shape or take place the same way all over the globe (or at least not in the same way, which is part of the point), but they come from all over the globe and intersect in individuals persons lives, with the result that, biographically, they may be more or less common instances. Whether religious or cultural or social in form, whether conflicting or integrating in effect, whether regional, neighborhood-level or familial in scope - these dynamics are part of our lives together now on this globe.

How do these developments change what theorists and their theories *do*, change the work of teachers for future religious practitioners in the local contexts and their specific faith perspectives? What does university theology contribute to society?

Well, there is a somewhat changed obvious challenge and also *goal* for such theology: theological work – its methods and research *desiderata* – will have to examine the changing nature of religious communications in the context of the transcultural, which is to say, the shifting, overlapping and mutually compounding social, political and economic conditions that mediate understanding in pluralistic societies.

For this reason, in universities also the exchange with neighboring sciences in research on religious communication is important. With theologies of other Christian denominations, doing ecumenical theology together – and with sciences that work on theories of the cultural, the sociological, and the psychological dimensions of religious communications. That includes also in theory a greater conformity in reflection about religious practice – continuous interdisciplinary interaction would lead to a set of shared methodological standards and generate shared insights into forms of social complexity

So we can observe certain *tasks* generated in this "trans-" situation regarding what theology does. I count four of them:

Task 1) There are shared tasks for all academic research on phenomena related to religion. Research on religion is one area, too, that shows the *value of the university for society*. The point of seeking understanding through study is, in the end, not simply to gain knowledge and expertise, though that may help you to find a well-paying job. The point of understanding is to improve capabilities in supporting work toward justice and peace in such culturally and religiously plural societies and in a globalized world. Such a change-sensitive way of doing theology matters for society.

Task 2) The task of theology, especially of practical theology is to engage in a certain kind of reflection. Its practice can be described as drawing attention to and reflecting on the action-oriented and communication-oriented character of what theology does. From this perspective, the things theology "does" or produces might be viewed in ways similar to everyday art and artefacts. Practitioners, those involved in religious communication, are cooperative artists. That is the reason why *the job of practical theory, and the job for theorists, is a specific communicative art itself*: to develop such practical theological theory which functions in analogy to, for example, what music theory does for future musicians and composers. To make them aware of what patterns can be described when it comes to a certain field of artistic practice – in our case, that of religions communication.

Task 3) The task of the academic discipline of Practical Theology is to *produce insights which assist* professional and non-professional religious *practitioners* in their local settings. What is required there, especially from educated professionals, but also from other leading non-professionals and in cooperation with religious persons and in public media? The *production of artefacts of religious communication*, for their situation and in their contexts, whatever they may be like. It is a contextual and situational art even when it is performed in established settings. Be it through giving a sermon or celebrating or by mourning together, be it in organizing public social action or by constructively listening to the private life-story of someone who is lonely.

On the theoretical side, theology is meant to improve the artistry of the students for use in future practice. So it is to improve reflection by artists in the field, reflection on their cooperative way of art production, their leadership in religious social bodies, whether those of a religious movement, a classical church institution or religious non-profit organization. This artful communication may, in everyday life, constitute a kind of uniquely religious contribution to cultivating peaceful and mutually enriching forms of shared life in contemporary societies.

4) Thus, academic theological theory itself is not just about giving details and results and knowledge. All of this is important and theological science can never do without it. However, it is also *artistry* in producing works of art – artefacts, if you will – by talks and in learning settings, and in academic debates, and, yes, also by articles and books. And it seems to me that this is a potential of all humane scientific work.

Doing theology in its established academic and scientific settings – for example, seminars and symposia – is just this: The production of *temporary* artefacts about religion for contemporary contexts, artefacts which even dare to relate to the religious dimension of communication – not in such a way that this requires participants in the communication to proclaim or confess belief, but that merely facilitates interest in understanding how religion works and its potential for the common good.

5. Conclusion

What does theology actually do? That is the question asked in the title of the symposium, which gave occasion for the writing of this chapter. As a *practical* theologian, my answer is: *Practical* theology supports religious life as found contextualized in its various settings, and it does this in a theoretical and academic way by developing theory of religious communication for the present. These two tasks do not contradict each other. At least, not in theory.

Bibliography

Watzlawick, Paul, Janet H. Beavin, and Don D. Jackson. *Menschliche Kommunikation: Formen, Störungen, Paradoxien*. Bern: Hogrefe AG, 2017 [1969].

Pew Research Center. "Christian Population by Country." Feb 25, 2020. http://www.globalreligiousfutures.org/religions/christians.

Part 4 How Public is Theology? How is Theology Public?

What Does Theological Ethics Do?

Toward an Account of Theological Ethics as Tropology

Esther D. Reed (Exeter, UK)

I. Introduction

The question: "What does theological ethics do?" invites answers that range from the descriptive and comparative (for example, what happens in universities where theological ethics is taught) to the doctrinal and hermeneutical (for example, why theological ethics is dependent utterly upon the self-revealing grace of the triune God revealed in the bible), and the contextual and constructive (why and how the places and politics, etc., of where theological ethics is done, is related intrinsically to decision-making that bears upon action). Mindful of Karl Barth's reported words in a *Time* magazine piece that, 40 years previously, he had advised young theologians "to take your Bible and take your newspaper, and read both. But interpret newspapers from your Bible" (Friday, May 31, 1963), this essay offers a doctrinally-informed, constructive answer: theological ethics does tropology.[1]

Tropology is rarely discussed in Christian ethics today but has a lineage in Christian tradition of interconnecting aesthetic, political and moral practice. Tropology is everyday striving after the moral sense of the bible that allows the diverse witness to the self-revealing grace of the triune God revealed in its pages to bear upon the praxis of life. In a short study entitled *The Book that Reads Me: A Handbook for Bible Study Enablers* (1995), Hans-Ruedi Weber invites bible-study enablers to re-experience the bible as an oral rather than literary tradition through story-telling and singing, drama and symbolic actions. His point is that generations of Western Christians have flattened the bible to merely a literary document to be read and/or listened to. A striking front cover shows a wood carving of a beautiful and strong African woman whose arms are raised in prayer and dramatic representation of the scriptures. The message conveyed by the image is that bible is more like the script for many dramas than simple prose text and comes with an expectation of dramatization; this book must be lived. This is the essence of tropology. Theological ethics that does tropology moves between newspapers and the bible, as

---

[1] *Time*, "Barth in Retirement," Friday, May 31, 1963 https://content.time.com/time/subscriber/article/0,33009,896838,00.html (Accessed 19 July, 2019).

Barth summons young scholars, in ways that expect deep hermeneutic relation between the logos of the text and lifestyle, judgment and action.

2. What is Tropology?

Tropology (from Gr. trépō + -os, meaning turn, way, manner or style) is one of the classic models for the interpretation of scripture employed variously throughout the history of the churches, and is associated especially with John Cassian's (c. 360-435) multiple senses of scripture. A Latin ascetic monk whose *Institutes* and *Conferences* became normative accounts of 5th century monastic life and the history of the Desert Fathers, Cassian taught his readers to interpret scripture with scripture, to stay focused hermeneutically on the person of Christ Jesus, and to expect that spiritual knowledge has several dimensions including the tropological: "[O]f spiritual knowledge there are three kinds, tropological, allegorical, anagogical .... The tropological sense is the moral explanation which has to do with improvement of life and practical teaching."[2] Tropological readings of biblical texts are found throughout the *Institutes* which describe and prescribe the lives of monks in minute detail – the cords and capes of their robes, the canonical system of the nocturnal prayers and psalms, the election of those in authority, how to struggle against faults including gluttony, covetousness, anger, dejection, accidie, vain glory and pride. The *Conferences* similarly recount the teachings of various abbots especially for those individuals who renounce the world and aim at perfection in love through ascetic practices.

Gaining insight and wisdom with respect to moral explanations of the bible demands much of the monastic institution and of individuals: "[H]oly lessons should be read in the Cœnobia,"[3] that is, within the community of the monastery such that all hear the words of scripture. The institution is variously expected to set the conditions within which constant meditation upon the bible's teaching yields practical knowledge with respect to the improvement of morals and purification from faults.[4] The monk or anchorite living alone is

---

[2] John Cassian, *Conferences,* trans. by C.S. Gibson (Buffalo: Christian Literature Publishing, 1894); revised and edited for New Advent by Kevin Knight. <http://www.newadvent.org/fathers/350814.htm>. Conference 14, ch.8. Note also that A.M.C. Casiday's Tradition and Theology in St. John Cassian (Oxford: Oxford University Press, 2006) is an excellent guide to Cassian's Chalcedonian Christology. A strong emphasis on the humanity of the incarnate Christ informs Casiday's account of how spiritual knowledge holds together *praktikê and theorêtikê* knowledge, ascetic struggle and thoughts of God.

[3] John Cassian, *Institutes,* trans. by C.S. Gibson (Buffalo: Christian Literature Publishing, 1894.) Revised and edited for New Advent by Kevin Knight. <http://www.newadvent.org/fathers/350704.htm>. Book IV, ch. 17.

[4] Cassian, *Conference* 14, ch.1.

expected to pursue this practical knowledge in close association with their striving also after theoretical knowledge, that is, the most sacred truths with respect to the nature of the triune God and things divine: "Whoever then would arrive at this theoretical knowledge must first pursue practical knowledge with all his might and main. For this practical knowledge can be acquired without theoretical, but theoretical cannot possibly be gained without practical."[5] In the *Institutes*, examples are given of Abbots who sought understanding of the scriptures with prayer "until he discovered by a revelation from the Lord the solution of the question propounded."[6] The challenge for the monks both communally and individually is to adapt their own life or understanding to the meaning of the scripture rather than making its meaning correspond to their own views. Thus, the bible is read for inspiration to banish the incentive to anger and to reserve no occasion whatever for indignation.[7] Where biblical texts yield answers that could be understood to vary, the challenge is to "understand the drift of Scripture" mindful that the end of the monk's way of life is the kingdom of God.[8]

Tropology for Cassian entails constant meditation on the scriptures for the treasures of wisdom in order better to grasp knowledge of spiritual things.[9] It also requires certain attitudes of heart and mind. Anyone seeking a vision of God must shun the stain of sin, have peace of mind, a steadfast purpose of heart that they should constantly aspire after this vision and ever cleave to God and to heavenly things.[10] In so doing, all should be careful to see that no wrong interpretation is fixed on to the pure gold of scripture thereby deceiving them as to the value of the metal. When the devil tempted Jesus, he twisted the precious sayings of scripture into a dangerous sense. Likewise, he will try "to cheat us with counterfeits."[11] The monk must return again and again to the scripture for guidance in matters of mindset and behaviour, seeking the guidance of the Holy Spirit mindful that there might be multiple senses of scripture:

> Wherefore on those passages which are brought forward with a clear explanation we also can constantly lay down the meaning and boldly state our own opinions. But those which the Holy Spirit, reserving for our meditation and exercise, has inserted in holy Scripture with veiled meaning, wishing some of them to be gathered from various proofs and conjectures, ought to be step by step and carefully brought together, so that their assertions and proofs may be arranged by the discretion of the man who is arguing or supporting them. For sometimes when a dif-

---

[5] Cassian, *Conference* 14, ch.2.
[6] Cassian, *Institutes*, Bk V, ch.33.
[7] Cassian, *Institutes*, Bk VIII, ch. 21.
[8] Cassian, *Institutes*, Bk VIII, ch. 21.
[9] Cassian, *Institutes*, Bk VIII, ch.2.
[10] Cassian, *Conference 1*, chs. 7 and 8.
[11] Cassian, *Conference 1*, ch. 20.

> ference of opinion is expressed on one and the same subject, either view may be considered reasonable and be held without injury to the faith either firmly, or doubtfully, i.e., in such a way that neither is full belief nor absolute rejection accorded to it, and the second view need not interfere with the former, if neither of them is found to be opposed to the faith [. . .][12]

Continual prayer and the guidance of those wise persons acknowledged by the Cœnobia is required, although no guarantee of protection is given against how heretics pervert scripture or how the devil might lead astray.[13] As A.M.C. Casiday summarises: "Cassian is calling for a reading of Scripture that is holistic rather than fragmentary. [. . .] Cassian has already committed himself to the proposition that a right and life-giving explication of Scripture is possible only for those who are leading a holy life; and that the holiness in question, while it may be found in diverse callings, is authenticated by the Church."[14] Adoration, love and worship of Christ as God properly results in a life of service learned from the bible, which is a testament to God's actions in history.[15]

Augustine's four senses of scripture did not include the tropological but had a built-in moral test. He outlined the four senses of scripture as follows:

> Four ways of expounding the law have been laid down by some scripture commentators, which can be named in words derived from the Greek, while they need further definition and explanation in plain Latin; they are the way of history, the way of allegory, the way of analogy, the way of aetiology. History is when things done by God or man are recounted; allegory when they are understood as being said figuratively; analogy, when the harmony of the old and new covenants is being demonstrated; aetiology, when the causes of the things that have been said and done are presented.[16]

Individual believers and the church should test readings of the bible against the criterion of whether the resulting practice tends to build up love: "The fulfillment and end of the law and all the divine scriptures is to love the thing which must be enjoyed and the thing which together with us can enjoy that thing[. . .] Anyone who thinks that he has understood the divine scriptures or any part of them, but cannot by his understanding build up this double love of God and neighbor, has not yet succeeded in understanding them."[17] For example, in a letter to Jerome about his work of translation, Augustine foresees division between the Latin and Greek churches if the languages of the biblical

---

[12] Cassian, *Conference* VIII, ch.4.
[13] Cassian, *Institutes, Bk VII*, ch.14.
[14] Casiday, *Tradition and Theology*, 247.
[15] Casiday, *Tradition and Theology*, 242.
[16] Augustine, *On Genesis* (New York: New City Press, 1990), 5.
[17] Augustine, *On Christian Teaching*, trans. by James Shaw (Buffalo: Christian Literature Publishing, 1887); revised and edited for New Advent by Kevin Knight. <http://www.newadvent.org/fathers/12021.htm>, 1.36.41.

texts available to each were different.[18] He knew of discrepancies between the text supported by the Hebrew codices and the Greek Septuagint version, as well as Latin versions, such that "one has no confidence in either quoting it or proving anything by its help."[19] The dangers of mistaken interpretations were multiple but like many of his predecessors Augustine taught readers to expect multiple meanings of any text of scripture.[20] Alongside seeking the harmonization of the meaning of any given text with predominant meanings elsewhere in the bible, the test of whether the reading produces the fruit of love was, in effect, a tropological guide.

That Augustine's four senses of scripture should be understood to include a moral sense is affirmed by Aquinas in answer to whether, in holy scripture, a word may have several senses.[21] The objection countered is that Augustine's fourfold division as to history, etiology, analogy and allegory does not include tropology, and so perhaps excludes a moral sense. Aquinas's reply refutes such nonsense: "Therefore, so far as the things of the Old Law signify the things of the New Law, there is the allegorical sense; so far as the things done in Christ, or so far as the things which signify Christ, are types of what we ought to do, there is the moral sense."[22] One kind of truth in scripture does not contradict other kinds of truth. To ask about the moral meaning(s) of scripture is to inquire into the humanity of Christ. As Robert J. Dobie is clear: "Implicit in Aquinas ... is the insight that to uncover the true meaning of Scripture is to uncover the self-subsistent Word, Christ, in and through whom all things were created."[23] Tropological readings allow the soul to discover

---

[18] Augustine, *Letter 71*, trans. J.G. Cunningham (Buffalo: Christian Literature Publishing, 1887); revised and edited for New Advent by Kevin Knight. <http://www.newadvent.org/fathers/1102071.htm>. Manuscripts would have been in Old Latin and Greek, and Augustine was aware of issues of interpretation arising from uncertain translation. Augustine, *Retractions*, 2, 12, 39.

[19] Augustine, *Letter 71*, ch.4.

[20] The idea that the bible yields many and diverse readings, including moral readings, was familiar to Justin Martyr (c. 114-165), Irenaeus (c. 130-200), Tertullian (c. 160-225), the exegetical schools of Alexandria (including Clement of Alexandria, c.180-215 and Origen, c.185-253) and Antioch (including Theodore of Mopsuestia c.350-428 and John Chrysostom). See Elizabeth A. Clark, "Scripture and Asceticism," in *The Oxford Handbook of Early Christian Biblical Interpretation*, ed. by Paul M. Blowers and Peter W. Martens (Oxford: Oxford University Press, 2019), ch. 31; Frances M. Young, *Biblical Exegesis and the Formation of Christian Culture* (Cambridge: Cambridge University Press, 1997), John J. O'Keefe and R. R. Reno, *Sanctified Vision: An Introduction to Early Christian Interpretation of the Bible* (Baltimore: Johns Hopkins University Press, 2005), Karlfried Froehlich, *Biblical Interpretation in the Early Church* (Nashville: Augsburg Fortress, 1959).

[21] Thomas Aquinas, *Summa Theologia*, 1.1. art. 10.

[22] Thomas Aquinas, *Summa Theologia*, 1.1. art. 10, sed contra.

[23] Robert J. Dobie, "Thomas Aquinas and Meister Eckhart on Exodus 3:14: Exegesis or Eisegesis?" *Medieval Mystical Theology* 24, no. 2 (2015): 124-36, here 124.

what is true of Christ and required of the believer such that truth becomes a lived reality. While Aquinas says relatively little about the practice of hermeneutics, his bible commentaries constitute a significant corpus and his two most cited works, the *Summa Contra Gentiles* and the *Summa Theologiae*, are, in many respects, both commentaries on the bible. Reasoned argument is required to make sense of the scriptures and this includes attention to the literal sense of the texts. Beyond this, the spiritual sense – divided into the allegorical, moral, and anagogical – is found in relation to Christ. Consider how Aquinas unfolds an allegorical reading of Jesus' plucking ears of corn on the sabbath (Mk 2.23), to yield moral meaning:

> But in a mystical sense these disciples pass through the corn fields, when the holy doctors look with the care of a pious solicitude upon those whom they have initiated in the faith, and who, it is implied, are hungering for the best of all things, the salvation of men. But to pluck the ears of corn means to snatch men away from the eager desire of earthly things. And to rub with the hands is by examples of virtue to put from the purity of their minds the concupiscence of the flesh, as men do husks. To eat the grains is when a man, cleansed from the filth of vice by the mouths of preachers, is incorporated amongst the members of the Church. Again fitly are the disciples related to have done this, walking before the face of the Lord, for it is necessary that the discourse of the doctor should come first, although the grace of visitation from on high, following it, must enlighten the heart of the hearer.[24]

The line between the literal meaning of the text and spiritual truth seems relatively insignificant as Aquinas seems almost to riff, that is, to improvise a call-and-response routine intended to awaken the hearers' own responses.

Nor is tropology a reading practice confined in Christian tradition to the great scholars of the church. Tropology, says Ryan McDermott in *Tropologies: Ethics and Invention in England, c. 1350–1600,*

> might be thought of as the church's circulatory system," that is, the process by which belief that "All scripture is inspired by God and is useful for teaching, reproof, for correction, and for training in righteousness, so that everyone who belongs to God may be proficient, equipped for every good service" (2 Tim. 3:16-17)

---

[24] I am indebted to John F. Boyle for this example. See "St. Thomas Aquinas and Sacred Scripture," https://www3.nd.edu/~afreddos/papers/Taqandss.htm (accessed 26 April 2019). From *Catena aurea in quatuor Evangelia*, in Mk 2:23-28, vol. 1, ed. by A. Guarienti (Turin: Marietti, 1953), 450. The translation is taken from St. Thomas Aquinas, *Catena aurea. Commentary on the Four Gospels, Collected out of the Works of the Fathers*, vol. 3 (Oxford and London: James Parker, 1870), 52. Boyle observes that Thomas himself has taken this interpretation from the Venerable Bede.

> becomes the flesh and blood of everyday practice, "channeling the meanings of scripture into readers" lives.[25]

Tropology is an everyday striving after the moral sense of scriptural interpretation which allows biblical meaning to bear upon the believers own "actions on the way to the kingdom of heaven."[26] McDermott studies how literal and tropological readings of the bible interweave to contribute to literary invention in the period. Of interest especially is how crowds of people become ethical agents participating in the world of scripture without being absorbed by it. So McDermott:

> In the Pentecost episode in Piers Plowman, Will and Conscience find themselves on the scene in first-century Jerusalem, inventing with the gathered crowd one of the most famous hymns of the liturgy, the sequence *Veni, Creator Spiritus*. Like the apostles who are speaking in tongues, the crown invents a completely new song – indeed, invents the Christian liturgy – but it is already a copy of the Holy Spirit's gift. Such a "copy" defies classical rhetorical models, according to which an invention must vie with and displace its model.[27]

Tropological participation in the daily (re-)invention of the church's liturgy links reading of the bible to the history recounted within its pages and performance of the church's liturgical year, it links to poetry and biblical dramas, especially the Passion plays, and to the pastoral work of inspiring hearers to the good. By attending to medieval practices of tropology, McDermott accesses a rich history of interconnecting exegesis, artistic creativity, spirituality, poetic invention, moral philosophy, and more. McDermott's central point is that the bible presents its readers with the tropological imperative to turn its words into works.[28] Tropology is ordered toward participation in salvation history, and, says McDermott, much more intimately in touch with *sacra scriptura* (sacred scripture) and therefore more fundamental than the *scientia divina* (theology as a science) and *pastoralia* (pastoral and spiritual care) than developed later.[29]

McDermott's claim is that tropology as a practice of moral invention survived "as the most important principle of continuity between 'medieval' and Reformation cultures," for example, inspiring exegesis, poetry, and drama even in the court of the radical reformist King Edward VI.[30] Tropology helped bridge the spiritual and ecclesial gap opened by the Reformation between personal piety and the teaching of the church in the public practice, for in-

---

[25] Ryan McDermott, *Tropologies: Ethics and Invention in England*, c. 1350–1600 (Notre Dame: University of Notre Dame Press, 2016), 12.
[26] McDermott, *Tropologies*, 2.
[27] McDermott, *Tropologies*, 7.
[28] McDermott, *Tropologies*, 12.
[29] McDermott, *Tropologies*, 13. 17-18.
[30] McDermott, *Tropologies*, 4.

stance, of poetic paraphrases of biblical passages. Consider the continuing use of the *Patience* poem, an alliterative paraphrase of the biblical Book of Jonah where the prophet's psychological struggles with Yahweh are played out powerfully. More than this, says McDermott, tropology is moral in the Thomistic sense of uniting theological and philosophical aspects, empirical concepts, reason and will. It is the spiritually powerful invoking of the judicial gaze of God from the end of history through dramatic media.

In other words, McDermott's focus on the Doomsday pageant of the York Passion Play serves theologically to remind readers that the moral work of tropology in Christian tradition is not about individual agents stepping into salvation history and playing a role but, rather, being about swept up into the work of God: "This anagogical approach to ethical participation in salvation history exerts a salutary counter-pressure on tropological invention, keeping it from devolving into what Protestants would call works-righteousness."[31] In this tradition, tropology is a reading practice that invites the activity of making or doing something not planned beforehand, whether as narrative creation, homily, sacramental practices of penance, imaginatively dramatic renderings of bible passages or moral argument.

3. Tropology Today

Even this brief survey of the history of tropology in Christian tradition yields preliminary findings.

First, tropology is inseparable from doctrine, the church's confession of the gospel of Christ, the pastoral nurture of believers, formation in his service and for the sake of his coming reign, and more. Just as, for John Cassian, spiritual knowledge holds together *theorêtikê* and *praktikê* knowledge, doctrinal exposition and judgment oriented toward action, so too tropology today derives its lifeblood from Christian doctrine and is the practical outworking of the beliefs of the church. The pattern is found repeatedly in the New Testament: "Let the same mind be in you that was in Christ Jesus, who, though he was in the form of God did not regard equality with God .... Therefore (Gr. ὥ···) my beloved." (Phil 2: 5-6, 12) The practical dimensions of Christian living are secondary to, and derive from, what is believed. The substance of a Christian ethics is given by God's love for the world: "[S]ince (Gr. ·ἰ) God loved us so much, we also ought to love one another." (1 Jn 4:11 NRSV) The ground of theological ethics is the nature of God, beyond human conception, unconfined to human ideals, rules, or concepts, and revealed as love: "So if you have been raised with Christ [. . .]" – this is the premise from which implications for Christ's disciples stem – "seek the things that are above," – that is, grow in their knowledge of matters spiritual – and "[p]ut to death, therefore, whatever in you

[31] McDermott, *Tropologies*, 291.

is earthly: fornication, impurity, passion, evil desire, and greed, which is idolatry." (Col 3:1) Tropology is doctrinally-rooted description of the human condition and destiny informed by reading of the bible; tropological readings of the biblical texts link the lives of communities of believers and individuals to God's purposes for all creation.

Second, tropology is inseparable from spiritual formation. At least as understood by Cassian, tropological readings of bible texts require a fixing of the spiritual eye upon God in the hope that divine assistance on the path toward perfection will be given through the written words. In many respects, tropology is not primarily an academic but spiritual endeavour undertaken by the believer who seeks only to follow the example of Christ's life and be formed in his image. His rhetoric is harsh on the ear today but can be re-appropriated if the basic point is taken that tropological readings of bible texts are expected to have formative effects upon the believer and are undertaken by communities and believers in the expectation of change. While Cassian's wrote for monks and anchorites, there is no reason to suppose that striving to discern the moral sense of scripture, which has to do with improvement of life and practical teaching, is delimited to the monastic life. Nor is it necessary to suppose that discernment of the moral sense of scripture is somehow dependent upon human efforts with respect to spiritual discipline and achievements in prayer. While Cassian taught that the most appropriate posture or attitude of the heart before the word of God revealed in scripture is untiring perseverance and humility, there was no assumption that such attitudes and behaviour would guarantee some kind of result. He walked the narrow path between urging those in his care to be diligent with respect to their own spiritual formation whilst not turning such efforts into a merit system. With this proviso, the believer is expected to renounce love of self that leads astray and fear only the Lord who is love incarnate, mindful that the devil always lies wait for every human being's downfall. Those reading the bible for its moral sense are expected to pray that their minds might be purged from all carnal desires and daily lifted towards spiritual things, until the whole of life and all the thoughts of the heart become one continuous prayer.[32]

Third, tropology is inseparable from the work of the moral imagination. Imagination is variously involved in our knowledge of the self, world and other people, and in constructions of possibility and hope. The allegorical poems and passion plays of medieval and Reformation England exemplified this expectation in dramatic ways and are a powerful example of how tropology is inherently creative as the ethicist envisions the world, or their tiny part therein, in the light of the coming reign of God. Discussion could easily widen at this point into reflection on how the arts play a vital role in Christian discipleship or why aesthetic philosophy has a role in the social sciences, law, and

---

[32] Cassian, *Conference 10*, ch.7.

psychology.[33] A more expansive consideration would include the work of imagination in enabling a person to comprehend something of the experiences, motives, joys and pains of others, the work of imagination in opening vistas of possibility, and mediating between the universal and the particular.[34] For the moment, it must be enough to observe that seeking the moral sense of the bible or, indeed, anything which has to do with improvement of life and practical teaching, invites the imaginative capacity to revision the world such that once again God might declare it good (Gen. 1:31). The seeming aesthetic dimension to which the creation narratives bear witness is integral to the capacity to reflect, form judgments and act in ways that embody the love of God for the world. Approaching theological ethics as tropology entails the claim that theological ethics is helpfully conceived, at least in part, as aesthetic creativity, perception and appreciation.

Fourth, theological ethics as tropology demands interdisciplinary engagement across the academy. It is allowable - indeed, unavoidable and desirable - for moral theologians and Christian ethicists to engage across academic disciplines if their own discipline is to be adequately attentive to the world in which we live. Enacting the movement described by Barth between newspapers and the bible requires theological ethicists to be intelligently aware of, and responsive to, the complexity of contemporary life and of the interplay of cultural, economic and psychological influences that shape human experience.[35] Interdisciplinarity is necessary if theologians and ethicists are to contribute to public debate, "to recover the contribution of faith" or to "deepen its contribution" in the public arena. As Dan Hardy wrote:

> theological inquiry through interdisciplinary study would attempt to rediscover the distinctness and relation of the spheres of understanding and life, religious and 'non-religious,' theological and interdisciplinary for the good of humankind, and in that way to recover their intrinsic connection to the truth of God and God's purposes.[36]

---

[33] For a sustained consideration of how the arts are essential to citizenship, see Martha Nussbaum, *Cultivating Humanity: A Classical Defense of Reform in Liberal Education* (London: Harvard University Press, 1997), esp. 85. For consideration of beauty in international law, see Mary Ellen O'Connell, *The Art of Law in the International Community* (Cambridge: Cambridge University Press, 2019), esp. 33-4.

[34] Paul Ricoeur, From Text to Action: Essays in Hermeneutics II (Evanston: Northwestern University Press, 2007). For an excellent review that sets the book within the context of Ricoeur's philosophical career, see Robert P. Scharlemann, *Language and Society* 22, no. 1 (1993): 157-60.

[35] I acknowledge indebtedness to Daniel W. Hardy's unpublished piece "The Logic of Interdisciplinary Studies and the Coherence of Theology," (November 1995) Report to the Center of Theological Inquiry, Princeton.

[36] Hardy, "The Logic," 9 [unpublished]. For Hardy, the predominant image in this essay was the refraction of light into bands of color as it passes through a glass prism; the

Such interdisciplinarity will avoid unwarranted suspicion of the value of other disciplines for understanding or benefitting theology and seek instead to develop fruitful and appropriate interaction.

4. Tropology Evaluated

Evaluation of some kind is required if theological ethics as tropology is to produce "good fruit." Jesus is reported in various New Testament texts as evaluating words and actions in terms of what fruit is produced (Matt 7:15-20; Matt 11:2-15; Matt 21:18-22; Mark 11:12-14). Matthew's report of Jesus' warning against false prophets seems to suggest that the community operate a rule of thumb whereby they expect the difference between true and false prophets to be recognizable in the character of what results from their words and other actions. "Fruit" was commonplace as a metaphor for the consequences of deeds.[37] Hence the signs by which false prophets will be recognized are their works. While the meaning of the metaphor becomes eschatological when referring to the fire that will burn in final judgment, the ideas running across the pericope are that judgment will come, that hearers are called to consider the relationship between words and what results from them, inner and outer lives, and whether "evil" (πονηρός) or "good" (ἀγαθός) issues from how people speak and behave. While the immediate application in Matt 7:15-20 is false prophets - identified by Ulrich Luz as Christian, not Jewish, miracle workers and exorcists - whose words and deeds will produce fruit recognizable as good or evil, and questions may be asked about what constitutes "good" or "evil" fruit, whether the metaphor may pressed with questions about different kinds of tree, the limits of the metaphor, and more specifically, the expectation that the falsity of prophets will be recognizable in their works has wider application as a pragmatic principle of expectation with respect to the evaluation of personal behaviours, ecclesial polity, public witness, etc.[38]

Failure to make a strong theological case for evaluation as something inherent in the renewal of tropology would leave us in a precarious position. Church history is too filled with atrocities committed in Jesus' name for an account of theological ethics as tropology to proceed much further without

---

colors in this refraction represent how "God's truth is to be found present in and through the dynamics of human understanding and life in the world." (15; emphasis original) This is no "pretense" of theology in interdisciplinarity, nor a half-way house in which the mutual benefits of each discipline are never fully engaged, but a mode of approach that "should have as its goal the uncovering of the dynamic of the work of the Triune God in the refraction of modern life and understanding as that occurs in other disciplines." (15; emphasis original)

[37] Ulrich Luz, *Matthew 1-7* (Minneapolis: Augsburg Fortress, 2007), 378.

[38] Luz, *Matthew 1-7*, 376. See further 380-3 for notes on the history of interpretation of this passage.

attention to evaluation, that is, to how judgments are made with respect to what counts as "good." How, then, is theological ethics, undertaken as tropology, to understand and map the kind of evaluation(s) that will satisfy the "good fruit" criterion without turning Jesus' words into a full-blown Christian pragmatism that clarifies and corrects the validity of textual readings with reference only to outcomes? How is Christian ethics as tropology to be evaluated without reducing theological ethics to a justification of means by reference to ends?[39] At issue is the scope and kind of evaluation required as reading the bible produces judgment and decision-making with respect to action. While not advocating an anti-foundationalist, Dewey-like pragmatism which resists appeal to an eschatological end or transcendent good, the "good fruit" criterion suggests that a built-in expectation of evaluation is something required and not an optional, nice-to-have extra. How, then, are we to conceive of and map the various dimensions of the evaluative task?

Four dimensions of the task require consideration. First is the doctrinal dimension of the evaluative task whereby tropology itself is understood as possessing an internal, evaluative dimension when the bible is read canonically as ordering all judgments to the cross of Christ. Striving after the moral sense of the bible for the improvement of life and specifics of decision-making presupposes that the meaning of "good" in theological ethics is given by the goodness of God revealed in Christ Jesus (2 Chron 7:3; Ps 34:8; Mk 10:18; Lk 18:19). Tropology is only ever about seeking to live according to the "mind of Christ" (Phil 2:5) and as "the body of Christ" (1 Cor 12:27; Eph 4:12; Col 1:18), and so evaluating tropology requires a working relationship between the two concepts of revelation and evaluation. The scope of the question of what this working relationship entails is potentially vast. Questions come into play about hierarchically construed ecclesial authority versus more discursive accounts of how divine revelation is discerned, how God's word addresses sinful creatures, how dogmatic prejudices bear upon perceptions of the moral sense of the bible, when to distrust tropological claims that tend toward the subjective or intuitive, how to discern the true prophetic voice when contested by the community, and so on. For the moment, we note merely that tropology today must entail something like a living dialectic whereby enquiry into the goodness of God revealed in Christ Jesus is understood as inherently polyphonous and polysemic because given through communities of faith in which every believer is, at once, both justified and a sinner, *simul justus et peccator*.

Second, meeting the "good fruit" criterion in tropology today invites creative reengagement with the existential dimension pertaining to spiritual formation. John Cassian and those for whom he wrote expected individuals to

---

[39] For a nuanced account of why Reinhold Niebuhr's pragmatism should not be characterized in this problematic way, see Mark L. Haas, "Reinhold Niebuhr's 'Christian Pragmatism': A Principled Alternative to Consequentialism," *The Review of Politics* 61, no. 4 (1999): 605-36.

grow in their spiritual lives, including in moral discernment and discipline. Today, it is more common for debates about maturation, about how adults – and not only children – grow in self-understanding and moral awareness, and about capacities for meaning-making, ethical judgment, and effective leadership, etc., to happen within developmental psychology than theological ethics.[40] Hence our question is whether theological ethics should find better ways of conceiving and talking of the ethical dimensions of spiritual formation as entailing personal growth and increasing capacity for moral rigour. More specifically, should revisiting the ancient tropological interest in spiritual development manifesting itself in progress in the moral life urge theological ethics toward cognitive and developmental psychology with a view to understanding better how developmental research has bearing upon spiritual formation and accompanying moral decision-making and behaviour? Words of caution are necessary. Developmental psychology takes many forms but may be broadly conceived as empirically-based scientific investigation intended to explain growth, change and consistency across the human lifespan, and to analyse how moral development is experienced. The psychologist's questions are different from the questions of theological ethics or moral philosophy;[41] our interest is in the points at which respective interests overlap. At issue is the extent to which spiritual formation is deemed to entail developmental change, the morally appropriate direction of that change, and whether there is scope for theological ethics to expect somehow that discipleship is developmental.

Third, evaluating tropology today needs better understanding of the philosophico-aesthetic dimension of tropology pertaining to moral imagination. Having noted the wealth of witness in Christian tradition to benefits entailed in dramatizing and otherwise giving artistic expression to readings of the bible, and how the products of their labours – plays, music, paintings, stories, sculptures, etc. – variously give imaginative form to the moral sense of biblical texts in given situations, questions arise with respect to what happens in

---

[40] For example, Robert Kegan, *The Evolving Self: Problem and Process in Human Development* (Cambridge: Harvard University Press, 1982) was significant in advancing a constructive-developmental theory of meaning-making influenced especially by the child developmental psychologist Jean Piaget but with application to adults. Judith Stevens-Long, *Adult Life* (Palo Alto: Mayfield, 1988) included ethical and committed behaviour in her typology of development across the adult lifespan whereby a person matures from behaviour driven by a desire to conform to behaviour driven by principles, includes assisting others, and ability to meet one's own needs without using others instrumentally. See esp. 66. More recently *The Oxford Handbook of Reciprocal Adult Development and Learning* (Oxford: Oxford University Press, 2011).

[41] Note, for instance, moral philosopher Gertrud Nunner-Winkler's critique of the moral universalism held by Lawrence Kohlberg. Lawrence Kohlberg, "Moral Relativism and Strict Universalism," in *The Moral Domain: Essays in the Ongoing Discussion between Philosophy and the Social Sciences*, ed. Thomas E. Wren (Cambridge: MIT Press, 1990), 109-26.

theological ethics as the moral imagination creates space for judgement and various kinds of critique. The same conceptual space was in view when, in his report of Abbot Moses's reply to a question regarding the goal and end of the monk, John Cassian urged monks and hermits to fix their spiritual eye on the coming reign of God:

> The end of our profession indeed, as I said, is the kingdom of God or the kingdom of heaven: but the immediate aim or goal, is purity of heart, without which no one can gain that end: fixing our gaze then steadily on this goal, as if on a definite mark, let us direct our course as straight towards it as possible, and if our thoughts wander somewhat from this, let us revert to our gaze upon it, and check them accurately as by a sure standard, which will always bring back all our efforts to this one mark, and will show at once if our mind has wandered ever so little from the direction marked out for it.[42]

Note how Cassian both affirms the imaginative work of fixing one's gaze upon the goal of the coming reign of God whilst alluding also to "a sure standard" and bringing efforts back "to this one mark." He holds in tension both the creative work of imagination and its discipline. Reflection at this point could burst into contemplation of how beauty awakens and enlarges human capacity to act for the sake of God/the good, psycho-cognitive considerations of how empathy is experienced and whether and/or why visualization renders the experience more intense, why moral imagination is required to conceive of something different from the status quo, and more; we note merely that tropology entails moral reasoning as a study of the creative and beautiful.

Fourth, the "good fruit" criterion in tropology requires extended conversation across academic disciplines, language, cultures, etc. This might seem self-evident but warrants mention because of the (often justified) complaint against the tradition of theologico-ethical engagement with the bible marked by Karl Barth and Eduard Thurneysen's attempt in the period 1916-1921 to learn their "theological ABC all over again, beginning by reading and interpreting the writing of the Old and New Testament, more thoughtfully than before."[43] The complaint is that this kind of doctrinal commitment squeezes out serious socio-political and other academic engagement. Robin Lovin makes the point:

> For all its theological integrity, Barth's position is impossible for a public ethics. If we are to choose our actions by reason and defend them publicly by argument, we

---

[42] Cassian, *Conference 1*, ch.2.

[43] Eberhard Busch and Karl Barth, *His Life from Letters and Autobiographical Texts*, trans. by John Bowden (Philadelphia: Fortress Press, 1976), 97.

> must either limit the freedom of God or abandon the metaethics that bases all moral meanings on God's will.[44]

Lovin's concern is that appeals to the Word of God are too often made at such a level of abstraction that they mean very little practically.

> Obedience to the requirements of the moment is all that marks a faithful ethics. Moral argument, moral uncertainty, and moral justifications belong to that closed-off realm of human speech untouched by the Word.[45]

While not sharing Lovin's view that "Barth's position is impossible for a public ethics," I recognize difficulties entailed in, on the one hand, not reducing God's word to a divine object that may be discussed at will and somehow manipulated by human reason such that obedience to divine command becomes a method for making moral judgments and, on the other, speaking about the moral sense of the bible in meaningful degrees of specificity and certainty. There is no single response to this challenge, only repeated demonstration that holding tropological readings of the bible to the full range of academic standards is consistent with affirming that bible remains a purposive means of divine self-communication that is understood only with holding that the bible is still "sufficient to declare the truth" in matters of both doctrine and morals.[46]

5. Conclusion

In a *TIME Magazine* piece published April 20, 1962, Barth is reported as saying:

> There can be [. . .] no question of "disproving" the authority of the Scriptures, for the church today must take the "risk" of accepting the witness of the early Christians who established the canon of the Scripture, and the Reformation fathers who revised it. God still speaks within the Bible: In the light of faith, the church and her theologians must listen and undertake the ever-unfinished task of finding out what He is saying.[47]

My answer today to the question: "What, then, does theological ethics do?" is to reaffirm Barth's urging of the risk to keep listening for how God speaks

---

[44] Robin W. Lovin, *Christian Faith and Public Choices: Social Ethics of Barth, Brunner, and Bonhoeffer* (Philadelphia: Fortress, 1984), 42.

[45] Lovin, *Christian Faith*, 42.

[46] Athanasius, *Against the Heathen*, trans. by Archibald Robertson (Buffalo: Christian Literature Publishing, 1892); revised and edited for New Advent by Kevin Knight. <http://www.newadvent.org/fathers/2801.htm>, Part I, §2.

[47] "Witness to an Ancient Truth," *TIME Magazine*, 20 April 1962, 59-63, http://content.time.com/time/covers/0,16641,19620420,00.html (Accessed 7 August, 2019).

within the Bible and, as per long-standing witness in Christian tradition, to do so for its moral sense. To this end, I have reflected on various dimensions of the tropological task in this essay: the doctrinal (concerning the substance of "the good"), the existential (concerning personal growth in relation to "the good"), the philosophico-aesthetic (how "the good" is seen as beautiful and otherwise perceived) and the discursive (how perceptions of "the good" must be subjected to the rigor of cross-disciplinary investigation).

Bibliography

Aquinas, Thomas. *Summa Theologiœ of St. Thomas Aquinas.* Translated by Fathers of the English Dominican Province. Second and Revised Edition, 1920. Online Edition, 2017 by Kevin Knight. http://www.newadvent.org/summa/.

Augustine. *On Genesis: A Refutation of the Manichees.* Translated by Edmund Hill. Unfinished Literal Commentary on Genesis; the Literal Meaning of Genesis. The works of St. Augustin: A Translation for the 21st Century, I.13, edited by John E. Rotelle, O.S.A.. Translated by O.P. (New York: New City Press, 1990).

Augustine. *On Christian Teaching.* Translated by James Shaw. From Nicene and Post-Nicene Fathers, First Series, vol. 2, edited by Philip Schaff (Buffalo, New York: Christian Literature Publishing Co., 1887.) Revised and edited for New Advent by Kevin Knight. http://www.newadvent.org/fathers/12021.htm.

Boyle, John F. "St. Thomas Aquinas and Sacred Scripture." In *Catena aurea in quatuor Evangelia. In Mk 2:23-28,* vol. 1, edited by Angelici Guarienti. Turin: Marietti, 1953.

Busch, Eberhard. *Karl Barth: His Life from Letters and Autobiographical Texts.* Translated by John Bowden. Philadelphia: Fortress Press, 1976.

Cassian, John. *Conferences.* Translated by C.S. Gibson. From Nicene and Post-Nicene Fathers, Second Series, vol. 11, edited by Philip Schaff and Henry Wace. Buffalo: Christian Literature Publishing, 1894. Revised and edited for New Advent by Kevin Knight. http://www.newadvent.org/fathers/350814.htm.

Cassian, John. *Institutes.* Translated by C.S. Gibson. From Nicene and Post-Nicene Fathers, Second Series, vol. 11, edited by Philip Schaff and Henry Wace. Buffalo: Christian Literature Publishing, 1894. Revised and edited for New Advent by Kevin Knight. http://www.newadvent.org/fathers/350704.htm.

Dobie, Robert J. "Thomas Aquinas and Meister Eckhart on Exodus 3:14: Exegesis or Eisegesis?" *Medieval Mystical Theology* 24, no. 2 (2015): 124-36.

Haas, Mark L. "Reinhold Niebuhr's 'Christian Pragmatism': A Principled Alternative to Consequentialism." *The Review of Politics* 61, no. 4, Christianity and Politics: Millennial Issue 1 (1999): 605-36.

Luz, Ulrich. *Matthew 1-7.* Minneapolis: Augsburg Fortress, 2007.

McDermott, Ryan. *Tropologies: Ethics and Invention in England, c. 1350–1600.* Notre Dame: University of Notre Dame Press, 2016.

Kohlberg, Lawrence. "Moral Relativism and Strict Universalism." In *The Moral Domain: Essays in the Ongoing Discussion between Philosophy and the Social Sciences,* edited by Thomas E. Wren, 109-126. Cambridge: The MIT Press, 1990.

Ricoeur, *Paul. From Text to Action: Essays in Hermeneutics II.* Evanston: Northwestern University Press, 2007 [1968].

On Doing Public Theology

Reflections Towards a More Public Praxis

Florian Höhne (Berlin, Germany)

1. Introduction

Because theology deals with questions thought to be relevant to all persons, theologians have often understood their work as inherently public. Although the liberal theologian might call it "religion", "feeling" or ground of existence, and the Barthian theologian might talk about revelation, the kingdom of God and the Christ-event – both take themselves to be dealing with matters of universal significance and thus relevance. Accordingly, public theologians all over the world have identified various reasons for regarding their theology as essentially public.[1]

But let's be honest: Theology, at least in Germany, is not really that public. How many people read a theological dissertation that is printed 150 times to be securely stored in libraries? How many people read a theological journal article? What was the last theological book that was widely discussed like, for example, Yuval Harari's work is right now in multiple contexts? When was theology last a trendsetter in public debate for a large number of people, as, for example, Hartmut Rosa's terminology of "Resonanz" was in Germany for instance? Sober reflection on these questions will – at least for the German context – probably lead to the plain truth: Theology is not really that public. It is therefore more than a little ambitious to speak of a "Public Theology".

Of course, in another sense, referring to institutions, theology is quite public in Germany: Academic theology profits from its traditional public status as a discipline also taught and researched at state-financed universities. Even in times of decreasing numbers of church members and of those studying theology, this public status is still legally secured (though it is also being publicly challenged). The public character of theology in this sense does not reflect the theological sensibilities of any given theologian. Its public charac-

---

[1] While Wolfgang Huber for example has argued with reference to the church's commission to be public (Wolfgang Huber, *Kirche in Der Zeitenwende: Gesellschaftlicher Wandel und Erneuerung der Kirche* (Gütersloh: Verlag Bertelsmann Stiftung, 1998), 102), Robert McElroy has drawn on the catholic natural law tradition (Robert W. McElroy, *The Search for an American Public Theology: The Contribution of John Courtney Murray* (New York: Paulist Press, 1989), 157).

ter – or lack thereof – is due rather to complex and powerful dynamics in society. But as part of these dynamics the way theology is done most certainly plays a role. Since theology has theological as well as institutional reasons to understand itself as public, it seems worth asking: What hinders theology from being more public in a quantitative sense? That is what I want to focus on in this chapter: I want to suggest a theory of social practice and imagination that provides a useful heuristic for reflecting on those obstacles. My basic thesis is that theology's imaginaries of the public sphere tend to keep its practices from being more public. In closing, I will offer some practical suggestions.

2. The Public of Theology as Social Practice

What does it mean to understand something or oneself as public? I begin with a very broad understanding of "public" which Horst Pöttker has suggested:[2] Something is public insofar as there are no obstacles to see, hear, or understand it – in other words: "public" refers to being non-exclusive and to the claim to reduce excluding factors.[3] The term qualifies a "mode of communication".[4] This makes it possible to understand "public" as a set of social practices.

I borrow my understanding of "practice" in this sense from the sociology of practice, particularly from the work of Theodore Schatzki, Andreas Reckwitz, Charles Taylor, and Pierre Bourdieu, as well as the overviews of Frank Hillebrandt, Jan Schmidt und Robert Schmidt.[5] So to speak of a "theory of social practices" as I am proposing here does not refer to one coherent theory of

---

[2] Cf. Horst Pöttker, "Der Beruf Zur Öffentlichkeit: Über Aufgabe, Grundsätze und Perspektiven des Journalismus in Der Mediengesellschaft aus der Sicht Praktischer Vernunft," *Publizistik* 55 (2010): 110-11.

[3] Cf. Pöttker, "Beruf," 110-11.

[4] Pöttker, "Beruf," 110, my translation.

[5] Cf. Theodore R. Schatzki, *Social Practices: A Wittgensteinian Approach to Human Activity and the Social* (Cambridge: Cambridge University Press, 1996); Andreas Reckwitz, "Grundelemente Einer Theorie Sozialer Praktiken: Eine Sozialtheoretische Perspektive," *Zeitschrift für Soziologie* 32, no. 4 (2003); Charles Taylor, *Modern Social Imaginaries, Philosophy social theory* (Durham: Duke University Press, 2004); Pierre Bourdieu, *Sozialer Sinn: Kritik Der Theoretischen Vernunft* (Frankfurt am Main: Suhrkamp, 1993); Pierre Bourdieu, *Die Feinen Unterschiede: Kritik Der Gesellschaftlichen Urteilskraft, with the assistance of Bernd Schwibs, and Achim Russer* (Frankfurt am Main: Suhrkamp, 2014); Frank Hillebrandt, *Soziologische Praxistheorien: Eine Einführung* (Wiesbaden: Springer, 2014); Jan-Hinrik Schmidt, *Das Neue Netz: Merkmale, Praktiken Und Folgen Des Web 2.0, 2.* (Konstanz: UVK, 2011); Robert Schmidt, *Soziologie Der Praktiken: Konzeptionelle Studien Und Empirische Analysen* (Berlin: Suhrkamp, 2012).

the social but more to a "pool of ideas".[6] They convene in the attempt to understand the social with primary focus on practices – in a way that is distinct from (though not contrast with) discourse, interaction, communication or systems.[7]

What is a social practice? Andreas Reckwitz defines it as follows: A Practice is a "routinized 'nexus of doings and sayings' (Schatzki) [. . .], which is connected by an implicit understanding"[8]. Consider an example common to the German academic's every-day life: riding a bike. This practice includes doing certain things – I move my legs to push the pedals down, my hands to move the handlebar – and saying things as well – occasionally I need to yell at pedestrians who loiter on the bikepath. All of that is held together by/as knowing-how-to-ride-a-bike.[9]

Three features of practices are important here; the first two are summarized by Reckwitz, and the third is discussed by Jan Schmidt. Practices involve materiality, two kinds of material in particular: bodies and things.[10] Saying this might sound self-evident, though theoretical reflection complicates matters:[11] The bike is a thing and my body is my body. Hence, a practice includes implicit knowledge my body has incorporated, namely, my bodily "knowing how to".[12] To use a concept from Bourdieu: The acquired habitus that I have incorporated performs a certain practice.[13] A practice also includes the material structure of things that allows for a certain set of practices:[14] bikes allow for the practice of riding a bike. Reckwitz' decisive argument at this point says, that it is neither the structure of the material that determines the practice one-sidedly nor the agent determining the material. Rather, the practical "meaningful use" thereof makes the material into something that enables the practice:[15] The bike allows for the practice of riding only insofar as and while I use it for riding.

Secondly, practices include practical knowledge.[16] The decisive point about practical knowledge is its being implicit; it also includes, routines, com-

---

[6] Reckwitz, "Grundelemente," 283, 289, the latter quote is my translation.
[7] Cf. Reckwitz, "Grundelemente," 290.
[8] Reckwitz, "Grundelemente," 290, my translation.
[9] For the term "knowing how to" and "understanding of X-ing" and their meaning see Schatzki, *Practices,* 91. The example already shows a problem of this definition: it's never unambiguously clear what belongs to one particular practice. We may abstain from this problem in the context of this paper.
[10] Cf. Reckwitz, "Grundelemente," 290.
[11] Cf. Reckwitz, "Grundelemente," 290.
[12] Cf. Reckwitz, "Grundelemente," 290. Quote: Schatzki, *Practices,* 91.
[13] Cf. Bourdieu, *Unterschiede,* 277–86.
[14] Cf. Reckwitz, "Grundelemente," 291.
[15] Reckwitz, "Grundelemente," 291, my translation of "sinnhafter *Gebrauch*".
[16] Cf. Reckwitz, "Grundelemente," 292.

petences that are not made explicit.[17] I am able to ride a bike, but I cannot explain to you how to do that. Reckwitz points to three elements of practical knowledge: it includes a "routinized attribution of meaning" to things and bodies, methodological knowledge of how to do something, and motivational knowledge of what to want in a particular situation.[18] Such practical knowledge is situated in what Charles Taylor has called "the social imaginary" that "extends beyond the immediate background understanding that makes sense of our particular practices:"[19] Implicit imaginations of who I am socially, how I relate to other, what is expected of me and what I can expect from others – a knowledge carried on in "images, stories, and legends", rather than in theories.[20]

Thirdly: Implied by their situatedness in things and bodies, and by the ways that the knowledge used in practices is practical, implicit and embodied, practices are always socially situated[21]: They are situated in a social, economic, and cultural context, in a given country, a given habit of doing things, a given lifestyle, a given class.[22] Even the practice of riding a bike is more common in one class than in another.

These categories drawn from theories of social practice offer help in asking about the practice of theology. I do not mean the practices theology observes, like the practices of ethical conduct, of religious rituals, of preaching and spiritual formation. I mean the practice that is theology itself or the practice we see when we observe people doing theology: What does one person at a German public university do when she or he does systematic theology at the dawn of the 21st century? Probably the following: reading books and articles, thinking, talking and listing to others in conversations, teaching, applying for funds, answering emails, traveling to conferences, organizing conferences, grading papers, and so on. For the purpose of my argument, let me group a couple of these activities into three types:[23]

There are *practices of exposure:* Theologians present their thoughts in front of an audience: a presentation, a book, or a peer-reviewed article. Practices of exposure are public, insofar as they make the exposed content acces-

---

[17] Cf. Reckwitz, "Grundelemente," 292.

[18] Reckwitz, "Grundelemente," 292., my translation.

[19] Taylor, *Imaginaries*, 25.

[20] Cf. also for the quote Taylor, *Imaginaries*, 23.

[21] Cf. Schmidt, *Netz*, 41–44.

[22] Cf. Schmidt, *Netz*, 42.

[23] For the first two sets of practices see also Florian Höhne, "Öffentlichkeit" als Imagination und Ensemble Sozialer Praktiken. Zur Relevanz einer Schlüsselkategorie Öffentlicher Theologie in digitalen Kontexten," *Ethik und Gesellschaft*, no. 1 (2019), https://doi.org/10.18156/EUG-1-2019-ART-1, http://www.ethik-und-gesellschaft.de/ojs/index.php/eug/article/view/1-2019-art-1/653.

sible to a public. The measure for publicness is accessibility. Accessibility[24] requires things that cost money: publication-possibilities or rooms. It also requires practical knowledge: knowing how to say something, having the courage to do so publically. Practices of exposure are situated in a certain academic culture in which it is common to talk and listen.

Secondly, there are *practices of conversation:* Theologians discuss topics, orally and in writing. Practices of conversation are public, insofar as people can participate[25] in them. The measure for publicness is participation in discourse. How many people discuss, who discusses, and who is excluded? Who may speak and who then actually speaks? This requires the practical knowledge of knowing what kind of comments, questions, jokes, and answers are appropriate, what kind of voice and words to use: Do you yell or whisper? It also requires the emotional capacity to deal with criticism and counterarguments.

Thirdly, there are *practices of retreat:* Theologians read, think for themselves, write for themselves notes that nobody might ever read. Practices of retreat are not public themselves but they are more or less directed to practices of conversation and exposure: Is the question one deals with in private relevant to a public discourse? Practices of retreat require the practical knowledge to focus, to think, to create a certain inner distance, to observe, to make the body rest and sit for hours, to distance oneself from feelings about texts and phenomena. It requires literacy. It requires relief from the pressing necessities of life, actually and mentally, at least for a while.

On this background, we can distinguish at least three senses in which theology is practically public: Accessibility of the exposed, participation in the discourse, directedness of the quiet work-process. At least the first two senses are been discusses theologically: Clemens Wustmans for example has discussed whether "plain language" could make theological texts more accessible and better understandable.[26] Public theologians have tested concepts of bilin-

---

[24] For this notion of accessibility see also Torsten Meireis's work on the moral right to access [. . .] the public sphere" (Torsten Meireis, "Recht Auf Zugang: Sozialethische Überlegungen zur Gentrifizierung des Öffentlichen Raums," in *Stadtluft macht reich/arm: Stadtentwicklung, soziale Ungleichheit und Raumgerechtigkeit,* ed. by Bernhard Emunds, Claudia Czingon and Michael Wolff, *Die Wirtschaft der Gesellschaft Jahrbuch* 4 (Marburg: Metropolis-Verlag, 2018), 211, my translation of the quote). Meireis distinguishes between taking part ("Teilnahme") and having part ("Teilhabe"): While "taking part" refers to the conditions for taking part in the formation of a social entity, "having part" refers to the access to material resources (Meireis, "Recht auf Zugang," 211–13).

[25] For the notion of participation see also Torsten Meireis's work on the "moral right to access [. . .] the public sphere": Meireis, "Recht auf Zugang".

[26] Cf. Clemens Wustmans, "Plain Language as Empowerment Beyond a Faithful Middle-Class Public: Contributions of Public Theology to the Capability Approach of Social

guality and translation as ways to make theological arguments more accessible and hence more public.[27] Benedict Friedrich, Hanna Reichel and Thomas Renkert are developing a citizen theology that focusses on participation in the theological discourse.[28]

3. The Public of Theology Imagined

If it makes sense to understand theology as a practice itself, one cannot only ask for how publicly this practice is performed. It will also make a difference what kind of public the participants in that very practice of theology imagine themselves to be in. Charles Taylor described the "social imaginary" as the implicit broader imaginations of context, purpose, role and situation that inform practices.[29] The social imaginary, which Taylor clearly distinguishes from a social theory, is "carried in images, stories, and legends" and it "makes possible common practices".[30] What imaginaries of the public and publicness[31] inform the performance of theology? Let me begin an open list with three examples that are specific to cultural context, history, and habits.

The Kerygmatic Imaginary

I want to read a passage of an article published by the German theologian Martin Plieninger in 1948 as an illustration of one social imaginary concerning how proclamation of the Gospel works. Plieninger starts with the "silent, hidden experience that 'God looks at me friendly again'"; this experience

---

Justice," in *Religion and Democracy: Studies in Public Theology*, ed. by Torsten Meireis and Rolf Schieder (Baden-Baden: Nomos, 2017), 2018.

[27] Cf. Friederike van Oorschot and Simone Ziermann, eds., *Theologie in Übersetzung? Religiöse Sprache und Kommunikation in heterogenen Kontexten* (Leipzig: Evangelische Verlagsanstalt, 2019).

[28] Benedikt Friedrich, Hanna Reichel, and Thomas Renkert have recently sketched the concept of a "citizen theology" that tries to make theology a "collaborative, participatory, and explorative" praxis in the digital age (Benedikt Friedrich, Hanna Reichel, and Thomas Renkert, "Citizen Theology: Eine Exploration zwischen Digitalisierung und theologischer Epistemologie," in *Digitaler Strukturwandel der Öffentlichkeit: Interdisziplinäre Perspektiven auf politische Partizipation im Wandel*, ed. by Jonas Bedford-Strohm, Florian Höhne, and Julian Zeyher-Quattlender (Baden-Baden: Nomos, 2019), 175.

[29] Taylor puts it as follows: "By social imaginary, [. . .] I am thinking, rather, of ways people imagine their social existence, how they fit together with others, how things go on between them and their fellows, the expectations that are normally met, and the deeper normative notions and images that underlie these expectations." (Taylor, *Imaginaries*, 23.)

[30] Taylor, *Imaginaries*, 23.

[31] Taylor himself sees the public sphere also as imagination: "That a conclusion 'counts as' public opinion reflects the fact that a public sphere can exist only if it is imagined as such." (Taylor, *Imaginaries*, 85).

made in private solitude would seek public expression.[32] He describes a movement from the inner heart, the hidden interior, to the exposed exterior, to the public, and uses a biblical image for that, which was quite common in that time.[33]

> Jesus says to his disciples: "What I tell you in the dark, say in the light, and what you hear whispered, proclaim on the housetops." (Mt 10, 27, ESV)[34]

That is an imaginary which has not only informed practices of preaching but also of doing theology: Practices of retreat are imagined to be the place where theology is fabricated, where new thoughts are thought, where the hard work is done, ideas are produced, insights happen, are evaluated, checked, tested, and considered. After a thought, a theory, a model, a narrative, an interpretation has been found reliable in the darkness of the private study, it is carried into the light, exposed in publications. The whispered insight is proclaimed on the housetops.

This imaginary of theology going public works with the named basic dichotomies: from the dark into the light, from hearing a whisper into proclaiming, from private to public. Practically, other parallel dichotomies are added: from the private safe space where imperfect thoughts, vulnerable expressions, and dilettante concepts are allowed and can be played with, to the light of the public sphere, where concepts need to be perfect, well informed, sealed against all kinds of possible criticism, where references need to be acknowledged in an interdisciplinary dialogue; from vulnerable production to armed presentation. In those dichotomies between the inner and the outer, the inner always comes first and the public is secondary. Plus, the public has something hostile and menacing to it: One needs to shield oneself before one dares to go public.

Of course, as a social or philosophical theory this imaginary would be incoherent, because it makes one oversee the public nature of thinking and reasoning itself. Volker Gerhard has impressively and convincingly argued that human consciousness is genuinely public because it has always already drawn on a shared world.[35] But theoretical incoherence is not an obstacle for an imaginary to make a practical impact.

---

[32] Martin Plieninger, "Der Öffentlichkeitsauftrag der Kirche," in *Auf dem Grunde der Apostel und Propheten*, ed. Max Loeser (Stuttgart: Quell-Verlag, 1948), 253, my translation.

[33] Cf. Plieninger, "Öffentlichkeitsauftrag," 253.

[34] Cf. Plieninger, "Öffentlichkeitsauftrag," 253.

[35] Cf. Volker Gerhardt, *Öffentlichkeit: Die Politische Form des Bewusstseins* (München: Beck, 2012), 13-14. (Accessed September 5, 2018)

The Ecclesial Imaginary[36]

A couple of theologians have suggested to imagine the church itself as a public sphere or a counter public: drawing on Reinhard Hütter, Bernd Wannenwetsch has spoken of the church as "a peculiar public generated in worship service".[37] William Cavanaugh has explicitly used the term "imagination" in this context.[38] Therefore, I will refer to one of his books to paint one version of this imaginary: the church as public.

In the "Theopolitical Imagination," Cavanaugh summarizes what he sees as the founding-narrative of modern secular states:

> When the religious consensus of civil society was shattered by the Reformation, the passions excited by religion as such were loosed, and Catholics and the newly-minted Protestants began killing each other in the name of doctrinal loyalties. [. . .] The modern secular state and the privatization of religion was necessary, therefore, to keep the peace among warring religious factions.[39]

Against this background, the imagination of a secular nation-state and a civil society of free citizens succeeded – according to Cavanaugh – the imagination of the body of Christ.[40] Cavanaugh claims to debunk this modern narrative and imagination by saying: "The 'Wars of Religion' were not the events that necessitated the birth of the modern state; they were in fact themselves the birth-pangs of the state."[41] Accordingly, he criticizes public theologies for having bought into those secular imaginations of the public sphere and civil society.[42] Opposed to that, he wants to reimagine the body of Christ: He sees the practice of Eucharist as "an alternative imagining of space and time which builds up a body of resistance to violence, the body of Christ"[43], in which national borderlines, the "dichotomy of centre and periphery," and private property were overcome.[44]

While this imagination might sound very plausible and attractive, particularly in times of shrinking congregations, it is problematic for at least two reasons: First, it overlooks the worldliness inside the church. Second, it tends

---

[36] A more developed account of this point may be found in: Florian Höhne, "Wo noch? Kirche in gesellschaftlichen Öffentlichkeiten. Anmerkungen zu theopolitischen Imaginationen." In *Krisen - Aufbrüche - Transformationen,* ed. by Traugott Jähnchen, *Jahrbuch Sozialer Protestantismus* 12 (2019): 255-282.

[37] Bernd Wannenwetsch, *Gottesdienst als Lebensform - Ethik für Christenbürger* (Stuttgart, Berlin, and Köln: Kohlhammer, 1997), 242, my translation.

[38] William T. Cavanaugh, *Theopolitical Imagination: Discovering the Liturgy as a Political Act in an Age of Global Consumerism* (London and New York: Clark, 2002).

[39] Cavanaugh, *Imagination,* 20f.

[40] Cf. Cavanaugh, *Imagination,* 5f., 9-46; 53, 55.

[41] Cavanaugh, *Imagination,* 22.

[42] Cf. Cavanaugh, *Imagination,* 3, 6.

[43] Cavanaugh, *Imagination,* 7.

[44] Cf. Cavanaugh, *Imagination,* 50f., 90, 49, 47. Quote on page 49.

to leave society's public a blank or equally dark space: Imaging the eucharistic community as the decisive community as opposed to state and society entails the danger of stripping theology of categories and narratives to interpret contemporary politics in a differentiated and nuanced way. If theology's guiding categories for describing social phenomena are only taken form Christian traditions and only fit to describe Eucharistic community, they might make one overlook differences, nuances and positive developments outside the church.

The Discursive Imaginary

The catholic theologian David Tracy has famously argued, "that all theology is public discourse."[45] He starts with the social reality of the academic theologian and distinguishes three publics addressed by the theologian – "the wider society, the academy and the church."[46] Tracy attributes "proper criteria for publicness" and different forms of publicness – argumentative, hermeneutic and meditative reason – to these different publics.[47] Two features of his arguments are particularly interesting:

In doing so, Tracy includes a differentiated understanding of the different public spheres into his imagination of the theologian: How a theologian speaks, will then depend on the public he addresses. Hence, he imagines not only a movement from some interior reflection to some outward expression but includes the different structures of different outwards in his imagination. Tracy's imagination of publicness entails a higher sensitivity of social context than the kerygmatic one. But it's not only that.

Of course, one can get the sense from many of Tracy's formulations that theology is made in private before it is brought out into the public light of day.[48] But in understanding "theology as public discourse" he integrates a hermeneutical as opposed to merely instrumental understanding of the public into his theology:[49] Strictly speaking, theology for him is not only brought to

---

[45] David Tracy, *The Analogical Imagination: Christian Theology and the Culture of Pluralism* (London: SCM Press, 1981), accessed August 14, 2012, 3; David Tracy, "Theology as Public Discourse," *The Christian Century*, 1975.

[46] Tracy, *Analogical*, 5.

[47] Cf. David Tracy, "Three Kinds of Publicness in Public Theology," *International Journal of Public Theology* 8, no. 3 (2014): 330, https://doi.org/10.1163/15697320-12341354.

[48] He asks for the "addressee of the theologian's reflections" (Tracy, *Analogical*, 4) and formulates systematic theology's main question as follows: "What systematic model [. . .] will allow a specific historical community of faith to articulate its particular vision of reality in a manner that makes it available for the wider community [. . .]?" (Tracy, "Theology as Public Discourse").

[49] For this distinction between instrumental and hermeneutical with reference to rhetoric cf. Albrecht Grözinger, "Das Verständnis von Rhetorik und Homiletik: Bemerkungen zum Stand der Diskussion," *Theologia Practica* 14 (1979): 266–67. On Habermas, specifically, in this context, cf. Grözinger, "Verständnis," 272.

the public discourse after having been produced – it is produced in public discourse. Like public discourse in Jürgen Habermas's, sense for example, theological assertions take the form of claims, which become subject to open discussion.[50] In another sense, religious resources are offered for public contemplation.[51] In the middle between the two stands the "candidate, especially appropriate for understanding the public dimensions of the ineluctable particularity of religion":[52] "the hermeneutical phenomenon of dialogue or conversation with all classic expressions."[53] At this point, the public dimension refers not only to the product of theology, but also to its development: theological insight happens in conversation, which is a special kind of interaction: "Yet what is authentic conversation as distinct from idle chatter, mere debate, gossip or non-negotiable confrontation? [. . .] Real conversation occurs only when the participants allow the question, the subject matter, to assume primacy. It occurs only when our usual fears about our own self-image die: whether that fear is expressed in either arrogance or scrupulosity matters little."[54]

Insofar as such conversation is itself a form of publicness, some public spheres are imagined as a productive space, where insights can happen, opinions can be transformed, and the vulnerability of a fragmented or even personal thought may be exposed. Accordingly, this public is imagined as a less menacing space, at least as safe enough to enter the conversation and become vulnerable enough for the subject matter to take over.[55]

A theologian who imagines her or his theology as public discourse has to imagine it as changeable, as open to critique, as public not only in its presentation but also in its development, as in flux, as an imperfect fragment of the uncontrollable, unforeseeable and communal way of conversation. One might ask with Maluleke where to find such a public sphere, where it is safe to do that, "where strangers meet with civility"[56] and the criticism this question leads to is a very valid one – but again: it is not about social reality yet, but about the imaginary of a public that form the performance of public practices.

---

[50] Cf. Tracy, "Publicness," 331-32.
[51] Cf. Tracy, "Publicness," 334.
[52] Tracy, "Publicness," 331-32.
[53] Tracy, "Publicness," 332.
[54] Tracy, *Analogical,* 101.
[55] Not only Tracy's notion of conversation, that comes from Gadamer (Tracy, *Analogical,* 101), but already the Habermasian sense of discourse entails such elements of vulnerability and openness: To formulate a claim – as opposed to a nonnegotiable sentence or command – to provide warrants for it and to listen to one's critics opens up for transformation of one's former point.
[56] Tinyiko S. Maluleke, "The Elusive Public of Public Theology: A Response to William Storrar," *International Journal of Public Theology* 5 (2011): 85.

4. On Doing Public Theology

Mark Lewis Taylor, a postcolonial thinker and theologian, has summarized a dilemma of academic theology at universities: Practices at universities "create and sustain" subalternity in many ways.[57] For Taylor and Beverly, that includes material financial exclusion as well as the discipline of discourse.[58] Animated by their work, I am interested in how much it is particularly theology's imaginations of the public that make practices informed by theses imaginations exclusive and hence less public: less accessible, less participatory, and less directed to the public sphere. The intuition behind this approach is that where theology excludes certain ideas and people, it is likewise excluded from discourses in which these people and ideas matter. Thus, exclusion makes theology less public in two ways, by excluding and being excluded. Firstly, I will revisit the summarized imaginations in order to suggest practical changes afterwards.

Imaginations Revisited

As described above, the *kerygmatic imaginary of the public* works with the dichotomy of inner and outer sphere. This imaginary creates a filter between the private and the public that leads practically to the exclusion of the vulnerable, the fragmentary or the unready idea from theology's public: Practices of conversation informed by this imaginary are less public because they accordingly exclude people and thoughts from discourse whose statements are not elaborate enough. Exclusion happens in two ways: Informed by this imaginary and its claimed precondition for going public, one might not dare to participate in the public discourse. If one dares, one might be excluded or not taken seriously because of one's unscientific style or one's inappropriate diction. Practices of exposure informed by this imagination are less public because their complex elaboration will tend to be less understandable for many people and hence less accessible.

The approach of a "citizen theology" rightly points to the witness of the most vulnerable which is privileged in Christian narratives and hence needs to be privileged by Christian theology.[59] In this perspective, the effects of the

---

[57] Cf. Mark L. Taylor, "Subalternität und Fürsprache als Kairos für die Theologie," in *Postkoloniale Theologien: Bibelhermeneutische und kulturwissenschaftliche Beiträge*, ed. by Andreas Nehring and Simon Tielesch (Stuttgart, 2013), 289. See there also for the following description. My translation.

[58] Taylor, "Subalternität und Fürsprache als Kairos für die Theologie," 289.

[59] The previously mentioned authors of a citizen theology – Benedikt Friedrich, Hanna Reichel, and Thomas Renkert – infer from a theology of the cross that the corresponding community will have to include the vulnerable and epistemically favor the least privileged: "Das Bekenntnis zum gekreuzigten Christus, der von allen gesellschaftlichen Sicherungsinstanzen verurteilt und exkludiert auf Golgatha gestorben ist, kann daher nur um den Preis eines theologischen Selbstwiderspruchs

described kerygmatic imagination are particularly problematic. On the other hand, there are good ethical reasons for a professional academic theology that maintains certain standards in methodology, transparency of methodology, rational argumentation and distanced observation: For example, professional theology is helpful to make subtle oppression visible, to question what seems self-evidently given, and to liberate from the bondage of fundamentalism. There is no easy solution to this tension between the intention to privilege the perspective of the most vulnerable and to benefit from a professionalized theology.

The *ecclesial imaginary of the public* tends to see the religious community as the decisive public of theology. As the numbers of church-members decrease, imaginaries like these might become more attractive. Practices informed by ecclesial imaginaaries will not only exclude non-Christian perspectives. They also imagine religious communities in an idealizing way as non-violent, border-transcending, and participatory. These imaginaries are in danger of making the reality of violence, contextuality, and exclusion invisible. Accordingly, theological practices of exposure informed by this imaginarymight tend to hide the injustice and violence in religious communities. Practices of conversation might tend to silence the voices of those whose perspective does not fit the imagination of the church.

The *discursive imaginary of public theology* is favorable in the perspective of a public theology that wants to understand itself as genuinely public. Paradoxically, even this imaginary can lead to exclusion where it is actualized practically: Firstly, such imaginations, for example, when informed by Habermas' theory of discourse will favor a certain mode of speech, in Habermas' case: argumentative speech. While this helps to render the search for political or ethical consensus more inclusive and emancipative, it also excludes certain other forms of expression: untranslated, explicitly religious reasons[60] or protest.

Secondly, having its practices of exposure informed by such discourse-imaginaries, theology excludes itself from the publics that do not even vaguely

---

nicht auch den Charakter vermeintlicher Ohnmacht in der Gemeinschaft der Zeug*innen anerkennen." (Friedrich, Reichel, and Renkert, "Citizen Theology," 179). Consequently, they see theology not as purely academic endeavor, but as a form of rational reflection that happens in the academy as well as among non-professionals: They emphasize the practical knowledge embedded in the communal practices of the community of witness and the epistemic prevalence of the vulnerable; In all that, they think of the community of witness as embedded and participating in the broader society and culture (Friedrich, Reichel, and Renkert, "Citizen Theology," 180). The practical consequences of these theological reflections is a citizen theology that needs to include non-professional und privilege the vulnerable. Cf. Friedrich, Reichel, and Renkert, "Citizen Theology," 185.

[60] Cf. Jürgen Habermas, *Zwischen Naturalismus und Religion: Philosophische Aufsätze* (Frankfurt am Main: Suhrkamp, 2009), 136.

work like a Habermasian discourse: those publics created by mass media and social media. 800-page-books might not be the appropriate publication form for the age of twitter. This is ambivalent: While it is necessary, to have nuanced, differentiated, complex and rational argumentations, a broader audience might help theological ideas to have more impact. Again, there is no easy solution to this tension between the quality of a piece of work and the quantity of a public.

5. Conclusion: Towards More Public Theological Practices

How to do theology in these tensions? Let me bring this chapter to a close with three practical suggestions that try to address this question.

Theology needs more filter bubbles. Given the critic of filter bubbles[61] in digital communication, this appeal might sound odd on the one hand. On the other hand, Bernhard Pörksen has convincingly described the reality of a "*Filter Clash*" in digital networks[62]: Different perceptions, discourse-cultures, and lifestyles collide on twitter, Facebook and others platforms. The public sphere as created by mass and digital media is a rough spot, battered by shit storms. It is not necessarily the right occasion to show vulnerability and give up control of the subject matter. Precisely that is needed for what Tracy has described as conversation: a theological practice that leads to new, interesting, authentic, disturbing insights. Therefore, an exciting and inspiring public theology needs (more) non-public places, to explore thought-possibilities, to listen, to have a safe space to expose vulnerability, to formulate fragmented ideas in an environment of trust. One way to foster such places would be, to inscribe a discursive self-understanding into theological practices of retreat: Those non-public practices in which theology is produced can be imagined and instituted as discursive themselves.

Theology in Germany needs a positive imagination of dilettantes. Of course the term as strong negative connotations, so let me be precise about what I mean with it: At least the German word *Dilettant* started out with a positive meaning, referring to somebody who is enthusiastic about a field she or he does not master professionally.[63] That's a positive image for doing theology:

---

[61] For the term and its meaning see Eli Pariser, *Filter Bubble: Wie wir im Internet entmündigt werden* (München: Hanser, 2012).

[62] Bernhard Pörksen, *Die große Gereiztheit: Wege aus der kollektiven Erregung* (München: Carl Hanser Verlag, 2018), 118-123.

[63] The German word "Dilettant" refers to a "Liebhaber einer Kunst oder Wissenschaft, der sich ohne schulmäßige Ausbildung, nicht berufsmäßig damit beschäftigt. Der Begriff wurde 1774 eingedeutscht und hatte rd. für ein Jh. diese positive Bedeutung." (See "Dilettant," in Brockhaus Enzyklopädie in vierundzwanzig Bänden, 19. völlig neu bearbeitete Auflage, Band V COT-DR, Mannheim 1988, 506).

taking joy in an art one does not master. Not infrequently arguments publicly presented by public theologians are neither surprising nor unexpected.[64] The intention, to present only a "perfectly" elaborated and nuanced product tends to produce theological statements that are not very exciting. The same applies to highly sophisticated theological arguments that are insulated against all possible critiques. Of course, a well-argued, professionalized, well informed, complex, and interdisciplinary theology is needed and to be appreciated. But that could be combined with the appreciation for theological dilettantes in the public square: for those, who take joy in the art of theology they do not master professionally. The dilettantes' statements might be less informed, but sometimes more interesting. To be sure, this is not an invitation for pretenders. It is rather a call to picture the dilettante as a member of a community of theologians that are all learning at different stages in their career and life: let's imagine the dilettante not as a failure over against the "real" expert, but as a role of its own right: She or he can draw threads together, inspire with new ideas, and provide unexpected perspectives. What might practices of exposure look like that are informed by appreciation for dilettantes?

Theology may appreciate its particularities. If the theologian's participation in practices of conversation is informed by the imagination of public theology as discourse, the role of the theologian need not be limited to the position of a moderator of the discourse. As discourse and as part of discourse, theologians are free to take particular positions and to draw on their particular traditions with all their particularities. In this sense, the urge to be public is also the urge to take a position – a genuinely theological position. Maybe it is not the translation of theological insights into supposedly secular language that makes theology public – but the exposition of the wisdom, disturbance and beauty of the untranslated.

---

[64] Christian Albrecht and Reiner Anselm have rightly pointed to this danger of being "überraschungslos erwartbar" (Christian Albrecht and Reiner Anselm, *Öffentlicher Protestantismus: Zur aktuellen Debatte um gesellschaftliche Präsenz und politische Aufgaben des evangelischen Christentums* (Zürich: Theologischer Verlag Zürich, 2017), 32; Thomas Wabel, Florian Höhne, and Torben Stamer, "Klingende öffentliche Theologie: Plädoyer für eine methodische Weitung," in *Öffentliche Theologie zwischen Klang und Sprache: Hymnen als eine Verkörperungsform von Religion*, ed. by Thomas Wabel, Florian Höhne, and Torben Stamer (Leipzig: Evangelische Verlagsanstalt, 2017), 13).

Bibliography

Albrecht, Christian and Reiner Anselm. *Öffentlicher Protestantismus: Zur Aktuellen Debatte Um Gesellschaftliche Präsenz und Politische Aufgaben des evangelischen Christentums.* Zürich: Theologischer Verlag Zürich, 2017.

Bourdieu, Pierre. *Sozialer Sinn: Kritik Der Theoretischen Vernunft.* Frankfurt am Main: Suhrkamp, 1993.

Bourdieu, Pierre. *Die feinen Unterschiede: Kritik der gesellschaftlichen Urteilskraft.* With the assistance of Bernd Schwibs and Achim Russer. Frankfurt am Main: Suhrkamp, 2014.

Cavanaugh, William T. *Theopolitical Imagination: Discovering the Liturgy as a Political Act in an Age of Global Consumerism.* London and New York: Clark, 2002.

Friedrich, Benedikt, Hanna Reichel, and Thomas Renkert. "Citizen Theology: Eine Exploration Zwischen Digitalisierung und Theologischer Epistemologie." In *Digitaler Strukturwandel der Öffentlichkeit: Interdisziplinäre Perspektiven auf politische Partizipation Im Wandel*, edited by Jonas Bedford-Strohm, Florian Höhne and Julian Zeyher-Quattlender. 1. Auflage, 175–91. Baden-Baden: Nomos, 2019.

Gerhardt, Volker. *Öffentlichkeit: Die Politische Form des Bewusstseins.* München: Beck, 2012.

Grözinger, Albrecht. "Das Verständnis Von Rhetorik Und Homiletik: Bemerkungen Zum Stand Der Diskussion." *Theologia Practica* 14 (1979): 265–74.

Habermas, Jürgen. *Zwischen Naturalismus und Religion: Philosophische Aufsätze.* Frankfurt am Main: Suhrkamp, 2009.

Hillebrandt, Frank. *Soziologische Praxistheorien: Eine Einführung.* Wiesbaden: Springer, 2014. https://doi.org/10.1007/978-3-531-94097-7.

Höhne, Florian. "Öffentlichkeit" als Imagination und Ensemble sozialer Praktiken. Zur Relevanz einer Schlüsselkategorie Öffentlicher Theologie in digitalen Kontexten." *Ethik und* Gesellschaft, no. 1 (2019): 1–31. https://doi.org/10.18156/EUG-1-2019-ART-1. http://www.ethik-und-gesellschaft.de/ojs/index.php/eug/article/view/1-2019-art-1/653.

Höhne, Florian. "Wo noch? Kirche in gesellschaftlichen Öffentlichkeiten. Anmerkungen zu theopolitischen Imaginationen." In Krisen – Aufbrüche – Transformationen, ed. by Traugott Jähnchen, Jahrbuch Sozialer Protestantismus 12 (2019): 255-282.

Huber, Wolfgang. *Kirche in der Zeitenwende: Gesellschaftlicher Wandel und Erneuerung der Kirche.* Gütersloh: Verlag Bertelsmann Stiftung, 1998.

Maluleke, Tinyiko Sam. "The Elusive Public of Public Theology: A Response to William Storrar." *International Journal of Public Theology* 5 (2011): 79–89.

McElroy, Robert W. *The Search for an American Public Theology: The Contribution of John Courtney Murray.* New York: Paulist Press, 1989.

Meireis, Torsten. "Recht auf Zugang: Sozialethische Überlegungen zur Gentrifizierung des Öffentlichen Raums." In *Stadtluft Macht Reich/arm: Stadtentwicklung, soziale Ungleichheit und Raumgerechtigkeit*, edited by Bernhard Emunds, Claudia Czingon, and Michael Wolff, 201–20. Marburg: Metropolis-Verlag, 2018.

Pariser, Eli. *Filter Bubble: Wie wir im Internet entmündigt werden.* München: Hanser, 2012.

Plieninger, Martin. "Der Öffentlichkeitsauftrag der Kirche." In *Auf dem Grunde der Apostel und Propheten*, edited by Max Loeser, 250–64. Stuttgart: Quell-Verlag, 1948.

Pörksen, Bernhard. *Die Große Gereiztheit: Wege aus der Kollektiven Erregung*. München: Carl Hanser Verlag, 2018. Accessed June 20, 2018.

Pöttker, Horst. "Der Beruf zur Öffentlichkeit: Über Aufgabe, Grundsätze und Perspektiven des Journalismus in der Mediengesellschaft aus der Sicht Praktischer Vernunft." *Publizistik* 55 (2010): 107–28.

Reckwitz, Andreas. "Grundelemente einer Theorie Sozialer Praktiken: Eine Sozialtheoretische Perspektive." *Zeitschrift für Soziologie* 32, no. 4 (2003): 282–301.

Schatzki, Theodore R. *Social Practices: A Wittgensteinian Approach to Human Activity and the Social*. Cambridge: Cambridge University Press, 1996.

Schmidt, Jan-Hinrik. *Das Neue Netz: Merkmale, Praktiken und Folgen des Web 2.0*. Konstanz: UVK, 2011.

Schmidt, Robert. *Soziologie Der Praktiken: Konzeptionelle Studien und Empirische Analysen*. Erste Auflage. Suhrkamp Taschenbuch Wissenschaft 2030. Berlin: Suhrkamp, 2012.

Taylor, Charles. *Modern Social Imaginaries*. Durham: Duke University Press, 2004.

Taylor, Mark Lewis. "Subalternität und Fürsprache als Kairos für die Theologie." In *Postkoloniale Theologien: Bibelhermeneutische und kulturwissenschaftliche Beiträge*, edited by Andreas Nehring and Simon Tielesch. 276–99. Stuttgart: Kohlhammer, 2013.

Tracy, David. "Theology as Public Discourse." *The Christian Century*, 1975, 280–84.

Tracy, David. *The Analogical Imagination: Christian Theology and the Culture of Pluralism*. London: SCM Press, 1981. (Accessed August 14, 2012)

Tracy, David. "Three Kinds of Publicness in Public Theology." *International Journal of Public Theology* 8, no. 3 (2014): 330–34. https://doi.org/10.1163/15697320-12341354.

van Oorschot, Friederike, and Simone Ziermann. *Theologie in Übersetzung? Religiöse Sprache und Kommunikation in Heterogenen Kontexten*. Öffentliche Theologie (ÖTh) 36. Leipzig: Evangelische Verlagsanstalt, 2019.

Wabel, Thomas, Florian Höhne, and Torben Stamer. "Klingende Öffentliche Theologie: Plädoyer für eine Methodische Weitung." In *Öffentliche Theologie zwischen Klang und Sprache: Hymnen als eine Verkörperungsform von Religion*, edited by Thomas Wabel, Florian Höhne and Torben Stamer. 9–40. Leipzig: Evangelische Verlagsanstalt, 2017.

Wannenwetsch, Bernd. *Gottesdienst als Lebensform - Ethik für Christenbürger*. Stuttgart, Berlin, Köln: Kohlhammer, 1997.

Wustmans, Clemens. "Plain Language as Empowerment Beyond a Faithful Middle-Class Public: Contributions of Public Theology to the Capability Approach of Social Justice." In *Religion and Democracy: Studies in Public Theology*, edited by Torsten Meireis and Rolf Schieder, 143–53. Baden-Baden, Germany: Nomos, 2017.

Public Theology in Ethiopia

State, Church, and Neighbour-Love

Andrew DeCort (Chicago, USA; Addis Ababa, Ethiopia)

1. Introduction: What Does Christian Theology Do in Ethopian Public Life?

What does theology do in Ethiopia? More specifically for this chapter, what does Christian theology do in Ethiopian public life?

Theology can numb people to injustice and train them to comply with tyranny. It can do this by teaching that God is with the powerful and calls us to obey them as his representatives. Theology can train people to pray and hope for a miracle while they mind their own business and accept a status quo that causes suffering for others. It can do this by teaching that only God can intervene and change our circumstances. Theology can also remind people that they are neighbours and called to love one another across every division. It can do this by teaching that God created and loves each and every person across the human-made identities and divisions we construct. In this way, theology can give us new lenses for seeing the world as God's gift, the other as a reflection of God's own dignity, and thus our life together as a sacred calling to respect and serve the poorest and most vulnerable. Here we are energized with a practical commitment to work for a new future in which responsibility is reborn and hope comes alive.

This question – what does Christian theology do in Ethiopian public life? – is practical, important, and even urgent for at least three interrelated reasons.

First, Ethiopians are overwhelmingly religious people. In 2017, the Pew Forum found that 98% of Ethiopian Orthodox Christians (approximately 50 million people or 44% of the population) answered that their faith is "very important" to them.[1] This makes Ethiopia one of the most intensely religious countries in the world. There is little reason to assume that Ethiopian Muslims (approximately 34%) and Evangelicals (approximately 19%) would attribute less importance to their respective faiths. Taken together, 97% of Ethiopians claim identity-shaping allegiance either to Orthodox Christianity, Islam, or

[1] See Pew Forum, "Orthodox Christians Are Highly Religious in Ethiopia," November 8, 2017 at http://www.pewforum.org/2017/11/08/orthodox-christians-are-highly-religious-in-ethiopia-much-less-so-in-former-soviet-union/.

Evangelical Christianity.[2] By 2050, estimates indicate that Ethiopia will be home to the largest Orthodox population in the world and one of the five largest Evangelical populations in the world.[3] It is impossible to understand Ethiopian society without appreciating the profound influence of religious faith and the theology that defines it.

Second, Christian theology in Ethiopia is understood as the preaching of God's absolute will, and it is held in great reverence. Theology is literally "the word of God," and the role of human mediation, interpretation, and potential distortion of God's word is not emphasized. This means that theology as it is preached and taught in churches, schools, stadiums, televisions, and computer screens wields enormous authority for shaping Ethiopian attitudes, opinions, and actions. Theology is the primary normative guide for how people think they ought to feel, speak, and behave.

Third, Ethiopia is passing through an extended national crisis dating back to 2015 and before. Some analysts fear civil war or genocide remains possible, and disturbing comparisons have been made between Ethiopia now and Rwanda in 1994.[4] The Ethiopian New Testament scholar and theologian Dr. Desta Heliso has written, "While I try to remain hopeful, I feel that our country is in mortal danger."[5]

Ethnic hostility is rapidly spreading and causing massive polarization, conflict, and suffering.[6] The Internal Displacement Monitoring Centre reported on May 11 that Ethiopia has the highest level of displacement in the world with over three million Ethiopians living as internally displaced persons to-

---

[2] These numbers are dated, since the last national census took place in 2007. An updated census was scheduled for 2019 but has been postponed for a third time due to political instability. For perspectives on these traditions, cf. Ephraim Isaac, *The Ethiopian Orthodox Tawahido Church* (Trenton: Red Sea Press, 2012); Patrick Desplat and Terje Østebø, *Muslim Ethiopia: The Christian Legacy, Identity Politics, and Islamic Reformism* (New York: Palgrave Macmillan, 2013); Tibebe Eshete, *The Evangelical Movement in Ethiopia: Resistance and Resilience* (Baylor: Baylor University Press, 2009).

[3] Cf. Patrick Johnstone, *The Future of the Global Church* (Downers Grove: Intervarsity Press, 2011), 75, 107, 109, 145.

[4] On the twenty-fifth anniversary of the Rwandan genocide, The Reporter, a respected newspaper in Ethiopia, published a sobering editorial entitled "Lest the Rwanda Genocide Be Repeated in Ethiopia!," *The Reporter*, April 13, 2019, https://www.thereporterethiopia.com. For a more controversial perspective, cf. Dawit Woldegiorgis, "Ethiopia: A Country on the Brinks," borkena.com, April 10, 2019, https://borkena.com.

[5] Desta Heliso, "Warlordism in Ethiopia?," *The Reporter*, July 6, 2019, https://www.thereporterethiopia.com/article/warlordism-ethiopia.

[6] Temesgen Tiruneh, national security advisor to Prime Minister Abiy Ahmed, has said, "It is radical nationalism that is the current national security threat of Ethiopia." Cf. Brook Abdu, "Ethnic Politics: The Peril of Ethiopia?," *The Reporter*, April 13, 2019, https://www.thereporterethiopia.com/article/ethnic-politics-peril-ethiopia.

day.[7] Photographs from 2018 of public killings in urban centres (for example, Shashemane and Hawassa), in which individuals were dragged through the streets, lynched, and burned alive with large crowds watching, graphically illustrate the severity of the problem. According to the Inter-Religious Council of Ethiopia, "Our Ethiopian value, which accepts others based on their humanity, is being eroded at an alarming rate."[8]

Amidst this larger crisis of ethnic conflict and displacement, violence and lawlessness are rising.[9] Mass corruption has been exposed, and government control is weakened in various parts of the country.[10] The thirty million youth between the ages of fifteen and twenty-nine are facing a crisis of joblessness and discontent, which is fuelling frustration and unrest.[11] With nearly one in three Ethiopians living on under $1.25 a day, poverty and human suffering remain enormous challenges attacking human dignity, wellbeing, and hope.[12]

In this very serious situation, the way people feel, think, speak, and act is extremely important and has enormous significance for the future of Ethiopia. And the way people feel, think, speak, and act is profoundly influenced by their religious or theological convictions – what they believe to be the will and word of God for themselves and their society.

In short, then, theology does enormous work in Ethiopia, for better and worse. Like any other context, some people may be nominal and/or committed to competing interpretations of what their theology requires. But theology has great power and potential to shape how Ethiopian people understand and engage their society in a crucial transitional moment, amidst the larger human quest for truth. This is indicated in Prime Minister Abiy's decision to appoint a religious leader, Cardinal Berhaneyesus Demerew Souraphiel of the Ethiopi-

---

[7] Cf. IDMC, "Ethiopia," released May 11, 2019, http://www.internal-displacement.org/countries/ethiopia.

[8] Untitled press release from the Ethiopian Catholic Secretariat on behalf of the Inter-Religious Council of Ethiopia on January 1, 2019. For the Amharic text, cf. http://www.ecsethiopia.com.

[9] Cf. Woldegiorgis, "Ethiopia." On April 5, 2019, the UN Department of Safety and Security published a "Security Advisory" with the subject line "Crime incidents mounting in Addis Ababa." Cf. https://mereja.com.

[10] Cf. Hayalnesh Gezahegn, "Security Forces Ordered to Take Measures as Weekend Violence Claims Lives," *Addis Standard*, April 8, 2019, https://addisstandard.com. On recent corruption, cf. George Obulutsa, "Ethiopia Arrests 59 Officials over Corruption, Economic Sabotage," *Reuters*, April 12, 2019, https://www.reuters.com.

[11] Cf. Samuel Alemu, "Unemployment in Ethiopia: Socio-Political Implications," *The Reporter*, July 28, 2018, https://www.thereporterethiopia.com. Cf. also USAID, "Fact Sheet: Developing Ethiopia's Youth," July 2017, https://www.usaid.gov.

[12] Cf. The World Bank's "Ethiopia Poverty Assessment" from 2014 at http://www.worldbank.org/en/topic/poverty/publication/ethiopia-poverty-assessment.

an Catholic Church, to head Ethiopia's recently established Reconciliation Commission.[13]

So, we can sharpen our question: What does Christian theology do in a time of national socio-political crisis?

2. The Kairos Document as Framework: State, Church, and Prophetic Theology

South African theologians wrestled with this question during Apartheid, and we can use their 1985 Kairos Document as a loose framework for interpreting Ethiopian public theology today.[14]

In short, the Kairos theologians analysed three kinds of theology with three different effects on society in the midst of what they call "life and death conflict."[15] They wrote, "we sit in the same Church while outside Christian policemen and soldiers are beating up and killing Christian children or torturing Christian prisoners to death while yet other Christians stand by and weakly plead for peace." (252) They see these three different theologies as explaining these societal contradictions and conflicting theological effects within Christianity itself.

First, "state theology" is a "justification of the status quo" that "canonizes the will of the powerful and reduces the poor to passivity, obedience, and apathy." (252) State theology misuses Scripture and theology "to give an absolute and 'divine' authority to the State." (252) The Kairos theologians argue that state theology errs in prioritizing the strong over the weak against God's will revealed in Christ. (Luke 1:51-52)

Second, "church theology" is cautiously critical of apartheid's injustice, but it consists of a superficial repetition of "stock ideas" like "reconciliation" without being committed to real justice for the oppressed. The Kairos theologians see "church theology" as rooted in a spirituality that is otherworldly, individualistic, and passive (261). It seeks change only through divine intervention via prayer and doesn't engage human agency and responsibility. It

---

[13] Cf. Fana Broadcast Corporate, "Reconciliation Commission Announces Three-Year Plan," April 30, 2019, https://fanabc.com. This news article outlines the powers and duties of the Commission.

[14] I am grateful to Dr. Theodros A. Teklu, lecturer in theology and ethics at the Ethiopian Graduate School of Theology, for suggesting that I use the Kairos Document as a framework for thinking about Ethiopian public theology. Cf. his *Public Theology and the State, African Public Theology* (Carlisle: Langham Publishers, forthcoming).

[15] "The Kairos Document," in *Between Christ and Caesar: Classic and Contemporary Texts on Church and State*, ed. by Charles Villa-Vicencio (Grand Rapids: W. B. Eerdmans and Cape Town, South Africa: David Philips, 1986), 251. Parenthetical numbers henceforth refer to this text.

sees "social and political matters[. . .]as worldly affairs that have nothing to do with the spiritual concerns of the Church," and the result is "paralysis." (261)

Third, "prophetic theology" is characterized by four practices: (1) contextual social analysis rather than abstract principles, (2) the embrace of the Bible's critique of oppression and identification of God with the oppressed, (3) the embrace of the Christian tradition's condemnation of tyranny and affirmation of the right of resistance for the sake of just government, and (4) the declaration of ultimate hope in God's promise of true liberation and his presence with the oppressed now. The Kairos theologians do not use the language of "public theology," but their "prophetic theology" is clearly committed to envisioning and serving "a just society" in which all people can flourish as God's image-bearers (267).[16] It calls upon the church to condemn evil, to call for repentance, and to mobilize practical action to resist injustice and serve the common good.

The Ethiopian context may be more complicated than South African apartheid, since the Kairos Document's binary of oppressors and oppressed has become more ambiguous as non-state injustice and violence take place in Ethiopian society, largely along ethnic lines. Still, we can use the Kairos Document as a helpful framework for interpreting Ethiopian public theology.

3. The Work of Christian Theologies in Ethiopian Public Life: Three Options

Orthodox Theology as a State Theology

First, the Ethiopian Tewehado Orthodox theological tradition can be broadly described as a state theology, which may authorize the status quo and teach believers to be submissive to the state. Of course, the Orthodox tradition is not monolithic or static, and it has produced inspiring prophetic leaders. Still, this broad description may be applicable.

This state theology helps explain why the hierarchy of the Orthodox Church has made limited responses during several years of public crisis.[17] Its

[16] When I use "public theology," I have in mind Max Stackhouse's broad description in "Civil Religion, Political Theology, and Public Theology: What's the Difference?" *Political Theology* 5, no. 3 (2004): 284: "[Public theology] was rooted in the interaction of biblical insight, philosophical analysis, and the responsibility of the ecclesial community to engage in historical discernment of and constant reformation of the social order because it believed that certain kinds of [non-utopian] progress could be made in human affairs."

[17] For example, cf. Zecharias Zelalem, "Woldia Massacre: Ethiopian Security Forces Kill a Dozen, Turning a Holiday Procession into Nightmare," *OPride*, January 22, 2018, https://www.opride.com: "there have been no public statements or messages of condolences by anyone affiliated to the Church's governing body or the Patriarch Abune Mathias."

few public statements have not boldly challenged state injustice or called for practical action among the faithful in addition to fasting and prayer.[18] Soon after a nation-wide state of emergency ended in 2017, the New York Times reported that a rural Orthodox priest was telling his village "that they will 'benefit in heaven and on earth,' if they join the governing party."[19] Of course, this is a single anecdote that should not be over-interpreted. Still, Orthodox Christians have expressed concern that their church may be too closely aligned with political power.

This state theology is rooted in the *Kebra Negast* (*Glory of Kings*) saga, which is among the most authoritative theological texts for the Ethiopian Orthodox Church outside the Bible. In the *Kebra Negast*, God is the King of the universe, and God has appointed human kings to rule on God's behalf over earthly kingdoms.[20] Its central narrative tells the famous story of the Queen of Sheba's visit to King Solomon in Jerusalem, how Queen Makeda became pregnant with Solomon's son, how the Ark of the Covenant was taken to Ethiopia, and how God's covenant with Israel was transferred to the Ethiopian monarchy beginning with Makeda's son David II or Menelik I.

In the thirty-sixth chapter, the elders of Israel submissively ask King Solomon, "Who can resist the command of God and the King?"[21] They vow that even if the king were to ask them to sell their children as slaves, they would obey. In the thirty-seventh chapter, David II is then anointed king of Ethiopia with "the oil of kingship" in the Holy of Holies.[22] The chief priest Zadok promises that for the obedient king, "God shall perform your will in everything that you desire," making the king's enemies "terrified at the sight of your dreadful

---

[18] Cf. Mengisteab Teshome and Haftu Gebreegziabher, "Religious Fathers Convey New Year's Messages," *Ethiopian Herald*, September 11, 2016, http://www.ethpress.gov.et; Francesca Merlo, "16 Days of Prayer for Peace in Ethiopia," *Vatican News*, August 8, 2018, https://www.vaticannews.va/en; untitled press release (Amharic) from the Ethiopian Catholic Secretariat on behalf of the Inter-Religious Council of Ethiopia on January 1, 2019, which made a ten-point statement concerning "Peace for All by All" at http://www.ecsethiopia.com.

[19] Kimiko de Freytas-Tamura, "'We Are Everywhere': How Ethiopia Became a Land of Prying Eyes," *New York Times*, November 5, 2017.

[20] Cf. *Kebra Negast*, trans. Miguel Brooks (Kingston: LMH Publishing, 2001), 57: "And the whole earth, the heavens, and the ends of the world, the sea and the dry land are the kingdom of God. He judges. And he has given the earth to the King to be subject unto him, that he may judge those who do evil, and those who do good he may reward them with good."

[21] *Kebra Negast*, 45.

[22] *Kebra Negast*, 45. The priests declare in the hearing of the city that the Law of God will be the king's guide and that, "All your enemies and foes shall be overthrown before you, and completion and perfection shall be unto you and your seed after you; you shall judge many nations and none shall judge you. The blessing of heaven and earth shall be your blessing."

majesty."[23] Chapter 41 elaborates this theology of kingship: "the Spirit of God rests in the heart of the king, and [God's] hands are in his mind, and His knowledge is in his understanding."[24]

Chapter 42 spells out the theological and profoundly political implication: "It is not a good thing to revile the king, for he is the anointed of God[. . .] It is not a good thing for any of those who are under the dominion of a king to revile him, for retribution belongs to God."[25] The king is God's sovereign representative, and he must not be challenged. The *Fetha Negast* (*Law of Kings*) – Ethiopia's medieval Christian law code – adds, "he who rises against the king deserves punishment, even if he is his son or friend."[26]

Here we see a clear articulation of state theology. God is the cosmic King; the human king is God's earthly representative; thus, the king must not be challenged, because obedience to the king means obedience to God. The people must be exclusively submissive and obedient to political authority. It was precisely on this theological basis that Emperor Haile Selassie (r. 1930-1974) declared in his 1931 Constitution, "the person of the Emperor is sacred, His dignity inviolable, and His power indisputable."[27]

The *Kebra Negast* allows one exception to this theological vision of indisputable power. Priests are given permission to hold the king accountable to God's word: "a priest who has in him understanding rebukes the king concerning the work he has seen[. . .] O priest, if you see sin in a well-known man, do not hesitate to rebuke him; let neither sword nor exile make you afraid."[28] However, accounts of critical priests being suppressed, tortured, and killed by the state and church hierarchy may not have encouraged the exercise of this priestly duty.[29] Aba Estifanos (1380-1450), who used Scripture to publicly critique the absolutist rule of Emperor Zara Yaqob and died of torture, is a notable example.[30] Abuna Petros (1892-1936) and Abuna Tewoflos (1910-

[23] *Kebra Negast*, 48.
[24] *Kebra Negast*, 57.
[25] *Kebra Negast*, 57.
[26] *Fetha Nagast*: The Law of the Kings, ed. by Peter Strauss (Jamaica: Miguel Lorne Publishers, 2008), 56. Ch. XII "On Mass" (see page 83) requires that the king be prayed for at Mass.
[27] Constitution of Ethiopia (1931), Article 5, https://www.worldstatesmen.org.
[28] *Kebra Negast*, 57-58. The *Fetha Negast* states that "any bishop or minister of the church" who approaches the king without the permission of his ecclesial superior will be excommunicated and "deprived of the honor he used to have" (41, 45). To what extent would this regulation discourage priests from carrying out their divine duty of critiquing the king for injustice?
[29] The *Kebra Negast* also notes that "the people must not revile the priests, for they are the children of God and the men of His house" (58). The *Fetha Negast* also reinforces the unquestionability of priests. See 56 (Ch. IX On Priests, Section III On Ranks).
[30] Cf. *The Ge'ez Acts of Abba Estifanos of Gwendawende*, trans. by Getachew Haile, Scriptores Aethiopici Tomus 111 (Leuven: Aedibus Peeters, 2006); Maimire Mennasemay, "A Critical Dialogue Between Fifteenth and Twenty First Century

1979) are examples of Orthodox Patriarchs who have courageously challenged state (foreign and domestic) injustice at the cost of their lives.[31]

Of course, much has changed over the centuries, and Ethiopia is now governed by a secular regime whose ideology is called "revolutionary democracy." But the *Kebra Negast* remains authoritative in the Orthodox Church, and its "state theology" of near total submission to the ruler may help make sense of the Church's limited public leadership during these years of crisis when religious leadership has been urgently needed. The implicit and sometimes explicit message of the church has been, "Be silent and accept the way things are as God's will," as noted above. We are seeing that the vacuum of strong Church leadership has not resulted in peace but increased anger, lawlessness, and violence.

Evangelical Theology as a Church Theology

Second, the Evangelical and/or Pentecostal theological movement can be broadly described as promoting a church theology in Ethiopian society. Again, it is important to be wary of monolithic and static interpretations. Still, Ethiopian Evangelical spirituality has emphasized otherworldly, individualistic, and passive orientations. It frequently affirms that the world is not our home and that change is only possible through God's intervention. Thus, rather than calling for prophetic speech or organizing action beyond the walls of the church for justice in society, it calls the faithful to pray, fast, and hope for a miracle.[32]

This theology helps explain why the leading Protestant denominations in Ethiopia have been largely silent and invisible during these years of crisis. The few denominational statements that were made came late, avoided referring to any specific injustices, and neglected to map any concrete action plans for real change.[33]

Ethiopia," *The International Journal of Ethiopian Studies* 5, no. 1: 1-37; and Andrew DeCort, "Authority, Martyrdom, and the Question of Axiality in Ethiopian Political Theology: From Ancient Aksum to Abba Estifanos toward Addis Ababa," *The Journal of Ethiopian Religious Studies* (forthcoming).

[31] Cf. Mersha Alehegne, "Abune Petros," *Encyclopedia Aethiopica* 4, ed. by Siegbert Uhlig (Wiesbaden: Harrassowitz Verlag, 2011), 140-41, and Dirshaye Menberu, "Tewoflos (B)," on the Dictionary of African Christian Biography website at https://dacb.org.

[32] Cf. Rich Hansen (former professor of systematic theology at the Ethiopian Graduate School of Theology), "Transforming the Dualistic Worldview of Ethiopian Evangelical Christians," *International Bulletin of Missionary Research* 39, no. 3 (2015): 138-41.

[33] For an outline and discussion of official church responses, cf. Andrew DeCort, "On Human Flourishing: A Call for Public Responsibility in Contemporary Ethiopian Christianity," in *A Church for The World: The Church's Role in Fostering Democracy and Sustainable Development*, ed. by Samuel Yonas Deressa and Josh de Keijzer (Minneapolis: Fortress Press, forthcoming). The Ethiopian Catholic Church issued "A Call for Peaceful Dialogue to Resolve Conflicts" in a press conference led by Cardinal

I taught theology and ethics at the Ethiopian Graduate School of Theology in Addis Ababa from 2016 to 2018. During this time, Ethiopia suffered two states of emergency, the public killing of hundreds of citizens, and the arrest of thousands of others. In each of my classes, I required all of my students to conduct and write up an "ecclesiography." These compact studies of their churches' preaching and practice were based on fifteen weeks of detailed participant observation in their local congregations and represented the major denominations and independent churches in Ethiopia, including Mulu Wongel, Mekane Yesus, and Kale Heywet. In over eighty reports, I cannot remember a single paper that described a local church with any active preaching or practice related to social justice and how Ethiopian Christians should respond to the socio-political crisis. Students repeatedly reported that their churches were either silent on the crisis or restricted themselves to calling for prayers for peace.

Several of my students were frustrated by this and wrote critical evaluations of their churches' silence and passivity in the face of the extreme injustice and human suffering in their society. A student who worked as a federal prosecutor articulately summarized the dominant pattern among my students' ecclesiographic research. Their observations are worth quoting at length:

> There is great chaos in the country [. . .] which resulted in great suffering for millions of people, including women and children [. . .] But I have never seen the church trying to help, collect offerings, sending clothes or anything to anyone who suffered from natural or manmade crisis [. . .] the church is not serving her purpose, and I am afraid God is not accepting our rituals (Amos 5:21-24) [. . .] The church is so passive in relation to the socio-political concerns of the society. All the church has been doing is pray, and the church has used the prayer as an excuse for her inactiveness. The leaders and the congregations don't realize that prayer doesn't replace action. Some of the leaders and members who have some affiliations with the ruling party somehow try to influence others to believe everything is ok. But injustice and violence is not ok.[34]

Berhaneyesus on August 15, 2016 many months into the crisis and eleven days after the first State of Emergency was declared. In mid-September 2016, the Full-Gospel Believers' Church posted a 3-page "Statement of the EFGBC Concerning the Current Situation of Our Country." On February 24, 2018 – during the second State of Emergency and long after various public massacres – the Ethiopian Evangelical Churches Mekane Yesus (EECMY) published a 2-page statement on its social media platform entitled "A Call from EECMY regarding the Current Situation of our Country." On March 26, 2018, the Ethiopian Kale Heywet Church posted to its social media platform a statement with an introduction and ten paragraphs on "the current problems of our country."

[34] Ecclesiography from Introduction to Christian Ethics. No further information is given to protect the author's anonymity.

I experienced a dramatic example of "prayer replacing action" at a large and influential church in Addis on the Sunday of September 16, 2018. In what later came to be known as the Burayu massacre, a major political demonstration was taking place in the city that weekend, and the night before reports started emerging that youth were killing people from certain ethnic groups in specific areas of the city and its outskirts. At church that Sunday, this is how a pastor responded to the situation from the stage:

> I got some calls and texts this morning. There have been a few conflicts and some displaced people and whatnot on the outskirts of the city. It's God's job from now on. We leave it in God's hands. We just watch You [God] fight for us. Let's sing a prophetic song. We put an end to it right now. We declare that it is over right now.[35]

It was later revealed that as many as two hundred people were slaughtered that weekend with gruesome pictures of bodies dumped in the streets and garbage cans.[36] But the pastor's response was only to call the church to sing more passionately in church and "leave it in God's hands."

To be fair, the pastor may not have known the full scope of what was unfolding. But his response was revealing and crystalized what the Kairos theologians called "church theology." The message was clear that God alone has real agency and that we trigger God's intervention by singing and praying. When the Sunday service ended, nothing further was said about the massacre taking place in the city. In the logic of this theological outlook, it had already been forgotten or simply solved by the congregation's singing to God in the safety of the church on the other side of town. No invocation of human responsibility or call for action was made. In the church's weekly updates thereafter, no mention was made of the Burayu massacre.

This example illustrates how "church theology" can do powerful work in Ethiopian public life. It encourages millions of Evangelical Christians to fast, pray, and sing in church in the face of socio-political crisis. It doesn't appear to call them to speak or act for justice and the defence of vulnerable neighbours. Its interventionist vision of God de-emphasizes a thick view of human agency and responsibility. As a Christian myself, I believe in the great importance and power of prayer. But as Dr. Martin Luther King, Jr. noted, prayer is a "necessary supplement" to but a "dangerous substitute" for our human responsibility to serve God's will for justice.[37]

---

[35] From field notes I recorded at the service on September 16, 2018.

[36] The numbers are highly disputed. The official death count was around sixty. An official at the U.S. Embassy told me that representatives from local hospitals said the number was as high as two hundred.

[37] Martin Luther King, Jr., "The Answer to a Perplexing Question," *Strength to Love* (Minneapolis: Fortress Press, 2010), 133-43, 138. For the prophets' critique of prayer without advocacy for justice and mercy in society, see Isaiah 1:10:17 and 58:1-14.

Neighbour-Love as a Prophetic Public Theology

Third, prophetic public theology can expand our vision of human responsibility and energize speech and action for human flourishing in Ethiopian public life. It can do this by re-voicing the radical biblical theology of neighbour-love: "Love your neighbour as yourself."[38]

The way we see others produces the society we see, and neighbour-love calls for a fundamental transformation in how we see others. Through the lens of neighbour-love, we no longer see others as insiders, outsiders, and enemies based upon ethnic, religious, and political identity markers. Instead, we see each and every person as a neighbour who bears precious value in the image of God. Every person is our neighbour across every manmade division. We hear a call from God to will and work for our neighbours' wellbeing in all that we say and do, for this is the biblical meaning of "love".[39]

This theology of neighbour-love has profound implications for public life. In the same way that we desire justice under the law when we are mistreated or oppressed, neighbour-love calls us to promote and defend justice under the law courageously for our neighbours when they experience mistreatment and injustice. In the same way that we desire generosity and empowerment when we are vulnerable and in need, neighbour-love calls us to organize and energize action for our neighbours' protection and wellbeing. More broadly, neighbour-love calls for speech and action marked by respect, kindness, and compassion between people in everyday life and work. It breaks down stereotypes, suspicion, and separation by calling us to know and love one another in our human uniqueness and universality.

Yes, we should respect authority under the law (the emphasis of state theology) and, yes, we should pray without ceasing (the emphasis of church theology). But as we do so, loving our neighbours as ourselves does not allow us to remain silent, passive, or detached when injustice and suffering attack our neighbours' wellbeing, especially neighbours who are different from us or seen as "enemies" in wider culture (see Luke 10:25-37). Neighbour-love means that the people outside our church and beyond our ethnic group must matter to us as equally as ourselves.

Rather than a sectarian message, the theology of neighbour-love powerfully unites the Orthodox, Islamic, and Evangelical traditions of Ethiopia in a

---

[38] Cf. Leviticus 19:18, 34; Matthew 5:38-48; Matthew 7:12; 19:16-30; 22:39-40; 28:19-20; Luke 6:27-46; 10:25-37; Mark 12:31-35; John 13:34-34-35; Romans 13:9-10; 15:1-7; Galatians 5:6, 13-15; 1 Corinthians 13:1-3; 16:14; James 2:1-13; 4:12.

[39] Cf. Lenn Goodman, *Love Thy Neighbour As Thyself* (New York and Oxford: Oxford University Press, 2008), and Mark Labberton, *The Dangerous Act of Loving Your Neighbour: Seeing Others Through the Eyes of Jesus* (Downers Grove: Intervarsity Press, 2010).

shared moral imagination and imperative.[40] Neighbour-love is also at the heart of democratic values in which each and every life matters equally under the law. In this way, neighbour-love has rich potential to put theology to work for a public life of responsibility and flourishing for all people in Ethiopia.

In the Orthodox tradition, we see seeds of this theology in the Kebra Negast's call for priests to hold public leaders accountable to justice and in the ministry of the 15th century monk Aba Estifanos who challenged the authoritarianism of the emperor on the basis of neighbour-love.[41] The Fetha Negast powerfully declares,

> Respect others more than yourself, and be the brother of all[. . .] A person shall not consider himself a Christian nor say he is a Christian, while he himself is given to quarrels and does not obey the precepts of Christ. Such a person is like one who takes a bath in a place full of dirt.[42]

In the Evangelical tradition, we see seeds of prophetic public theology in the ministry of Gudina Tumsa, "Ethiopia's Bonhoeffer," who was killed by the Marxist Derg in 1979.[43] The theological statements of the Protestant churches today have called for peace, justice, and respect between people, and these should be built upon. Evangelical theologians are emerging who are exploring the implications of faith for human relationship, ethnic identity, academics, and society.[44]

Dr. Christoph Schneider-Yattara, country director of Bread for the World in Ethiopia, has articulated the importance of fresh theological imagination for Ethiopia's present and future:

> New [theological] ideas are absolutely needed. The mainline churches are not prophetic. The last prophetic leader in Ethiopia was Gudina Tumsa [d. 1979][. . .] The young people are moving out and it's getting worse – to the prosperity gos-

---

[40] Cf. Leviticus 19:18; Matthew 22:39-40; Quran an-Nisa 4:36; *Fetha Nagast, 78 and James Walters, Loving Your Neighbour in an Age of Religious Conflict: A New Agenda for Interfaith Relations* (London: Jessica Kingsley Publishers, 2019).

[41] Cf. *The Ge'ez Acts of Abba Estifanos of Gwendawende*, trans. by Getachew Haile, Scriptores Aethiopici Tomus 111 (Leuven: Aedibus Peeters, 2006), 28. Estifanos is a fascinating figure, because he is claimed as an inspiration for both Orthodox and Evangelical Christians.

[42] Fetha Nagast, *The Law of the Kings* (Jamaica: Miguel Lorne Publishers, 2008), 78.

[43] Cf. Samuel Yonas, *The Life, Works, and Witness of Tsehay Tolessa and Gudina Tumsa, the Ethiopian Bonhoeffer* (Minneapolis: Fortress Press, 2017).

[44] Cf. Theodros Teklu, *The Politics of Metanoia: Towards a Post-Nationalistic Political Theology in Ethiopia* (Frankfurt am Main: Peter Lang, 2014); Desta Heliso, "The Relevance of the Study of Religion in Ethiopian Context," *The Reporter*, July 28, 2017, https://www.thereporterethiopia.com; Yodit TARIKU, "Political Theology of the Neighbour: Reflections from Saint Maximus the Confessor Towards Challenging Violence" (Addis Ababa: Unpublished MABTS thesis at the Ethiopian Graduate School of Theology, 2016).

> pel. Ethiopia is at an already-but-not-yet: the old is gone, but the new hasn't come yet. Everything is emotional and resorts to violence. You can watch history pass you by, or you can be part of it.[45]

"Being part of it" is what my colleague Dr. Tekalign Nega Angore and I are attempting to do. We are currently developing the Neighbour-Love Movement ("Balinjeraye," Amharic for "My Neighbour"), which aims to promote the theological vision of neighbour-love in Ethiopia's theological institutions and public life through teaching, dialogue, and social media.[46] We are launching an Amharic video course on neighbour-love, the first Amharic book on neighbour-love, and workshops around the country.[47] Our vision is to use ecumenical theological resources and democratic values to inspire Ethiopian youth to become ambassadors of neighbour-love in this critical moment when the future of Ethiopia is being decided. Our mission is to inspire love, justice, and flourishing for all neighbours across every boundary.

4. Conclusion: "Do This and You Will Live"

In this chapter, I have tried to unpack three claims.

First, theology does profound work in shaping Ethiopian attitudes, opinions, and actions in relation to public life. Theology has enormous power in Ethiopia, particularly because it is commonly understood as the preaching of God's absolute word and thus the primary source for normative moral imagination and order.

Second, following the Kairos theologians' framework, the dominant strands of Ethiopian public theology can be described broadly as "state theology" or "church theology." One way or another, Orthodox and Evangelical theologies too often lead to silence and passivity in the face of injustice and public crisis. This has been observed in the void of compelling Christian leadership in these recent years of alarming upheaval. I have also pointed out inspiring counter-examples and promising seeds of growth in both traditions.

Third, an important task for Ethiopian theologians across traditions today is to articulate a prophetic public theology. I have suggested that the Bible's theology of neighbour-love may serve as a uniting, energizing core for this public theology. Neighbour-love can help Ethiopian Christians, Muslims, and all citizens understand the value of others as neighbours across differences of

---

[45] Christoph Schneider-Yattara, unpublished interview with the author on October 19, 2018 at Bread for the World's office in Addis Ababa.

[46] Cf. Andrew DeCort, "Ethics During Crisis: From Missed Chances to Neighbour-Love," *The Ethiopian Herald*, February 20, 2018, www.press.et.

[47] Cf. www.balinjeraye.org and #Balinjeraye on Facebook, Twitter, Instagram, YouTube, and Telegram.

identity. It can also guide us into the practical exercise of compassion and justice, and motivate us with passion and courage to do this work when hatred and injustice seem insurmountable. It would be exciting to see Ethiopian theologians produce their own Kairos Document and for the Neighbour-Love Movement to flourish.

Theology can be a transformative, deeply inspiring discipline that reminds us that we are not self-created and not meant to live solely for ourselves. It calls us to ask self-transcendent questions like who is God, what does God desire for humanity, and how should we live in relation to others? And it can offer profound and practical answers: God is the Creator of all people, God desires for humanity to flourish, and we become fully alive when we love one another as neighbours across every division.

In these dark times, we are given courage by the promise of Jesus, who said, "Do this [love God and your neighbour], and you will live" (Luke 10:28).

Bibliography

n.b. Ethiopians use their first names to refer to their work. This custom has been followed here. Also, due to the instability of weblinks to the Ethiopian news media and ecclesiastical materials cited in this chapter, only links to the sources' main sites are given. For copies of any of those materials, readers are invited to contact the author

Brook Abdu. "Ethnic Politics: The Peril of Ethiopia?" *The Reporter*, April 13, 2019. https://www.thereporterethiopia.com/article/ethnic-politics-peril-ethiopia.

Constitution of Ethiopia (1931), https://www.worldstatesmen.org.

Dawit Woldegiorgis. "Ethiopia: A Country on the Brinks," *borcena.com*, April 10, 2019, https://borkena.com.

de Freytas-Tamura, Kimiko. "'We Are Everywhere': How Ethiopia Became a Land of Prying Eyes." *New York Times*, November 5, 2017.

DeCort, Andrew. "Ethics During Crisis: From Missed Chances to Neighbour-Love." *The Ethiopian Herald*, February 20, 2018. www.press.et.

DeCort, Andrew. "Authority, Martyrdom, and the Question of Axiality in Ethiopian Political Theology: From Ancient Aksum to Abba Estifanos toward Addis Ababa." *The Journal of Ethiopian Religious Studies* (forthcoming).

DeCort, Andrew. "On Human Flourishing: A Call for Public Responsibility in Contemporary Ethiopian Christianity." In *A Church For The World: The Church's Role in Fostering Democracy and Sustainable Development*, edited by Samuel Yonas Deressa and Josh de Keijzer. Minnesota: Fortress Press, forthcoming.

Desplat, Patrick and Terje Østebø. *Muslim Ethiopia: The Christian Legacy, Identity Politics, and Islamic Reformism*. New York: Palgrave Macmillan, 2013.

Desta Heliso. "Warlordism in Ethiopia?" *The Reporter*, July 6, 2019. https://www.thereporterethiopia.com.

Desta Heliso. "The Relevance of the Study of Religion in Ethiopian Context." *The Reporter*, July 28, 2017. https://www.thereporterethiopia.com.

Dirshaye Menberu. "Tewoflos (B)." The Dictionary of African Christian Biography,2006. https://dacb.org.

Ephraim Isaac. *The Ethiopian Orthodox Tawahido Church*. Trenton: Red Sea Press, 2012.

Ethiopian Catholic Secretariat on behalf of the Inter-Religious Council of Ethiopia on January 1, 2019. Untitled Press Release at http://www.ecsethiopia.com.

Fetha Nagast: The Law of the Kings, edited by Peter Strauss. Jamaica: Miguel Lorne Publishers, 2008.

Merlo, Francesca. "16 Days of Prayer for Peace in Ethiopia." *Vatican News,* August 8, 2018. https://www.vaticannews.va/en.

Ge'ez Acts of Abba Estifanos of Gwendawende. Translated by Getachew Haile. Scriptores Aethiopici Tomus 111. Leuven, Belgium: Aedibus Peeters, 2006.

Goodman, Lenn. *Love Thy Neighbour As Thyself*. New York: Oxford University Press, 2008.

Hansen, Rich. "Transforming the Dualistic Worldview of Ethiopian Evangelical Christians." *International Bulletin of Missionary Research* 39, no. 3 (2015): 138-41.

Hayalnesh Gezahegn. "Security Forces Ordered to Take Measures as Weekend Violence Claims Lives." *Addis Standard,* April 8, 2019. https://addisstandard.com.

International Displacement Monitoring Centre. "Ethiopia," May 11, 2019. http://www.internal-displacement.org.

Johnstone, Patrick. *The Future of the Global Church*. Downers Grove: IVP, 2011.

"Kairos Document." In *Between Christ and Caesar: Classic and Contemporary Texts on Church and State,* edited by Charles Villa-Vicencio. Grand Rapids: W. B. Eerdmans and Cape Town, South Africa: David Philips, 1986.

Kebra Negast: The Glory of Kings. Translated by Miguel Brooks. Kingston, Jamaica: LMH Publishing, 2001.

King, Jr., Martin Luther. "The Answer to a Perplexing Question." *Strength to Love*. 133-43. Minneapolis: Fortress Press, 2010.

Labberton, Mark. *The Dangerous Act of Loving Your Neighbour: Seeing Others Through the Eyes of Jesus*. Downers Grove: IVP Books, 2010.

"Lest the Rwanda Genocide Be Repeated in Ethiopia!" *The Reporter,* April 13, 2019. https://www.thereporterethiopia.com.

Maimir Mennasemay. "A Critical Dialogue Between Fifteenth and Twenty First Century Ethiopia." *The International Journal of Ethiopian Studies* V, no. 1 (2010): 1-37.

Mengisteab Teshome and Haftu Gebreegziabher. "Religious Fathers Convey New Year's Messages." *Ethiopian Herald,* September 11, 2016. http://www.ethpress.gov.et.

Mersha Alehegne. "Abune Petros." *Encyclopedia Aethiopica* 4, edited by Siegbert Uhlig, 140-41. Wiesbaden: Harrassowitz, 2010.

Obulutsa, George. "Ethiopia Arrests 59 Officials over Corruption, Economic Sabotage." *Reuters,* April 12, 2019. https://www.reuters.com.

Pew Forum. "Orthodox Christians Are Highly Religious in Ethiopia." November 8, 2017. http://www.pewforum.org.

"Reconciliation Commission Announces Three-Year Plan." *Fana Broadcast Corporate*, April 30, 2019. https://fanabc.com.

Samuel Alemu. "Unemployment in Ethiopia: Socio-Political Implications." *The Reporter*, July 28, 2018. https://www.thereporterethiopia.com.

Samuel Yonas. *The Life, Works, and Witness of Tsehay Tolessa and Gudina Tumsa, the Ethiopian Bonhoeffer*. Minneapolis: Fortress Press, 2017.

Stackhouse, Max. "Civil Religion, Political Theology, and Public Theology: What's the Difference?" *Political Theology* 5, no. 3 (2004): 275-93.

Theodros A Teklu. "Public Theology and the State." In *African Public Theology*. Carlisle: Langham Publishers, forthcoming.

Theodros A Teklu. The Politics of Metanoia: Towards a Post-Nationalistic Political Theology in Ethiopia. Frankfurt am Main: Peter Lang, 2014.

Tibebe Eshete. *The Evangelical Movement in Ethiopia: Resistance and Resilience*. Baylor: Baylor University Press, 2009.

UN Department of Safety and Security. "Crime Incidents Mounting in Addis Ababa." https://mereja.com/forum.

USAID Ethiopia. "Fact Sheet: Developing Ethiopia's Youth." July 2017. https://www.usaid.gov.

Walters, James. *Loving Your Neighbour in an Age of Religious Conflict: A New Agenda for Interfaith Relations*. London: Jessica Kingsley Publishers, 2019.

The World Bank. "Ethiopia Poverty Assessment." 2014. http://www.worldbank.org.

Yodit Tariku. "*Political Theology of the Neighbour: Reflections from Saint Maximus the Confessor Towards Challenging Violence*." Addis Ababa: Unpublished MABTS thesis at the Ethiopian Graduate School of Theology, 2016.

Zecharias Zelalem. "Woldia Massacre: Ethiopian Security Forces Kill a Dozen, Turning a Holiday Procession into Nightmare." *OPride*, January 22, 2018. https://www.opride.com.

In Need of Differentiation

The "Public Sphere" as a Challenge for Theology

Constantin Plaul (Halle, Germany)

1. Introduction

Faith and religion fundamentally deal with a reality that transcends daily life, and they aim at the inner core of human existence. In modern times, these characteristics have sometimes been used to declare religion as something private and private alone. Originally, of course, the differentiation of a private sphere of religion was not intended to make religion exclusively a private matter. Establishing a private dimension rather had the function of emphasizing the freedom of the individual from forced absolute conformity with religion's public appearance, but the existence of religion in public remained an unquestioned matter of social life. Later, however, the notion of the private character of religion virtually became a means to justify calls for the public absence of religion, and these calls appeared in very different contexts and with very different intentions: in intellectual debates and in concrete sociopolitical structures. At times, such perspectives were also articulated from a theological perspective, but not least the experiences of the civil catastrophes in the 20th century and the totalitarian political regimes brought forth a broad recognition of the importance of a faith that does not withdraw from the public sphere, but engages with it critically and constructively. How far this involvement should go has been a matter of critical debate and some controversy – what it should look like, and how it should concretely be implemented – but in principle the idea of a publicly engaged religion is broadly accepted.

It is therefore reasonable to claim that religion and Christianity can, do, and should play a public role in society. The theological understanding of the public sphere, however, sometimes shows a lack of differentiation. This can be shown exemplarily in reference to Wolfgang Huber's influential work "Kirche und Öffentlichkeit", published in 1972,[1] which also became one of the main sources for 'public theology' in Germany. In "Kirche und Öffentlichkeit" Huber identifies various dimensions of the public sphere, and he searches for possible fields of activity in which the church may exercise influence. He thus argues for the social responsibility of the Protestant church as something inscribed in it from the very beginning and which it can only evade at the price

[1] Wolfgang Huber, *Kirche und Öffentlichkeit* (München: Chr. Kaiser, 1991).

of its social segregation. But as much as I agree with this general perspective, I question whether his understanding of the public sphere is theologically sufficient. Because, even though Huber recognizes the fundamental differentiation between the social public sphere in general and the public character of ecclesiastical life, he does not really take into account that the public sphere itself already contains a manifold of (Christian-)religious expressions and communication that exist relatively independent from church action. This social and cultural situation can be considered as an effect of a transformation process which began during the Enlightenment, which altered the appearance of Christianity in Western culture quite significantly, and in the course of which Christianity ceased to appear merely in its ecclesiastical formation, but also started to exist in its own public sphere which has emancipated itself from the church.

In the following, I aim to explore this dimension of the "public sphere" which seems to be crucial for theology as well as for the churches. First, I want to focus on that process of differentiation. To do so, I apply Jürgen Habermas's model of the structural transformation of the public sphere. Despite the fact that the problem of religion plays no role in his theory, his concept can be meaningfully related to the history of Christianity, at least in its Protestant appearance. After that and a short interim summary, I will draw attention to some productive approaches in recent and current theology which have dealt with the problem of how the post-Enlightenment situation of Christianity might be rendered categorically. Following this, I point out three general problems which should be considered in this context, before in the end I come to my final conclusion.

2. Differentiation and the Public Sphere

In his postdoctoral thesis "The Structural Transformation of the Public Sphere,"[2] Habermas convincingly emphasizes that the "public sphere" underwent a profound transformation process in the so-called Age of Enlightenment. As is well known, Habermas describes this process as a shift from a "representative" to a "bourgeois public sphere". He characterizes this transformation in the form of a historical description that gains its plausibility through recourse to various phenomena, but whose main goal is to point out a *structural* process of change. Notwithstanding some criticism from a historical point of view,[3] the core of Habermas's theory has proven to be convincing to this day and is still widely recognized.

[2] This and all subsequent translations of German texts are my own.

[3] One critique has been that Habermas relies in his historical description mainly on developments in the British context. That makes it at least questionable, whether the

Habermas mainly identifies the representative public sphere with the socio-cultural formation of the European Middle Ages, where no differentiation between a public and a private sphere can yet be observed. Although an idea of the public existed, it was limited to the representation of feudal and later absolutist rule. And this is precisely wherein its representative character can be seen. As much as this public sphere depended on a broader environment of subjects which it appeared, all groups and actors outside the authorities were excluded from all public dignity associated with representation. In addition to that, this public sphere unfolded in a culture of fixed attributes, assigned to their bearers independently of concrete places and functions, accompanied with a practice of the mysterious Arcanum.

Since the 17th century, however, this social structure has undergone a profound transformation that led to a distinction between the public and private spheres. The historical background can be seen in the emergence of the new class of the "bourgeois", who became the primary audience of princely announcements, due to the concentration of power at court and the associated demotion of the landed gentry. This was accompanied by the emergence of new forms of long-distance trade, which simultaneously led to the expansion of news and newspapers. These became the leading media of communication, which the authorities soon sought to use for their administrative purposes. The more the new class became aware of its social position, the more it began to use these media for its own communication. This resulted in the constitution of a "bourgeois public sphere", in which the "public interest in the private sphere of bourgeois society is no longer perceived only by the authorities, but by the subjects as their own."[4] Hereby it is important to note that even though the bourgeois public sphere was constituted by intersubjective processes of reflection, these processes remained in an inner relation to the private sphere, in which the appropriation of the objects of discourse took place.[5] And this still applied when the literary public evolved into a political public. To quote Habermas again: "The bourgeois public sphere unfolds in the field of tension between state and society, but in such a way that it itself remains part of the private sphere."[6] Even more: "The model of the bourgeois public sphere counted on the strict separation of the public and private spheres, whereby the public sphere [. . .] was itself part of the private sphere."[7]

---

patterns found in that way are significant enough to serve as the basis for a structural theory. However, every structural theory needs a inductive basis from which it develops its theoretical network. And as it is mentioned above, Habermas took a constructive grasp here.

[4] Jürgen Habermas, *Strukturwandel der Öffentlichkeit: Untersuchungen zu einer Kategorie der bürgerlichen Gesellschaft* (Frankfurt am Main: Suhrkamp, 2015).

[5] Cf. Habermas, *Strukturwandel der Öffentlichkeit*, 260f.

[6] Habermas, *Strukturwandel der Öffentlichkeit*, 225.

[7] Habermas, *Strukturwandel der Öffentlichkeit*, 268.

The structural change Habermas describes can also and especially be observed with regard to religion.[8] The concept of the public played a decisive role for the theologians of Protestant reformations. One exemplary instance may be found in the "publice docere" of the *Confessio Augustana* (CA XIV), according to which the sermon in worship is regarded as a public process. From the perspective of Habermas's differentiation, it seems appropriate to describe this kind of public as a representative one: It is the institution of the church alone that possesses and contributes the media of salvation in their cultic forms of sacrament and sermon. Hereby, sacraments and sermon function as a mediation of institutionally administered norms of teaching which are communicated in the form of official directives and which have their main support in church and university. This "representative" restriction of religious communication was strengthened even more by the fact that in the course of the Reformation the political authorities soon became heads of the church, and that they were the only Christians allowed to live out this - indirect - political dimension of the faith. Although the idea of the general priesthood is a key element of the Protestant matrix, the socio-cultural preconditions which would allow its realisation did not exist in the earlier stages of Reformation period. This started to change, however, in the Age of Enlightenment.

To bring this change into view, I refer to the well-known distinction between private and public religion made by Johann Salomo Semler[9] in the 18th century.[10] This distinction already reflects a clear awareness of the fact that religious life is no longer absorbed in ecclesiastic theological directives and guidelines, but that it also appears in its own critical form in the private sphere, wherein Semler found an important source for religious progress.[11] Semler, however, was reluctant to directly relate private reasoning to the pub-

---

[8] Cf. Ulrich Barth, "Sichtbare und unsichtbare Kirche: Die Tragweite von Luthers ekklesiologischem Ansatz," in *Kritischer Religionsdiskurs*, ed. by Ulrich Barth (Tübingen: Mohr Siebeck, 2013), 1–51, here 30.

[9] Cf. Johann Salomo Semler, *Neuer Versuch die gemeinnützige Auslegung und Anwendung des neuen Testaments zu befördern* (Halle, 1786), 1; Johann Salomo Semler, *Ueber historische, geselschaftliche und moralische Religion der Christen* (Leipzig, 1786), Vorrede (without pagination).

[10] Cf. Marianne Schröter, *Aufklärung durch Historisierung: Johann Salomo Semlers Hermeneutik des Christentums* (Berlin and Boston: De Gruyter, 2012).

[11] On the possibility of carrying forward the idea of progress into the field of the history of religion under the intellectual conditions of late modernity cf. Jörg Dierken, *Fortschritte in der Geschichte der Religion? Aneignung einer Denkfigur der Aufklärung* (Leipzig: Evangelische Verlagsanstalt, 2012). Cf. also forthcoming, Constantin Plaul, "Die Irritation des Fortschritts. Kritisch-konstruktive Beurteilung einer klassischen Kategorie der Religionsgeschichte," in *Freiheit Denken: Protestantische Transformationen in der Gegenwart, Festschrift für Jörg Dierken*, ed. by Malte D. Krüger, Christian Polke, Constantin Plaul, and Arnulf von Scheliha (Frankfurt am Main et al: Peter Lang, 2020).

lic sphere of pulpit and lectern. Rather, he trusted that the critical force of the private religion would communicate itself indirectly to the public religion.

As Trutz Rendtorff later pointed out, the entire scope of transformative dynamics is not fully covered yet by the way Semler reflects on it. "In truth," writes Rendtorff, "it was about the fact that in the area of the so-called private or undogmatic Christianity, another public sphere has formed."[12] This formation can certainly be described analogously to Habermas's notion of a new type of the public sphere. A decisive precondition can be seen in the newly forming journalism, which found its media in a variety of new publication organs. In his book about the Enlightenment, Albrecht Beutel cites a whole series of corresponding phenomena:[13] For example, the moral weekly journals, which had become increasingly widespread since the first half of the 18th century and in which religious questions were discussed in a literary and public context. These discourses were fuelled by the publishing and book market; a prominent example in the German context is the publisher and writer Friedrich Nicolai, who pursued the project of a moral-religious enlightenment by taking a stand against orthodox and pietist movements. Another example is the theologically oriented *Popular Enlightenment*, which was initially supported by the clergy itself, and which found its expression in very different publication formats. Finally, the new literary genre of *Popular Theology* should be mentioned here, which was also concerned with the factual and contemporary treatment of religious questions about life. While it initially aimed primarily at the so-called teachers of religion, who should become enabled to effectively represent popular theology, this professional boundary was soon crossed, so that unbiased laymen also advanced to the circle of addressees. When Habermas notes that during the Enlightenment the lay judgement of literarily interested private people had become institutionalized,[14] this can also be said with regard to the field of Protestant religion. Thus, Albrecht Beutel speaks of the emergence of "a lay Christian religion emancipated from ecclesiastical supervision",[15] which led to the fact that the "religious discourse had been democratized programmatically".[16] It makes sense to consider this democratization of religious discourse as a realisation of the early Protestant idea of a "priesthood of all believers" which could not have been realized under the socio-cultural circumstances of the 16th century.[17]

---

[12] Trutz Rendtorff, *Christentum außerhalb der Kirche: Konkretionen der Aufklärung* (Hamburg: Furche-Verlag, 1969), 79.

[13] Albrecht Beutel, *Aufklärung in Deutschland* (Göttingen: Vandenhoeck & Ruprecht, 2006), 283–287.

[14] Cf. Habermas, *Strukturwandel der Öffentlichkeit*, 257.

[15] Albrecht Beutel, *Aufklärung in Deutschland*, 286.

[16] Albrecht Beutel, *Aufklärung in Deutschland*, 287.

[17] Of course, such a perspective implies the differentiation of a real history and a history of ideas. It can already be found in historical thinking of progressive theologians during the Age of Enlightment. In the later history of theology, a

3. Christianity and Publicness in the Wake of Differentiation

The process of the emergence of a lay Christian religion does not mean that the former public appearances of Christian life – the ecclesiastical and the political one – had ceased to exist. The transformation from a "representative" to a "bourgeois" public sphere should therefore not be understood as a simple sequence. In the course of this transformation, the public appearance of Christian life began to unfold in varying and interconnected ways. Maybe instead of speaking of a "transformation" of the public sphere it would be more accurate to speak of a "differentiation". In the context of the analysis presented above, at least four different dimensions should be mentioned which prove to be essential regarding the living expression of Christian life.

First, there is the public dimension of ecclesiastic action itself. Not least the public character of church services that has played an important role for the Protestant church from the beginning should be mentioned in this connection. The "publice docere" of the fourteenth article of the *Confessio Augustana* was already quoted above. This article claims that nobody should publicly teach, preach or administer the sacraments in a church without a regular call, that is, without having been properly ordained and installed as a minister. With that claim, the CA seeks to set up an organisational element in religious life and practice to prevent religious communication and action from dissolving into chaos. Due to the core idea of the general priesthood, the ecclesiastic structure which arises with this "supervision of the church" (ordo ecclesiastico) does not aim to establish a new clergy which would, then, have a higher dignity than the so-called laypeople, but rather seeks only to regulate religious life in a functional manner. Most of the main branches of the different Protestant denominations employed organisational concepts similar to this one, and this concept designates an important element in many of the Protestant churches right down to the present day. Regardless of whether the organisational element is stressed more or less, ecclesiastical action forms a special part of the public sphere in Protestant life. Most likely, Protestant churches will always include some kind of "representative" element, even though most are no longer aligned with political authorities as they used to be.[18]

The socio-political dimension of the public sphere also plays an important role for Christian life. Christians have always lived as members of political systems and societies. Furthermore, the task of shaping the world according to

---

prominent scholar who rendered his historical judgment on the basis of such a differentiation was Albrecht Ritschl.

[18] Of course, there are quite significant differences regarding the historical developments and the current situation if one compares America and Europe, in addition to there being varying models within Europe.

ideas of what is good and right has been a formative element of biblical and Christian belief since Christianity's earliest beginnings. But for a long time, only the (Christian) authorities were allowed to act out this indirect dimension of the faith. This started to change during the period of the Enlightenment, but it took a long time before individuals significantly contributed to the political process. In Germany, this development was only broadly realized in the second half of the 20th century.

Third, an entire area of religious discourses exists, which are of a public character, but do not necessarily appear to be the result of ecclesiastical action. It is worth noting that even during the Reformation, a vast distribution of pamphlets and leaflets already started to constitute a kind of religious public sphere of its own. However, this public sphere was still widely dominated by the emerging confessional boundaries including their institutional backgrounds, an aspect which became even stronger during the later "Confessional Age". As shown above, significant changes occurred during the Age of Enlightenment with its emancipation of a lay Christian religion, whose participants set up new forms of religious-theological communication – a differentiation which was also assisted by the growth and differentiation of new media formats. This development has continued to the present. Moreover, the establishment of modern liberal societies and the development of electronic and digital media have rather advanced this whole process quite dramatically. There is a huge publishing and book market with a wide range of more or less sophisticated expressions of belief and faith. And the internet and social media have made it possible in principle for everyone to express their (Christian) religious ideas and concerns freely in blogs, chatrooms, videos and so on.

Fourth and finally, it is necessary to refer to the vast field of direct and indirect effects of Christianity in society and culture. Just to mention a few, this starts with the way the calendar works in the West, counting the years before and after Christ. It continues with the structuring of the year with Christian holidays, such as Christmas, Good Friday, Easter, Pentecost and so on, though this may be more noticeable in many European countries than in the United States. Furthermore, there is a vast field of cultural expressions in the arts, literature, music and so on. The history of Western culture is simply not comprehensible without any knowledge about basic Christian ideas, which have found various articulations over time. Exhibits and performances of classic works continue to perpetuate these cultural sedimentations. In addition, Christian ideas, symbols and notions still play a big role in all kinds of current cultural productions, from pop songs to movies.[19] Finally, a last important

---

[19] To scan cultural life for expressions of this kind and to reconstruct their more or less hidden (Christian-)religious meaning, a theological research program within the field of practical theology has been established in the last decades, which is normally referred to as a "theological hermeneutics of culture". For a historic-systematic reconstruction of a theological hermeneutics of culture cf. Andreas Kubik, *Theologische*

effect of Christianity on society and culture can be seen in the implementation of different moral-ethical norms and ideas which may have originated from Christianity, but have become a self-evident part of social life and societies.

4. Publicness Inside and Outside the Church: Observations and Consequences

Theology is integrally related to a concrete religious practice which it seeks to perceive, to describe, to analyze, to critically question, and to explicate constructively. Therefore, theology does not carry out its business in an intangible place of merely supernatural divine truths. Instead, it is connected to historical and cultural realizations in which religion – in this case, Christianity – articulates itself practically. For this reason, theology must also take into account the socio-cultural transformation processes in which religion develops.[20] A striking result of the history of Christianity in the Age of Enlightenment consists – at least in its Protestant form – is a differentiation of Christian life, which no longer exclusively merges into an ecclesiastical representation, but also exists as a relatively independent public sphere. Theology should take this finding into account and accept the task of reflection that accompanies it. In the more recent history of theology, a series of interesting approaches can be found.

One of the most important theologians in this context is undoubtedly Trutz Rendtorff. His collection of essays, "Christianity outside the church" (Christentum außerhalb der Kirche, 1968), brought this problem emphatically

---

Kulturhermeneutik impliziter Religion: Ein praktisch-theologisches Paradigma der Spätmoderne (Berlin and Boston: De Gruyter, 2018).

[20] The cornerstone to of such an understanding of theology was laid by Friedrich Schleiermacher's theory of theology. In the *Brief Outline of Theology as a Field of Study* (Kurze Darstellung des theologischen Studiums), he characterizes theology as a "positive science" (positive Wissenschaft). This means that theology functions as a science, or better, as a human science, in the strict sense of the word, but all its different sub-disciplines are related more or less to the aim of solving a practical task. In a formal comparison, this structure is not unique to theology alone, but can also be found in other fields of the sciences and the humanities, especially in law and medicine. All these subjects have in common both that they treat their objects and questions methodologically and they deal with practical concerns of society and culture. What matters for present purposes is the fact that theology is related to a pre-scientific practical context: the individual and collective Christian life. Only the reference to this context makes it possible to speak of theology as an independent discipline. Of course, not only is theology *dependent* on its practical context, but theological reflection also has an *impact* on the practical level. Behind this distinction and relationship, one can easily recognize Semler's differentiation between religion and theology, according to which the former designates the practices of piety, while the latter refers to its scientific reflection.

into focus again. In these essays, he tries to bring to attention not least differentiation of Christian life which developed in the course of the structural change of the religious public sphere. He argues that theology cannot capitulate to the ecclesiastical form of Christian life if it really wants to encompass Christian life in its rich and full complexity. Although Rendtorff is making a contemporary argument, he also draws a historical arch from the Enlightenment period, which had brought forth the result – as I quoted before – that "in the area of the so-called private or undogmatic Christianity another public sphere had formed."[21] Despite its non-ecclesiastical character, this appearance of Christian life must by no means be delegitimized as un-Christian, but can be understood as a justified manifestation of Christianity. Beyond that, Rendtorff then expands the concept of the public to include not only Christian communication outside the church, but also the manifold and sometimes highly indirect objectifications of Christianity in society and culture. On this basis, he develops a theory of Christianity, which he presents as a form of cultural hermeneutics from a Christian theologian perspective.[22] In order not to misunderstand the intention of this project, however, it is important to point out that Rendtorff does not advocate a simple opposition: In spite of an openness to communication practices outside the church, his aim is not to discredit church life by any means. Not least his strong commitment in the context of the *Evangelische Kirche in Deutschland* testifies to this. Public sensibility and ecclesiastical interest must not be played off against each other.

Rendtorff's ideas were taken up and further developed constructively by Dietrich Rössler. He outlined an oft quoted triad of concepts, according to which modern Christianity realizes itself as ecclesiastical, individual, and public Christianity.[23] Although Rössler presented this distinction in the context of practical theology, it resonated beyond the boundaries of his discipline. Only recently, Traugott Jähnichen presented an article with the title "Public Christianity"[24] in which he follows Rössler's model[25] of differentiation in order to plead for a stronger consideration of its cultural, political, socio-ethical and pedagogical dimensions.[26] Another conceptual reminiscence of Rössler is par-

---

[21] Rendtorff, *Christentum außerhalb der Kirche*, 79.

[22] On Rendtorff's concept cf. Martin Laube, *Theologie des neuzeitlichen Christentums: Studien zu Genese und Profil der Christentumstheorie Trutz Rendtorffs* (Tübingen: Mohr Siebeck, 2006); Stefan Atze, *Ethik als Steigerungsform von Theologie?* (Berlin and New York: De Gruyter, 2008).

[23] Dietrich Rössler, *Grundriß der Praktischen Theologie* (Berlin and New York: De Gruyter, 1986), 79–83.

[24] Cf. Traugott Jähnichen, "'Öffentliches Christentum': Eine unterschätzte Dimension christlicher Präsenz im Kontext der Kirchenmitgliedschaftsuntersuchungen," *Evangelische Theologie* 75, no. 3 (2015): 166–78.

[25] Cf. Jähnichen, "Öffentliches Christentum", 166.

[26] Jähnichen does not explore the full implications regarding a theory of Protestantism as they are found in Rössler's concept of "public Christianity". Instead Jähnichen

ticularly prominent in the book by Christian Albrecht and Reiner Anselm, *Public Protestantism*.[27] Against the background of the current democratic crisis, the authors ask what contribution Protestant Christianity can make to support social and political communication processes in a productive way. In this regard, the focus is directed especially toward the public sphere of Protestantism in its relative difference to its ecclesiastical manifestations.

Despite all the differences in the initial questions and the objectives pursued, all the positions just mentioned are careful not to reduce modern Christianity to its ecclesiastical manifestation, but to remain attentive to its public appearances outside the church.[28]

In view of the ongoing socio-cultural transformations in modernity, a contemporary theory of Christianity needs considerable nuance in order to be able to unfold its constructive power as a theology which works responsibly in and for the present. At this point, I would only like to emphasize three aspects that seem essential. First of all, it is important to prevent a latent danger of over-identification in the field of normative concepts. Although the existence of a profound socio-cultural effect of Christianity is indeed indisputable, the perception of this effect can result in misleading ideas. Thus, the role Christianity played historically in developing concepts holding normative content still in the present cannot be identified with the claim that Christianity is the only and necessary precondition for the validity of these ideas. A good example is the concept of human dignity. As much as the latter is undoubtedly connected in a complex way with the history of the Christian tradition in the West, its religious symbolisation must not only be articulated by Christian belief. In principle this value also proves to be open to and identifiable in other basic religious perspectives.

Second, besides its cultural diagnostic function, "Christianity outside the church" calls for freedom from ecclesiastical supervision. Without questioning this view in principle, an exclusive emphasis on the necessity to process those public discourses *constructively* seems too one-sided. In addition, the need for *critical* reference will also have to be taken into account. This seems necessary, because the Christian-religious discourses and debates outside the church can unfold quite problematically, for instance when populist or fundamentalist misuses of Christianity occur. The right-wing slogan to save the

---

inclines toward the rather ecclesiastical model of "public theology". In doing so, he offers no further reflections on the question of how both concepts could be taught together.

[27] Christian Albrecht and Reiner Anselm, *Öffentlicher Protestantismus: Zur aktuellen Debatte um gesellschaftliche Präsenz und politische Aufgaben des evangelischen Christentums* (Zürich: Theologischer Verlag Zürich, 2017).

[28] Cf. also Martin Fritz, "Kultivierung politischer Gefühle: Das Programm Martha Nussbaums als Anstoß für die öffentliche Theologie," in *Zwischen Diskurs und Affekt. Politische Urteilsbildung in theologischer Perspektive*, ed. by Thomas Wabel, Torben Stamer, and Jonathan Weider (Leipzig: Evangelische Verlagsanstalt, 2018), 47–67.

Christian Occident is an example of this. A critical examination of such developments is certainly not only the task of the churches, but also takes place within the relevant public spheres. Nevertheless, in this context reference to the church plays an important role.

Concerning the third aspect, I want to identify a problem rather than to offer a solution. This problem is related to two criteriological questions that lead further to rather complex issues. On the one hand, a manifold of religious expressions in modern culture exist. But their actual or potential Christian character is at stake: Which phenomena are part of Christian life or could become part of it – and which not? To deal with such questions, criteria of assessment are needed. The classical teaching norm of *CA VII* helps here at best partially. Might Jesus' own criterion – namely, that where two or three are gathered in the name of Jesus, their communion is further marked by his presence (Mt 18,20) – provide helpful orientation?[29] On the other hand cultural life generally bears a wide range of direct and indirect manifestations of Christianity. But how can it be decided whether and, if yes, where and when such manifestations stay at the mere cultural level – and where and when they function as media for authentic religious communication?[30] In the end, of course, ambiguity remains inevitable in both criteriological dimensions.

5. Conclusion

In this essay, I have examined the development of the religious public sphere(s) which had differentiated themselves from the church proper, with a particular focus on religious communication. In this analysis, Huber's juxtaposition of the church and the public sphere appears to be problematic, since it underestimates the fact that the public sphere is not a religiously blank area which seeks to fill theological-ecclesiastical action with Christian expressions. On the contrary, it already contains manifold forms of (Christian-)religious life and communication that exists relatively independently from church action.

Huber's concept of the public sphere has become one of the most important sources for the development of public theology in Germany, currently represented not least by the chairperson of the council of the EKD, Heinrich Bedford-Strohm.[31] In view of this connection I want to draw a line from my

---

[29] Cf. Barth, *Sichtbare und unsichtbare Kirche*, 41.

[30] I also discuss this problem in the course of a field study regarding Humperdincks opera "Hänsel und Gretel", cf. Constantin Plaul, "Bewahrtes Leben: Theologische Gedanken zu Engelbert Humperdincks 'Hänsel und Gretel'," in *Wege zum Menschen* 72, no. 1, (2020), 29–41, here 40f.

[31] Cf. Heinrich Bedford-Strohm, "Vorrang für die Armen. Öffentliche Theologie als Befreiungstheologie einer demokratischen Gesellschaft," in *Theologische Ethik der Gegenwart. Ein Überblick über zentrale Ansätze und Themen*, ed. Friederike Nüssel (Tübingen: Mohr Siebeck, 2009), 167–82; "Öffentliche Theologie und Kirche.

critique of Huber's approach to the critique of public theology in general, as it has been recently expressed from diverse theological sides and in various ways.[32] Apparently, the many critical aspects – forced unification of public discourses,[33] Christian-religious exaggeration of certain political positions,[34] moralization of the political,[35] or even clericalization of politics[36] – can be summed up to a basic reproach of church paternalism. And is it not a similar paternalism that also lays behind the ignorance of Christian manifestations outside the church? In both cases one finds an attempt to determine what can count as legitimized expressions of Christian faith, and what not, from a theological-ecclesiastical perspective; including strong claims concerning how people should live and act as Christians. But as shown above, it is questionable whether such a theological-ecclesiastical stance is appropriate in view of the appearance of Christianity in (late) modern times. Admittedly, with the affirmation of the differentiation of a religious public sphere we enter a confusing area. But to acknowledge it as such and to reflect it critically and constructively – that seems to be an important challenge of Protestant theology in the present.

Abschiedsvorlesung an der Universität Bamberg am 26. Juli 2011," *Landesbischof*, https://landesbischof.bayern-evangelisch.de/downloads/Abschiedsvorlesung_Bedford_Strohm.pdf (16. Dezember 2019); "Öffentliche Theologie und politische Verantwortung," in *Religion im öffentlichen Raum*, ed. by Karlies Abmeier, Michael Borchard, and Matthias Riemenschneider (Paderborn et al: Ferdinand Schöning, 2013), 27–39.

[32] A very good overview, including his own critique, can be found in Rochus Leonhardt, "Evangelische Spiritualität und Prophetie," in *Handbuch Evangelische Spiritualität: Band 2: Theologie*, ed. by Peter Zimmerling (Göttingen: Vandenhoeck & Ruprecht, 2017), 579-86.

[33] Cf. Johannes Fischer, "Gefahr der Unduldsamkeit: Die 'Öffentliche Theologie' der EKD ist problematisch," in *Zeitzeichen* 5, (2016): 43–5.

[34] Cf. Albrecht and Anselm, *Öffentlicher Protestantismus*, 31.

[35] Cf. Günter Thomas, "Radikaler moralischer Universalismus, begrenzte Verantwortung und partikulare Staatlichkeit: Fragen angesichts der Flüchtlingskrise. Ein Essay," in *Religion und Politik. Historische und aktuelle Konstellationen eines spannungsvollen Geflechts: Hartmut Ruddies zum 70. Geburtstag*, ed. by Jörg Dierken and Dirk Evers (Frankfurt am Main et al: Peter Lang, 2016), 353–79.

[36] Ulrich H. J. Körtner, *Für die Vernunft. Wider Moralisierung und Emotionalisierung in Politik und Kirche*, (Leipzig: Evangelische Verlagsanstalt, 2017). For a critical remark on Körtners identification of ethical theology with moralization cf. Constantin Plaul, "review of Für die Vernunft, by Ulrich H. J. Körtner," *Theologische Zeitschrift*, no. 75, 2019, 173-74.

BIBLIOGRAPHY

Albrecht, Christian and Reiner Anselm. *Öffentlicher Protestantismus: Zur aktuellen Debatte um gesellschaftliche Präsenz und politische Aufgaben des evangelischen Christentums.* Zürich: Theologischer Verlag Zürich, 2017.

Atze, Stefan. *Ethik als Steigerungsform von Theologie?* Berlin and New York: De Gruyter, 2008.

Barth, Ulrich. "Sichtbare und unsichtbare Kirche: Die Tragweite von Luthers ekklesiologischem Ansatz." In *Kritischer Religionsdiskurs*, edited by Ulrich Barth, 1-51. Tübingen: Mohr Siebeck 2013.

Bedford-Strohm, Heinrich. "Vorrang für die Armen. Öffentliche Theologie als Befreiungstheologie einer demokratischen Gesellschaft." In *Theologische Ethik der Gegenwart. Ein Überblick über zentrale Ansätze und Themen*, edited by Friederike Nüssel, 167-82. Tübingen: Mohr Siebeck, 2009.

Bedford-Strohm, Heinrich. "Öffentliche Theologie und Kirche. Abschiedsvorlesung an der Universität Bamberg am 26. Juli 2011." *Landesbischof.* https://landesbischof.bayern-evangelisch.de/downloads/Abschiedsvorlesung_Bedford_Strohm.pdf (16 Dezember 2019)

Bedford-Strohm, Heinrich. "Öffentliche Theologie und politische Verantwortung." In *Religion im öffentlichen Raum,* edited by Karlies Abmeier, Michael Borchard, Matthias Riemenschneider, 27-39. Paderborn et al.: Ferdinand Schöning, 2013.

Beutel, Albrecht. *Aufklärung in Deutschland.* Göttingen: Vandenhoeck & Ruprecht: 2006.

Dierken, Jörg. *Fortschritte in der Geschichte der Religion? Aneignung einer Denkfigur der Aufklärung.* Leipzig: Evangelische Verlagsanstalt, 2012.

Fischer, Johannes. "Gefahr der Unduldsamkeit: Die 'Öffentliche Theologie' der EKD ist problematisch." *Zeitzeichen* 5 (2016): 43-45.

Fritz, Martin. "Kultivierung politischer Gefühle: Das Programm Martha Nussbaums als Anstoß für die öffentliche Theologie."In *Zwischen Diskurs und Affekt. Politische Urteilsbildung in theologischer Perspektive,* edited by Thomas Wabel, Torben Stamer, Jonathan Wieder, 47-67. Evangelische Verlagsanstalt: Leipzig, 2018.

Thomas, Günter. "Radikaler moralischer Universalismus, begrenzte Verantwortung und partikulare Staatlichkeit: Fragen angesichts der Flüchtlingskrise. Ein Essay." In *Religion und Politik. Historische und aktuelle Konstellationen eines spannungsvollen Geflechts: Hartmut Ruddies zum 70. Geburtstag,* edited by Jörg Dierken and Dirk Evers, 353-79. Frankfurt am Main et al: Peter Lang, 2016.

Habermas, Jürgen. *Strukturwandel der Öffentlichkeit: Untersuchungen zu einer Kategorie der bürgerlichen Gesellschaft.* Frankfurt am Main: Suhrkamp, 2015.

Huber, Wolfgang. *Kirche und Öffentlichkeit.* München: Chr. Kaiser, 1991.

Jähnichen, Traugott. "'Öffentliches Christentum': Eine unterschätzte Dimension christlicher Präsenz im Kontext der Kirchenmitgliedschaftsuntersuchungen." *Evangelische Theologie* 75, no. 3 (2015): 166-78.

Körtner, Ulrich H. J. *Für die Vernunft. Wider Moralisierung und Emotionalisierung in Politik und Kirche.* Evangelische Verlagsanstalt: Leipzig, 2017.

Kubik, Andreas. *Theologische Kulturhermeneutik impliziter Religion: Ein praktisch-theologisches Paradigma der Spätmoderne.* Berlin and Boston: De Gruyter, 2018.

Laube, Martin. *Theologie des neuzeitlichen Christentums: Studien zu Genese und Profil der Christentumstheorie Trutz Rendtorffs*. Tübingen: Mohr Siebeck, 2006.

Leonhardt, Rochus. "Evangelische Spiritualität und Prophetie." In *Handbuch Evangelische Spiritualität: Band 2, Theologie*, edited by Peter Zimmerling, 579-86. Göttingen: Vandenhoeck & Ruprecht, 2017.

Plaul, Constantin. "Bewahrtes Leben: Theologische Gedanken zu Engelbert Humperdincks 'Hänsel und Gretel'." *Wege zum Menschen* 72, no. 1 (2020): 29–41.

Plaul, Constantin. "Die Irritation des Fortschritts. Kritisch-konstruktive Beurteilung einer klassischen Kategorie der Religionsgeschichte." In *Freiheit Denken: Protestantische Transformationen in der Gegenwart, FS Jörg Dierken*, edited by Malte D. Krüger, Christian Polke, Constantin Plaul, and Arnulf von Scheliha. Frankfurt am Main et al: Peter Lang, 2020. Forthcoming.

Plaul, Constantin. "Review. Für die Vernunft, by Ulrich H. J. Körtner." *Theologische Zeitschrift* 75 (2019): 173–74.

Rendtorff, Trutz. *Christentum außerhalb der Kirche: Konkretionen der Aufklärung*. Hamburg: Furche-Verlag, 1969.

Rössler, Dietrich. *Grundriß der Praktischen Theologie*. Berlin and New York: De Gruyter 1986.

Schröter, Marianne. *Aufklärung durch Historisierung: Johann Salomo Semlers Hermeneutik des Christentums*. Berlin and Boston: De Gruyter, 2012.

Semler, Johann Salomo. *Neuer Versuch die gemeinnüzige Auslegung und Anwendung des neuen Testaments zu befördern*. Halle, 1786.

Semler, Johann Salomo. *Ueber historische, geselschaftliche und moralische Religion der Christen*. Leipzig, 1786.

Part 5 What will Theology Do?
From the Present to Possible Futures

What Does Biblical "Exegethics" Do?

Method, Trajectories, and Reflections from an African Context

Dogara Ishaya Manomi (Jos, Nigeria)

1. Introduction

Two primary tasks undergird the focus of this chapter, namely, (1) identifying current trajectories in biblical scholarship and (2) describing appropriate methodologies in the light of current academic trends toward transdisciplinarity and current global realities characterized by transculturality. Nonetheless, these tasks are undertaken with a focus on African Christian contexts.

2. "Script" and "Scripted": Forms and Functions of Scripture

Allen Verhey's description of Scripture as "scripted" and "script" provides an appropriate point of departure for the present chapter. Scripture as "scripted," on the one hand, simply refers to it as an object, a given, a written text at a certain time in history, by certain persons who did things with words, and for certain purposes.[1] Interpreting Scripture as "scripted," therefore, basically refers to exegetical interpretation of scripture, which is primarily the task of biblical scholars.[2] To refer to Scripture as "script," on the other hand, is simply to draw an analogy between Scripture and a script to be performed by actors; an instrument.[3] Performance is an act of interpretation, and interpreting Scripture as "script," therefore, refers to the "performance interpretation" (and evaluation) which is primarily the work of moral theologians.[4]

According to Verhey, engaging Scripture in the faith community or "the church" involves both of these two disciplines of "scripted interpretation" (exegesis) and "script interpretation" (hermeneutics). By implication, it involves the work of biblical scholars and moral theologians. Nevertheless, Ver-

---

[1] Allen Verhey, "Scripture as Script and as Scripted: The Beatitudes," in *Character Ethics and the NT: Moral Dimensions of Scripture*, ed. by Robert L. Brawley (London: Westminster John Knox Press, 2007), 20-28.

[2] Verhey, "Scripture," 19.

[3] Verhey, "Scripture," 19, 25.

[4] Verhey, "Scripture," 19.

hey argues further, Scripture as "script" and "scripted" must be interpreted in the light of the whole "canon."[5] And in carrying out their tasks, biblical scholars and moral theologians must listen to each other, and not only so, they must listen to the faith community, as they all belong in the faith community (church).[6]

Verhey notes that biblical scholars, moral theologians, and the church depend on one another, and continue to shape and correct one another in this context. For example, form and source critical studies of the Beatitudes are examples of "scripted interpretation," while preaching a sermon from the Beatitudes, making a prayer or confession out of it, honoring those who exemplify the virtues therein (for example, peace and meekness), and personal efforts to live out the virtues in daily life are all examples of performance interpretation of Scripture as a "script" in the church.[7]

While Verhey's concept of interpreting the Scripture as "script" and "scripted" is apt, it poses methodological questions when it comes to the practical interpretation of Scripture as "script" and as "scripted" in African contexts and in the light of current transdisciplinary and transcultural realities. It is noteworthy that Verhey's concept is developed within an interdisciplinary framework of interdependence between biblical studies and moral theology on the one hand, and within intercultural interaction between the biblical world and its culture(s) and contemporary Western world and its culture(s) on the other hand. However, my concept of *exegethics*, as reflected in this essay, argues that for Scripture to be interpreted as "scripted" and "script," especially in African contexts, it requires more than an interdisciplinary and intercultural framework, but a transdisciplinary and transcultural one, reflecting the realities of globalization and glocalization simultaneously.

3. Exegethics: A Transdisciplinary and Transcultural Methodology

Hence, moving beyond Verhey's interdisciplinary and intercultural framework into transdisciplinary and transcultural ones, this essay asks and seeks to answer the question: What practical steps need to be taken at the "scripted" and "script" levels of interpretation of Scripture in an African context? To answer this, the paper heuristically proposes three broad interpretive categories, namely, *analytical*, *performative*, and *transformative* categories, under which the practical tasks of biblical exegesis and application in an African context will be described. Nonetheless, rather than a general focus on theological concepts like the concept of God, salvation, justification, etc. in African

[5] Verhey, "Scripture," 26.
[6] Verhey, "Scripture," 26–27.
[7] Verhey, "Scripture," 29–31.

Christian contexts, this paper limits its discussion to the methodology required for interpreting and appropriating biblical ethical norms as "scripted" and "script" in an African context. This narrowed focus on ethics informs the description of my methodology as "exegethics."

The "exegethics" methodology is an adapted version of Ruben Zimmermann's "implicit ethics"[8] methodology of reading biblical texts ethically.[9] Zimmermann describes his model as "implicit" because what the biblical ethics reader seeks to do is to unearth both implicit and explicit ethical norms embedded in a given biblical text. At the background of this concept of implicit ethics is Zimmermann's conclusion that even though the Bible is a book of ethics, no biblical book or text presents an organized or reasoned ethical structure consistent with an ethical theory of action. Such a structure is to be critically analyzed, recognized, and presented in forms consistent with modern ethical theories.[10]

Exegesis and ethics, being two-dimensional categories, constitute the two major inter-disciplinary categories integrated and the tasks to be undertaken in my *exegethics* methodology, which explains the rationale behind the coined term *exegethics*—exegesis and ethics.

While the "implicit ethics" and "exegethics" methodologies are applicable to a wide range of contexts, this essay presents it with focus on exegetical analysis of biblical ethics and hermeneutical appropriation of such ethics in African contexts. Particularly, the exegethics approach proposes and illustrates that African biblical interpretation in its "scripted" and "script" forms

---

[8] See Ruben Zimmermann, "Ethics in the New Testament and Language: Basic Explorations and Eph 5:21–33 as a Test Case," in *Moral Language in the NT: The Interrelatedness of Language and Ethics in Early Christian Writings*; eds. By Ruben Zimmermann, Jan G. Van Der Watt, and Susanne Luther (Tübingen: Mohr Siebeck, 2010), 26. For the detailed discussion and application of the "Implicit Ethics," see Ruben Zimmermann, *The Logic of Love: Discovering Paul's "Implicit Ethics" Through 1 Corinthians,* trans. by Dieter T. Roth. (Lanham et al: Lexington Books/Fortress Academic, 2018). See also Ruben Zimmermann, *Die Logik der Liebe: Die ,implizite Ethik' der Paulusbriefe am Beispiel des 1. Korintherbriefs,* (Neukirchen-Vluyn: Neukirchener Theologie, 2016).

[9] In order to achieve this, Zimmermann presents eight ways to analyze and recognize ethical norms in biblical texts, which include: linguistic forms, norms and maxims for action, moral agents, history of tradition of individual norms, values and the priority of values, ethical reflection (generating moral significance), moral agents, range of application.

[10] The differences between the two methodologies can be summarized thus: While the implicit ethics approach applies the eight ways of reading a passage or pericope, the exegethics approach applies them in reading only the virtue-ethical norms generated from the text. While the broad passage or pericope is the focus of the implicit ethics approach, the specific virtue-related norms in the passage are the focal points in the *exegethics* approach, reading the virtue-ethical norms out of the text, not into the text.

(should) involve(s) eight overlapping tasks. Such multiplicity of tasks is best undertaken using transdisciplinary and transcultural lenses.

4. Analytical Tasks

Task 1: Textual Analysis

This task involves, primarily, historical-critical, linguistic, literary, and rhetorical analyses of biblical texts to understand the texts, the co-texts, the contexts in which they were written, the message they sought to convey, and the effect or impact they sought to have. This task is what Verhey describes as interpreting Scripture as "scripted."[11]

Task 2: Cultural Analysis

This task analyzes the written and non-written "texts"[12] of African ethics and culture at large, being, to a large extent, an oral culture up to now. Unlike simplistic attempts to apply biblical ethics into African contexts with little or no commitment to analyzing African moral reasoning, this task is based on the recognition that African ethics is or should no longer be regarded as "the cradle" and "experimental space"[13] of ethics, but a developed ethical space with its complete resources, which can offer valid ethical reasoning to global ethical discourse.

Judith Gruber identifies cultural analysis as one of the threefold tasks of intercultural theology.[14] She notes that in cultural analysis, intercultural theology regards cultures as "*loci theologici* that provide the specific languages it needs to be able to formulate the Gospel in its inescapable culturality."[15] The cultural analysis of theology in contextual specificity (whether defined by locality or other markers) can be carried out reconstructively, referring to reconstructing postcolonial identities, or deconstructively, deconstructing Western cultural notions that have dominated theology, giving a voice to "non-Western cultural meaning systems."[16] Not only intercultural theology, however, but exegetical theology also needs to engage actively in cultural analysis. The central question in this task is, what are African[17] understandings of mo-

---

[11] Verhey, "Scripture," 20–25.

[12] By this, I mean the oral as well as documented cultural artefacts of African peoples.

[13] Kenneth Ngwa, *Exodus and Exile as Doors of (no) Return? Moses, Sundiata and the Constructions of Afro-Spatial-Genealogies* (Paper presented at the Annual Conference of the Society of Biblical Literature 2017, Boston, MA, USA), 1.

[14] Judith Gruber, *Intercultural Theology: Exploring World Christianity After the Cultural Turn* (Göttingen: Vandenhoeck & Ruprecht, 2017), 42.

[15] Gruber, *Intercultural*, 42.

[16] Gruber, *Intercultural*, 42.

[17] It is worth noting that ethical discourse among Christians in African churches, especially among the Christians in the Northern and Middle Belt Nigeria where I come

rality, virtue, and in particular cases, of ethical issues such as adultery, humility, hospitality, etc.?

The cultural analysis referred to here includes the analysis of both the historical and current (popular) aspects of African culture. Cultural analysis is necessary at the initial stage because, appropriating or constructing an African biblical or Christian ethics requires, first of all, understanding African Traditional Religion (ATR) and ethics in their pre-colonial, pre-Christian or pre-Islamic conceptions. In other words, understanding African religion and ethics in its form and shape before and/or without the influence of colonialism, Christianity and Islam, especially in the sub-Saharan Africa, is necessary for applying biblical ethics in an African context.

Cultural analysis of African cultures and ethics is an accountable way to understand the worldview of the Africans, their sense of reality, personality, identity, solidarity, and of course, morality. Thereafter, one could begin to seek to identify distinctive African religious worldviews about God, gods, sin, etc. which have made their way into the African Christians' interpretation and application of Scripture and its application in liturgy and worship and which could be described as African Christian theology. And it is also on this basis that one should seek to identify African ethical worldviews, judgments, and senses of an ethical *telos* which have made their way into the African Christians' interpretation, application and judgment of acceptable or unacceptable Christian behavior – all of which could fall under the category of African Christian ethics.

Task 3: Synthetic Analysis

At this level, the task is synthetic in the sense that it synthesizes the results of the first and second tasks above by identifying points of correlation and disparity, or tandems and tensions between biblical ethics and African ethics. The guiding question for this task is, what aspects of the two "understandings/views" (the biblical view and African views) are in tandem or tension with each other? Identifying and describing the tensions and/or tandems enables the interpreter of the Bible to appropriate the message of the text accountably.

---

from, is still heavily influenced by the worldview of the traditional African religion and ethics. As such, studying African religion and ethics is important for understanding why and how African Christians behave the way they do, and also how they order their liturgy, worship, communion, prayers, church music, and so on the way they do. And if one understands that through a study of African ethics/religion, it is a step further in an attempt to appropriate biblical ethics in a Christian context as I have proposed above. But for the reasons given above, suffice it to say that I shall be referring to African ethics in general, and where need be, shall make reference to African Christian ethics.

Task 4: Appropriative Analysis
This task bridges the gaps between the analytical tasks and the performative ones. It seeks to reconcile or harmonize the tensions identified from task three, namely, the points of departure between African ethical worldview or practices and biblical ethical worldviews and practices. The task here involves identifying what negotiations, concessions or appropriations need to be made in order to arrive at an ethic that is biblically accountable and relevantly African. Specific questions that need to be asked include: What aspects of African understanding of ethical issues that are in tension with the biblical understanding need to be conceded? Or how can traditional understandings be modified or appropriated to retain some African distinctive but still hold true to the biblical understanding to which African Christians seek to remain faithful? On the other hand, what implicit aspects of the biblical understanding need to be explicated in order to be relevant in African Christian ethics? These, I am convinced, are the tasks of Christian biblical scholars/ethicists in Africa.

The four analytical tasks described above show that the skills required to do biblical exegesis are no longer historical critical methods alone, but include other skills also such as cultural analysis, contextual hermeneutics, and systematic theological skills. In this enterprise lies the future of biblical exegesis. We shall now turn to the performative tasks, which build on the analytic tasks described above.

5. Performative Tasks

Task 5: Performance of Scripture
This fifth task is homiletical. This task engages interpreters like pastors, missionaries, preachers, and so on (whom I will henceforth refer heuristically as "non-academic" biblical interpreters) who apply the results of the work of "academic interpreters" in and through preaching, teaching, liturgy, songs, Sunday schools programs, different church groups, etc. in the context of church congregations. In this way, the task of non-academic biblical interpreters depends on (or should depend on) and benefits from the tasks of the biblical ethicists.

At this level, theology interprets the Scripture through communal worship, liturgy, songs, and prayer, but also films, podcasts, devotional books, and captions, or slogans on clothes, hand bands, emblems, cards, inscriptions on cars, buildings, on cups and plates, jewelries, etc. There are myriad media printed with Scripture and thus performing Scriptural interpretation by means of their movement and interaction in embedded contexts.

Observing trends among current biblical scholars, one wonders whether there is a growing concern to make the results of exegetical work available for general readership. To mention only three representative examples of contemporary New Testament scholarship seeking to engage a general rather than an academic audience, I think of N.T. Wright's *Simply Christian* and *After You Believe,*[18] Ruben Zimmermann's forthcoming book on the "Ethics of Relinguishing,"[19] and Danny McCain's *Tough Tests for Top Leaders.*[20] One other trend can be seen in theology's increasing interdisciplinarity. This is evident in the way faculties are continuing to organize interdisciplinary conferences (for example, between biblical ethics and medical or bio-ethics), hold lectures for popular audiences, and establish interdisciplinary doctoral and post-doctoral programs, which require participants to undertake research that is intentionally and convincingly interdisciplinary in methodology and content.[21] The more interdisciplinary theology becomes, the more the possibility for it to be fully transdisciplinary, as described in this book.

Observing these trends, we could say that the future of theology, broadly stated, in our intensely utilitarian and consumer-oriented culture, lies in its ability to integrate analytical and performative efficiency. One indication of this is the way that funding for theological research continues to decline in favor of other disciplines that are considered, consciously or unconsciously, more empirical and more practical for directly addressing immediate needs and problems. This situation has put a burden of proof on many humanities faculties – for example, theology and philosophy, to name only two – to demonstrate the relevance of their academic disciplines. Thus, the further the divide between the *academia* and the *ecclesia,* the more likely that in the future, not only states and universities, but even churches may withdraw their funding from rigorous academic theological studies, replacing them perhaps with online basic theological and ministry trainings that have immediate and direct relevance for the community. Formats for learning beyond traditional institutional structures constitute yet another performative trend already in development in theological work, and serve as a good example of the way

---

[18] Tom N. Wright, *Virtue Reborn* (London: SPCK, 2010); Tom N. Wright, *After You Believe: Why Christian Character Matters* (New York: Harper One, 2010); Tom N. Wright, *Simply Christian,* (London: SPCK, 2011).

[19] See a Q & A section with Ruben Zimmermann about the project, which is culminating in a book: http://enhancinglife.uchicago.edu/blog/enhancing-through-relinquishment-a-q-and-a-with-dr-ruben-zimmermann. Or http://enhancinglife.uchicago.edu/people/ruben-zimmermann.

[20] Danny McCain, *Tough Tests for Top Leaders: God's Strategy for Preparing Africans to Lead Global Christianity* (Jos: MoreBooks, 1984).

[21] For example, the doctoral program I am admitted into at the faculty of Protestant Theology, University of Mainz, is called "Interdisciplinary Studies in Theology and Religion." This doctoral track admits only students whose research proposals are intentionally and unambiguously interdisciplinary in nature, which would necessitate a second supervisor from another distinct discipline and faculty other than the theological disciplines.

transcultural forces (here, the reach of technology) provide new opportunities while creating new pressures.

To keep up, biblical exegesis needs to evolve continuously, at least methodologically, to be actively involved in inter or transdisciplinary interactions that challenge and enable exegesis to reflect on practical ways of applying the results of its endeavors in answering current questions and meeting current needs. This does not in any way mean that academic theology is or will not be relevant at any time. Instead, it means that theological study must keep reconstructing itself and evolving for its performative roles in both Christian and non-Christian social contexts. The interest among academic theologians in writing popular books, being socially sensitive, engaging in inter-disciplinary research, and similar "performative" endeavors give hope for the future of academic biblical exegesis.

Task 6: Performance Evaluation

Like any art, theology in general, and biblical exegesis in particular, has to be deliberately open to self-criticism, self-evaluation, and criticisms from the church and society. It must always be ready to return to the drawing board, review, reformulate, re-strategize, and present its content to the performing community (church and society) in a way that addresses current concerns.

6. Transformative Tasks

Task 7: Identification and Description of Transformation

This task seeks to identify, name, and describe specific evidences of transformation that result from the analytical and performative tasks discussed above. In other words, this task intentionally looks for evidence demonstrating the concrete impact of correct exegesis, hermeneutics, and homiletics. Moreover, it looks out for the vivid impact of the performance of Scripture in worship, liturgy, prayer, and so on. Such concrete impact could be qualitatively assessed, in the form of spiritual growth, more commitment to Christian faith and praxis, more knowledge of Scripture, more peaceful co-existence in homes and society, and the like. Or it could be quantitatively measured, in the form of numerical growth of the church, creativity and initiation of new life-transforming church programs, mission strategy, and so on.

The transforming effect of biblical exegesis and application is to be observed and evaluated at three levels: at a personal level, at an institutional level, and at a societal level. I will consider the latter two together first and then add a few thoughts concerning the personal level. Finally, I will conclude by assuming a posture of humility before the unknown mysteries that lie ahead.

Institutional and Societal (Trans-) Formation

An example of how exegesis has had an institutional effect on generations is seen in its interpretation of the NT "household codes" (Col 3:18–4:1; Eph 5:21–6:9; 1 Pet 2:18–3:7; 1 Tim 2:8–15 and Titus 2:1–10).[22] Two outstanding negative impacts the interpretation of these texts has had on the church and family as institutions may be seen (1) in the way that submission of the wife to her husband has been overemphasized over and against the husband's love for his wife and (2) in the way that many church institutions do not ordain women based on their understanding of some of these texts. It is, therefore, no surprise that feminist biblical interpreters now heavily indict "the household codes," especially those in the pastoral epistles. For example, Frances Young argues that the household codes in the pastoral epistles "have shaped a world in which women and others have been subordinated and devalued on the authority of God's word."[23] She concludes that in a democratic society which has a totally different view of women, lay people, and slaves, the pastorals epistles cannot but become "texts of terror."[24] Lilian Portefaix likewise laments that the pastoral epistles' instruction regarding women have been "causing oppression inside and outside the church from late antiquity up to the present time."[25] Elisabeth Schüssler Fiorenza, too, has indicted the pastoral epistles of advocating the patriarchal order of submission and subordination.[26] Linda M. Maloney also posits that from a feminist point of view, the pastorals epistles are "the most revealing part of Christian Testament[. . .]and the most frustrating."[27] She, therefore, indicts them of "heavy and unmistakable misogyny."[28] These

---

[22] See David L. Balch, *Let Wives be Submissive: The Domestic Code in 1 Peter* (Chico: Scholars Press, 1981), 1.

[23] Frances Young, *New Testament Theology: The Pastoral Epistles* (Cambridge: Cambridge University Press, 1994), 146.

[24]Young, *New Testament Theology*, 146 n.3.

[25] Lilian Portefaix, "'Good Citizenship' in the Household of God: Women's Position in the Pastorals Reconsidered in the Light of Roman Rule," in *A Feminist Companion to the Deutero-Pauline Epistles*, ed. by Amy-Jill Levine and Marianne Blickenstaff (London: T & T Clark International, 2003), 157–58. Portefaix laments that instead of considering them as admonitions by the author to a few communities during the reign of Trajan in the eastern part of Aegean, they have overtime been directly applied to all Christian women of all periods. Young also notes that to a large extent the teachings in the pastoral epistles are culture-specific, and women readers have found much there that has tended to marginalize them in church structures. Cf. Young, *Theology of the Pastoral Epistels*, 2.

[26] Elisabeth Schüssler Fiorenza, *In Memory of Her: A Feminist Theological Reconstruction of Christian Origins* (New York: Crossroad, 1983), 289.

[27] Linda M. Maloney, "The Pastoral Epistles," in *Searching the Scriptures: A Feminist Commentary*, vol. 2, ed. Elisabeth Schüssler Fiorenza (New York: Crossroad, 1994), 361.

[28] Maloney, "The Pastoral Epistles," 363.

are just few examples of contemporary voices seeking to depatriarchalize the NT "household codes" in the light of the transcultural realities of our time.

Beyond indicting these texts, biblical scholars are now reinterpreting the texts with more careful attention to linguistic and theological details, the socio-historical background, and the intended range of application of the texts. For example, the present passive indicative verb ὑποτάσσεται in Eph. 5:24 has been interpreted as pointing to the Church's submission to Christ as being a model for the wife's submission to her husband.[29] However, patriarchal interpretations over centuries have mostly presented wife's submission to her husband as a command or an imperative to be unconditionally obeyed rather than an admirable virtue to be desired, acquired, and creatively and contextually applied, modelled after the relationship between Christ and the church.

Nonetheless, current biblical scholars, paying attention to linguistic details, now argue that in the Greek text, there is neither an imperative verb commanding, nor a subjunctive verb admonishing wives to submit to their husbands. Many translations deduce a third person imperative ("'so let wives also be subject' in everything to their husbands" RSV) or a subjunctive nuance ("'so also wives should submit' to their husbands in everything" NIV) as an implied message based on the context, and not an explicit (linguistic) command to wives to submit to their husbands. On the other hand, however, there is an imperative verb ἀγαπᾶτε (Eph 5:26), commanding husbands to love their wives. Zimmermann rightly argues, on this basis, that Eph 5:21–31 "is not primarily admonishing women, but rather that men are being instructed on their obligation to love."[30] Zimmermann's argument finds validation in the argument that the first pointer to an ethical instruction is in the language itself. Hence, if the author intended to command wives to submit to their husbands, he would have chosen to use an imperative verb to express that, as he has done for the instruction to men to love their wives.

---

[29] See Harry O. Maier, *Picturing Paul in Empire: Imperial Image, Text and Persuasion in Colossians, Ephesians and the Pastoral Epistels* (London: Bloomsbury, 2013), 164–66. According to Maier, "the Pastorals present the harmoniously functioning household as the blueprint for faithful religious practice and belief." This is the context of "household codes" that many modern interpreters express their discontent with the Pastorals. The letters repeatedly return to traditional female gender roles as mark of a rightly worshipping and behaving household of God. Maier notes that ancient Greek writers described the household as the most basic element of civic rule and harmony, and this is the tradition underlying the "household codes" in the NT and other extracanonical materials (Maier, *Picturing Paul*, 165). However, the Pastorals expand and adapt "Haustafel topos" in a new and dynamic way by equating a properly governed church with a properly governed household (1 Tim 3:1–12, Titus 1:5–9). In the Pastorals, the household church and imperial ideals have been successfully wedded that good citizenship, traditional gender performance, and being a Christ-follower had become identical (Maier, *Picturing Paul*, 166).

[30] Zimmermann, *How to Read Biblical Texts Ethically*, 8.

Observing trajectories, we could therefore say that while biblical theology over the centuries has interpreted the "household codes" as "archetypes," with patriarchal structures that have formed institutional traditions, current biblical scholarship, by paying attention to linguistic, theological, and ethical details, interprets them as "prototypes,"[31] thereby de-patriarchalizing them and transforming husband-wife relationships and the roles of women in church as an institution.

This example of how the NT "household codes" have been patriarchally interpreted over the years and how it is being re-interpreted and de-patriarchalized today illustrates one of the things that biblical exegesis does. It transforms institutions such as church and family, identifies and names the transforming effects it had had, and re-interprets the texts where necessary in order to promote tranquil and just human relations in family, church, and society at large.

Personal (Trans-)Formation

It is important, at this point, to make further comments on evaluating personal transformation at an individual level, especially of and by biblical scholars and moral theologians, because it seems to be often neglected. It can be easy for biblical scholars and moral theologians to have a "hero" mentality, seeing themselves more as those who work "for" the church to help the laity understand and apply Scripture than those who seek to understand and apply Scripture by and for themselves. The danger in this "hero" mentality is that it could keep the scholar busy looking out for the fruit or visible impact of his or her labor or heroism (displayed in scholarly works, preaching, teaching, etc.) in the lives of others while forgetting to let the tasks he or she has engaged in transform him-/herself; this busyness can lead to forgetting to identify and describe the transformative effect exegesis can have on her-/himself as an individual. To correct this shift in focus, I refer to the transformative task included in my concept of exegethics. The transformative effect of biblical interpretation (both at analytical and performative levels) addresses both the biblical scholar who interprets Scripture as "scripted" and the moral theologi-

[31] According to Schüssler Fiorenza (Schüssler Fiorenza, *In Memory of Her*, 33), feminist theology challenges biblical theological scholarship to develop a paradigm for biblical interpretation which presents the NT not "as an archetype but as a prototype," understanding archetype as presenting an ideal, unchanging, and timeless pattern while prototype presents biblical ethics as "critically open to the possibilities of its own transformation." Even though the methodological approach to this research is different from the feminist approach, the interpretation of the' "household codes" in Titus responds positively to Schüssler Fiorenza's challenge. The virtue-ethical approach adopted here understands the household virtues in Titus 2:1–10 as not "archetypes" but "prototypes" for a functional Christian household, on the basis that there is no concrete ethos for action but virtues for acquisition and creative application.

an who interprets Scripture as "script." It is when the scholar identifies and describes the transformative effect of the Scripture on his or her own life as an individual that he or she can credibly look out for, identify, and appreciate the transformative effect of her or his own endeavors on other individuals in the church congregation, on the church as an institution, on culture, and on the society at large.

Hence, when undertaking academic theological exercises, there are two kinds of questions the exegete should be asking, namely, academic questions and moral questions. Academic questions include, for example, historical-critical questions like, who is the author of this text? Who were and are the recipients? What was the occasion or purpose of writing? What is the intended message of the text? Why does the author use a certain tense or mood instead of another? What does, for example, the word λόγος ("word/reason") in John or δικαιοσύνη ("righteousness/justice") in Paul mean? How are these terminologies used in the LXX, apocryphal books, other parts of the NT, and other writings of the time? What is the history of reception of this concept in the medieval era, 20th century, and the like?

The moral questions, on the other hand, include: What does this text or concept that I have analyzed linguistically mean to me today? What does the message of this text, or the meaning of this word, say to my life today? How does it transform my relationship with my spouse, partner, children, relatives, colleagues, neighbors, strangers, refugees? How does it influence my priorities in life?

Broader moral questions might include: How does the knowledge I have gained from my analysis of biblical texts or my reflection on theological concepts affect my attitude towards the Bible and its message? Does the knowledge inspire pride in me to disregard the authority of Scripture because I think I have analyzed and concluded that, for example, a portion of a given text was the author's adaptation of secular materials and does not have anything distinctively Christian to it – and is therefore not "inspired"? Or does it inspire humility in me, making me to see that even with my academic skills and analysis, I have only known just a little portion of the Scripture, that my knowledge is finite and therefore insufficient to finalize judgment about its authority? Does it inspire humility in me to see that God is bigger and greater than any written text, and no analyses of text can faithfully contain who God is in his entirety? Am I not doing a disservice to my sponsors, my family, the church, and society if I do shabby and lazy work after spending so much money and time on the research?

In the context of personal transformation where opinions could be presented subjectively and/or subjunctively, it is helpful to illustrate the moral questions I have described above with my personal experience, gained mostly through and during my doctoral research on virtue or character ethics in the letter to Titus. In my analysis of σωφροσύνη "self-control," δικαιοσύνη "justice," εὐσέβεια "godliness," καλά ἔργα "good works," ἐπιεικής "humility," φιλόξενος "hospitality," ἀνέγκλητος "blamelessness," etc. in Titus, I have continuously reflected on how I should apply these virtues in my daily life. I do ask myself, for example, am I becoming more just, humbler, more honest, and more self-controlled in my behavior towards my wife, children, colleagues, and everyone? Whenever I am confronted with any practical life situation that challenges me to compromise my humility, or my honesty, self-control, or justice, I do remember to reflect: What sort of a hypocrite would I be if I devote years to study these virtues in the Scripture, and yet fail to apply them in practical daily life?

If biblical scholars and theologians engage in such honest self-evaluation of the moral transformative effects of their scholarly work on their own lives, it will engender fidelity and provide a more credible basis for calling other Christians and the society to responsible living.

Task 8: The "Unknown" Task

Finally, biblical exegethics recognizes that our scholarly endeavors today have future impact beyond our generation. Including the "unknown" task is important because, while we can identify, describe, correct, and even control the impact of our biblical interpretation on people, institutions, and cultures, we have no control on what the future generations may do with the work we produce or how they will use that work in interpreting Scripture. One cannot help but imagine that Paul, for example, had no idea the number of academic doctors and professors that would emerge from engaging with his writings, neither had he a clue as to the number of books that would be written out of his writings. He probably had no idea that analyzing or interpreting his letters, which are sometimes very simple with personal notes to close associates, would become a profession or occupation that provides employment to hundreds of thousands of people around the world, from one generation to another. Similarly, it is possible that biblical interpreters like Luther, Schleiermacher, Bultmann, Bonhoeffer (to mention just a few) had no idea to what extent their exegetical endeavors would impact future generations, including ours. Nevertheless, lots of academic societies, research groups, conferences, symposia, doctoral and post-doctoral theses have emerged and are still emerging from their works. Such imaginations or thoughts should spring up when we, as biblical exegetes, are analyzing biblical texts. Knowing that the future effect of our analytical, performative, and transformative tasks on the generations to come is unknown to us should call us, all exegetes and theologians, to fidelity and to humility.

7. Summary and Conclusion

The eight tasks of biblical interpretation in African contexts that we have discussed in this chapter are summarized as follows:

Analytical Tasks

- Task 1: Textual analysis or exegesis, interpreting Scripture as "scripted."
- Task 2: Cultural analysis, analyzing both historical and contemporary African culture.
- Task 3: Synthetic analysis, analyzing the tandems and tensions between ethical perspectives.
- Task 4: Appropriative task, negotiating and appropriating a new ethical space.

Performative Tasks

- Task 5: Performative interpretation. Preaching, liturgy, songs, and Sunday school but also vast quantities of material culture that (re)present Scripture in manifold ways.
- Task 6: Performative evaluation. Review, re-evaluation, re-interpretation of interactions with Scripture.

Transformative Tasks

- Task 7: Transformation Identification and Description. Identifying and describing concrete moral transformation that result from all the interpretive tasks discussed above.
- Task 8: The "Unknown" Task. Fidelity with humility in view of the future unknown impact of our current theological efforts.

The future of exegetical theology seems to be in its transdisciplinary structure, which also implies that, its relevance in a comity of text-related disciplines depends on its ability to develop transdisciplinary methodologies. As it stands, the continuous shift towards a transcultural and transdisciplinary function of theology itself seems to have outpaced exegesis. Trying to catch up, theological exegesis could be said to be currently at the level of interdisciplinary approaches, which is still a rather new horizon in exegesis – at least in many European settings.

To meet the challenges of the transcultural and transdisciplinary that contemporary society and academic disciplines have introduced, exegetical theology needs to develop appropriate methodologies beyond historical critical ones. This chapter has, therefore, proposed exegethics as a viable methodology, with reflections from an African Christian context.

Bibliography

Balch, David L. "Household Codes." In *Greco-Roman Literature and the New Testament: Selected Forms and Genres*, edited by David E. Aune, 25-50. Atlanta Georgia: Scholar Press, The Society of Biblical Literature, 1988.

Balch, David L. *Let Wives be Submissive: The Domestic Code in 1 Peter*. Society of Biblical Literature Monograph Series. Volume 26. Chico: Scholars Press, 1981.

Bond, Lucy. "Types of Transculturality: Narrative Frameworks and the Commemoration of 9/11." In *The Transcultural Turn. Interrogating Memory Between and Beyond Borders*, edited by Lucy Bond, and Jessica Rapson, 61-80. Berlin and Boston: De Gruyter, 2014.

Carrier, Peter, and Kobi Kabalek. "Cultural Memory and Transcultural Memory – a Conceptual Analysis." In *The Transcultural Turn. Interrogating Memory Between and Beyond Borders*, edited by Lucy Bond, and Jessica Rapson, 39-60. Berlin, Boston: De Gruyter, 2014.

Carson, Don A. *What is Biblical Theology? And Do We Need It?* An interview with D.A.Carson. Desiring God Episode 644. July 21, 2015: https://www.desiringgod.org/interviews/what-is-biblical-theology-and-do-we-need-it.

Schüssler Fiorenza, Elisabeth, ed. *Searching the Scriptures: A Feminist Commentary*, vol. 2. New York: Crossroad, 1994.

Schüssler Fiorenza, Elisabeth. *In Memory of Her: A Feminist Theological Reconstruction of Christian Origins*. New York: Crossroad, 1985.

Young, Frances. *New Testament Theology: The Pastoral Epistles*. Cambridge: Cambridge University Press, 1994.

Gruber, Judith. *Intercultural Theology: Exploring World Christianity After the Cultural Turn*. Göttingen: Vandenhoeck & Ruprecht, 2017.

Maier, Harry O. *Picturing Paul in Empire: Imperial Image, Text and Persuasion in Colossians, Ephesians and the Pastoral Epistles*. London: Bloomsbury, 2013.

Maloney, Linda M. "The Pastoral Epistles." In *Searching the Scriptures: A Feminist Commentary*, vol. 2, edited by Elisabeth Schüssler Fiorenza, 361-378. New York: Crossroad, 1994.

Ngwa, Kenneth. *Exodus and Exile as Doors of (no) Return? Moses, Sundiata and the Constructions of Afro-Spatial-Genealogies*. Paper presented at the Annual Conference of the Society of Biblical Literature 2017, Boston, MA, USA.

Portefaix, Lilian. "'Good Citizenship' in the Household of God: Women's Position in the Pastorals Reconsidered in the Light of Roman Rule." In *A Feminist Companion to the Deutero-Pauline Epistles*, edited by Amy-Jill Levine and Marianne Blickenstaff, 147-158. London: T & T Clark, 2003.

Verhey, Allen. "Ethics in Scripture." In *Dictionary of Scripture and Ethics*, edited by Joel B. Green, 5-11. Grand Rapids: Baker, 2011.

Verhey, Allen. "Scripture as Script and as Scripted: The Beatitudes." In *Character Ethics and the NT: Moral Dimensions of Scripture*, edited by Robert L. Brawley, 19-34. London: Westminster John Knox Press, 2007.

Young, Frances. *New Testament Theology: The Pastoral Epistles*. Cambridge: Cambridge University Press, 1994.

Zimmermann, Ruben, and Stephen Joubert. *Biblical Ethics and Application*. Tübingen: Mohr Siebeck, 2017.

Zimmermann, Ruben, Jan G. Van Der Watt, and Susanne Luther. *Moral Language in the New Testament: The Inter-relatedness of Language and Ethics in Early Christian Writings*. Tübingen: Mohr Siebeck, 2010.

Zimmermann, Ruben. *How to Read Biblical Texts Ethically: The New Methods of "Implicit Ethics" in Dealing with Biblical Ethics*. A paper presented at the SBL, USA, 2014.

Zimmermann, Ruben. *The Logic of Love: Discovering Paul's "Implicit Ethics" Through 1 Corinthians*. Translated by Dieter T. Roth. Lanham et al: Lexington Books/Fortress Academic, 2018.

As Many Theories as Phenomena

Practical Theology as Theory of Theology

Inja Inderst (Bonn, Germany)

1. Introduction

Conducting pastoral conversations, leading a church, teaching classes – these are not the things practical theology actually deals with. Not concretely, not abstractly, not generally. So, at the risk of being the bearer of bad news, I want to challenge a common misconception here at the outset: Practical theology (PT) is actually theory, not practice. The theory-practice question is a classical topic that arises at the university, and, particularly as it concerns the discipline of practical theology, in practical theology one learns how theology works in practice.

In saying that practical theology is "only" theory I am not trying to make an appeal for recognition in the context of a research university. Rather, the claim refers to reflection on the significant challenges arising for religious practice in the presence of social and religious diversity. Practical theology takes as its task both to *understand* religious and ecclesiastical practice and to make it *understandable*. An overview of the entire field of practice is needed. This, in turn, requires that practical theology be able to render practice visible, that is, that it create structures which make practice accessible for analysis. And here we're already becoming theoretical, when we've only just begun.

Our theoretical work can be divided into three main approaches: historical and systematic theology combined with empirical research. With historical theological methods, we ask: What was it like in the past? How have things changed? Where does change come from? With systematic theological reflection its methods, we ask: What does religion mean? What do human beings need? Is there right and wrong or good and bad religion? With empirical research – and this is probably where practical theology distinguishes itself the most from other theological disciplines – we ask, how do we quantify these questions and make them tangible? For example, data might be collected on church membership numbers to see if it is really the case that worship services are being attended less. Practical theology uses sociology and psychology to better understand this phenomenon and make it understandable.

One can basically say that as theory PT wants to make the increasing complexity of culture tangible and understandable. This is due to a significant extent to the fact that PT in it present forms has developed alongside the development of the human sciences themselves. The sub-disciplines within practical theology of church theory, homiletics, liturgy, pastoral care and religious education reflect that development. They comprise the breadth and complexity in which Christian and ecclesiastical themes evolve. Practical theology can therefore be regarded as a product of social pluralization, which it in turn reacts to. Practical theology is thus multidimensional and multi-perspectival.

Practical theology as theory is therefore about understanding religious and ecclesiastical practice and the ways these require making oneself understood. Although it makes use of historical, systematic, and empirical methods, it is with a hermeneutical posture that it lives and moves and has its being.[1]

So then, with that being said: "What does Practical Theology do?"

I would like to use practical theology itself to outline an answer to this question. First, I will summarize the beginnings and history of practical theology. Then, second, I will look at whether PT does what it says it does, or in other words, take a critical look at PT's account of itself as a discipline. This is where empirical research comes into play. Third, I address the question: "What is PT [doing] when it does what it does?" And therein lies my thesis: Practical Theology *is* hermeneutics and theory of communication that is closely related to hermeneutics. And hermeneutics is the interface at which all the theological disciplines run out. This leads me to conclude, third, practical theology amounts to theory of theology.

2. Where Does Practical Theology's Doing Come From? A Look at its History

The theological discipline of practical theology in its modern form was founded by Friedrich Daniel Ernst Schleiermacher (1768-1834), and the first textbook published in the field was written by his student, Carl Immanuel Nitzsch (1787-1868).[2] Schleiermacher's and Nitzsch's approaches stand in the context of the separation of church and state. The 18th and 19th centuries faced the challenge of the divergence of ecclesiastical and secular social orders, so that it was no longer obvious what religion, interwoven with a variety of cultural practices, actually was and how church practice might be changing or need to change as a result. In his Philosophical Ethics, Schleiermacher developed a theory of society that attempted to give an account of the evolution of society in terms of differentiation into what today are referred to as social systems as that was unfolding in his day. The central task of practical theology in that

---

[1] Cf. Michael Meyer-Blanck and Birgit Weyel, *Studien- und Arbeitsbuch Praktische Theologie* (Göttingen: Vandenhoeck & Ruprecht, 22008), 259ff.

[2] Cf. Christian Grethlein and Michael Meyer-Blanck, *Geschichte in der Praktischen Theologie: Dargestellt anhand ihrer Klassiker* (Leipzig: Evangelische Verlagsanstalt, 1999), 1-65.

context became the study of the differentiation of church, individual Christianity and society as well as their interactions.[3]

Schleiermacher thus approached religion at the intersections of science, culture and society and demanded that it be understood there, rather than separated from them, and PT emerged as a subject exactly with and in response to the pluralization of practice. To an extent, the same can be said of the concept and study of religion itself: "Religion" formed as an object of inquiry at the intersection of science, culture and society and thus in response to social differentiation and pluralization. Somewhat paradoxically one can say: the reason we cannot separate out religion from science, politics and culture is because they *are functionally* separated. The functional differentiation of society has brought about this complex overlapping. And this insight constitutes the organizing principle and focus of the discipline of practical theology.

It is for this reason that I would suggest the "transcultural" presents itself as a more helpful concept than the intercultural for analyzing Schleiermacher's context as well as our own due to its ability to recognize and address various levels and forms of social complexity, including but not limited to the meeting of two discrete "cultures." Social environments consist of different, evolving contextual complexities: In Schleiermacher's day these included pietistic influences and the projects of the enlightenment; numerous and overlapping contexts fill our own social environment today. In this evolutionary or developmental process there always arise questions of "What to say" and "how to say it": But "How to *do* it" is a theoretical question that began with Schleiermacher – and he began asking that question in response to the perception of the pluralization of practice. Starting with Schleiermacher, PT has been understood as a science of perception and understanding that is not content merely to carry exegetical and dogmatic insights into practice.

3. Perception of Religious Practice as a Challenge from an Empirical Perspective

Springing forward, the empirical turn in practical theology around 1970 led to the realization of the necessity of bringing theological questions to bear on empirical research findings. The aim was to overcome the growing distance between the church and the real situations of people's lives and society. And this led PT to specialize its work further in distinction from, though still not competition with, systematic theology.[4]

Within PT, empirical action serves as a solution to the problem of perception. Here PT becomes a kind of "early warning system" in theology, when the

[3] Cf. Meyer-Blanck and Weyel, *Studien- und Arbeitsbuch*, 9-10.
[4] Cf. Meyer-Blanck and Weyel, *Studien- und Arbeitsbuch*, 46.

"desire to do better" is approached too hastily. Practical theology first asks descriptively: "What is *really* happening here?" Using empirical methods, PT creates "texts" from data that can be read and interpreted. And in fact, one way of interpreting the question "What does Theology do, actually?" - at least from a practical-theological perspective - is to read it as a question about the relation of theology to its object in the present situation: To what extent do religion in general and Christianity in particular still find expression and relevance in a plural and secular society?

The Church Membership Surveys (KMU) of the Protestant Church in Germany (EKD) are examples of empirical work on this question. The first KMU Survey "How stable is the church?"[5] stands against the background of the rising number of people giving up their formal church membership since the end of the 60s. As formulated, the question implies concern about a collapse of church practice- which would make theological reflection superfluous in the long run. Today the wording is more positive: The V.KMU bears the title "Networked Diversity".[6] Pluralism no longer seems to be interpreted primarily as a danger. But it becomes clear that also in this empirical research of practical theology above all "social and ecclesiastical change [. . .] is decisive for the interpretation of the results."[7] The focus remains social pluralisation and, coincidentally, religious pluralisation.[8] The multitude of contemporary lifestyles and models, the understanding of the roles of men and women and the understanding of family and work are just a few examples of this. It "means on the whole an increasing differentiation of very different milieus, lifestyles and subcultures."[9] The experience of individuals shaping their own lives and being able and having to decide for themselves (!) also affects religious understanding. And within and alongside these social changes, religious and cultural pluralization becomes more and more visible in everyday life.[10] It is a logical consequence that both in practice and in theory more and more differences become visible that must be dealt with in practical theology.

---

[5] Cf. the title of the book Helmut Hild, *Wie stabil ist die Kirche? Bestand und Erneuerung: Ergebnisse einer Meinungsbefragung* (Gelnhaus: Burckhardthaus, 1974).

[6] Heinrich Bedford-Strohm and Volker Jung, *Vernetzte Vielfalt: Kirche angesichts von Individualisierung und Säkularisierung: Die fünfte EKD-Erhebung über Kirchenmitgliedschaft* (Gütersloh: Gütersloher Verlagshaus, 2015).

[7] Jan Hermelink and Birgit Weyel, "Vernetzte Vielfalt: Eine Einführung in den theoretischen Ansatz, die methodischen Grundentscheidungen und zentralen Ergebnisse der V. KMU," in *Vernetzte Vielfalt: Kirche angesichts von Individualisierung und Säkularisierung: Die fünfte EKD-Erhebung über Kirchenmitgliedschaft*, ed. Heinrich Bedford-Strohm and Volker Jung (Gütersloh: Gütersloher Verlagshaus, 2015), 16-32, 17.

[8] Cf. Hermelink and Weyel, "Vernetzte," 17-18.

[9] Hermelink and Weyel, "Vernetzte," 18.

[10] Cf. Hermelink and Weyel, "Vernetzte," 18.

Practical theological reflection, however, not only includes description, but also the interpretation of what is described. At this point, we approach the hermeneutic work of PT. Not only the data, but especially interpretations thereof are manifold and often divergent - even within practical theology itself. Thus, the interpretations of the data of the V.KMU developed "in [. . .] contradictory directions."[11] On the one hand, some interpreted the V.KMU data to imply an increasing secularization, in which "religious communication [. . .] hardly finds itself without church."[12] The data of the V.KMU had refuted the view that all people have a religious interest. On the other hand and contrary to this, there were those who found the classical parish office continued to play a key role and considered and regarded the increase in conventional justifications for church memberships as a positive trend.[13] Instead of opting for one interpretation and excluding the other, there is a third that is more compelling interpretation under present circumstances: Claudia Schulz, Tabea Spieß, and Eberhard Hauschildt interpret such contradictions "from the perspective of a theory of the church as hybrid"[14] which finds those interpretations "neither surprising nor unfortunate"[15] per se. For it can also be assumed that in the Protestant church several logics, which also run contrary to each other, stand side by side.[16] If these differences of the different ways of life, as identified by the V.KMU, contrast with each other, it is true that the church remains in its hybrid structure.[17] This suggests that the situation of the churches - and probably this holds for other religious communities as well - is not wholly or best explained by only *one* theory, approached using a single methodology. Instead theoretically and methodologically diverse approaches

---

[11] Claudia Schulz, Tabea Spieß and Eberhard Hauschildt, "Zwischen kirchlichem Mainstream und der Macht der Mileudifferenzen: Lerneffekte aus der Analyse von Mileus, Lebensstilen und Lebenslagen," in *Vernetzte Vielfalt. Kirche angesichts von Individualisierung und Säkularisierung. Die fünfte EKD-Erhebung über Kirchenmitgliedschaft,* ed. by Heinrich Bedford-Strohm and Volker Jung (Gütersloh: Gütersloher Verlagshaus, 2015), 219-235, 234.

[12] Gerhard Wegner, *Religiöse Kommunikation und Kirchenbindung: Ende des liberalen Paradigmas?* (Leipzig: Evangelische Verlagsanstalt, 2014), 7f.

[13] Cf. Jan Hermelink, Anne Elise Liskowsky, and Franz Grubauer, "Kirchliches Personal," in *Engagement und Indifferenz: Kirchenmitgliedschaft als soziale Praxis: V.EKD-Erhebung über Kirchenmitgliedschaft,* ed. by EKD (Hannover: Evangelische Kirche Deutschland, 2014), 96-105. Cf. the contribution of Schulz, Spieß and Hauschildt, "Zwischen," 234.

[14] Schulz, Spieß and Hauschildt, "Zwischen," 235, (translation mine).

[15] Schulz, Spieß and Hauschildt, "Zwischen," 235, (translation mine).

[16] Cf. Eberhard Hauschildt and Uta Pohl-Patalong, *Kirche* (Gütersloh: Gütersloher Verlagshaus, 2013), 138-219; cf. Schulz, Spieß, and Hauschildt, "Zwischen," 235.

[17] Hauschildt and Pohl-Patalong develop church as "hybrid", which networks the seemingly contradictory images of church within itself. See Hauschildt and Pohl-Patalong, *Kirche,* 216-21.

are needed that are appropriate to the social diversity of the phenomena being interpreted.[18]

In the presence of the complex social trends (and often seeming incoherencies) brought about by pluralisation and secularisation, one needs almost as many theories as possible constellations of phenomena. In this way it is possible to let the diversity and contrariness of experiences, views and scientific approaches stand side by side, that they might come into constructive dialogue with one another without playing one off against the other. For practical theology, this could mean that it itself forms a kind of hybrid of different disciplines and sciences. Practical theology pays attention to subtle differences, discovers small incoherencies and diversities and reacts to them in detail, and in so doing it draws on sciences such as sociology and psychology, that look at important social trends at both the societal and individual level.

What does this mean for the occurrence of religion in society? Even though the V.KMU puts questions of church sociology at the centre of its analysis, it also allows conclusions to be drawn about religious practice as a whole.[19] It is obvious that religion is *no longer obvious* in today's society – it is no longer something to be assumed or taken for granted. It is also much less institutionally bound. What is meant by religion is not fixed. And groups of people who regularly make use of church services may not extensively reflect on theological questions.[20] According to scholars like Weyel and Hermlink, religion is "first and foremost and ever anew identified and emblematized in social practices – or not in which case it remains implicit."[21] Either way, "Religion is essentially to be regarded as communication."[22] And rendering religion visible or legible for research requires that these religious communications be transcribed. The consequence of this is to understand interviewees, for example, in the context of empirical studies "as religious subjects, who each form their own relationship to the convictions as well as to the practice of the church on their own, and, indeed, in the context of their entire way of life as well as their world and self-interpretation."[23] Here the understanding of the church in the Protestant sense, "as a social, communicative, and at the same

---

[18] Cf. Schulz, Spieß, and Hauschildt, "Zwischen," 235.

[19] Cf. Hermelink and Weyel, "Vernetzte," 21.

[20] Schulz, Spieß, and Hauschildt, "Zwischen," 233: "'Social' church members are not at the same time more religious because of their tendency to socialise. Church sociability, however, gives them a contact surface, while it certainly does not address fewer sociable people who are close to the church. It is not appropriate to identify church socializing practice with a theological understanding of Christian and church 'fellowship'." (translation mine).

[21] Hermelink and Weyel, "Vernetzte," 21 with reference to Thomas Luckmann, *Die unsichtbare Religion*, (Frankfurt am Main: Suhrkamp, 1991 [1967]).

[22] Hermelink and Weyel, "Vernetzte," 21.

[23] Hermelink and Weyel, "Vernetzte," 22.

time reflected practice shaped by multiple perspectives"[24] does not first refer to the church office, but to the "communication of the gospel."[25] This means: If "theology as a whole [. . .] is to develop perspectives of interpretation and action for the life of Christian people which have to do with real decisions and actions and not only with conceptual distinctions,"[26] and if there is no such thing as a single "Christian practice", then empirical work as a description of Christian practices is a necessity.

But it also is not sufficient. Although many religious persons' expressions of faith may not be explicated wholly with reference to specific religious traditions and communities, the hermeneutical work requires contextualizing these descriptions within such framings. This is not, strictly speaking, a *prescriptive* kind of work, but neither is it to be regarded as wholly neutral or indifferent. To the extent that it draws distinctions with, about and for a particular tradition or community and makes interpretations about continuities and changes, it requires unavoidably the responsible exercise of judgement.

4. Practical Theology as Hermeneutics and Science of Communication

So far it has been shown exemplarily with the two methods of historical contemplation and empirical research what practical theology does, namely, to find an answer to a question on a theoretical level by looking at practice - in this case: "What does practical theology do?" From its history it showed itself as an "observational science" of a given present situation or context, which becomes accessible to it above all through use of empirical methods. When considering empirical data, the question about the relevance of the question "What does theology do, actually?" arose - that is, whether theology's own actions have any meaning at all. This question might be answered with a "yes", on the understanding, however, that religion never appears unambiguously and without contradiction in the face of pluralization and secularization. And this means that theology's own meanings, significances, purposes, and "doings" will reflect those ambiguities and contradictions.

At this point the hermeneutic competence of practical-theological reflection becomes relevant.

In practical theology, one encounters different contexts empirically, *in situ*, so-to-speak, and it is indispensable to perceive and take seriously their differences. In other words, at a certain level, it is not about finding out and deciding what is right and better, but about perception and discussion. And so it is about hermeneutics and communication.

---

[24] Hermelink and Weyel, "Vernetzte," 22 (translation mine).
[25] Hermelink and Weyel, "Vernetzte," 22 (emphasis in original; translation mine).
[26] Meyer-Blanck and Weyel, *Studien- und Arbeitsbuch*, 47 (translation mine).

Therefore, the relationship of practical to systematic theology in situations of transcultural complexity such as our own needs to be rather fundamentally reconsidered. If practical theology is understood in Schleiermacher's sense as theory and not as a system for pastoral training, then practical theology is only possible "as theory of religion and thus with strong systematic components."[27] In contrast to systematic theology, however, practical theology asks more about the empirical and current conditions of Christian faith, while systematic theology refers most often to philosophical analyses in relation to the history of ideas - although it cannot be thought of without a practical reference.[28] This allows practical theology to think less in the structure of the "or" than in the "and", such that, for it, empirical research and systematic theology do not have to represent competing alternatives.

In Michael Meyer-Blanck's words, practical theology is "hermeneutics of Christian practice."[29] If theology as a whole has the claim "to develop perspectives of interpretation and action for the life of Christian people which have to do with actual expressions [i.e., of belief and/in practice] and not only with conceptual distinctions,"[30] then a mere description of the diversity of Christian practice"[31] does not go far enough. Therefore, PT is also hermeneutics of Christian practice, which reflects this "with regard to new theological understanding and changed church action."[32] In other words, practical theology comes from the systematic and thinks towards it.[33] It works at the same time with descriptive and normative sentences. The description, as an indispensable, characteristic part of its reference to the present, characterizes practical theology as *practical*. Through its normative self-assurance, it becomes practical *theology*.[34] Consequently it does not - as in former times - have to decide between the alternatives of the orientation to systematic theology and the human sciences and empiricism, but as hermeneutics it cannot avoid looking at all these in a multi-perspectival way - giving particular attention to complexity and plurality in our transcultural present.

It is obvious that it cannot do this on its own, but in close exchange with all the other (theological) disciplines. It is therefore interdisciplinary. It is based on the biblical traditions from which the Gospel unfolds - not only through exegetical work, but through the hermeneutical work "in its life significance for people of the present by means of communicative acts of inter-

[27] Meyer-Blanck and Weyel, *Studien- und Arbeitsbuch*, 40, (translation mine).
[28] Cf. Meyer-Blanck and Weyel, *Studien- und Arbeitsbuch*, 40. Cf. also Michael MEYER-BLANCK, 79-80.
[29] Meyer-Blanck and Weyel, *Studien- und Arbeitsbuch*, 47 (translation mine).
[30] Meyer-Blanck and Weyel, *Studien- und Arbeitsbuch*, 47 (translation mine).
[31] Meyer-Blanck and Weyel, *Studien- und Arbeitsbuch*, 47 (translation mine).
[32] Meyer-Blanck and Weyel, *Studien- und Arbeitsbuch*, 47 (italics in original; translation mine).
[33] Meyer-Blanck and Weyel, *Studien- und Arbeitsbuch*, 47-80.
[34] Meyer-Blanck and Weyel, *Studien- und Arbeitsbuch*, 48.

pretation and communication,"[35] as Wilhelm Gräb concludes. Hermeneutical analysis thus proves to be not only the apex of practical theology, but also an intersection of all theological disciplines.

Furthermore, PT provides language that makes it possible to communicate (existential) situations. Practical theology must therefore learn to understand communication through communication. This aspect of communication is currently a focal point within the practical-theological discourse, which elevates "communication of the Gospel"[36] to the core task of practical theology. As shown above, interpretations of the empirical data lead to the view that the understanding of the church in the Protestant sense, "as a social, communicative, multifariously shaped and at the same time reflected practice"[37] does not first refer to the church office, but to the "communication of the gospel"[38].

In 2014 an anthology entitled *Communication of the Gospel. Guiding Concept of Practical Theology*[39] was published. This is dedicated to the practical theologian Christian Grethlein, who in his work developed "a theory of communication of the Gospel in the present."[40] According to Grethlein, Practical

---

[35] Cf. Wilhelm Gräb, "Kommunikation des Evangeliums. Religionstheologische Ansichten und Anfragen," in *Kommunikation des Evangeliums: Leitbegriff der Praktischen Theologie,* ed. Michael Domsgen and Bernd Schröder (Leipzig: Evangelische Verlagsanstalt, 2014), 68 (translation mine).

[36] German: "Kommunikation des Evangeliums". The phrase was developed especially by Ernst Lange in the 1960s and 1970s. Cf. Ernst Lange, "Aus der 'Bilanz 65'," in *Kirche für die Welt. Aufsätze zur Theorie kirchlichen Handelns,* ed. by Rüdiger Schloz (München and Gelnhausen: Burckhardthaus, 1981), 101-29. Relevant titles include: Christian Grethlein, *Kommunikation des Evangeliums in der Mediengesellschaft* (Leipzig: Evangelische Verlagsanstalt, 2003); Christian Grethlein, *Grundinformation Kasualien: Kommunikation des Evangeliums an den Übergängen des Lebens* (Göttingen: Vandenhoeck & Ruprecht, 2004); Ingolf U. Dalferth, *Evangelische Theologie als Interpretationspraxis: Eine systematische Orientierung* (Leipzig: Evangelische Verlagsanstalt, 2004), 90-113, 149-53; Reiner Preul, "Kommunikation des Evangeliums unter den Bedingungen der Mediengesellschaft (2000)," in *Die soziale Gestalt des Glaubens: Aufsätze zur Kirchentheorie,* ed. by Reiner Preul (Leipzig: Evangelische Verlagsanstalt, 2008), 65-103; Hauschildt and Pohl-Patalong, *Kirche,* 411-415; Tobias Kläden, Judith Könemann and Dagmar Stoltmann, *Kommunikation des Evangeliums: Festschrift Udo Schmälzle* (Berlin: LIT, 2008); Cf. Domsgen and Schröder, Kommunikation, 8. n. 7.

[37] Hermelink and Weyel, "Vernetzte," 22, (translation mine).

[38] Hermelink and Weyel, "Vernetzte," 22 [italics in original], (translation mine).

[39] Domsgen and Schröder, *Kommunikation des Evangeliums: Leitbegriff der Praktischen Theologie* (Leipzig: Evangelische Verlagsanstalt, 2014).

[40] Christian Grethlein, Praktische Theologie, (Berlin and Boston: De Gruyter, 2012), 157, 167, (translation mine). His understanding is discussed by practical theologians in Domsgen and Schröder, *Kommunikation.* The debates revolve in particular around the definition of "gospel" and what significance the "concept of religion" has when - as Grethlein's understanding suggests - all these concepts are only negotiated in communication.

Theology aims at "providing insights for the promotion of communication of the Gospel,"[41] so that he calls PT pointedly "theological communication science."[42] At this point the question arises as to the meaning of "communication" and "gospel", as well as their union as "communication of the gospel".

"Communication"[43] is not only reflected in an interdisciplinary way but is also a term used in everyday language.[44] Therefore, the concept of practical theological work, which aims to reflect scientifically, interdisciplinarily and at the same time realistically, is useful.

Ernst Lange, who coined the leading concept of "communication of the gospel" in the 1960s and 1970s, replaced the concept of proclamation with communication, because in communication all participants must be actively involved in it.[45] People are not regarded with him as passive, proclamation-receiving recipients, but are taken seriously as acting, communication-producing subjects.[46] Consequently, the diversity of these subjects must also be perceived and taken into account. All of them differ in their perception and communicate differently. Communication can react adequately to this. Watzlawick's basic idea "one cannot not communicate" refers to the diversity of communication that takes place where two entities can perceive each other. It provides different sign systems and includes interpersonal communication not only of a verbal but also of a non-verbal nature, that is, also signs, aesthetics, music, it takes place explicitly as well as implicitly.[47]

Because "communication of meaning [. . .] is always related to certain contents,"[48] communication in the ecclesiastical context and thus in the context of practical theology "cannot be detached from its genitive 'of the gospel', which logically names both cause and object of communication."[49] "Gospel meets in the form of religion, as speech of the unavailable and the whole, of transcendence in human languages."[50] Religion is for practical theology "ineluctable".[51]

---

[41] Grethlein, *Praktische,* 136.

[42] Grethlein, *Praktische,* 141, (italics in original).

[43] At this point, only the most important characteristics of communication are dealt with for the purposes of this essay. For a clear explanation of the term and its advantages for the practical-theological context, cf. Hauschildt and Pohl-Patalong, *Kirche,* 411-415.

[44] Cf. Hauschildt and Pohl-Patalong, *Kirche,* 412.

[45] Cf. Lange, "Aus der Bilanz," 101.

[46] Cf. Hauschildt and Pohl-Patalong, *Kirche,* 412.

[47] Cf. also Wilfried Engemann, *Personen, Zeichen und das Evangelium: Argumentationsmuster der Praktischen Theologie* (Leipzig: Evangelische Verlagsanstalt, 2003), 15.ff; Cf. Hauschildt and Pohl-Patalong, *Kirche,* 412.

[48] Hauschildt and Pohl-Patalong, *Kirche,* 413, (translation mine).

[49] Hauschildt and Pohl-Patalong, *Kirche,* 413, (translation mine).

[50] Michael Meyer-Blanck, "Gebildete Routine: Das Evangelium in der pastoralen Berufspraxis," in *Kommunikation des Evangeliums: Leitbegriff der Praktischen Theologie,* ed. Michael Domsgen and Bernd Schröder (Leipzig: Evangelische Verlagsanstalt, 2014), 101-10, 103, (translation mine).

As Meyer-Blanck explains, communication of religion gives practical theology a "theoretical access"[52] through "decisive contents and experiences."[53] According to this understanding of religious communication, practical theology reflects not only that communication in which the Gospel and religion explicitly (here meaning, "traditionally") have expressed themselves – think of the parish office in its multidimensionality, but also that in which religion reveals itself between the lines – in those areas not traditionally identified as religious, where empirical investigations provide information. What is particularly relevant in this context is the unavailability and "unplanability" of successful communication. The meaning of a text, a liturgical act or a spoken word are not necessarily understood in the way they were meant, but are given a new/individual meaning in the discussion of them by the recipients. They always understand the perceived semiotics against the background of their own context.[54] It is the task and opportunity of hermeneutical analysis to make oneself aware of this and to interpret and provide communication accordingly.

It can be said that the theological disciplines can provide language that makes it possible to communicate (existential) situations. It is precisely then that a contemporary hermeneutics becomes significant, as Gräb conceives it, in which existential-religious questions are decisive.[55] Such language transforms itself from the biblical traditions, where a conversation between PT and exegetical-theological subjects becomes indispensable in order to be able to communicate the biblical narratives scientifically (not arbitrarily), but in a meaningful way through the path of hermeneutics and to make them available for transformation and performance (for example, in sermon and liturgy).[56]

5. Conclusion

In summary, it can be said for the *doing* of PT, as highlighted in the question "What does practical theology *do*, actually?" that it asks about implicit and

---

[51] Meyer-Blanck, "Gebildete Routine," 103, (translation mine).
[52] Meyer-Blanck, "Gebildete Routine," 103, (translation mine).
[53] Meyer-Blanck, "Gebildete Routine," 103.
[54] Cf. Hauschildt and Pohl-Patalong, *Kirche*, 414-15.
[55] Cf. Wilhelm Gräb, "Kommunikation des Evangeliums: Religionstheologische Ansichten und Anfragen," in *Kommunikation des Evangeliums: Leitbegriff der Praktischen Theologie*, ed. by Michael Domsgen and Bernd Schröder (Leipzig: Evangelische Verlagsanstalt, 2014), 61-85, here 69.
[56] Statements such as "Jesus died for our sins" or "God forgives everyone" must be made accessible exegetically and hermeneutically before they are communicated. Otherwise they are ineffective because, as Michael Meyer-Blanck explicates, they are mis-communicated as general truth, (cf. Meyer-Blanck, *Gottesdienstlehre*, 112). Whereby the effect of communication always also contains a passive moment, it is not completely plannable, cf. also Pohl-Patalong and Hauschildt, *Kirche*, 414; similary Gräb, "Kommunikation," 68.

explicit relevance of religion in an interdisciplinary way in relation to the present. From the perspective that practical theology, in recourse to the past, perceives and interprets its present (specifically of Christian and ecclesiastical practice), it also asks about future. It does not presume to decide what is right and what is wrong in general. Practical theology is at its best the more it perceives and absorbs changes rather than predicting them. It perceives, reflects and interprets implicit Christian practice and explicit church practice and seeks to place them in a horizon of understanding. Practical theology can then formulate alternatives and approach what is absolutely not going to work. But it will not be able to provide a great explanation of the world and general practical guidance. It is hermeneutical in its actions so that it is closely related to systematic theology and with it makes the Gospel accessible. It is communication science because it grasps language and creates language that expresses the Gospel - be it explicit and aesthetic in preaching and liturgy, be it implicit in pastoral care conversations or in everyday life, where faith and religion are not always the starting point and content of conversation for the other.

Bibliography

Bedford-Strohm, Heinrich and Volker Jung. *Vernetzte Vielfalt: Kirche angesichts von Individualisierung und Säkularisierung: Die fünfte EKD-Erhebung über Kirchenmitgliedschaft.* Gütersloh: Gütersloher Verlagshaus, 2015.

Dalferth, Ingolf U. *Evangelische Theologie als Interpretationspraxis: Eine systematische Orientierung.* Leipzig: Evangelische Verlagsanstalt, 2004.

Domsgen, Michael and Bernd Schröder. *Kommunikation des Evangeliums: Leitbegriff der Praktischen Theologie.* Leipzig: Evangelische Verlagsanstalt, 2014.

Engemann, Wilfried. *Personen, Zeichen und das Evangelium: Argumentationsmuster der Praktischen Theologie.* Leipzig: Evangelische Verlagsanstalt, 2003.

Gräb, Wilhelm. "Kommunikation des Evangeliums: Religionstheoretische Ansichten und Anfragen," In *Kommunikation des Evangelium. Leitbegriff der Praktischen Theologie*, edited by Michael Domsgen and Bernd Schröder, 61-74. Leipzig: Evangelische Verlagsanstalt, 2014.

Grethlein, Christian. *Grundinformation Kasualien: Kommunikation des Evangeliums an den Übergängen des Lebens.* Göttingen: Vandenhoeck & Ruprecht, 2004.

Grethlein, Christian. *Kommunikation des Evangeliums in der Mediengesellschaft.* Leipzig: Evangelische Verlagsanstalt, 2003.

Grethlein, Christian. *Praktische Theologie.* Berlin and Boston: De Gruyter, 2012.

Grethlein, Christian and Michael Meyer-Blanck. *Geschichte der Praktischen Theologie: Dargestellt anhand ihrer Klassiker.* Leipzig: Evangelische Verlagsanstalt, 1999.

Hauschildt, Eberhard and Uta Pohl-Patalong. *Kirche.* Gütersloh: Gütersloher Verlagshaus, 2013.

Hermelink, Jan, Anne Elise Liskowsky, and Franz Grubauer. "Kirchliches Personal." In *Engagement und Indifferenz: Kirchenmitgliedschaft als soziale Praxis: V.EKD-Erhebung über Kirchenmitgliedschaft*, edited by EKD, 96-105. Hannover: Evangelische Kirche in Deutschland, 2014.

Hermelink, Jan, and Birgit Weyel. *"Vernetzte Vielfalt: Eine Einführung in den theoretischen Ansatz, die methodischen Grundentscheidungen und zentralen Ergebnisse der V. KMU." In Vernetzte Vielfalt: Kirche angesichts von Individualisierung und Säkularisierung: Die fünfte EKD-Erhebung über Kirchenmitgliedschaft,* edited by Heinrich Bedford-Strohm and Volker Jung, 16-32. Gütersloh: Gütersloher Verlagshaus, 2015.

Hild, Helmut. *Wie stabil ist die Kirche? Bestand und Erneuerung: Ergebnisse einer Meinungsbefragung*. Gelnhaus: Burckhardthaus, 1974.

Kläden, Tobias, Judith Könemann, and Dagmar Stoltmann. *Kommunikation des Evangeliums: FS Udo Schmälzle*. Berlin: LIT, 2008.

Lange, Ernst. *"Aus der 'Bilanz 65'." In Kirche für die Welt: Aufsätze zur Theorie kirchlichen Handelns*, edited by Rüdiger Schloz 101-129. München and Gelnhausen: Burckhardthaus, 1981.

Luckmann, Thomas. *Die unsichtbare Religion*. Frankfurt am Main: Suhrkamp, 1991 [1967].

Meyer-Blanck, Michael. *"Gebildete Routine: Das Evangelium in der pastoralen Berufspraxis." In Kommunikation des Evangeliums: Leitbegriff der Praktischen Theologie.* Leipzig: Evangelische Verlagsanstalt, edited by Michael Domsgen, and Bernd Schröder, 101-10. Leipzig: Evangelische Verlagsanstalt, 2014.

Meyer-Blanck, Michael. *Gottesdienstlehre*. Tübingen: Mohr Siebeck, 2011.

Meyer-Blanck, Michael, and Birgit Weyel. *Studien- und Arbeitsbuch Praktische Theologie*. Göttingen: Vandenhoeck & Ruprecht, [2]2008.

Preul, Reiner. "Kommunikation des Evangeliums unter den Bedingungen der Mediengesellschaft (2000)." In *Die soziale Gestalt des Glaubens: Aufsätze zur Kirchentheorie*, edited by Reiner Preul, 65-103. Leipzig: Evangelische Verlagsanstalt, 2008.

Schulz, Claudia, Tabea Spieß, and Eberhard Hauschildt. "Zwischen kirchlichem Mainstream und der Macht der Mileudifferenzen: Lerneffekte aus der Analyse von Milieus, Lebensstilen und Lebenslagen." In *Vernetzte Vielfalt: Kirche angesichts von Individualisierung und Säkularisierung: Die fünfte EKD-Erhebung über Kirchenmitgliedschaft*, edited by Heinrich Bedford-Strohm, and Volker Jung, 219-35. Gütersloh: Gütersloher Verlagshaus, 2015.

Wegner, Gerhard: *Religiöse Kommunikation und Kirchenbindung: Ende des liberalen Paradigmas?* Leipzig: Evangelische Verlagsanstalt, 2014.

Church History

Past, Present, and Context

Gianna Zipp (Mainz, Germany)

I. Introduction

This chapter aims to provide an overview of the methods and goals of Church History as a discipline, more specifically from a German point of view and with a view to the questions what Church History did, does, and might possibly do in the near future.

Therefore, it uses a historical approach to the question, "What does theology do, actually?" beginning with a historical sprint from the fourth century CE to the 1900s. Obviously, not all the important Church historians, theologians who concerned themselves with history, and historians who concerned themselves with theology can be discussed, but rather only a small selection.[1] Authors who provided the foundation for modern scholarship will then be contrasted with modern scholars who have followed and shaped the field as it is known today. These modern scholars have ensured that the subject area has been able to detach itself from other theological and historical disciplines and maintain a distinct identity. Yet Church History still shares methods and questions with other disciplines and has a great concurrence with History, for example, signaling the question concerning where Church History differs from History. Is it a difference in methods, style of writing, topic or approach? In a next step, this chapter will examine some of those methods and topics that Church History deals with, but it will also add a very recent attempt to define it in contrast to the aforementioned disciplines. Finally, this chapter will ask how Church History is placed within Theology. In the end I want to pinpoint a few difficulties and problems we face within the discipline and close, not with a conclusion, but with several open questions.

---

[1] This chapter will not give an overview, even in summary outline, of everything Church History is, can or can be defined as. See for example Wolfram Kinzig, Volker Leppin, and Günther Wartenberg, eds., *Historiographie und Theologie. Kirchen und Theologiegeschichte im Spannungsfeld von geschichtswissenschaftlicher Methode und theologischem Anspruch. Konzeption von Kurt Nowak* (Leipzig: EVA, 2004).

2. Historical Background – From Laktantius and Eusebius to Troeltsch, Hauschild, and Harnack

Some might argue that Acts is the earliest form of Church History,[2] and I would agree with that. Yet for the sake of argument I want to exclude biblical evidence from this paper and focus on Church History that was written as history with Christianity as the officially accepted *religio licita* in the Roman Empire.[3]

That leads us to Lactantius (ca. 250–320 A.D.) as the first church historian,[4] closely followed by Eusebius (ca. 260–339).[5] Both follow guidelines for historiography: They intend to tell the truth and not omit anything.[6] They tell what happened, why, and to what end.[7] These two write history to show how God rules the world and can be seen in history.[8] Later authors follow their lead

---

[2] See Martin Hengel, *Acts and the history of earliest Christianity* (Eugene: Wipf and Stock Publishers, 2003), 36-37; Plümacher, Eckhard. "Geschichtsschreibung IV. Biblisch." In *Religion in Geschichte und Gegenwart,* 4th edition http://dx.doi.org/10.1163/2405-8262_rgg4_COM_08523, 3, 807ff.; Martin Dibelius, "der erste christliche Historiker," in *Aufsätze zur Apostelgeschichte,* ed. by Heinrich Greeven (Göttingen: Vandenhoeck & Ruprecht, [4]1961), 108-119; Daniel Marguerat, *The First Christian Historian. Writing the Acts of the Apostels,* (Cambridge: Cambridge University Press, 2002); Jens Schröter, "Actaforschung seit 1983 III. Die Apostelgeschichte als Geschichtswerk," *Theologische Rundschau* 72, no. 2 (2007): 383-419, here 403-419; Jörg Frey, Clare K. Rothschild, and Jens Schröter, eds., *Die Apostelgeschichte im Kontext antiker und frühchristlicher Historiographie, Beihefte zur Zeitschrift für die neutestamentliche Wissenschaft 162,* (Berlin and New York: Walter DeGruyter, 2009).

[3] See Lact. mort. 48, 2–12; Euseb. Hist. Eccl. X, 5,2-14.

[4] There is still some debate about the genre of *Death of the Persecutors.* See for example, John McGuckin, *The Problem of Lactantius the Theologian* (Leuven: Peeters Publishers, 2017) 17–34, 19; Marcia L. Colish, *The Stoic Tradition from Antiquitiy to the Early Middle Ages. II. Stoicism in Christian Latin Thought through the Sixth Century* (Leiden: Brill, 1985), 38; Oliver Nicholson, *The Christian Sallust: Lactantius on God, Man and History,* (Leuven: Peeters Publishers, 2017), 119–38; Eve-Marie Becker, ed., *Die antike Historiographie und die Anfänge der christlichen Geschichtsschreibung,* (Berlin and New York: De Gruyter, 2005); Ulrich Eigler, "Geschichtsschreibung IV. Christentum B. Lateinisch," *Der Neue Pauly* 4 (1998), 1000–1004, here 1002; Wolfgang Kirsch, Triebkräfte der historischen Entwicklung bei Laktanz, *Klio* 66/2 (1984), 624–30, here 625. I would argue that *Death of the Persecutors* is a mixture of genres with a large share of historiography.

[5] See Aaron P. Johnson, *Eusebius* (London, Tauris & Co Ltd, 2014), 1–24; Devin Singh, "Eusebius as Political Theologian: The Legend Continues," *Harvard Theological Review,* 108, no.1 (2015): 129–54; Sabrina Inowlocki and Claudio Zamagni, eds., *Reconsidering Eusebius: Collected Papers on Literary, Historical, and Theological Issues* (Leiden and Boston: Brill, 2011).

[6] Cicero proclaims these to be the major criteria for *historia* (Cic. de orat. II, 15,62).

[7] This, too, is demanded by Cicero (Cic. de orat. II, 15,64).

[8] See Lact. mort. pers. 1,7. Lact. mort. pers. 52,1; see also Eus. Hist. Eccl. I, 1,1–2.

and focus on the connection between God and events in history. This focus remained valid throughout the Middle Ages.[9]

In the 18th century, the previous tried and tested approach was challenged by philosophers like Immanuel Kant (1724-1804). In the Age of Enlightenment, Theology as an academic enterprise had to question its methods and so did Church History, which, at the time, was not a discipline of its own but either integrated into the faculties of Philosophy or (systematic) Theology. The focus shifted from God's place in history to what is often referred to as History of Christianity and History of Dogma. From now on Church History tried to explain how certain dogmas and events came into place.[10] Still it often focused on demonstrating superiorities: Now the apologetic task was not to show which god was superior to others but which denomination. With the rise of historicist paradigms, another great shift happened. Church Historians wanted to find out "what really happened". First and foremost, Leopold von Ranke (1795-1886) who demanded: "The highest demand from an historical work remains that it is true; that things really did happen as they are presented."[11] Johann Gustav Droysen (1808-1884) objected strongly to this approach and stated that there is more to history than mere research on sources (*Quellenforschung*) and being open about one's goals. A historian, Droysen argued, must interpret history and classify it into his philosophy of life.[12]

Ernst Troeltsch (1865-1923) suggested that knowledge of events should to be tested against their probability. Even if something seemed to be the case according to sources it still had to be tested by probability.[13] He showed that sources are influenced by myths or bias - today we might add "discourse" as

---

[9] See for example, *Ottonis episcopi Frisingensis chronicon*, ed. by Adolf Hofmeister, MGH SS rer. Germ. 45 (Hanover and Leipzig, 1912), 180.

[10] See for example, Ferdinand Christian Baur, *Die christliche Lehre von der Versöhnung in ihrer geschichtlichen Entwickelung von der ältesten Zeit bis auf die neueste* (Tübingen: C.F. Osiander, 1838). Especially his Vorrede underlines the role of history of dogma in Baur's opinion.

[11] "Allein die vornehmste Forderung an ein historisches Werk bleibt doch immer, daß [a History] wahr sei; daß die Dinge sich so begeben haben, wie sie dargestellt werden," in *Französische Geschichte vornehmlich im sechzehnten und siebzehnten Jahrhundert*, ed. by Leopold Ranke (Stuttgart: J. G. Cotta'scher Verlag, 1861), 7. Translation of this and other quotations in the present chapter by Matthew Ryan Robinson. See also Helmut Berding, "Leopold von Ranke," in *The Discovery of Historicity in German Idealism and Historism, Studies in Economic Ethics and Philosophy*, ed. by Peter Koslowski (Berlin and Heidelberg: Springer 2005, 41-58).

[12] See Johann Gustav Droysen, *Grundriss der Historik* (Leipzig: Verlag con Veit & Com. 1868), 3-6.

[13] See Ernst Troeltsch, "Über historische und dogmatische Methode in der Theologie," [1908] in *Zur religiösen Lage, Religionsphilosophie und Ethik. Gesammelte Schriften Bd.*, 729-53 (Tübingen: Mohr, 1913).

an important factor. Individual events must be placed in a larger historical context to determine their influence on the present.[14]

These theologians had a lively exchange of views on the methods of history and this phase in the development of the discipline is known as historicism. With historicism, a more methodical approach to research developed. A set of skills and methods gained pride of place that are supposed to make findings verifiable. The period of their refinement was also the time when History as a field of study became independent and separated from Theology. Both subjects, however, shared their set of methods.[15] Adolf von Harnack (1851–1930) accelerated the separation between Church History and Systematic Theology by founding the series *Kirchenhistorische Gesellschaft, Texte zur Untersuchung zur Geschichte der altchristlichen Literatur*, and critical Editions like *Griechische Christliche Schriftsteller.*

3. 1950 to Today

Even though the skills and methods developed in the historicist period remain standard to this day, nevertheless, since the 1900s, Church History has further evolved. In the aftermath of World War II, Historians everywhere decided to shift their attention from the former "search for truth" as the ultimate goal of Church History to a broader approach. They tried to find out how and why things happened and what influenced opinions and decisions. The movement was slow and is still going on, but the ideal shifted from historicism to cultural studies (*Kulturwissenschaften*). With this shift, the questions change significantly: Instead of "who was the first to do this?" the narrative is more like "What socioeconomic background influenced this actor to decide in a certain way?" In the process, the whole field of Church History came into question. Karl Barth's infamous definition of Church History as an "indispensable auxiliary science"[16] and Gerhard Ebeling's definition of Church History as the "his-

[14] Troeltsch, "Über historische und dogmatische Methode," 94

[15] In 1927 Emil Clemens Scherer scrutinised the History of Church History and History at German Universities: Emil Clemens Scherer, *Geschichte und Kirchengeschichte an den deutschen Universitäten. Ihre Anfänge im Zeitalter des Humanismus und ihre Ausbildung zu selbstständigen Disziplinen* (Freiburg im Breisgau: Olms Verlag, 1927).

[16] German, "unentbehrliche Hilfswissenschaft." Karl Barth, *Die kirchliche Dogmatik 1 I.* (Zürich: EVZ-Verlag, 1932 [=1986]), 3.

tory of the interpretation of Holy Scripture"[17] are said to have changed the importance of Church History in Theology.[18]

Further, at the same time as the relationship between the theological disciplines gained more attention, it also become more important to address the question of the differences between Church History and History.

While I would argue that the difference consists mainly in the university faculty in which each may be found. Mainly, but not completely. And the differences we can determine are important ones. However, maybe in focusing on the similarities first, we can then see the differences more clearly: Both try to paint a picture of the past using mostly text-based evidence, but also include archaeological findings where applicable. Both try to be as comprehensive as possible and use a special pool of methods to work with their material. Both take into consideration socioeconomic and political reasonings for decision making processes.

Church History seems to be a little bit narrower in the topics it researches as it is always at least somehow connected to religious topics, but what does Church History do, actually, that History does not? Volker Leppin offers a definition of Church History within Theology and in contrast to History, suggesting an understanding of religion as a system of semiotic symbols helps to define the research object of Church History. Modifying Thomas Luckmann,[19] Leppin proposes:

> The object of Church History is a "socially formed system of symbols that offers orientation in the world by means of a reality constructed socially from theology, ritual, and life experience or practice" that provide the individual as well as the society with "an interpretation of transcendence."[20]

This means, Church History always investigates an object, person, group, text, system, or event, that in and of itself is oriented toward God and a heavenly

---

[17] German: "Geschichte der Auslegung der Heiligen Schrift". Gerhard Ebeling, "Kirchengeschichte als Geschichte der Auslegung der Heiligen Schrift," in *Wort Gottes und Tradition. Studien zu einer Hermeneutik der Konfessionen*, ed. Gerhard Ebeling (Göttingen: Vandenhoeck & Ruprecht, 1964), 9-27.

[18] See Wolf-Friedrich Schäufele, "Theologische Kirchengeschichtsschreibung als Konstruktionsaufgabe. Ein Plädoyer," *Theologische Literaturzeitung* 7 (2014): 831–50. Michael Basse, "Theologiegeschichtsschreibung und Kontroverstheologie: die Bedeutung der Scholastik für die protestantische Kirchengeschichtsschreibung," *Zeitschrift für Kirchengeschichte* 107, no. 1 (1996): 50-71.

[19] Thomas Luckmann, "Einleitung," in Bronislaw Malinowski, *Magie, Wissenschaft und Religion und andere Schriften*, ed. by Thomas Luckmann (Frankfurt am Main: Fischer S., 1973), xi.

[20] "Gegenstand der Kirchengeschichte ist ein 'sozialgeformtes Symbolsystem', das durch Theologie, Ritus und Lebenspraxis Weltorientierung in Bezug auf die sozial verfasste Wirklichkeit bietet und [den Einzelnen wie die Gesellschaft] transzendierende Sinngebung' stiftet." Volker Leppin, "Kirchengeschichte," 229.

kingdom. And, while Church Historians today do not seek to prove its existence, scholars can accept the truthfulness of its scientific object.[21] We do not have to understand God and religion merely as social constructs, but can work with the understanding that is innate to religion as a semiotic system. This definition gives us the freedom to use a description that has been utilized across the theological disciplines for quite a while and is anchored outside of Theology as well.

Thus, perhaps it is easier to locate ourselves in the broad spectrum of humanities research employing the help of cultural symbols. Findings from historical studies can then help Church historians to understand and even rethink approaches from other theological disciplines. A systematic theologian working on Augustine of Hippo for example may develop a deeper understanding of Augustine's writing when he includes research on the author from a different point of view, namely a historical one. He or she may then come to different conclusions with, say, an analysis of Augustine's concept of monasticism than without such analysis.

The relationship between Church History and other fields of Theology like Exegesis, Practical Theology, and Systematic Theology is, again, not yet fully determined. It still seems to lack a definition to which all involved are ready to consent. Church History offers Theology the perspective of a Historian, scrutinizing similar questions from a very different point of view and with historical methods. Wolf-Friedrich Schäufele sees another difference between history in a theological context and history in a non-theological context in the exchange between the theological disciplines. He argues that the historical knowledge produced and exchanged in universities must prepare students for employment. A preacher or teacher should know how to make use of Church History in his or her profession, and Church Historians have to communicate not only the importance of knowledge of historical events for general educational purposes but also for practical use.[22] For example a Church Historian might ask "How can God let tyranny happen?" and against the background of this question analyse Lactantius' "Death of the Persecutors". The answer will be contextualized in a historical perspective and can vary vastly depending on the examined subject. But the research findings can be integrated into wider theological discourse and influence other theological disciplines as they interact with one's findings. They can also be integrated into research and training in the field of religious education. Church History offers, just as any theological discipline, an equal, unique perspective on questions concerning theological discourse with theoretical as well as a specific practical relevance.

---

[21] See Leppin, "Kirchengeschichte",231.

[22] See Wolf-Friedrich Schäufele, "Theologische Kirchengeschichtsschreibung als Konstruktionsaufgabe. Ein Plädoyer," in *Theologische Literaturzeitung* 7 (2014): 831–50.

This leads me to turn now specifically to the question of how Church History does the theology that it does, that is, to the question of which methods Church History uses.

4. Cultural Turn and/vs. Historical Critical Methods: Thinking about Space in Church History as an Example

Like scientists across all fields of research, we in Church History are susceptible to trends and ever shifting fashions in research methodologies. Over time the questions we ask shift depending on what we think is important, and what we find important is of course culturally influence by attitudes toward, for example, what is modern or fashionable. Contemporary economic, social, political or popular-cultural phenomena shape our day to day life and form our personal interests, and in this way they influence our work as scientists as well.[23] It can happen that a certain aspect of a question comes to carry more weight than others throughout our field of study simply because a generation of scholars get influenced in the same way. When large segments of the scientific community pay attention to these aspects and dedicate their work to it, certain issues gain more weight than others within the scientific community - or at least it seems like they get talked about more for a certain time. Such developments can be called turns[24], and there are many of them, including the so-called cultural turn, spatial turn, material turn, and digital turn, to name just a few. Moreover, within current scholarship in different disciplines of the humanities the question arose whether there is only one cultural turn or one spatial turn. It is probably more precise to speak of various turns that developed differently in each discipline. When I speak of a turn in Church History, I am referring only to the theological discourse, keeping in mind that those turns are nevertheless connected, somehow.

---

[23] This is true for political ideologies, as well. Although historians and church historians try to be neutral and often probably think they are free from bias, this cannot be the case. See: Evans H. Carr, *What is History?* (London: Palgrave Macmillan, 1961); this problem is very obvious in studies about WWII and has been critiqued recently: Rüdiger Hohls, ed., *Versäumte Fragen. Deutsche Historiker im Schatten des Nationalismus*, (Stuttgart and Wien: DVA, 2000).

[24] Jörg Döring and Tristan Thielmann state, rightfully so I'd say, that *turns* are often proclaimed but scientists are rarely sure they'd locate themselves within a special turn. See Jörg Döring, Tristan Thielmann, "Einleitung: Was lesen wir im Raume? Der Spatial Turn und das geheime Wissen der Georgraphen," in *Spatial Turn. Das Raumparadigma in den Kultur- und Sozialwissenschaften*, ed. Jörg Döring, Tristan Thielmann, (Bielefeld: Transcript, 2008). In this essay a *turn* is not seen as a strict model of research questions but more like a trend. There is not necessarily a shift in paradigm but a bigger interest in certain aspects.

Turns usually stem from one field of study but then make their way into different disciplines and get interpreted according to the discipline's self-understanding. So, the spatial turn, for example, developed in Geography, but then was adapted in nearly all fields of the humanities.[25] The main theses driving the spatial turn are that space is a social construct and that analyzing this social construct can benefit the understanding of texts or material. Questions arise like "Where did this happen?", "What space is attributed to a certain person/group/event?", "Does space get mentioned at all?". Or if we focus on a theological use of the spatial turn: "Where is God located?", "What place of worship is described and how?", "How can we define space for practical use?", "Where did these people meet, and did their location influence their theology?". Of course, one might say that questions concerning where to locate God and whether God's space would be within this world or somewhere outside it loom over the whole history of Christianity.[26] So what's new about this spatial turn? The difference is very nuanced. Reading Lactantius, being one of my areas of research focus, I myself ask how the description of a certain location helps or shapes the narrative. Whereas philologists or historians have asked, for example, how Lactantius could relate a private conversation between two emperors, a Church historian might ask, rather, how this fictitious conversation helps to paint a picture of God as an entity that is responsible for the world as it is. What does this secluded conversation – one which Lactantius obviously never heard – add to the reader's understanding of God's work in history? To return to Leppin's definition: As a Church historian, I do not just want to know how this author who participates in received social constructs while also reproducing them knows what happened (historical), how he tells it (philological) or before what socio-cultural background is he is telling it (culture studies). I also inquire after the transcendental force, namely God, that he wants to show.

---

[25] A very broad overview over spatial turn throughout different fields is given by: Barney Warf, Santa Arias [eds.], *The Spatial Turn: Interdisciplinary Perspectives, Routledge Studies in Human Geography*, (Routledge: London/New York 2008), and Jörg Döring, Tristan Thielmann, eds., *Spatial Turn. Das Raumparadigma in den Kultur- und Sozialwissenschaften*, (Bielefeld: Transcript, 2008). Doris Bachmann-Medick explains why it is more useful to speak about various *turns* than just the one cultural or spatial turn. (see: Doris Bachmann-Medick, *Cultural Turns, Neuorientierung in den Kulturwissenschaften* (Reinbeck bei Hamburg: Rohwolt Taschenbuch, 2009). For further critical reading of turns and methods, see: Michael Gubo, Martin Kypta, and Florian Öchsner, eds., *Kritische Perspektiven: "Turns", Trends und Theorien*, (Münster: LIT, 2011). In 2016 Angela Kaupp edited a volume showing different theological approaches to space concepts. In this volume practical, exegetical, ethical, and historical approaches are combined. See Angela Kaupp, ed., *Raumkonzepte in der Theologie. Interdisziplinäre und interkulturelle Zugänge*, (Ostfildern: Matthias-Grünewald, 2016).

[26] See for example Augustin's *civitas dei*.

5. WHAT WILL HAPPEN NEXT?

But not only what we focus our research on differs based on personal background, experience and preference, but also – and this is especially important for historians – where we begin our research. This chapter has focused on work in Church History in the German research context. International discourse, however, is a completely different field to discover.[27]

In Germany, we mostly interact with scholars from across Europe or the USA. I by no means want to say that German scholarship in Church History does not interact with people from other areas of the world, but our focus usually lies on European Church History. Our focus tends to be rather Eurocentric. This is not to say that we have to shift our attention immediately, but we should be able to acknowledge our background and take it into consideration. Somewhat ironically, precisely this self-limitation might lead to a wider approach to Church History done in Europe by enhancing our understandings of wider circles of events even more. This can also encourage cooperation across the world and foster new relationships. We then might find links we never thought possible. The conference from which this chapter emerged, for example, was exemplary work in this regard.

In summary, it remains an abidingly important question for Church History how it defines itself. I have tried to show in this chapter that there is still a lot of work to do in regard to paint a more nuanced picture of our self-understanding: How much of a Historian am I as a Church historian? What can I add to the conversation, that cannot be said by historians, philologists or other theologians? I hope it is clear that this remains a very necessary conversation.

There surely is a new turn coming soon. I for myself am excited to see what it may bring and how my colleagues and I might react to it.

BIBLIOGRAPHY

Bachmann-Medick, Doris. *Cultural Turns: Neuorientierung in den Kulturwissenschaften.* Reinbeck bei Hamburg: Rohwolt Taschenbuch Verlag, 2009.

Barth, Karl. *Die kirchliche Dogmatik 1 I.* Zürich: EVZ-Verlag 1986 [1932].

Basse, Michael. "Theologiegeschichtsschreibung und Kontroverstheoogie: die Bedeutung der Scholastik für die protestantische Kirchengeschichtsschreibung." *Zeitschrift für Kirchengeschichte* 107, no. 1 (1996): 50-71.

Baur, Ferdinand Christian. *Die christliche Lehre von der Versöhnung in ihrer geschichtlichen Entwickelung von der ältesten Zeit bis auf die neueste.* Tübingen: C.F. Osiander, 1838.

---

[27] I am aware of my own gaps in tracing back Church Historiography. Nevertheless, a comparative study of different approaches to the study of Church History or History of Christianity does appear to be an important research *desideratum* – and one which I hope to make a subject of more focused inquiry in the near future.

Berding, Helmut. "Leopold von Ranke." In *The Discovery of Historicity in German Idealism and Historism, Studies in Economic Ethics and Philosophy*, edited by Peter Koslowski, 41-58. Berlin and Heidelberg: Springer 2005.

Becker, Eve-Marie, ed. *Die antike Historiographie und die Anfänge der christlichen Geschichtsschreibung*. Berlin and New York: De Gruyter, 2005.

Carr, Evans H. *What is history?* London: Palgrave Macmillan, 1961.

Colish, Marcia L. *The Stoic Tradition from Antiquitiy to the Early Middle Ages. II. Stoicism in Christian Latin Thought through the Sixth Century*. Leiden: Brill, 1985.

Devin, Singh. "Eusebius as Political Theologian: The Legend Continues." *Harvard Theological Review* 108, no. 1 (2015): 129–54.

Dibelius, Martin. "Der erste christliche Historiker." In *Aufsätze zur Apostelgeschichte*, edited by Heinrich Greeven, 108-19. Göttingen: Vandenhoeck & Ruprecht, 1961 [1953].

Döring, Jörg, and Tristan Thielmann. "Einleitung: Was lesen wir im Raume? Der Spatial Turn und das geheime Wissen der Georgraphen." In *Spatial Turn. Das Raumparadigma in den Kultur- und Sozialwissenschaften*, edited by Jörg Döring, and Tristan Thielmann. Bielefeld: Transcript 2008.

Droysen, Johann Gustav. *Grundriss der Historik*. Leipzig: Verlag con Veit & Com, 1868.

Ebeling, Gerhard. "Kirchengeschichte als Geschichte der Auslegung der Heiligen Schrift." In: *Wort Gottes und Tradition. Studien zu einer Hermeneutik der Konfessionen*, edited by Gerhard Ebeling, 9-27. Göttingen: Vandenhoeck & Ruprecht, 1964.

Eigler, Ulrich. "Geschichtsschreibung IV. Christentum B. Lateinisch." *Der Neue Pauly* 4 (1998), 1000–1004.

Frey, Jörg Clare K. Rothschild, and Jens Schröter, eds. *Die Apostelgeschichte im Kontext antiker und frühchristlicher Historiographie, Beihefte zur Zeitschrift für die neutestamentliche Wissenschaft 162*. Berlin and New York Walter: DeGruyter, 2009.

Johnson, Aaron P. *Eusebius*. London: Tauris & Co Ltd, 2014.

Inowlocki, S., and C. Zamagnı [eds.]. *Reconsidering Eusebius: Collected Papers on Literary, Historical, and Theological Issues*. Leiden/Boston: Brill 2011.

Gubo, Michael, Martin Kypta, and Florian Öchsner [eds.]. *Kritische Perspektiven: "Turns", Trends und Theorien*. Münster: LIT, 2011.

Hengel, Martin. *Acts and the history of earliest Christianity*. Eugene Oregon: Wipf and Stock Publishers, 2003.

Hohls, Rüdiger, ed. *Versäumte Fragen. Deutsche Historiker im Schatten des Nationalismus*. Stuttgart and Wien: DVA, 2000.

Kaupp, Angela, ed. *Raumkonzepte in der Theologie. Interdisziplinäre und interkulturelle Zugänge*. Ostfildern: Matthias-Grünewald, 2016.

Kinzig, Wolfram, Volker Leppin, and Günther Wartenberg, eds. *Historiographie und Theologie. Kirchen und Theologiegeschichte im Spannungsfeld von geschichtswissenschaftlicher Methode und theologischem Anspruch. Konzeption von Kurt Nowak*. Leipzig: EVA, 2004.

Kirsch, Wolfgang. "Triebkräfte der historischen Entwicklung bei Laktanz." *Klio* 66, no. 2 (1984): 624–30.

Leppin, Volker. "Kirchengeschichte zwischen historiographischem und theologischem Anspruch." In *Historiographie und Theologie. Kirchen und Theologiegeschichte im Span-*

nungsfeld von geschichtswissenschaftlicher Methode und theologischem Anspruch. Konzeption von Kurt Nowak, edited by Wolfram Kinzig, Volker Leppin, and Günther Wartenberg, 223-34. Leipzig: EVA, 2004.

Luckmann, Thomas. "Einleitung." In Bronislaw Malinowski, *Magie, Wissenschaft und Religion und andere Schriften*, edited by Thomas Luckmann. Frankfurt am Main: Fischer S. Verlag, 1973.

Marguerat, Daniel. *The First Christian Historian. Writing the Acts of the Apostels*. Cambridge: Cambridge University Press, 2002.

McGuckin, John. *The Problem of Lactantius the Theologian*. Leuven: Peeters Publishers, 2017.

Nicholson, Oliver. "The Christian Sallust: Lactantius on God, Man and History." Studia Patristica 80 (2017): 119–138.

Plümacher, Eckhard. "Geschichtsschreibung IV. Biblisch." In *Religion in Geschichte und Gegenwart*. http://dx.doi.org/10.1163/2405-8262_rgg4_COM_08523.

Ranke, Leopold v. *Französische Geschichte vornehmlich im sechzehnten und siebzehnten Jahrhundert*. Stuttgart: J. G. Cotta'scher Verlag, 1861.

Schäufele, Wolf-Friedrich. "Theologische Kirchengeschichtsschreibung als Konstruktionsaufgabe. Ein Plädoyer." *Theologische Literaturzeitung* 7 (2014): 831–50.

Scherer, Emil Clemens. *Geschichte und Kirchengeschichte an den deutschen Universitäten. Ihre Anfänge im Zeitalter des Humanismus und ihre Ausbildung zu selbstständigen Disziplinen*. Freiburg im Breisgau: Olms Verlag, 1927.

Schröter, Jens. "Actaforschung seit 1983 III. Die Apostelgeschichte als Geschichtswerk." *Theologische Rundschau* 72, no. 2 (2007): 383-419

Troeltsch, Ernst. "Über historische und dogmatische Methode in der Theologie." [1908] In *Zur religiösen Lage, Religionsphilosophie und Ethik. Gesammelte Schriften Bd. II*, 729-53. Tübingen: Mohr, 1913.

Warf, Barney, and Santa Arias, eds. *The Spatial Turn: Interdisciplinary Perspectives, Routledge Studies in Human Geography*. London/New York: Routledge, 2008.

Contemplating Christ and/in His People

The Practice of a Socially Transformation-Oriented Christology – in Africa

Chukwuemeka Anthony Atansi (Leuven, Belgium / Nigeria)

> The preacher [we substitute "theologian"] also needs to keep his ear to the people and to discover what it is that the faithful need to hear. A preacher [theologian] has to contemplate the word, but he also has to contemplate his people and their experiences. In this way he learns "of the aspirations, of riches and limitations, of ways of praying, of loving, of looking at life and the world, which distinguish this or that human gathering," while paying attention "to actual people, to using their language, their signs and symbols, to answering the questions they ask." He needs to be able to link the message of a biblical text to a human situation, to an experience which cries out for the light of God's word.
>
> –Pope Francis[1]

1. Introduction: Searching for a Transformative Christology

Jesus Christ is an important reality among Africans today.[2] Many Africans experience Jesus as being present to them, and not just as a historical personage or as a socio-cultural icon, but, very importantly, as the abiding gift of God's own life. So, Christ is proclaimed as good news, as the subject of living

---

[1] Pope Francis, "Apostolic Exhortation on the Proclamation of the Gospel in Today's World, *Evangelii Gaudium*, 24 November 2013," *AAS* 105, no. 12 (2013): no. 154. As I will discuss in what follow, Pope Francis's statement here could also be said of theologians in general, in particular those working on Christology.

[2] In this essay, the names Jesus, Christ, Jesus Christ, Jesus the Christ, and Christ Jesus are used interchangeably with no theological distinction intended. The creed followed in this study is faith "in the *one* Lord Jesus Christ," which represents the basic statement of Christian belief in the unity and identity of Christ confessed by the apostle Paul (1 Cor 8:6). For a recent and remarkably fine discussion of this basic christological confession of the *one* Christ, see Aaron Riches, *Ecce Homo: On the Divine Unity of Christ* (Grand Rapids: W. B. Eerdmans, 2016), xvi.

faith in Africa.[3] This faith is lived within the context of challenging social realities like curable illnesses, enduring systemic social injustice, and unbearable poverty. Such realities that move one, as Jon Sobrino says in speaking of the Latin American social situation, "to think a lot about Jesus Christ."[4] But there is more to simply *thinking* about the meaning and significance of Christ necessitated by these realities. The realities bear in them the capacity of bringing one to also *contemplate* the reality of Christ, present and acting amongst his people, who, in their daily battle for human well-being, continue to wrestle with faith and hope in him.[5] Thus, I consider that returning to where the people are, the grassroots Christian communities, and articulating therefrom the meaning and implications of this contemplative exercise for the life of faith and human flourishing in Africa is the primary task of Christology in that context and, perhaps, elsewhere in today's world.

Christologizing as such in Africa, and even in the so-called prosperous nations where there exist other forms of, often, concealed deprivation and alienation, also offers a vision of (doing) Christian theology that is not cut off from

---

[3] The reference to, or my use of, "Africa" and the "African" context and experience is meant in a certain quantitative and qualitative sense. Of the former, that is, the quantitative sense, I refer to Africa in terms of a geographical delimitation that focuses on four English speaking African countries where Christianity is dominant. The countries are Nigeria, Ghana, Uganda and Kenya. Most of the authors I shall be citing have engaged in empirical research in these countries on the experience and understanding of Christ that are popular among theologians and ordinary people. As regards the qualitative sense, I agree with Michael Cook, who proposes that, "it is still useful to speak of Africa and the African experience or context, however much what is said must be qualified and applied to different concrete situations." Hence there is a "shared sense of Africanness." See Michael L. Cook, "The African Experience of Jesus," *Theological Studies* 70 (2009): 668-692, at 671.

[4] Jon Sobrino, *Jesus the Liberator: A Historical-Theological Reading of Jesus of Nazareth*, translated from the Spanish by Paul Burns and Francis McDonagh (Maryknoll: Orbis Books, 1993); Tunbridge Wells, Kent: Burns and Oates, 1994), 8. See also Jon Sobrino, *Christ the Liberator: A View from the Victims*, translated from the Spanish by Paul Burns (Maryknoll: Orbis Books, 2001), 2-8.

[5] Thinking and contemplation, of course, share a certain co-inherence of meanings. They bear essential relationship with each other as intrinsic components of one other. The art of thinking can be, or rather, is, a profoundly spiritual activity. Likewise, contemplation is also a deeply intellectual practice, for it is not just directed to the spiritual component of a human person nor carried forward only by it; it is also directed to and fostered by the mental faculty as well. For some theological insights on this idea, see Andrew Prevot, *Thinking Prayer: Theology and Spirituality amid the Crises of Modernity* (Notre Dame: University of Notre Dame Press, 2015). However, the distinction I wish to highlight here is the understanding in some scholarly circles that see "thinking" as *the* only proper mode of christological investigation, and which sometimes is presented as foreclosing the contemplative exercise. I am therefore suggesting that contemplation is also *a* way of doing Christology.

the real lives, issues, and questions of the women and men of our time.[6] As Nigerian theologian, Agbonkhianmeghe Orobator, rightly expresses, theology has to speak *to* real lives.[7] Obviously, Orobator would mean the lives of people, especially those suffering under the burden of underdevelopment and all forms of oppression.[8] Such speaking to real lives with greater clarity and energy requires, I suggest, a speaking *to* Christ. He is the One who has gone before us into, has sought, and who still seeks to transform the situations of human suffering experienced by a vast majority of Africans, Christians and non-Christians alike.

There is no gainsaying that African theologians have long been involved in this christological venture of either speaking to or about Christ, in relation to the concrete issues of social deprivation in the continent. Many early and contemporary African scholars, south of the Sahara, have produced a body of literature dealing with the subject of christological belief and its relation to social transformation in Africa. When one surveys the christological landscape, it is obvious that there has been a concern for social situations and for the formation of christological judgments and proposals in response to them.[9] But these judgements and proposals often tend to be far removed from the

---

[6] For a similar line of argumentation see Anselm K. Min, ed., *The Task of Theology: Leading Theologians on the Most Compelling Questions for Today* (Maryknoll: Orbis Books, 2014); Christopher Southgate, *Theology in a Suffering World: Glory and Longing* (Cambridge: Cambridge University Press, 2018); Miroslav Volf and Matthew Croasmun, *For the Life of the World: Theology that Makes a Difference* (Grand Rapids: Brazos Press, 2019).

[7] See Agbonkhianmeghe Orobator, *Theology Brewed in an African Pot* (Maryknoll: Orbis Books, 2008); Agbonkhianmeghe Orobator, *Religion and Faith in Africa: Confessions of an Animist* (Maryknoll: Orbis Books, 2018).

[8] See Agbonkhianmeghe Orobator, "*Caritas in Veritate* and Africa's Burden of (Under)Development," *Theological Studies* 71 (2010): 320-334. See also Orobator (with Elias Opongo), *Faith Doing Justice: A Manual for Social Analysis, Catholic Social Teaching and Social Justice* (Nairobi: Paulines, 2007).

[9] Some of the recent theological (christological) works are those of the proponents of African theology of reconstruction. Advocates of African theology of reconstruction – one of the three main trends of African theology – called for the reconstruction of Africa, based not on the inculturation and liberation motifs, but on the biblical motifs of the New Testament Resurrection-Event. They insist that the building of a new society "be based not on the logic of market economy, but on the logic of Christological-Resurrection-Event of Jesus Christ." In their works, they place special emphasis on the social transformation of Africa. These include the works of Jesse N. K. Mugambi, *From Liberation to Reconstruction: African Christian Theology After the Cold War* (Nairobi: East African Educational Publishers, 1995); *The Church and Reconstruction of Africa: Theological Considerations* (Nairobi: AACC, 1997); "Christian Mission and Social Transformation After the Cold War," *Journal of Constructive Theology* 4, no. 2 (1998): 65-86; *Christian Mission and Social Transformation* (Nairobi: Acton, 2003). See also Charles Villa-Vicencio, *A Theology of Reconstruction: Nation-Building and Human Rights* (Cambridge: Cambridge University Press, 1992).

concrete realities of life of people who seek to follow Christ in situations of deprivation and suffering, which most of the theologians claim inform their christological reflections. This gap is largely due to their governing foundational presuppositions, – such as their methodological, hermeneutical, and epistemological frameworks. Their reflections on the images of Christ in response to the issue of social transformation appear in such forms as mere christological adaptationism, transposition, and re-narration. These include the reworking and translation of the cultural (Aylward Shorter),[10] as well as biblical (Jean Marc Éla and Mercy Amba Oduyoye),[11] kerygmatic-ethical (Mana),[12] and doctrinal-notional (Ezigbo)[13] perspectives about the life and mission Christ and how they find application, predominantly, in the pastoral activities of Church hierarchy in Africa.

Such christological undertakings, surprisingly, as Aylward Shorter himself once remarked, still operate in "an ideological sphere."[14] They mainly come across as the products "of scholars working in the libraries of universities and seminaries."[15] In other words, their Christologies "have been a notional theology and not couched (to use John Henry Newman's terminology) in the grammar of real assent – the imaginative expression of popular faith."[16] The consequence is that in academic discussions, marginal attention is paid to the vibrant christological imagination of African Christian consciousness, particularly at the grassroots level. As Kenneth Ross captures it:

Such discussion can make little headway until we have clearer picture of "grassroots" Christology, that is, of how ordinary people understand the identity and meaning of Jesus Christ. For the life and worship of the people of God is always an important formative factor in theological [christological] recon-

---

[10] Aylward Shorter, *Jesus and the Witchdoctor: An Approach to Healing and Wholeness* (Maryknoll: Orbis Books, 1985). See also Aylward Shorter, "Foreword," in Fernando Dominigues, *Christ Our Healer: A Theological Dialogue with Aylward Shorter* (Nairobi: Paulines Publications Africa, 2000).

[11] Jean Marc Éla, *African Cry* (Maryknoll: Orbis Books, 1991); "Christianity and Liberation in Africa," in *Paths of African Theology*, ed. Rosino Gibellini (Maryknoll: Orbis Books, 1994), 136-153; Mercy Amba Oduyoye, *Beads and Strands: Reflections of an African Woman on Christianity in Africa* (Maryknoll: Orbis Books, 2004).

[12] Kä Mana, *Christians and Churches of Africa Envisioning the Future: Salvation in Christ and Building a New African Society* (Maryknoll: Orbis Books, 2004).

[13] Victor Ezigbo, *Re-imagining African Christologies: Conversing with the Interpretations and Appropriations of Jesus in Contemporary African Christianity* (Eugene: Pickwick Publications, 2010).

[14] Aylward Shorter, "Folk Christianity and Functional Christology," *African Ecclesial Review* 24, no. 3 (1982): 133-137, here 135.

[15] Shorter, "Folk," 135.

[16] Shorter, "Folk," 135.

struction. It is a necessary source for the theological task required in Africa today.[17]

From this perspective, the urgent need then becomes not simply the creation of a "new" African Christology, but the inspiration of a new Christian disposition (knowing and loving), a form of Christian discipleship (embodied practices of ecclesial-social solidarity) that will bring about the transformation of African society. And contemplation is a key for such christological (re)envisioning or, if you like, re-orientation. For contemplation, as I hope to show, consists in the *practice* of a social, transformation-oriented Christology in Africa – a Christology that flowers in a silent and sympathetic gazing upon Christ and (amongst) his suffering people.

In order to spell out the argument, I will proceed in the following ways. First, I begin with a look at the grassroots level, and how Christ is imagined there as the subject of living faith and hope. With the example of the image of Christ as healer that is popular in the grassroots Christian communities, I show that the christological imagination of the African Christian consciousness is both a proclamation of faith in Jesus Christ and a longing for the transformation of the social reality, which informs the invocation of Christ in such an image. That is to say that, taking grassroots Christologies seriously is important in the enterprise of pursuing a social, transformation-oriented Christology. Second, I try to work out how this christological dynamics of faith and longing constitute the sources for contemplative practice, which in turn helps towards the pursuit of a social, transformation-oriented Christology. Third, I flesh out the implications of the practice for repositioning Christology within the context of the community called Church, and more importantly, in the wider society. This will lead me to concluding remarks on how a social, transformation-oriented Christology helps us to rethink the meaning (and task) of Christology as a whole.

2. At the Grassroots: Christological Imagination as Proclamation and Longing

I have already hinted at why there is need to return to the grassroots in exploring the meaning of Jesus' life, and its implications for societal transformation in Africa. I should like to add here that this need to take grassroots Christologies more seriously derives from the nature of the experience and expression of Christ at that level.[18] This can be gleaned, first, from the descrip-

---

[17] Kenneth Ross, "Current Christological Trends in Northern Malawi," *Journal of Religion in Africa* 27, no. 2 (1997), 160.

[18] See Patrick A. Kalilombe, "Doing Theology at the Grassroots: A Challenge for Professional Theologians. Part One," *African Ecclesial Review* 27, no. 3 (June 1985): 148-161; Idem., "Doing Theology at the Grassroots: A Challenge for Professional

tion of grassroots Christologies. By grassroots Christologies, I mean what many *people* - whether they are "ordinary" Christians or Christians who have had any formal academic (theological) training - think, believe, and confess about Jesus Christ within the African Christian and social context.[19] Grassroots Christologies are expressions of the identity and work of Jesus Christ that are found mainly within the community of believers and in the course of their daily living.[20] They "go beyond formal written expressions to include informal expressions, for example, in worship, prayer, preaching, artwork, drama, gesture, and symbols."[21] They are "Christologies of the people," for they are related with the experiences and aspirations of the people.[22] The experiences of

Theologians. Part Two," *African Ecclesial Review* 27, no. 4 (August 1985): 225-237; John S. Pobee, "In Search of Christology in Africa: Some Considerations for Today," in *Exploring Afro-Christology*, ed. John S. Pobee (Frankfurt: Peter Lang, 1992), 11; Sam Amirtham and John S. Pobee, eds., *Theology by the People: Reflections on Doing Theology in Community* (Geneva: WCC Publications, 1986), 2-7; and the whole issue devoted to grassroots Christologies, entitled "Christ in African Experience - Reflections from Homeland and Diaspora," *Journal of African Christian Thought* 8, no. 1 (June 2005). As cited in Diane Stinton, "Jesus-Immanuel, Image of the Invisible God: Aspects of Popular Christology in Sub-Saharan Africa," *Journal of Reformed Theology* 1 (2007): 6-40, here 38.

[19] I am aware that the category "people" can be an ambiguous term. For the purpose of this essay "people" is used and understood in the sense that connotes the plural unity of persons and communities that are "rooted in a common history, and projected forward toward a shared goal, namely, the common good (societal transformation for the flourishing of each and every human person)." See Juan Carlos Scannone, "Pope Francis and the Theology of the People," *Theological Studies* 77, no. 1 (2016), 121. See also the insightful articles in Carlos Mendoza-Álvarez and Po-Ho Huang, eds., *Wisdom and the People's Theology, Concilium* 3 (London: SCM Press, 2018).

[20] Diane Stinton, "Jesus of Africa: Voices of Contemporary African Christology," in *The Myriad Christ: Plurality and the Quest for Unity in Contemporary Christology*, ed. by Terrence Merrigan and Jacque Haers (Leuven: University Press and Peeters, 2000), 287.

[21] Ezigbo, *Re-imagining African Christologies*, 104-105. Henry Okullu had elaborated on the role and place of these sources. He maintained that in the search for African Christology, and a socially transformative one at that, "we should go first to the fields, to the village church, to Christian homes to listen to those spontaneously uttered prayers before people go to bed. [. . .] We must listen to the throbbing drumbeats and the clapping of hands accompanying the impromptu singing in the independent churches. We must look at the way in which faith in Christ is being planted in Africa through music, drama, songs, dances, art, paintings. We must listen to the preaching of the sophisticated pastor as well as that of the simple village vicar." Then Okullu asks a pointed question, "can it be that all this is an empty show?," "It is impossible," he responds. Henry Okullu, *Church and Politics in East Africa* (Nairobi: Uzima Press Limited, 1974), 53-54, cited in Stinton, "Jesus-Immanuel, Image of the Invisible God," 8.

[22] Stinton, "Jesus-Immanuel, Image of the Invisible God," 8.

faith in the midst of human suffering, and the aspirations for abundant life that comes from hope in Christ's transforming presence and act.

A survey of some recent, key publications on grassroots Christologies in contemporary African Christianity reveals an abundance of images of Christ.[23] Some of the images (among many others) that come to the fore include the following: Christ as Healer, Christ as Life-Giver or as Abundant Life, Christ as Liberator, Christ as King or Chief, and Christ as Provider. There are images such as Ancestor, Proto-Ancestor, Elder, Guest, and Master of Initiation, which are also considered to be popular in Africa,[24] in part, because they are informed by African worldviews. As Orobator says, they are "derived from categories which are authentically African and speak *im*-mediately to the African (traditional religious) consciousness."[25] There is no doubt that these images are important. As Robert Schreiter observes, they are "mediating images" that provide a way of relating Jesus more closely to African cultures and primal imagination.[26] Of these images, three are particularly pervasive in the present-day African Christian consciousness. They are Christ as healer, as liberator, and as king.

Scholars like Stinton, Goergen, and Ezigbo testify to the popularity of these images. For example, as Stinton notes, there is manifold evidence from sociological studies that the encounter and proclamation of Jesus Christ as

---

[23] Some of the main works that I shall rely extensively on in this essay are: Donald J. Goergen, "The Quest for the Christ of Africa," *African Christian Studies* 17 (2001): 5-51; Diane B. Stinton, *Jesus of Africa: Voices of Contemporary African Christology* (Maryknoll: Orbis Books, 2004), and also some of her in-depth articles and essays, "Encountering Jesus at the Well: Further Reflections on African Women's Christologies," *Journal of Reformed Theology* 7 (2013): 267-293; "Jesus Christ, Living Water in Africa Today," in *The Oxford Handbook of Christology*, ed. Francesca Aran Murphy (Oxford: Oxford University Press, 2015), 425-443; Ezigbo, *Re-imagining African Christologies*, 103-142; Clifton R. Clarke, *African Christology: Jesus in Post-missionary African Christianity* (Eugene, OR: Pickwick Publications, 2011); Paul Gifford, *Christianity, Development and Modernity in Africa* (London: C. Hurst and C. Publishers Ltd., 2015). These theologians have engaged in empirical research, particularly in the four Anglophone countries in Africa that form the scope of this essay - Kenya, Uganda, Ghana and Nigeria - as to images of Jesus Christ that are popular among ordinary people.

[24] For a discussion of some of these images, see Charles Nyamiti, *Christ as Our Ancestor: Christology from an African Perspective* (Gweru: Mambo Press, 1984); Enyi Ben Udoh, *Guest Christology: An Interpretative View of the Christological Problem in Africa*, Studies in the Intercultural History of Christianity 59 (Frankfurt am Main: Lang, 1988); Robert J. Schreiter, ed., *Faces of Jesus in Africa* (Maryknoll: Orbis Books, 1991); Idem, "Images of Jesus in Contemporary Culture," *Concilium* 3 (2008): 124-129.

[25] Agbonkhianmeghe Orobator, "The Quest for an African Christ: An Essay in Contemporary African Christology," *Hekima Review* 11 (September 1994): 75-99, at 81.

[26] Schreiter, "Images of Jesus in Contemporary Culture," 125. See also Kwame Bediako, *Jesus and the Gospel in Africa: History and Experience* (Maryknoll: Orbis Books, 2004), 85-96.

healer, liberator and king (leader) hold "a prime place in the imagination and in the lived experience of vast numbers of Christians."[27] They were by far the most "visible" christological images, in which Jesus Christ "is clearly perceived in terms of 'Immanuel' – God with us – in Africa, and in terms of being the 'image of the invisible God', or the one who puts a human face on the transcendent."[28] Donald Goergen, from his own empirical study while in Kenya, mentions that these images emerge from within context-aware, praxis-oriented, and socio-politically conscious theologies.[29]

For eleven years, between 2003 and 2014, I was a pastoral worker, actively involved in ministry with grassroots Christian communities in the South Eastern region of Nigeria. Some of the communities include people from other parts of Africa, like Kenya, Uganda, Ghana, Cameroon, Togo and Chad. I felt then, and I still feel today, very close to the members of these communities. In my sympathetic-critical attention to them, through sharing in their daily lives, which included participating in their lives of faith, I had a first-person encounter of their experience and understanding of Christ's identity and work. My close connection with the people themselves and, at the same time, my application of a critical analytic lens were both special avenues of insight into the *quality* of their lives of faith vis-à-vis the concrete realities of their daily lives. It became clear to me that the *immediate* expectations of the members of these grassroots communities were wholeness, liberation and benevolent care. These expectations led them to confess Christ in such images as healer, liberator, and king. They are images relating to their struggles for healing, abundant life, integral well-being, social justice, and good governance. So, in many of the liturgical celebrations and prayer gatherings, these believing communities confessed their unwavering faith in the healing, liberating, and saving power of Christ.

Therefore, against the view that grassroots Christologies are simply a "rhetoric of God's empowerment," forms of enchanted Christianity, or sheer "solution-oriented Christologies," I argue that they are the visible expressions of ordinary Christians' inmost understanding of the Christ-event in their midst. The images are the Christians' confessions of – faith and hope in – who Christ is and what he does and could do as "true God and true Man," within their challenging social situations. So, the images capture the Christians' way (though sometimes limited) of relating to the totality of Christ's divine and human identity within their African life context; a context in which one sees a profound, urgent longing by its people for health, life together in freedom, and social justice – indices of a transformed society, or, "pillars of authentic social development," as Pope Francis calls them, while re-counting the experience of

[27] Stinton, "Jesus-Immanuel, Image of the Invisible God," 38.
[28] Stinton, "Jesus-Immanuel, Image of the Invisible God," 38.
[29] Goergen, "The Quest for the Christ of Africa," 11.

his visits to Africa.[30] Let me illustrate this with the example of the image of Christ as healer.

Many African Christians proclaim Christ as healer because he is also portrayed as such in the Gospels. Stinton and the other authors underline the fact that the vast majority of Christians, who proclaim Christ as their healer, expect that, just as Christ in the Gospels healed all the sick people who were brought to him (cf. Mt 15:30, Lk 4:40), so also will he heal *them* – that is, now – of all diseases and their causes. Stinton particularly narrates some of her personal encounters with Christians who confess such beliefs. She tells, for instance, about Mary Kizito, a lecturer at Daystar University in Nairobi, who strongly holds to the belief that "Jesus as healer can take away all the diseases, like HIV/AIDS and malaria, which kill people in Africa."[31] Mary Kizito is representative of the vast numbers of Christians, who, not only uphold such a belief, but expect that their vibrant proclamation of Christ as healer will move him to cure them of their diseases, deliver them of all their ailments, and restore them to physical health and fullness of life.[32]

Stinton also provides other very vivid data regarding this way of understanding Christ's identity and work as healer.[33] In homes, churches, so-called healing ministries, streets, markets, offices, and astonishingly, in clinics and hospitals too, Christ is invoked in often loud tones to heal those who are sick.[34] Christ the healer is sought even in unexpected places as Stan Chu Ilo describes in a recent investigation into the search for health, healing, and wholeness among African Christians.[35] Paul Gifford draws on the writings and

---

[30] Pope Francis, *Address to the Members of the Diplomatic Corps Accredited to the Holy See for the Traditional Exchange of New Year Greetings*, Thursday, 9 January 2020. www.vatican.va/content/francesco/en/speeches [accessed January 12, 2020]. According to the Pope's pointed description, "increased security, reducing poverty, improving healthcare systems, favouring development and humanitarian assistance, promoting good governance and civil rights[. . .]are the pillars of authentic social development."

[31] Stinton, *Jesus of Africa*, 65.

[32] Duke professor of New Testament, Craig Keener, has assembled a massive two-volume work demonstrating that, in fact, millions of Christians in Africa even today hold such confessions and claim to have experienced a miracle through belief in Christ as healer. See Craig Keener, "Healing in Mainline Churches: Examples in Africa," in Idem, *Miracles: The Credibility of the New Testament Accounts*, vol. 1 (Grand Rapids: Baker Academic, 2011), 309-358.

[33] Stinton, *Jesus of Africa*, 64-71.

[34] Clarke, *African Christology*, 173-174.

[35] Stan Chu Ilo, "Searching for Healing in a Miraculous Stream: The Fate of God's People in Africa," in *Wealth, Health, and Hope in African Christian Religion: The Search for Abundant Life*, ed. by Stan Chu Ilo (Lanham: Lexington Books, 2018), 45-80. See also Ilo, "Interpreting the Search for Health and Healing Among African Charismatic and Pentecostal Groups: A Theological Bio-Social Approach," *Bigard Theological Studies* 38, no. 1 (2018): 1-36.

preaching of a popular African (Nigerian) pastor, David Oyedepo, in order to show how the image of Christ as healer is operative in some of these places aforementioned.[36] In these places, as Victor Ezigbo's researched-case in Nigeria also shows, there is an abundance of healing services with prayers and exorcism, with many healing claims and testimonies.[37] Ezigbo points to the readiness of many Christians across various denominations to locate Jesus-talk and doing, largely in terms and within the framework of healing and the quest to achieve total well-being.[38] Consequently, many African Christians engage in long all-night prayer vigils, protracted fasts, exuberant crusades, conventions, and "miraculous meetings" organized by prominent and "powerful men and women of God" believed to be healers in the name of Christ the healer. These exercises leave many Christians enervated, robbing them of the strength they need to become creative agents of Christ's ongoing healing presence and act.

The Christians and their leaders hope that by exercising their "agency" in and through these religious means, they will be healed, delivered and restored to fullness of life. I consider this sort of exercise of agency as one of the limits of grassroots christological imagination, precisely as what could be referred to as an "energetic passivity" of christological faith and hope. Some Christians might see these religious, or so-called spiritual exercises, as acts of their trust in what Jesus their healer will do *for* them. Yet, many of them do not come to terms with the fact that there is no example of healing in the New Testament, which does not involve some sort of *relationship* between Jesus and the one to be cured. And it is this relationship that sets the momentum for the healing (transformation) that occurs in the life of the sick person, and subsequently, through him or her, in the lives of other people with whom he or she comes into contact. The example of Jesus healing Peter's mother-in-law is a case in point (Lk 4:38-40). In every healing action of Jesus three – one could say "Christological" aspects – may be observed: enhanced relationship, empowered agency, and embodied actions.

Bracketing criticisms and concerns for the time being, my point here is that a constructive assessment nevertheless reveals that a popular gospel of health, so-to-speak, does form and inform a particular christological mindset – one that recognizes Jesus' identity as a saviour and his miraculous power to bestow blessings, particularly of health and wholeness.[39] It seems that it is a

---

[36] Oyedepo's works – all published by his Dominion Publishing House in Lagos – include: *Keys to Divine Health* (1986), *All You Need to Be Healed* (1990), *Breaking the Curses of Life* (1997), *Conquering Controlling Powers* (1997), *The Eternal Healer* (2000), *Commanding the Supernatural* (2006). For an extensive discussion of the meaning and operation of the image of Christ as healer in what Gifford refers to as "Oyedepo's Christianity," see Gifford, *Christianity, Development and Modernity in Africa*, 35-42.

[37] Ezigbo, *Re-imagining African Christologies*, 120-126.

[38] Ezigbo, *Re-imagining African Christologies*, 120-121.

[39] Ezigbo, *Re-imagining African Christologies*, 122-123.

way many Christians strive to make sense of, or as Ezigbo puts it, "to perceive and relate to", the acclamation of Christ as "a prophet mighty in deed and word" (Lk 24:19) and the doctrinal formulation about him as "true God and true man."[40] They believe that as "true man," Jesus represents what a good and full life is. He knows and shares in their experiences of brokenness wrought by sickness and disease. For the Gospels portrayed him as always having pity on individuals and people who were sick (Mk 1:41, Mt 9:36). As "true God," the one "in whom the fullness of God dwells" (Col 2:9), he has the power to take away all the diseases and to restore their physical health.

From these socio-christological encounters with, findings about, and perspectives on grassroots Christologies in African Christianity, focusing on the example of Christ as healer, it becomes obvious that such Christologies bespeak a proclamation and a longing – a proclamation of faith in the reality of Jesus' life and mission and a longing for the wholeness and flourishing life he brought and still brings. A sympathetic-critical attention and valuation of grassroots Christologies can help in disclosing the socially transformative potential of christological belief, and realigning it more with the effort to transform the social order in Africa. How to do this as a uniquely contemplative exercise is what I shall discuss in the next section.

3. Contemplating Christ and His People: Towards a Socially Transformative Christology

What Rowan Williams says of contemplative practice in itself as "the key" to Christian existence and living, can also be said of all our invocation of, and all our reflection on, the person of Christ. Williams admits it is a bold claim to be made, but is one we need to take seriously in our cultures and world today, and particularly in the African Christian and theological landscape. Let's listen to Williams:

> Contemplation is very far from being just one kind of thing that Christians do: it is the key to prayer, liturgy, art and ethics, the key to the essence of a renewed (transformed) humanity that is capable of seeing the world and other subjects in the world with freedom – freedom from self-oriented, acquisitive habits and the distorted understanding that comes from these[. . .]Contemplation is the only ultimate answer to the unreal and insane society that our financial systems and our advertising culture and our chaotic and unexamined emotions encourage us to inhabit. To learn contemplative practice is to learn what we need to live truthfully and honestly and lovingly in our world. It is a deeply revolutionary matter.[41]

[40] Ezigbo, *Re-imagining African Christologies*, 139.

[41] Williams, "Contemplation and Mission," in *Holy Living: The Christian Tradition for Today* (London: Bloomsbury, 2017), 96-97.

In contemplation, Williams goes on, "we learn how to look at one another and at the whole of created reality," which includes the realities of a suffering and believing people.[42] Thus, contemplative practice can be truly enhancing, empowering, and, consequently, transformative, for it gives rise to prophetic imagination and act. How does this happen? In what does this practice consist? These are questions I try to address in the discussion of the very closely related twofold encounter with Christ and Christ's people that will follow shortly. That is to say, this contemplative practice entails an attentiveness and openness to the reality of Christ and the realities of those who believe, hope in, and recognize him as the ground of a transformed society in which the human wellbeing of all is promoted.

Let me briefly note here that there is a theological premise to this contemplative practice. It is offered by Jon Sobrino in terms of "the isomorphism between Jesus and the crucified people."[43] This principle of "analogical isomorphism," as Sobrino calls it, is traced back to Oscar Romero and Ignacio Ellacuría. Romero and Ellacuría spoke of those who are poor and vulnerable as "the servant of Yahweh," "the crucified people," and "the pierced divinity."[44] These designations, according to Sobrino, mean that "the crucified people, the millions of poor and oppressed in the world are the historical sacrament of Christ, the Suffering Servant."[45] So that by gazing towards the (crucified) people, by contemplating on them, their griefs and their anxieties, their joys and their hopes, we are brought to contemplate Christ in them, and Christ in himself per se. And in contemplating Christ, we are drawn closer to the realities of the people, and become charged to engage, to confront, and to change those realities in a comprehensive and transformative way.[46] Representing these ideas more concretely, and suggesting the forms such a contemplative practice could take in the light of our consideration of a social, transformation-oriented Christology in Africa will be the focus of my attention in what now follows.

---

[42] Williams, "Contemplation and Mission," 96.

[43] Jon Sobrino, "Jesus of Galilee from the Salvadoran Context: Compassion, Hope, and Following the Light of the Cross," trans. by Robert Lassalle-Klein with J. Matthew Ashley, *Theological Studies* 70 (2009): 437-460, at 445-446.

[44] Sobrino, "Jesus of Galilee," 445-446. See also Sobrino, *Jesus the Liberator*, 275n4.

[45] Sobrino, "Jesus of Galilee," 446.

[46] See Sobrino, *Christ the Liberator*, 1. See also Sobrino, "Spirituality and the Following of Jesus," in *Mysterium Liberationis: Fundamental Concepts of Liberation Theology*, ed. by Ignacio Ellacuría and Jon Sobrino (Maryknoll: Orbis Books, 1993), 677-701; Matthew Ashley, "The Mystery of God and Compassion for the Poor: The Spiritual Basis of Theology," in *Hope and Solidarity: Jon Sobrino's Challenge to Christian Theology*, ed. by Stephen J. Pope (Maryknoll: Orbis Books, 2008), 63-75.

Contemplating the Mystery (Reality) of Christ

For my description of this aspect, I want to suggest two places where the mystery, or rather, the reality of Christ can be contemplated. They are in the Eucharistic service and in the practice of silence. The reason for my focus on the "where" rather than on the "what," is due to the fact that it is not often easy to give an account of the specific content and terms of the contemplative encounter, since it is an encounter between the individual or a community and God. I cannot speak of *how* God acts in the life of someone or a group of people. But one can suggest "places" within the Christian tradition where the transforming mystery of Christ does happen and can happen in an individual's or a community of believers' life. In such a manner that they can become themselves transformed, and then, using the transforming power of Christ in them, they are able to transform other people and their social sphere.

The first place is in the Eucharistic encounter. The Eucharist is the place where the transforming power of Christ is most strongly experienced. The experience emancipates and empowers the agency of the individual or community that participates in the encounter. It enables a form of living that is in keeping with Christ's own life and ongoing agency.[47] Within the context of this encounter, the gifts of Christ are given to us, not only for our sustenance, but as transforming energies for new lives and new encounters with fellow human beings.

Through our repeated engagement in Eucharistic practice, we manage to feed continually upon that life-giving and transforming Spirit coming to us through the gift of Christ's own humanity in the elements, so as to grow into and sustain under trial a Christ-like life. In the Eucharist the humanity of Christ gives to us the life-giving powers it has by way of the Spirit that rests upon it, enhancing and nourishing our lives as those powers enhanced and nourished his own humanity.[48]

These perspectives offer a more robust affirmation of the socially transformative reality of the Eucharist. This is not just because it is a sublime site of the Christian community's transforming relationship with God in Jesus Christ and with all those present, and even those that are absent. It is also because it has the potential to (re)create a community that is charged to actualize the transforming life and mission of Jesus. If this is so, why have the

---

[47] Kathryn Tanner, *Christ the Key* (Cambridge: Cambridge University Press, 2010), 199. See also Rowan Williams, "Christology, Ethics and Politics: Discourses of Transformation," in *Christ the Heart of Creation* (London: Bloomsbury, 2018), 204. Williams argues that the transformation of society is made possible by the life and action of those who have become so transformed as to live "radically" and "exhaustively" the ongoing agency of Christ. He expresses it this way: "The Christological transformation of humanity [society] is the transformation of all our constitutive relationships as humans so that they are now able to move more freely towards this maximal for-otherness."

[48] Tanner, *Christ the Key*, 200.

many Eucharistic encounters not been able to transform Africa and Africans, a growing number of whom participate in these encounters on a daily basis? There is no gainsaying that in African Christianity – Roman Catholicism to be precise – the Eucharist is at the heart of Christian worship, and it is not for me to judge here the transforming density or quality of Africans' Eucharistic encounter. However, there is an understanding of this sacrament among Christians and some theologians, which neither critically nor adequately explores its socially transformative potential. For instance, in some of the African political and liberation theologies, the Eucharist, and the Church as a Eucharistic community are taken as "instruments" for social change.[49] This is not just the case in theologies. It is also found in many places of worship in African Christianity where Eucharistic celebrations, or what is popularly known as "Eucharistic adoration", are "used" as instruments for demanding the change that only Christ as healer, liberator, and king, can and will bring about.

So, against such views and ensuing attitudes, I would like to argue here that the Eucharist is first and foremost a celebration of Christ's self-giving, which in turn, is an invitation to participate in his transforming life. It is a place of relationship with Christ and with other human beings who are both present and absent. From this perspective, Rowan Williams describes the place and role of the Eucharistic encounter for enhancing the relationship with Christ thus:

> The Eucharist is the primary locus of the listening Church, the place where it shows itself to be there in response to the call of God; and the Scripture that embodies that call has to be read as leading to precisely the point, the existence of a community that embodies Christ and does so by reflecting his kenotic act (and translating his transformative presence)."[50]

The reference to "listening" brings me to the second and much needed "place" – the practice of silence – of contemplating the transforming mystery and reality of Christ in Africa that I mentioned. Once again, Williams says that, "good liturgy is about silence."[51] A transformative Eucharistic encounter, and the contemplation of the transforming reality of Christ, "flower out of silence, patience and attention, and[. . .]lead us steadily back into silence and attention."[52] Williams cites the Anglican contemplative writer, Maggie Ross, who makes the point about the practice of silence well: "It is not a question of si-

[49] For such understanding of the Eucharist, even though it is articulated in a slightly nuanced fashion, see Emmanuel Katongole, *The Sacrifice of Africa: A Political Theology for Africa* (Grand Rapids: W. B. Eerdmans, 2011); Idem, *Born from Lament: The Theology and Politics of Hope in Africa* (Grand Rapids: W. B. Eerdmans, 2017).
[50] Williams, "The Bible Today: Reading and Hearing," in *Holy Living*, 46.
[51] Rowan Williams, "Silence and Human Maturity," in *Being Human: Bodies, Minds, Persons* (London: SPCK, 2018), 98.
[52] Williams, "Silence and Human Maturity," 99.

lence *or* speech, but rather that the transfiguring [transforming] energy given in silence is expanded and integrated by making us attempt interpretation through speech, while in the same moment insights that arise from such speech deepen and expand us again into silence."[53]

These thoughts help us in rethinking the dominant mode of (Eucharistic) worship and praying to Christ and in his name in many African churches. In these churches, the liturgical and other forms of religious practice are often highly-charged by an eardrum-bursting decibel-level of sound - sometimes literally. These noise levels can be undesirable to neighbours and disturbing to physical or psychological well-being as well as to the environment. To me, it also raises questions about the understanding of a trusting personal relationship with Christ involved. One alternative to these forms of religious practice is the rediscovery of the solitude and silence of forms of contemplative prayer found in early Christianity and its mystical tradition, which persons like the late Nigerian ecclesiastic, Archbishop Albert Obiefuna, championed within the course of his pastoral and social ministry.

Contemplating the reality of Christ, particularly in the Eucharist encounter and in practices of silence, opens us up, or as Williams puts it, lets "the reality of Jesus come alive in us."[54] This reality in turn outflows and flowers in sharing the burden of, and taking responsibility for, the realities of people.[55] It yields both in theologians and ordinary Christians alike what Richard Rohr calls "the contemplative mind" or disposition of knowing and loving.[56] This mindedness or disposition allows the reality of Christ to be seen in the light of the realities of people and allows the realities of the people to be seen in the light of the reality of Christ. How to *see* the realities of people, to sympathetically gaze upon their concrete social situations as another aspect of the contemplative practice of a socially transformative Christology, is what comes next.

Contemplating the Realities of (His) People

There have been discussions in recent times about including social theory as a necessary resource for, and sociological method in, understanding who Jesus is and what he represented - and still represents - for humanity.[57] There is a

---

[53] Williams, "Silence and Human Maturity," 98.

[54] Williams, "Contemplation and Mission," in *Holy Living,* 100.

[55] Williams, "Contemplation and Mission," in *Holy Living,* 100.

[56] Richard Rohr, "Transformation and Contemplation," in *The Universal Christ: How a Forgotten Reality Can Change Everything We See, Hope For, and Believe* (New York: Convergent Books, 2019), 203-220.

[57] See, for example, Francis Fiorenza, "Critical Social Theory and Christology," *Proceedings of the Catholic Theological Society of America* 30 (2012): 63-110. See also Michael Welker, "Who is Jesus Christ For Us Today," *Harvard Theological Review* 95 (2002): 129-146, at 129-130. Welker underlines the fact that there is a need to "develop a multi-systemic, polycontextual way of thinking" and speaking about Jesus.

possibility that these sound like the usual calls for the inter- and multi-disciplinarity that have come to be expected in humanities research. I have argued elsewhere that making use of sociological resources and method in theology is not simply a mechanical exploit.[58] The use of sociological resources could be better appreciated also as a contemplative exercise. This exercise involves two things: "descent and encounter,"[59] or as Orobator expresses it, "the forthright observation and experience of the situation in the life of the believing community wherein echoes the strong but gentle wind of the Spirit."[60]

What Orobator says in another place can be drawn upon to flesh out the meaning of this contemplative exercise, which demands sympathetic-critical attention to the concrete realities of the people, among whom and for whom those working on Christology should labour. Orobator writes:

> As a theologian (one) cannot float blissfully above the conditions and complexities of life on a continent that is chronically religious and yet so tragically impoverished. The engagement in theological activity, whether in a professional or lay capacity, demands a radical *descent* into context, of the theologian and his or her community, in order to engage vital issues and questions at the interstices of faith and life.[61]

I understand "radical descent" to mean a profoundly personal participation in the concrete experiences of people, and in their struggle to make sense of God's message of redemption (transformation) in Jesus Christ. This has the potential to awaken the empathy of the theologian who becomes moved to inspire, and to take on, *a Christological, transformational praxis,* "not on behalf of the people, but by the people themselves, as inventive agents moved by the spirit of God."[62]

Graham Ward also highlights the idea in his essay "Speaking of Jesus Today: Towards an Engaged Systematic Theology," in *Grace, Governance and Globalization*, ed. by Stephan van Erp, Martin G. Poulsom and Lieven Boeve (London: Bloomsbury T&T Clark, 2017), 91-101.

[58] Chukwuemeka Anthony Atansi, "The Method of Theology: By Way of Descent and Encounter," in "The Word is Among Us: Sketching the Contours and Significance of Lawrence Nwankwo's Contextualized-Constructive Theology," *Ministerium: Journal of Contextual Theology* 5 (2019), 64-66.

[59] Atansi, "The Method of Theology," 64-66.

[60] Agbonkhianmeghe E. Orobator, "The Sky is Wide Enough: A Historico-Critical Appraisal of Theological Activity and Method in Africa," *Hekima Review* 40 (2009), 41.

[61] Agbonkhianmeghe Orobator, "Method and Context: How and Where Theology Works in Africa," in *Shaping a Global Theological Mind*, ed. by Darren C. Marks (Aldershot: Ashgate Publishing Limited, 2008), 124-125.

[62] Georges De Schrijver, "Preface," in D.F. Pilario, *Back to the Rough Grounds of Praxis: Exploring Theological Method with Pierre Bourdieu*, (Leuven: University Press, 2005), x.

I say this with the conviction that the work of a theologian does not simply entail thinking about what God has revealed in Christ, but also feeling what it is, and what one and other people might be thinking about it, and doing so in relation to the location where the divine self-revelation in Christ continues to happen. Thus, in the practice of Christology, "it is necessary," says Pope Francis, "to reflect on what we are feeling and doing; to feel what we are thinking and doing; to do what we are thinking and feeling." In this way, christologizing becomes "an interplay of capacities at the service of the person and society."[63] The further implications of these insights for repositioning Christology within the Church and wider society are what I shall briefly reflect on in the next section.

4. Implications for Repositioning Christology within the Church and Society

The Christological insights we have fleshed out so far in the modest attempt to describe the practice of a socially transformative Christology as a contemplative practice, or what, by now, I could also refer to as a christological spirituality of social engagement, have a significant implication for thinking further about the primary places of Christology in Africa. For one thing obvious, the insights suggest an urgent need to reposition christological discourse within the context of the community called Church, and very importantly, the wider society in Africa. The argument needs some spelling out, especially in responding to the narrow view that the christological identity of the Church does not allow for engagement with the social order, that the Church has no space or role to play in the social sphere, or that the exercise of her divine mandate is a matter in and for the private.

In response to these views, the Dutch theologian, Edward Schillebeeckx reminds us of the Church's christological identity and mission, both within and outside of the Church. Schillebeeckx does so in these words: "The universal significance of Jesus' message which is affirmed in particular situations[. . .] requires to be made a reality ('actualized') in changed circumstances," or to borrow a phrase again from Jon Sobrino, in a transformed "good and just historical-social reality."[64] And for Schillebeeckx (as well as for Sobrino), the

---

[63] See Pope Francis, "Address to the Pontifical Catholic University of Chile (17 January, 2018)," http://w2.vatican.va/content/Francesco/en/speeches/2018/January/documents/papa-francesco_20180117_cile-santiago-pontuniversita.html [accessed September 15, 2019].

[64] Edward Schillebeeckx, *Jesus in Our Western Culture: Mysticism, Ethics and Politics* (London: SCM Press, 1986), 40, as cited in Graham Ward, "Speaking of Jesus Today," 94. See also Sobrino, *Jesus the Liberator*, 71.

community of the Church alive in every age and place should "bear witness to the living actuality" of Christ's personality and deeds.[65]

Graham Ward, in his constructive engagement with this idea, says something quite interesting, which paves the way for a second implication of a socially transformed Christology. According to Ward, it is not just the church communities that make the gospel of Jesus Christ a living word or actuality.[66] "Jesus-talk, once culturally embedded and culturally pervasive, spills over into the streets," into the social sphere.[67] So much so that, "we need to hear the ways Jesus-talk is circulating, and has, in fact, a life of its own, outside the ecclesia."[68] There is something more we could do with this "Jesus-talk", in addition to hearing it. We need to value and appropriate it so that it can become a resource for the Christian engagement in the public sphere where it is in circulation. The Jesuit systematic theologian, Michael Cook, describes the process of valuing and appropriating popular christologies in terms he refers to as "repristination and conscientization." According to Cook, they are the conditions for the possibility and pursuit of such a Christology, which I describe here as a social, transformation-oriented Christology.

The first condition is the provision of an in-depth theological account – and in light of the social dimension – of the popular expressions of the identity and work of Christ in grassroots Christian communities. Such a theological account is characterised by what Cook refers to as a "repristination" of the people's christological imagination expressed in images that are informed by their day-to-day struggles and hopes for a transformed African society.[69] By repristination, Cook means that the grassroots (popular) images of Christ must be valued for themselves, and through the "process of maturation at the grassroots," brought to expression in new and creative ways for engaging and responding to pressing social issues in Africa.[70] This was the christological move in the discussion of the grassroots christological imagination in Africa as both a proclamation and a longing that I outlined in the first section of this essay.

The second condition, according to Cook, involves a critical appropriation and creative incorporation of the popular expressions of the identity and work of Christ into the theologian's christological model. The model should be the kind that primes the christological imagination of ordinary believers, is able to enhance their relationship with Christ and with one another, opens the way to

[65] Schillebeeckx, *Jesus in Our Western Culture*, 41.
[66] Ward, "Speaking of Jesus Today," 95.
[67] Ward, "Speaking of Jesus Today," 95.
[68] Ward, "Speaking of Jesus Today," 95.
[69] See Cook, "The African Experience of Jesus," 672. Cook discusses a similar idea in an earlier article "Jesus from the Other Side of History: Christology in Latin America," *Theological Studies* 44 (1983): 258-287.
[70] Cook, "The African Experience of Jesus," 669, 679, and 682.

engaged and empowered human agency, orients them to confront their social realities, and, very importantly, inspires specific commitments of ecclesial-social solidarity. This second condition resonates with what Cook also refers to as "conscientization."[71] According to him, "conscientization" entails the "critical appropriation" of those images "through a specific politico-communal commitment."[72] Cook maintains that this second condition saves the first from being "romanticized or idealized."[73] The point here is that repristination and conscientization are the two processes for a socially-transformative Christology that privileges the experience and expressions of Christ within the Church and in the society.

5. By Way of Conclusion: Rethinking Christology and What it Can Do

What I have tried to do in this essay, as a way of pursuing a social transformation-oriented Christology in the African context, is in line with the fundamental assertion of liberation theology and of every theology that is true to its proper task in the face of suffering around the world today.[74] As Sobrino, drawing from Karl Rahner, articulates it: "It is the conviction that the poor – and God (Christ) in the poor – have broken into history."[75] To be sure, every human person, both ordinary Christians and the academic theologian, not least, the Christologist, has to respond to this reality, indeed correspond to it, and make an effort to change it.[76] This conviction is not the result of theoretical argument or dogmatic, self-determined abstractions; it comes, rather, from an honest and hopeful option to let the mystery of Christ be central, to let it speak, to let it guide, and to let it call forth response in the lived realities of (his) people.[77]

These ideas open up an insight into Christology as a whole. So that I am led towards a "new" way of thinking about the meaning of Christology – namely, Christology is the art of discerning, participating in, and collaborating with the ways Christ transforms the social order through loving encounter or relationship with Christ and with other people, through empowered agency,

---

[71] Cook, "The African Experience of Jesus," 672, and earlier in his book *Christology as Narrative Quest* (Collegeville: The Liturgical Press, 1997), 179-180.
[72] Cook, "The African Experience of Jesus," 672.
[73] Cook, "The African Experience of Jesus," 672.
[74] See, for example, Gustavo Gutiérrez, *A Theology of Liberation* (Maryknoll: Orbis Books, 1988); and Prevot, "The Contemplation of Liberation: Gustavo Gutiérrez," in *Thinking Prayer*, 235-241.
[75] Jon Sobrino, "Karl Rahner and Liberation Theology," *The Way* 43, no. 4 (October 2004): 53-66, at 58.
[76] Jon Sobrino, "Karl Rahner and Liberation Theology," 58.
[77] Jon Sobrino, "Karl Rahner and Liberation Theology," 59.

and through embodied practices of solidarity within and beyond ecclesial communities.[78] Rowan Williams expressed where and how Christology understood as such – in whatever context – can do that which is proper to it in the light of the foregoing discussions. His words shed further light on the hint I have just made about the meaning of Christology. And in their stirring unambiguity, they can also serve as a fitting conclusion to my contemplation here on the practice of a socially transformative Christology in Africa:

[. . .]Christology, in short, is done in the practice of a community that understands itself to be the Body of Christ, a [any] group of persons living and acting from the conviction that human community is most fully realized in the unconditional mutuality which is represented by the language of organic interdependence. Christology is done in the practice of lives that embrace their finitude and materiality without fear, lives that enact the divine self-identification with those who endure loss, pain and contempt. Christology is done in a practice of prayer and worship that does not approach God as a distant and distinct individual with a will to which mine must conform – as if in a finite relation of slave to master – but acts out of the recognition of adoptive filiation and the intimacy that flows from this. It is done when we see that the doing of God's will "in earth as in Heaven" means that the eternal will of God is for the life of the world – that God is "satisfied" when our flourishing is secured. Christology in this vein is the impetus for both the stillness and expectancy of prayer [contemplation] and the risk of action on behalf of the neglected or oppressed other.[79]

Bibliography

Amirtham, Sam, and John Pobee, eds. *Theology by the People: Reflections on Doing Theology in Community*. Geneva: WCC Publication, 1986.

Ashley, Matthew. "The Mystery of God and Compassion for the Poor: The Spiritual Basis of Theology." In *Hope and Solidarity: Jon Sobrino's Challenge to Christian Theology*, edited by Stephen J. Pope, 63-75. Maryknoll: Orbis Books, 2008.

Atansi, Chukwuemeka Anthony. "The Word is Among Us: Sketching the Contours and Significance of Lawrence Nwankwo's Contextualized-Constructive Theology." *Ministerium: Journal of Contextual Theology* 5 (2019): 47-69.

Bediako, Kwame. *Jesus and the Gospel in Africa: History and Experience*. Maryknoll: Orbis Books, 2004.

---

[78] Chukwuemeka Anthony Atansi, "Discerning and Collaborating with Christ's Solidarity with the World: Oscar Romero's Christological Spirituality and Its Methodological Dynamism," Presentation in the context of the interdisciplinary academy, *Romero: Memory – Activating Heritage of International Solidarity*, organised at the Katholieke Universiteit Leuven, Belgium, 4-8 November, 2019.

[79] Williams, *Christ the Heart of Creation*, 250.

Clarke, Clifton. *African Christology: Jesus in Post-missionary African Christianity*. Eugene: Pickwick Publications, 2011.

Cook, Michael. *Christology as Narrative Quest*. Collegeville: The Liturgical Press, 1997.

______. "Jesus from the Other Side of History." *Theological Studies* 44 (1983): 258-287.

______. "The African Experience of Jesus." *Theological Studies* 70 (2009): 668-692.

De Schrijver, Georges. "Preface." In Daniel F. Pilario *Back to the Rough Ground of Praxis: Exploring Theological Method with Pierre Bourdieu*, vii-xii. Leuven: University Press, 2005.

Éla, Jean Marc. "Christianity and Liberation in Africa." In *Paths of African Theology*, edited by Rosino Gibellini, 136-153. Maryknoll: Orbis Books, 1994.

______. *African Cry*. Maryknoll: Orbis Books, 1991.

Ezigbo, Victor. *Re-imagining African Christologies: Conversing with the Interpretations and Appropriations of Jesus in Contemporary African Christianity*. Eugene: Pickwick Publications, 2010.

Fiorenza, Francis. "Critical Social Theory and Christology." *Proceedings of the Catholic Theological Society of America* 30 (2012): 63-110.

Gifford, Paul. *Christianity, Development and Modernity in Africa*. London: C. Hurst & C. Publishers Ltd., 2015.

Goergen, Donald. "The Quest for the Christ of Africa." *African Christian Studies* 17 (2001): 5-51.

Gutiérrez, Gustavo. *A Theology of Liberation*. Maryknoll: Orbis Books, 1988.

Ilo, Stan Chu. "Interpreting the Search for Health and Healing Among African Charismatic and Pentecostal Groups: A Theological Bio-Social Approach." *Bigard Theological Studies* 38, no. 1 (2018): 1-36.

______. "Searching for Healing in a Miraculous Stream: The Fate of God's People in Africa." In *Wealth, Health, and Hope in African Christian Religion: The Search for Abundant Life*, edited by Stan Chu Ilo, 45-80. Lanham: Lexington Books, 2018.

Kalilombe, Patrick. "Doing Theology at the Grassroots: A Challenge for Professional Theologians, Part One." *African Ecclesial Review* 27, no. 3 (June 1985): 148-161.

______. "Doing Theology at the Grassroots: A Challenge for Professional Theologians, Part Two." *African Ecclesial Review* 27, no. 4 (August 1985): 225-237.

Katongole, Emmanuel. *Born of Lament: The Theology and Politics of Hope in Africa*. Grand Rapids: Eerdmans, 2017.

______. *The Sacrifice of Africa: A Political Theology of Africa*. Grand Rapids: Eerdmans, 2011.

Keener, Craig. *Miracles: The Credibility of the New Testament Accounts*, vol 1. Grand Rapid: Baker Academic, 2011.

Mana, Kä. *Christians and Churches of Africa Envisioning the Future: Salvation in Christ and Building a New African Society*. Maryknoll: Orbis Books, 2004.

Min, Anselm, ed. *The Task of Theology: Leading Theologians on the Most Compelling Questions for Today*. Maryknoll: Orbis Books, 2018.

Mugambi, Jesse. *Christian Mission and Social Transformation*. Nairobi: Acton, 2003.

______. *From Liberation to Reconstruction: African Christian Theology After the Cold War.* Nairobi: East African Educational Publishers, 1995.

______. *The Church and Reconstruction of Africa: Theological Considerations.* Nairobi: AACC, 1997.

______. "Christian Mission and Social Transformation After the Cold War." *Journal of Constructive Theology* 4, no. 2 (1998): 65-86.

Nyamiti, Charles. *Christ as Our Ancestor: Christology from an African Perspective.* Gweru: Mambo Press, 1984.

Oduyoye, Mercy Amba. *Beads and Strands: Reflections of an African Woman on Christianity in Africa.* Maryknoll: Orbis Books, 2004.

Opongo, Elias, and Agbonkhianmeghe Orobator, eds. *Faith Doing Justice: A Manual for Social Analysis, Catholic Social Teaching and Social Justice.* Nairobi: Paulines, 2007.

Orobator, Agbonkhianmeghe. "*Caritas in Veritate* and Africa's Burden of (Under)Development." *Theological Studies* 71 (2010): 320-334.

______. "Method and Context: How and Where Theology Works in Africa." In *Shaping a Global Theological Mind,* edited by Darren C. Marks, 121-126. Aldershot: Ashgate Publishing Limited, 2008.

______. *Religion and Faith in Africa: Confessions of an Animist.* Maryknoll: Orbis Books, 2018.

______. "The Quest for an African Christ: An Essay in Contemporary African Christology." *Hekima Review* 11 (September 1994): 75-99.

______. "The Sky is Wide Enough: A Historico-Critical Appraisal of Theological Activity and Method in Africa." *Hekima Review* 40 (May 2009): 34-44.

______. *Theology Brewed in an African Pot.* Maryknoll: Orbis Books, 2008.

Prevot, Andrew. *Thinking Prayer: Theology and Spirituality amid the Crises of Modernity.* Notre Dame: University of Notre Dame Press, 2015.

Rohr, Richard. *The Universal Christ: How a Forgotten Reality Can Change Everything We See, Hope For, and Believe.* New York: Convergent Books, 2019.

Ross, Kenneth. "Current Christological Trends in Northern Malawi." *Journal of Religion in Africa* 27, no. 2 (1997): 160-176.

Schreiter, Robert, "Images of Jesus in Contemporary Culture." *Concilium* 3 (2008): 124-129.

Schreiter, Robert, ed. *Faces of Jesus in Africa.* Maryknoll: Orbis Books, 1991.

Shorter, Aylward. *Jesus and the Witchdoctor: An Approach to Healing and Wholeness.* Maryknoll: Orbis Books, 1985.

______. "Folk Christianity and Functional Christology." *African Ecclesial Review* 24, no. 3 (1982): 133-137.

______. "Foreword." In *Christ Our Healer: A Theological Dialogue with Aylward Shorter,* Dominigues Fernando, 7-10. Nairobi: Paulines Publications Africa, 2000.

Sobrino, Jon. "Jesus of Galilee from the Salvadoran Context: Compassion, Hope, and Following the Light of the Cross." Translated by Robert Lassalle Klein with J. Matthew Ashley. *Theological Studies* 70 (2009): 437-460.

______. *Jesus the Liberator: A Historical-Theological Reading of Jesus of Nazareth*. Translated by Paul Burns and Francis McDonagh. Maryknoll: Orbis Books, 1993.

______. "Karl Rahner and Liberation Theology." *The Way* 43, no. 4 (October 2004): 53-66.

______. *Christ the Liberator: A View from the Victims*. Translated by Paul Burns. Maryknoll: Orbis Books, 2001.

______. "Spirituality and the Following of Jesus." In *Mysterium Liberationis: Fundamental Concepts of Liberation Theology*, edited by Ignacio Ellacuría and Jon Sobrino, 677-701. Maryknoll: Orbis Books, 1993.

Scannone, Juan Carlos. "Pope Francis and the Theology of the People." *Theological Studies* 77, no. 1 (2016): 118-135.

Southgate, Christopher. *Theology in a Suffering World: Glory and Longing*. Cambridge: Cambridge University Press, 2018.

Stinton, Diane. "Encountering Jesus at the Well: Further Reflections on African Women's Christologies." *Journal of Reformed Theology* 7 (2013): 267-293.

______. Jesus Christ, Living Water in Africa Today." In *The Oxford Handbook of Christology*, edited by Francesca Aran Murphy, 425-443. Oxford: Oxford University Press, 2015.

______. "Jesus-Immanuel, Image of the Invisible God: Aspects of Popular Christology in Sub-Saharan Africa." *Journal of Reformed Theology* 1 (2007): 6-40.

______. "Jesus of Africa: Voices of Contemporary African Christology." In *The Myriad Christ: Plurality and the Quest for Unity in Contemporary Christology*, edited by T. Merrigan and J. Haers, 287-313. Leuven: University Press and Peeters, 2000.

______. *Jesus of Africa: Voices of Contemporary African Christology*. Maryknoll: Orbis Books, 2004.

Tanner, Kathryn. *Christ the Key*. Cambridge: Cambridge University Press, 2010.

Udoh, Enyi Ben. *Guest Christology: An Interpretative View of the Christological Problem in Africa*. Frankfurt am Main: Lang, 1988.

Villa-Vicencio, Charles. *A Theology of Reconstruction: Nation-Building and Human Rights*. Cambridge: University Press, 1992.

Volf, Miroslav, and Matthew Croasmun. *For the Life of the World: Theology that Makes a Difference*. Grand Rapids, MI: Brazos Press, 2019.

Ward, Graham. "Speaking of Jesus Today: Towards an Engaged Systematic Theology." In Grace, Governance and Globalization, edited by Stephan van Erp, Martin G. Poulsom and Lieven Boeve, 91-101. London: Bloomsbury T&T Clark, 2017.

Welker, Michael. "Who is Jesus Christ for Us Today?" *Harvard Theological Review* 95, no. 2 (2002): 129-146.

Williams, Rowan. *Being Human: Bodies, Minds, Persons*. London: SPCK, 2018.

______. *Christ the Heart of Creation*. London: Bloomsbury, 2018.

______. *Holy Living: The Christian Tradition for Today*. London: Bloomsbury, 2017.

Afterword

Wanderings in Pedagogy as a Model-of Transcultural Theological Research

Matthew Ryan Robinson (Bonn, Germany)

I. Introduction

The following is an exercise in theological autobiography. I offer it not because I expect these personal glimpses will be especially interesting to readers, let alone because I regard my experience as a model for anyone else's. I do so, rather, because the concrete human person is such an important site for examining the intersections of the complex of issues addressed in this volume. One of the things theology does, I would suggest, is pursue self-understanding – yes: before God and in the world, but always with reference to particular communities and how they chart themselves in relation to God and world. Likewise, human beings constantly re-perform their understandings of the ways they fit in their own situation, their world and what they regard as ultimate reality. In this way, theologies, however much they seek to provide "models for" reality, remain nevertheless always also "models of", as discussed in the introductory chapter to this book[1]: theological work maps the experiences that they and their communities have had, always "from below" and beneath the horizons of human finitude. Regrettably, much theology leaves out the autobiographical element. I can understand why. From perspective of another, it might seem too subjective and not very objective or scientific; it may seem to call into question one's credibility or at least the generalizability of what one says. From one's own perspective, it can create an awareness of the limited, relative, even accidental nature of one's own experience; this can, in turn, create doubt – sometimes helpful, sometimes not – about the legitimacy or value of that experience, of one's tradition and past, or even of one's life.

But even though these concerns should be taken seriously, they do not eliminate what remains the case, namely, that the theological questions we ask about God, world, and self do not arise out of a contextless, laboratory-based course of study, but arise from bodily, sensory, emotional, rational,

---

[11] Clifford Geertz, "Religion as a Cultural System," in *The Interpretation of Cultures* (New York: Basic Books, 1973), 87-125, here 93.

relational human life embedded in the world. That embeddedness is "cultured" – that is, created and cultivated – in contexts structured by physical, social, political and historical experiences, all of which are distributed by weighted social values and attending social privileges. These physical-social intersections at the site of "my life", "your life" and the lives of others strictly shape the real possibilities, the possible realities even, that we as human beings inhabit. And theologians work with these intersections – in their very persons – no differently than anyone else. That is not say that theology therefore has a definite responsibility to serve or help this or that community; but neither am I, at least personally, very interested in theological work that ignores life in the world and allows who-knows-how-many theologians to dance on the head a needless point.[2] So one helpful approach for theologians who are interested in the functions of theological communications the world over today is to look to their own experience as a site of the intersection of religion, society, science, politics, and history, to consider the expectations, questions, and needs they encounter there in their own situations, and then to bring these into conversation with as many other people as possible who are interested in doing the same thing. Thus, it is my hope that, even while my experience will differ from the reader's – no doubt, significantly – it might provide signposts, helpful for orienting exploration of how theologies function in the world today to process the complex interconnectednesses of human life in particular communities before the Ultimate. And so, with that, let's hit the trail.

---

[2] The question of whether many angels might occupy a single place at one time, indeed, the point of a needle, is a metonym for the accusation that medieval scholastics often engaged in pointless debates. There is no evidence of any medieval scholastics actually posing this question, as Peter Harrison and others have argued convincingly. Harrison also offers a different etymology for the question, however, one which I find delightful. He refers to William Sclater (1575-1626), writing "English divine, William Sclater (1575–1626). Commenting in 1619 on medieval papists' predilection for 'doting about curious questions', he adduces the specific example of their enquiries about angels: '...they fell to Disputations about the time of their Creation; whether it were before, or with the visible World; whether on the first day, or when they were created. Touching their Orders, what, and how many they were, their number, whether more fell or stood: whether they did occupie a place; and so, whether many might be in one place at one time; and how many might sit on a Needles point; and six hundred such like needlesse points.'" On this basis, he concludes: "My suggestion is that the reason an English writer first introduced the 'needle's point' into a critique of medieval angelology is that it makes for a clever pun on 'needless point'." See Peter Harrison, "Angels on Pinheads and Needles' Points," *Notes and Queries* 63 (2016): 45-47.

2. Signpost I: Theological Research Needs a Critical Pedagogy

Like many other theologians and scholars of religion, one of the main paths I regularly travel is that of teaching, a road which, at least in theology, unavoidably wanders through the whole landscape of nature, religion, society, science, politics, and history. I would say that my thinking about WDTD as a programmatic question really grew out of conversations conducted in teaching. Or I should say more specifically, a certain kind of teaching: Sociologist of Religion, Grace Davie, who generously agreed to write the foreword to this book, reports that she would tell her students to "put the books down; go outside!" where things really happen.[3] Without meaning to undermine the value of long, silent hours in the library, I have to say I find Davie's pedagogical admonition energizing, especially for theological teaching and research. In my own teaching, I take much inspiration from Paulo Freire's vision of "education as the practice of freedom"[4] and from scholars like bell hooks (among others) who, following Freire, has advocated for a transgressive and engaged "critical pedagogy".[5] In Freire's and hooks's approaches, the teacher and the students learn together, from and with one another and embedded in a live, unfolding research field. One presupposition of this approach to teaching is that knowledge is not something that "exists" and must simply be transferred from one party to another. Freire famously described such an orientation as a "banking" model of education.[6] Rather, *knowledge* is produced as a kind *know-how,* as skills that help to realize possibilities for living in a certain way. Once I realized that, and once I acquired the tools necessary for approaching theology in that way, a whole new landscape of theological formations to explore and paths to follow opened up for me. I began looking for opportunities to leave the classroom – with and as students! – and I began thinking more *intentionally* about what it would mean to conduct on-the-ground theological surveys of the landscape of nature, religion, society, science, politics, and history in all the diversity of their mutually conditioning formations. The fol-

---

[3] Davie related this practice in "Understanding Religion in Modern Europe," the keynote address she gave at the 2019 conference of the European Society for the Study of Intercultural Theology and Interreligious Studies in Sarajevo. (24 April 2019)

[4] Paulo Freire, *Pedagogy of the Oppressed,* trans. by Myra Bergman Ramos, with an introduction by Donaldo Macedo (New York and London: Continuum, 2000 [1970]).

[5] bell hooks, *Teaching to Transgress: Education as the Practice of Freedom* (New York and London: Routledge, 1994).

[6] Freire, *Pedagogy of the Oppressed,* chapter 2. Freire writes that "education as the practice of freedom [. . .] denies that the world exists as a reality apart from people", but that this world is not simply to be observed but rather to "enter into" the student, such that the student is no longer a spectator of the world, but becomes a "co-creator" of full humanity. Cf. pages 81, 76, and 75 respectively.

lowing are pages from my own rough field guide in exploring this (to me) new territory.

3. Signpost 2: Theology Helps People Solve Problems

In Addis Ababa in 2016, I sat with fourteen American university students in the apartment of a development NGO manager-turned-entrepreneur. I was one of the "professors" on a cross-cultural immersion study program, designed and led by Andrew DeCort (who is also one of the contributors to this volume), but I felt distinctly non-professorial and much more like a beginning student. We listened as our dialogue partner told us how he had decided to pursue for-profit development work. Two things he said, which stood out to me at the time and have influenced my development as a theologian since, are relevant to the WDTD project: First, he described how locally-anchored for-profit development as a sustainable approach to devleopment, since a primary goal is independence from international financial backing and since it draws on local workforces as much as possible. Second, the jobs created further empower the local community by honing reusable, transferable skills. Business, he said, should help people solve problems, and good business practices can assist in reaching holistic, sustainable development aims.

I distinctly remember, as I sat there, starting to feel pretty disillusioned with my chosen line of work. In not so many words, I thought to myself, "but what does theology do?" The implied answer was "Nothing." But this person's mantra echoed in my thoughts – "business should help people solve problems" – until suddenly the coin dropped, and over the next few weeks, as we met with dozens of Ethiopian academics and activists, pastors, politicians, hospital workers, and other business persons, the wheels in my own theological consciousness were slowly beginning to turn. (Note: This was *after* I had received a doctorate in theology!) I saw, not only in these conversations in Ethiopia, but also in my teaching and research, that I had been struggling to process the reciprocal interplay between theological communications and the socio-political reverberations, effectivity, and agency of those communications for a long time: For example, in my first field-research experience in Kenya as a seminarian, studying the entrepreneurial formation of grassroots theological education institutions responding to the growing number of churches and attending need for pastoral training. Or, in seminars that I taught much later about the interwoven evolution of the theological doctrine of the priesthood of all believers, the political doctrines of toleration and freedom of conscience, and the religious wars in the (Post)Reformation period. Or, in a seminar I organized at the UN headquarters in New York on tolerance in interreligious perspectives. Or, in research I was just beginning that linked the history of German pietism to the first social solidarity organization in Germany, the

"Inner Mission".[7] In each of these examples, I saw that theology, too, was helping people solve problems. I had just never thought to put it exactly in those terms. Up until then, in my theological wanderings, I had simply had monument markers and a vague sense of direction to orient me. This new formulation now gave me a compass for theological orienteering.

4. Signpost 3: Theology Interrelates What is Ultimate with What is Actual in What is Immediate

Like a wilderness landscape, theological formations can surprise and seem unique in the surrounding environment and seem to possess a singular ability to withstand or even transcend that environment. But they are always also products of the environment, permanently situated before definite horizons. Theological ideas might appear to be inspired by, say, the Bible or the traditions of a church, and of course they are in significant ways. But they are not for that reason not *also* catalyzed by natural occurrences, political events, scientific developments. For example, as Ernst Troeltsch observed in his own re-thinking of theological method over 100 years ago, once the interconnectedness of all natural phenomena is recognized as a methodological principle, the religion of Yahweh and emergence of monotheism documented in the Hebrew Bible have to be seen in relation to geo-political contestations and -economic dynamics in the ancient near east; or again, the appearance of Christianity must also be interpreted in relation to prevailing apocalyptic ideas circulating in the Greco-Roman world and the socio-economic status of the first Christians.[8] These are just two examples of fundamental systematic-theological artifacts – one related to the doctrine of God and one related to the doctrine of the church – that document the problem-solving functions theological reflection and communication perform for communities.

I hasten to clarify that saying "theology helps people solve problems" is a descriptive observation rather than a prescriptive principle. It is by no means to say that theology always pursues justice, let alone ever achieves it; too much life-destroying theology has been propagated for that to be plausible. Much more cautiously than that, I mean to say that theological communications are one way in which groups process phenomena in their social envi-

[7] See chapter 1 of Matthew Ryan Robinson and Evan F. Kuehn, *Theology Compromised: Schleiermacher, Troeltsch, and the Possibility of a Sociological Theology* (Minneapolis: Lexington Books/Fortress Academic, 2019).

[8] Ernst Troeltsch, "Historical and Dogmatic Method in Theology," in Ernst Troeltsch, *Religion in History,* trans. by James Luther Adams and Walter F. Bense, ed. and with an introduction by James Luther Adams (Minneapolis: Fortress Press, 1991), 11-33, here 13, 15.

ronments that intersect with their group and which they perceive to be problematic in some way or another, whether as threatening to, inconsistent with, or incompatible with their self-understanding and way of life. In this way, "theology" and its expression in "theologies" might be understood along the lines of what sociologist Niklas Luhmann and others have theorized as a social "semantics".[9] Whatever else they can or should do – and this book has outlined many different observations – theologies at least help groups in their calibrations of their orientations toward what is ultimate with their experiences of an actual situation, as those two come together at the immediate site of the group, its community, its very self. One broad category of things that theology does might thus be summarized: *Theology conducts interrelations of the ultimate and the actual in the immediate.* I understand that the effects of what theology does may be "good" or "bad" on a number of registers and for a variety of constituencies. Walking through valleys of theological shadow and death only makes the compass more helpful for navigating difficult terrain, not less.

5. Signpost 4: Theological Semantics are Useful for Comparing Local Responses to Shared Transcultural Tensions

Equipped with this compass that pointed toward theology's problem-solving capacities, I set out to begin exploring and surveying territory, now intentionally rather than accidentally and, once again, with students.

On the one hand, in an attempt to chart some cross-contextual Cartesian coordinates, we have collectively examined what theology does in our respective contexts to process "transcultural pressures". As outlined in the introductory chapter, by "transcultural pressures" I mean social pressures that span large geo-political and geo-economic networks: for example, climate change and climate politics, digitalization, the 2020 Coronavirus pandemic. Attention to transcultural pressures in combination with the unique and locally effective ways that particular theologies respond to those pressures can make meaningful analysis across diverse contexts possible. I have challenged students to examine their own traditions' responses to themes common to multiple contexts, from topics as broad as "faith and flourishing" to more concretely defined topics like "protest movements". Throughout, I have enjoyed the tremendous privilege of working with students in ecumenical studies from around the world – three of whom contributed chapters to this book – from

[9] Luhmann's theorization of the evolving semantics of modernity and the ways the (re)produce contemporary global society's core systems of communicative exchange is presented in the studies of his four-volume work: *Gesellschaftsstruktur und Semantik. Studien zur Wissenssoziologie der modernen Gesellschaft, vols. 1-4* (Frankfurt am Main: Suhrkamp, 1980-1995).

Slovakia to Ukraine, South Korea to Hong Kong to the Philippines, Bangladesh to India, Togo to Ethiopia to Madagascar, and the USA. Our discussions have included study of Marian apparitions appearing in oven glass or a block of wood in the northeast mountains of Slovakia,[10] of the annual procession of the *Hesus Nazareno* through >200,000 of the faithful in the streets of Manila,[11] of Korean churches' struggles over how to respond to the pressure to accept Shinto religion during Japanese occupation and the divisions of Korean theologies after independence,[12] and of early African indigenous prophets like William Wadé Harris[13] among many, many other situations. In each case, our task has been, first, to identify and give a thick description of the issues experienced by the community as a problem: challenges to ethnic identity, tensions between colonial and indigenous religion, dictatorial threats to democratic practice or democratic threats to totalitarian regimes. Then, second, we have focused on the use of explicitly and classically "theological" language and symbols to work through these problems: divine and political sovereignty, true doctrine and apostasy, Scriptural exegesis and prophetic interpretation, and many others.

On the other hand, it quickly became clear that doing this kind of theological surveying, on the ground and attending to the use of theological communication in people's lived experience, meant we needed extra tools. Like the explorer's map, theoretical framings remain necessary for providing language to help us imagine the bigger picture of the phenomena in question – for example, the language of "lived religion" is helpful for starting to talk about

---

10 On Mary's appearance in the oven glass: "Ježiš na rúre v Batizovciach: Zjavenie v rómskej osade robí majiteľom sporáka problémy" https://www.youtube.com/watch?v=nsWMUZ0dIyg; on Mary's appearance in a block of wood: "javenia panny Márie na Slovensku -. Črepiny" https://www.youtube.com/watch?v=EfZ6OhRXaqQ (Accessed 22 May 2020)

11 Arnulfo Valderama Fortunado, "Feast of the Black Nazarene Draws Millions to Manila's Streets," Catholics and Culture (9 January 2016), https://www.catholicsandcultures.org/philippines/feast-black-nazarene (Accessed 22 May 2020); on the embodied theological devotionality in the translation of the Black Nazarene, cf. Mark Joseph T Calano, "Ginhawa as Ethic of Panatà: Body Politics and the Devotion to the Black Nazarene", *Budhi: A Journal of Ideas and Culture* 22, no. 2 (2018): 43-74.

12 See chapter 4 of Sebastian C. H. Kim/Kirsteen Kim, *A History of Korean Christianity* (Cambridge: Cambridge University Press, 2015), 107-156.

13 Surprisingly little has been written about William Wadé Harris, which may be explained by the lack of source materials, but David Shank is one standard reference for information on Harris: See David Shank, "Le Pentecôtisme de prophète William Wadé Harris", *Archives de Sciences Sociales des Religions* 44, no. 105 (1999): 51-70; and David Shank, "The Prophet Harris: A Historiographical and Bibliographical Survey", *Journal of Religion in Africa* 14, no. 2 (1983): 130-160.

devotional culture surround the appearance of Mary in the oven glass.[14] Textual analysis remains critical for assessing the distance, angles, and elevation in interpretation of the Biblical texts and church tradition – for example, in order to understand Indian Dalit theologians' theological identification of Christ's suffering and exclusion "outside the camp" with Dalit exclusion and oppression.[15] But, like the surveyor's chain, theodolite, and level, it becomes important to incorporate additional information-gathering instruments to process other forms of data like Wadé Harris's gourd rattle and walking stick,[16] umbrellas in the 2014 Hong Kong Umbrella Movement,[17] YouTube videos of news reports on the Slovakian apparitions, or inconsistent data and competing accounts of the 2013 and 2014 Maidan square protest movements from the Moscow and Kiev Patriarchy websites in Ukraine. And this requires the adaptation of qualitative, social-scientific methods for collecting and curating such theological artifacts.

In a related way, a two-semester seminar project in Bonn that explored ecclesiology in relation to practices of friendship with refugee youth was one of the first opportunities I had to devote extended attention to the use of participant observation and participant action methods in systematic-theological research.[18] Here, an explicitly systematic-theological *topos*, namely, ecclesiol-

---

14 In particular, the work of scholar of religion and American Catholicism Robert Orsi was helpful in that instance. See Robert A. Orsi, *Between Heaven and Earth: The Religious Worlds People Make and the Scholars who Study Them* (Princeton and Oxford: Princeton University Press, 2005); and Robert A. Orsi, *The Madonna of 115th Street: Faith and Community in Italian Harlem, 1880-1950* (New Haven: Yale University Press, 1985).

15 The phrase may be found in Hebrews 13:13 and refers to Jesus' suffering and exclusion, with which Dalit Christians identify from their own experiences of exclusion. See V. Devasahayam, *Outside the Camp: Biblical Studies in Dalit Perspective* (Madras: Gurukul Lutheran Theological College and Research Studies, 1994). I am thankful to Sam Sunny Anand Sigamani, from whom I have learned more about Dalit theology.

16 Ogbu Kalu, *African Pentecostalism: An Introduction* (Oxford and New York: Oxford University Press, 2008), 37.

17 Justin K. H. Tse and Jonathan Y. Tan, eds., *Theological Reflections on the Hong Kong Umbrella Movement* (New York: Palgrave Macmillan, 2016). In "The Umbrella Movement and Kairos: The Church's Theological Encounter with a Political Movement", Lap Yan Kung thematizes the umbrella as a solidifying symbol in the "conscientization" process in the Hong Kong protests, forming a sense of collectivity and purpose. Lap Yan Kung, "The Umbrella Movement and Kairos: The Church's Theological Encounter with a Political Movement", in *Theological Reflections on the Hong Kong Umbrella Movement*, ed. by Justin K. H. Tse and Jonathan Y. Tan, 107-130, here 110-111.

18 Matthew Ryan Robinson, "'Fake Friends': Zur Toleranz und Freundschaft als soziale und theologische Werte, oder wie Theologie Studierende Geflüchteten nicht Hilfe gaben, sondern mit ihnen Freundschaft fanden." *Pastoraltheologie* 107, no. 7 (2018): 333-352. This seminar was also a "transdisciplinary" effort, in that it was conducted in

ogy and the question of what "belonging" "in" the church means, was held up to ethnographic analysis. Students (many of them studying to become pastors) compared the stereotyped observation that Germans are less and less religious – as measured by traditional theological metrics like church membership and attendance – with the empirical observation that the numbers of people passing through the circle of church life every week actually might have increased tremendously after the arrival of 750,000 migrants in 2015, as thousands of migrants responded to the churches' assistance and relief efforts. From a traditional theological angle – let's say, church worship service attendance – the churches appear to be shrinking and society secularizing. But from a sociological angle, the church would appear to have grown – only, that growth includes many non-Christians. Empirical work describing what theology did in motivating, directing, or constraining the response-abilities of the churches revealed new systematic- and practical-theological questions of considerable significance: How might understandings of the church be changing in the course of these social-demographic changes, and what will it look like in the not-too-distant future to pastor what in effect are multi-religious congregations? To "work on" these questions, we read some introductory cultural-anthropological theory[19] and a few theological treatments of friendship,[20] but the primary texts were "living human documents"[21] and conversations conducted in the course of spending time with a group of young people in Bonn who had fled seeking refuge from war in Iraq, Iran, and Syria. The content of the "class sessions" included picnics, visits to one another's homes, shared celebration of one another's birthdays or holidays, and exchange of favorite foods and music. The effect for the theologians in our midst was to disrupt and expand the horizon of possibilities for understanding Christian and interreligious community, to gain clarity on the ways theological communications worked in an engaged and currently relevant context, and thereby also to be able to recalibrate the orientation toward theological study in relation to that challenge.

These efforts in a theological critical-pedagogy were injected with new life by a return to Ethiopia in 2018 with a different group of students, this time from Bonn. In preparation, we again read texts, both theological and "non-theological", in order to learn about Ethiopian history, religion, politics, and

---

collaboration with a colleague who worked for the office for children and family at the City of Bonn. The idea for a possible partnership must be credited to her vision and tireless efforts.

19 Specifically, Clifford Geertz, "Thick Description: Toward an Interpretive Theory of Culture," in *The Interpretation of Cultures: Selected Essays* (New York: Basic Books, 1973), 3-32.

20 Marco Hofheinz, Frank Mathwig, and Matthias Zeindler, eds., *Freundschaft. Zur Aktualität eines traditionsreichen Begriffs* (Zürich: TVZ, 2014).

21 Henri Nouwen, "Anton T. Boisen and Theology Through Living Human Documents", *Pastoral Psychology* 19, no. 7 (1968): 49-63.

culture, as well as to equip ourselves in at least a minimal way for conducting a kind of theological fieldwork. We examined Orthodox, Islamic, and Pentecostal theologies of Ethiopia and considered their functions in the complex negotiations of identity in a land with over 80 languages and people groups and one of the most ancient Christian churches in the world (in the Ethiopian Tewahedo Orthodox Church), but that is also processing intense modernization pressures from international political allies and actors with economic interests. The primary form of the *teaching,* though, was once again going outside of the classroom and *listening* to Ethiopians from all professional, political, and religious corners of the society. This collaborative teaching-learning effort also once again produced innovative theological research: Andrew DeCort, who had originally designed the program,[22] I, and the students working in teams wrote article contributions for a special issue of the journal *Pastoraltheologie* that explored their deepening understandings of traditional systematic-theological *topoi* like forgiveness, redemption, mission, and eschatology vis-à-vis the conversations and learning opportunities shared with their generous Ethiopian partners.[23]

6. Signpost 5: Good Theological Research Must be Concerned for the Liberation of Subjugated Theological Knowledges

An interesting kind of decentering takes place when this kind of theological exploring is done transculturally and with others hailing from and working on different local contexts: Namely, the map comes to be recognized as one representation among many existing representations, and in that process the map becomes dynamic and loses a center. This can come as a bit of a shock, particularly when talking about theology – when talking about the way something like "ultimate reality" might wholly render my immediate life in an actual situation. What does it mean to speak of more than one such thing? And yet, here we are, where we find ourselves having to do precisely that. This shock has the distinct benefit, however, of prodding one to look up from obsessed map-making and to enter back in to the world. In all of this wandering, *I* had been discovering new territory, but it was only *new* territory *for me.* In a knowledge-production system that rewards originality and innovation, it is perhaps not a very smart thing to say, but it is most likely on the reader's mind anyway: I understand that none of the foregoing points are original to

22 See Andrew D. DeCort, "Pilgrimage: An Ancient Model for Transformative Theological Education," *The Craft of Teaching in the Academic Study of Religion,* 5 March 2018, https://craftofteachingreligion.wordpress.com/2018/03/05/pilgrimage-an-ancient-model-for-transformative-theological-education/. (Accessed 22 May 2020)
23 *Pastoraltheologie* 108, no. 4 (2019).

me; they only record how *I* have learned of and about other theological knowledges.

And this reminded me of an important lesson about the way knowledges, including theological knowledges, function. As Ada María Isasi-Díaz and Eduardo Mendieta have argued in their decolonial epistemological approach, "Inasmuch as the stability and reach of knowledge is determined by its efficacy and dependability, its evocation is always a 'political move'."[24] The first peoples of North America did not first begin to exist upon "discovery" by Europeans; the expansion of a map does not correlate to expansion of physical territory. Furthermore, to adapt a well-known adage, not only is map not territory,[25] territory is not land (the semantic range of the Latin *terra* notwithstanding): Accounts of exploration and expansion of "territory" are reference-narratives about boundaries marking inclusions and exclusions. That is, they function by means of reference to the currently more powerful political, economic, and scientific interest-holders who have effected and can enforce the designated demarcations. As a child I was taught that Christopher Columbus "discovered the new world"; then I learned that, no, "actually" Norse seafarers had discovered it much earlier than Columbus. And I accepted these accounts even though I read about and visited dozens of times as a young person the Native American nations, who had been in the land for centuries upon centuries before Leif Eriksson. It was not until university that I understood that even the "actually" was still a European story – one that supported naturalization of the European settlement and expansion narrative, that erased horrors committed by European settlers, and that either aestheticized first peoples (usually as comically dumb or wildly violent) or simply ignored their presence altogether. To quote Isasi-Díaz and Mendieta again, "there is no knowledge claim that is not involved in some sort of power struggle."[26] For this reason, other peoples, the ways of life they have cultivated, and the narratives they tell are, analytically, to be distinguished from the narratives that a more powerful group tells about them, for the latter inevitably fit the encounter with otherness into categories that are perceptible and authorized by the more powerful (assuming it recognizes otherness at all).

The powerful exercise tremendous authority over what counts as knowledge – or, at least, knowledge worth having. Once more, Isasi-Díaz and Mendieta write: "the struggle between claims over, against, and despite politi-

---

24 Ada María Isasi-Díaz and Eduardo Mendieta, "Introduction: Freeing Subjgated Knowledge", in Ada María Isasi-Díaz/Eduardo Mendieta, *Decolonizing Epistemologies: Latina/o Theology and Philosophy* (New York: Fordham University Press, 2012), 10.

25 Jonathan Z. Smith, *Map is Not Territory: Studies in the History of Religion* (Chicago: University of Chicago Press, 1993 [1978]). The phrase is attributed to the Polish-American scholar Alfred Korzybski, who in turn credits Scottish-American mathematician Eric Temple Bell with giving him the idea.

26 Isasi-Díaz and Mendieta, "Introduction: Freeing Subjugated Knowledge", 10.

cal power" manifests itself in, among other things, "the struggle between knowledge and ignorance." The dark underside of this is that the powerful will themselves always be ignorant to the degree that the experiences of the non-powerful are silenced and erased. To the degree that knowledge is based on the exclusion of other resources, information, and perspectives, it is bad knowledge: unreliable, shifty, and likely to crumble under the impact of unforeseen consequences. With ignorance comes error, as decisions that must be made are made on the basis of incomplete and inaccurate information. And with error comes harm; erroneous judgements limit capabilities for achieving desired outcomes, resulting in injury, breakdown and collapse, loss, disease, and death – especially of the powerless. The production and maintenance of good knowledge is a highly ethically charged task that must be built on the liberation of subjugated knowledges and in reciprocity and mutuality.[27]

I have found that my approach to theological exploration, specifically, Christian theological study and research, increasingly follows this set of concern-vectors. For in theology, wherein matters of ultimacy come regularly into place, the epistemological vulnerabilities just outlined carry particularly catastrophic potential. In the context of a research university, research and attending knowledge-production about Christianity are given priority over questions of practice in the sense of training church leadership.[28] And yet, as I have been describing in this chapter, to prioritize theological research over the training of church leadership is not to prioritize seminars, conferences, and journal articles over lived Christian practice. And this leads me to the real crux of the matter for WDTD: If an epistemological goal is central in university-based theological research, then that research should be interested in all manifestations of Christian theologies, including the numerous "lived" theological expressions that take on more material and practiced forms. The map of my wanderings should aim at comprehensiveness. Good knowledge should also aim at correctness and accuracy in its representations of phenomena. I want my map to be a reliable guide.

---

27 See Walter Mignolo, "Decolonizing Western Epistemology / Building Decolonial Epistemologies", in Ada María Isasi-Díaz and Eduardo Mendieta, *Decolonizing Epistemologies: Latina/o Theology and Philosophy* (New York: Fordham University Press, 2012), 19-43.

28 Theological study traditionally has served the purpose of the training of church leadership; as a professional course of study it entails training both in theory and in the practice of church leadership, but it remains vocational training. I admit to being more interested, personally, in the task of descriptive research than cultivation of practice.

7. Conclusion: Good Theological Knowledge Requires Partnership and Methodological Agility

How are these *desiderata* to be achieved in mapping the landscapes of contemporary theological research? It seems to me that the minimal necessary (though not sufficient) epistemological conditions for preventing ignorance, error, and harm include, at least: (1) guaranteeing the ability of all affected parties to represent themselves before others in forms chosen by them; (2) a commitment of all other parties to listen to one another and to learn about others first from those others themselves; (3) the opportunity to "check" one's understanding of another by re-presenting what was learned to the presenters and asking whether the presenters are satisfied that the re-presenters have presented the presenters in such a way that they recognize themselves in the re-presentation; and (4) provisions for repeating steps 1-3 as necessary.

One of the biggest challenges facing theological research today, it seems to me, is that there is just *so much* theological data in the world to be collected, documented, and represented, and very little of that total "amount" (if I may be permitted to characterize theology so quantitatively) can be found or even accessed in one research context or format. Speaking from within Europe, this challenge is especially acute, first, for demographic reasons: The vast majority of Christians in the world today live outside of Europe, but the non-European theology represented in European theological faculties still constitutes an extreme minority of the theological work done - whether in terms of the proportion of European to non-European theologies engaged in required study or in terms of the ratio of European to non-European students, to say nothing of the numbers of non-European professors. If the purpose of theological study in Europe were only to train clergy in Europe, then this would be more understandable. But for theological research aimed at comprehensiveness and accuracy, a disproportionate focus on Europe or even the West can only produce incomplete, erroneous, and harmful theologies.

But it is a Gramscian situation, for while the old system is dying, the new cannot yet be born. The second factor making the challenge to theological research in Europe acute is that much theology outside of the West exists in forms not recognizable as "theology" within European theological knowledge production frameworks. Of course, Christians of the majority-world communicate their orientations in the nexus of ultimate-actual-immediate in reflected ways, just as any European believer does. As Gustavo Gutierrez famously wrote, "there is present [. . .] in every Christian community a rough outline of a theology [. . .] manifested in life, action and concrete attitude."[29] But while the European system of theological communication remains by and large text-focused (prioritizing monographs, articles, conferences, and the like), theolog-

---

[29] Gustavo Gutierrez, *A Theology of Liberation. 15th Anniversary Edition, with a New Introduction by the Author* (Maryknoll: Orbis Books, 1988 [1971]), 3.

ical communications in much majority-world Christianity also find expression in devotional objects, prayer cloths and anointing oil, CDs and DVDs, YouTube Channels, all manner of merchandise for sale in church shops, as well as social movements or even in extensive public service systems taken over by churches on behalf of the state, as in some West African Pentecostal megachurches who run banks, universities, restaurants, and extensive transportation routes. Are these things not "theology"? Why not? They may operate first on a material-experiential level, but they are nevertheless continuously calibrating what reality is ultimately like with the experience of how a social environment actually is in the immediacy of a particular community's life. This calibrating work, taking place in material and experiential registers, is the catalyst for the production of material and symbolic communications and norming practices, along with the texts and institutions that emerge to facilitate/regulate them. Renewed attention to material and experiential "primary sources" promises to be fruitful for future theological research.

This is not to say that "second-order", "model-for" theological observation and analysis are unnecessary or useless. To the contrary! Rather, it is to say that "second-order" theological reflection needs to find ways of attending also to "first order," lived theologies. It can do so, first, by forging creative partnerships that provide opportunities for self-presentation and, second, by approaching their theological self-understandings via social performances and artifacts that offer insight into communities' self-forming practice. The latter might be done using methods similar to those used by scholars of religion, cultural anthropologists, and sociologists in studying, for example, religion and ritual objects, religion and gendered bodies, religion and food, religion and animals, sacred space and architecture, and so on. Regarding the former, the WDTD symposia seeks to model one example of the formation of creative partnerships between the cultural scientists, academic theologians, and religious practitioners.

Combining the two, it seems to me that tremendous potential for research and learning about what theologies do around the world today and in the most diverse contexts lies along the path of qualitative theological research and fieldwork that engages in "observant participation" in and with communities, documenting, collecting, and curating reflected theological responses (in whatever form) to perceived problems and then comparing them cross-contextually in reference to identifiable transculturally shared pressures. In due course, "second-order" theological research can come to be recognized as itself an instance of "first-order" theology, one that, despite its ambitions to propose models-for what theology is and how to do it, nevertheless tentatively and humbly explores the vast landscape of theological communications around the world and seeks to chart ever new models-of social and ultimate realities, the vast horizons of which can never be finally drawn but beckon us forward all the same.

Bibliography

https://www.youtube.com/watch?v=nsWMUZ0dIyg;

https://www.youtube.com/watch?v=EfZ6OhRXaqQ

Chan, Simon. *Grassroots Asian Theology: Thinking the Faith from the Ground Up*. Downers Grove: Intervarsity Press. 2014.

"Christians Remain World's Largest Religious Group, but They are Declining in Europe". Pew Research Center. April 5, 2017. https://www.pewresearch.org/fact-tank/2017/04/05/christians-remain-worlds-largest-religious-group-but-they-are-declining-in-europe/ (Accessed May 3, 2020).

Calano, Mark Joseph T. "Ginhawa as Ethic of Panatà: Body Politics and the Devotion to the Black Nazarene." *Budhi: A Journal of Ideas and Culture* 22. no. 2 (2018): 43-74.

DeCort, Andrew D. "Pilgrimage: An Ancient Model for Transformative Theological Education". *The Craft of Teaching in the Academic Study of Religion.* 5 March 2018. https://craftofteachingreligion.wordpress.com/2018/03/05/pilgrimage-an-ancient-model-for-transformative-theological-education/. (Accessed 22 May 2020).

Devasahayam, V. *Outside the Camp: Biblical Studies in Dalit Perspective* (Madras: Gurukul Lutheran Theological College and Research Studies, 1994)

Freire, Paulo. *Pedagogy of the Oppressed,* trans. by Myra Bergman Ramos, with an introduction by Donaldo Macedo. New York/London: Continuum, 2000 [1970].

Geertz, Clifford. In *The Interpretation of Cultures: Selected Essays*. New York: Basic Books. 1973.

Gutierrez, Gustavo. *A Theology of Liberation. 15th Anniversary Edition, with a New Introduction by the Author.* Maryknoll: Orbis Books. 1988 [1971].

Harrison, Peter. "Angels on Pinheads and Needles' Points". *Notes and Queries* 63 (2016): 45-47.

Hofheinz, Marco, Frank Mathwig, and Matthias Zeindler, eds. *Freundschaft. Zur Aktualität eines traditionsreichen Begriffs*. Zürich: TVZ, 2014.

hooks, bell. *Teaching to Transgress: Education as the Practice of Freedom* (New York and London: Routledge, 1994)

Isasi-Díaz, Ada María and Eduardo Mendieta. "Introduction: Freeing Subjgated Knowledge". In *Decolonizing Epistemologies: Latina/o Theology and Philosophy*, edited by Ada María Isasi-Díaz and Eduardo Mendieta. 1-17. New York: Fordham University Press. 2012.

Kalu, Ogbu. *African Pentecostalism: An Introduction*. Oxford and New York: Oxford University Press. 2008.

Kim, Sebastian C. H. and Kirsteen Kim. *A History of Korean Christianity*. Cambridge: Cambridge University Press. 2015.

Kung, Lap Yan. "The Umbrella Movement and Kairos: The Church's Theological Encounter with a Political Movement". In *Theological Reflections on the Hong Kong Umbrella Movement.* Edited by Justin K. H. Tse and Jonathan Y. Tan. New York: Palgrave Macmillan. 2016. 107-130.

Luhmann, Niklas. *Gesellschaftsstruktur und Semantik. Studien zur Wissenssoziologie der modernen Gesellschaft, vols. 1-4* (Frankfurt am Main: Suhrkamp, 1980-1995).

Mignolo, Walter. "Decolonizing Western Epistemology / Building Decolonial Epistemologies". In Ada María Isasi-Díaz/Eduardo Mendieta, *Decolonizing Epistemologies: Latina/o Theology and Philosophy*. 19-43. New York: Fordham University Press. 2012.

Nouwen, Henri. "Anton T. Boisen and Theology Through Living Human Documents". *Pastoral Psychology* 19. no. 7 (1968): 49-63.

Orsi, Robert A. *Between Heaven and Earth: The Religious Worlds People Make and the Scholars who Study Them.* Princeton and Oxford: Princeton University Press. 2005.

Orsi, Robert A. *The Madonna of 115th Street: Faith and Community in Italian Harlem, 1880-1950.* New Haven: Yale University Press. 1985.

Pastoraltheologie 108. no. 4 (2019).

Robinson, Matthew Ryan. "'Fake Friends': Zur Toleranz und Freundschaft als soziale und theologische Werte, oder wie Theologie Studierende Geflüchteten nicht Hilfe gaben, sondern mit ihnen Freundschaft fanden." *Pastoraltheologie* 107. no. 7 (2018a): 333-352.

Robinson, Matthew Ryan. *Redeeming Relationship, Relationships that Redeem: Free Sociability and the Completion of Humanity in the Thought of Friedrich Schleiermacher*. Tübingen: Mohr Siebeck. 2018.

Robinson Matthew Ryan and Evan F. Kuehn, *Theology Compromised: Schleiermacher, Troeltsch, and the Possibility of a Sociological Theology* (Minneapolis: Lexington Books/Fortress Academic, 2019Sanneh, Lamin. *Whose Religion Is Christianity? Christianity Beyond the West.* Grand Rapids/Cambridge: W. B. Eerdmans. 2003.

Shank, David. "Le Pentecôtisme de prophète William Wadé Harris". *Archives de Sciences Sociales des Religions* 44. no. 105 (1999): 51-70.

Shank, David. "The Prophet Harris: A Historiographical and Bibliographical Survey". *Journal of Religion in Africa* 14. no. 2 (1983): 130-160.

Smith, Jonathan Z. *Map is Not Territory: Studies in the History of Religion*. Chicago: University of Chicago Press, 1993 [1978].

Troeltsch, Ernst. "Historical and Dogmatic Method in Theology." In *Religion in History,* edited and with an introduction by James Luther Adams. Translated by James Luther Adams and Walter F. Bense. (Minneapolis: Fortress Press, 1991), 11-33.

Tse, Justin K. H. and Jonathan Y. Tan, eds. *Theological Reflections on the Hong Kong Umbrella Movement*. New York: Palgrave Macmillan. 2016.

Contributors

Sara Abdella-Kedir (M.A. in Analytic Theology; University of Aberdeen) teaches theology and theological ethics at the Ethiopian Graduate School of Theology in Addis Ababa, Ethiopia. She studies theology and identity, with a particular interest in gender and nationalisms. She is currently working on a textbook for the Ethiopian context on ethnic diversity and moral responsibility.

Elorm Nick Ahialey-Mawusi (M.A. in Ecumenical Studies; University of Bonn) pastors the Living Generation Church in Hamburg. He served as the assistant coordinator of African Theological Training in Germany at the Academy of Mission at the University of Hamburg from 2011-2015, and as the director of African-European Theological Institute in Europe (AETIE) from 2013-2015. He has collaborated actively with the World Council of Churches (WCC), All Africa Conference of Churches (AACC), Evangelical Church in Germany (EKD), Association of Protestant Churches in Germany (EMW), Evangelical Lutheran Mission, and others on matters related to ecumenical relations, mission and intercultural theologies. Publications in the fields of ecumenical dialogue and ecclesiology in the context of migration include: "Reconciling the Odds: A Cross-Cultural Experience", in Amèle Adamavi-Aho Ekué, Pamela D. Couture, and Samuel George (eds.), *For Those Who Wish to Hear: Emerging Theologians on Mission and Evangelism* (World Council of Churches 2019), 31-42; and "Neo-Pentecostal Leadership of African Migrant Churches and the Abuse of Human Rights", in Theodor Ahrens/Werner Kahl (eds.), *Gegen Gewalt: Ökumeniche Bewährungsfelder* (Leipzig: Evangelische Verlangsanstalt 2012), 183-193.

Chukwuemeka Anthony Atansi (M.A., Master of Advanced Studies in Theology and Religion, S.T.L.; KU Leuven) is a research assistant at the Faculty of Theology and Religious Studies, Catholic University of Leuven, Belgium. He also holds previous graduate degrees in philosophy (2007) and theology (2012) from Bigard Memorial Seminary, Enugu, an affiliate of the Pontifical Urban University, Rome. His areas of research interest include Christology, Contextual Theology, Theology of Liberation and Transformation, and Christianity and Social Transformation. His doctoral dissertation is entitled *Christ the Image of Social Transformation: Towards a Transformative Christology in the African Context*. The work systematically explores the theological and practical significance of christological images, like healer, liberator and king for faith in Jesus Christ and societal transformation in Africa.

Che-wai Chan (M. Ed., M.A. plus) is completing the Extended Master of Ecumenical Studies at the University of Bonn. Before he started his study in Bonn in 2018, he worked as a school teacher in Hong Kong for 37 years. He taught Chinese History and advocated in working on Christian Life Education. Doing theological studies, to him, is a pilgrimage in search of identity.

Jayeel Cornelio (Ph.D. in Sociology; National University of Singapore) is Associate Professor and the Director of the Development Studies Program at the Ateneo de Manila University, Philippines. He is also Associate Editor of the journal Social Sciences and Missions and lead editor of the forthcoming Routledge International Handbook of Religion in Global Society. A sociologist of religion, he has written extensively on religious issues in relation to youth, politics, and development in the Philippines. Jayeel has held visiting posts at Lancaster University, the Chinese University of Hong Kong, and Lucian Blaga University of Sibiu and was a postdoctoral fellow at the Max Planck Institute for the Study of Religious and Ethnic Diversity in Göttingen.

Andrew DeCort (Ph.D. in Theology and Theological Ethics; University of Chicago) directs the Institute for Faith and Flourishing in Addis Ababa, Ethiopia, where he also founded and directs the Neighbor-Love Movement (www.balinjeraye.org). He has taught courses in ethics, theology, and Ethiopian studies at Wheaton College, the Ethiopian Graduate School of Theology, and the University of Bonn. He is the author of, among other other works, *Bonhoeffer's New Beginning: Ethics after Devastation* (Lexington Books / Fortress Academic 2018); "On Human Flourishing: A Call for Public Responsibility in Contemporary Ethiopian Christianity", in Samuel Deressa and Josh de Keijzer (eds.), *The Role of the Church in Fostering Democracy and Sustainable Human Development* (Lutheran University Press, Forthcoming 2020); and editor of Donald Levine, *Interpreting Ethiopia: Observations of Five Decades* (Tsehai Press 2014).

Martín Grassi (Ph.D. in Philosophy; University of Buenos Aires) is Professor at the Philosophy Department of the Pontifical Catholic University of Argentina and Research Assistant at the Buenos Aires National Academy of Sciences and the National Council of Scientific and Technical Research of Argentina (CONICET). From 2018-2020, he was an Alexander von Humboldt Research Fellow at the Institut für Hermeneutik at the Rheinische Friedrich-Wilhelms-University of Bonn. Further research stays include University of Oxford and Universität Bonn as an Oxford-Templeton Latin-American Fellow (2016) and in Université La Sorbonne (Paris I-Panthéon) within the Alexander von Humboldt Fellowship (2019). He has written several books, including: "Ignorare

Aude! La existencia ensazada" (2012); "(Im)posibilidad y (sin)razón: La filosofía, o habitar la paradoja" (2014); "La comunidad demorada: Ontología, Política y Teología de la vida en común" (2017). His current book project is a philosophical study of spirit and life in relation to political theology.

Eberhard Hauschildt (Dr.theol. in Practical Theology; Ludwig-Maximillians-University of Munich) is Professor of Practical Theology at the Rheinische Friedrich-Wilhelms-University of Bonn. His areas of research expertise include ecclesiology and pastoral care, including intercultural and interreligious pastoral care. He is currently a principal investigator in the DFG-FOR2686 research group "Resilience in Religion and Spirituality". Publications include: *Alltagsseelsorge. Eine sozio-linguistische Analyse des pastoralen Geburtstagsbesuchs* (Vandenhoeck & Ruprecht 1996); (with Uta Pohl-Patalong) *Kirche verstehen* (Gütersloher Verlagshaus 2016); (with Uta Pohl-Patalong) *Kirche* (Gütersloher Verlagshaus 2013); (with Claudia Schulz and Eike Kohler) *Milieus praktisch. Analyse- und Planungshilfen für Kirche und Gemeinde* (Vandenhoeck & Ruprecht 2008); and (with Claudia Schulz and Eike Kohler) *Milieus praktisch II. Konkretionen für Helfendes Handeln in Kirche und Diakonie* (Vandenhoeck & Ruprecht 2010).

Florian Höhne (Dr. theol. in Systematic Theology [ethics]; Friedrich-Alexander-Universität Erlangen-Nürnberg) is Research Assistant in Systematic Theology at the Humboldt University of Berlin. His teaching and research focus on current debates in theological ethics, with special emphases in public theology and digitalization. Recent publications include: Öffentliche Theologie. Begriffsgeschichte und Grundfragen (EVA 2015); Einer und Alle. Personalisierung in den Medien als Herausforderung für ein öffentliche Theologie der Kirche (EVA 2015); (with Jonas Bedford-Strohm and Julian Zeyer-Quattlender [eds.]) Digitaler Strukturwandel der Öffentlichkeit. Interdisziplinäre Perspektiven auf politische Partizipation im Wandel (Nomos 2019); (with Heinrich Bedford-Strohm and Tobias Reitmeier [eds.]) Contextuality and Intercontextuality in Public Theology (Lit 2013).

Inja Inderst (Practical Theology; RFW University of Bonn) is a research associate in practical theology in the Protestant Theological Faculty of the University of Bonn. Her main research interests are prison pastoral care, pastoral care and ethics.

Evan Kuehn (Ph.D. in Theology; University of Chicago) is a metadata specialist at Atla and interlibrary loan coordinator at North Park University, and has taught in the humanities and the history of philosophy at the University of Chicago and Trinity International University. He is the author of *Troeltsch's Eschatological Absolute* (Oxford University Press, 2020) and (with Matthew Ryan Robinson) *Theology Compromised: Schleiermacher, Troeltsch, and the*

Possibility of a Sociological Theology (Lexington Books / Fortress Academic 2019). His current work is focused on the development of ontologies and methods adequate to researching emerging problems in theology and the humanities more generally.

Dogara Ishaya Manomi (Ph.D. in New Testament; Johannes-Gutenberg-University of Mainz) is currently a lecturer in the Department of Linguistics and Bible Translation / Department of Biblical Studies at the Theological College of Northern Nigeria. Between March-April 2020, he was a visiting researcher at the Tyndale House, Cambridge. His research interests include New Testament interpretation and application, biblical ethics (historical, contemporary, and methodological), virtue ethics, and African ethics. His doctoral dissertation, which was awarded the prestigious Johannes Gutenberg University Dissertation Prize in 2019, conducted an interdisciplinary and comparative study of biblical ethics and virtue ethics theory. Dr. Manomi also leads the Initiative for Victims' Educational and Economic Development in Northern Nigeria.

Constantin Plaul (Dr.theol. in Systematic Theology; Martin-Luther-University Halle-Wittenberg) is Research Associate at the Institute of Systematic Theology at the Martin-Luther-University Halle-Wittenberg. He is the author of *Verstehen und Religion im Werk Wilhelm Diltheys. Theologische Dimensionen auf kulturphilosophischer Grundlage* (Mohr Siebeck 2019). He has edited several recent volumes on theology and social transformations, including: (with Anne Käfer und Florian Priesemuth) *Der reformierte Schleiermacher. Prägungen und Potentiale seiner Theologie* (DeGruyter 2020); (with Malte D. Krüger, Christian Polke, Arnulf von Scheliha) *Freiheit Denken: Protestantische Transformationen in der Gegenwart* (Peter Lang 2020); and (with Marianne Schröter and Christian Senkel) *Fundamentalismus. Vom Reiz des Einfachen in Religion, Politik und Wissen* (Mitteldeutscher Verlag 2020). He is currently writing a book on protestant media ethics in a digital age.

Esther D. Reed (Ph.D. in Theology; University of Durham, UK) is Professor of Theological Ethics at the University of Exeter, UK. Her research interests centre around the concepts of responsibility and citizenship – with particular reference to the many and complex issues associated with globalization, international law, human rights, social justice and citizenship, artificial intelligence and autonomy in weapons systems. She has written on Theology for International Law (2013) and The Ethics of Human Rights: Contested Moral and Theological. Her most recent book, The Limits of Responsibility: Engaging Dietrich Bonhoeffer in a Globalizing Era (2018), is about the concept of responsibility in an age when connections between agent, act and consequence fall apart.

Cornelia Richter (Dr.theol. in Systematic Theology; Philipps-University of Marburg) is Professor of Systematic Theology and Hermeneutics in the Protestant Theological Faculty of the University of Bonn, where she currently leads the transdisciplinary research group "Resilience in Religion and Spirituality" (DFG-FOR2686). She has authored and edited numerous books and articles, including recently: *Bodenloses Vertrauen. Performanzphänomen in Humanwissenschaften und Theologie* (Forthcoming from Mohr Siebeck); *Die Religion in der Sprache der Kultur. Schleiermacher und Cassirer - Kulturphilosophische Symmetrien und Divergenzen* (Mohr Siebeck 2004); (with Dietrich Korsch [eds.]) *Die heilende Kraft des Sinns. Viktor E. Frankl in philosophischer, theologischer und therapeutischer Betrachtung* (Kohlhammer 2018); *(ed.) Ohnmacht und Angst aushalten. Kritik der Resilienz in Theologie und Philosophie* (Kohlhammer 2017).

Matthew Ryan Robinson (Ph.D. in Theology and Religious Studies; Northwestern University) is Research Associate in the Protestant Theological Faculty of the University of Bonn, where he works at the intersections of Systematic Theology, Intercultural Theology and Religious Studies. Recent publications include: *Redeeming Relationship, Relationships that Redeem: Free Sociability and the Completion of Humanity in the Thought of Friedrich Schleiermacher* (Mohr Siebeck, 2018); (with Evan F. Kuehn) *Theology Compromised: Schleiermacher, Troeltsch, and the Possibility of a Sociological Theology* (Lexington Books / Academic Fortress 2019); (with Kevin Vander Schel [eds.]), *Beyond Tolerance: Schleiermacher on Friendship, Sociability and Lived Religion* (De Gruyter 2019). He is currently writing a book on hospitality and friendship in relation to theological method. He organizes the What Does Theology Do, Actually? project and book series.

Hadje Cresencio Sadje (M.A. in Ecumenical Studies; University of Bonn) is an associate member of the SOAS Center for Palestine Studies, University of London, UK. In 2016, Mr. Sadje obtained M.A. degrees in Crosscultural Theology degree at the Protestant Theological University, The Netherlands, and in ecumenical Studies from the University of Bonn. He is currently a graduate student in in Theology and Religious Studies at the Evangelical Theological Faculty in Leuven, Belgium. In the world of practice, he has worked with the Christian Peacemaker Team Greece, Caritas Brussels, World Student Christian Movement-Europe (WSCM-Europe), EAPPI-World Council of Churches (WCC), Society for Intercultural Pastoral Care and Counseling, PeaceBuilders Community Philippines, and Pananaw Pinoy.

Eva Youkhana (Ph.D. in Sociology; Johann Wolfgang Goethe-University Frankfurt) is Acting Director and Deputy Professor in the Department for Political and Cultural Change, Center for Development Research (ZEF) at the University of Bonn, where she works on migration, religion, development, and human-nature relationships in Colombia, Ecuador and Spain using actor network theory and spatial theory. Recent publications include: "Die Untersuchung von Akteursnetzwerken in der kritischen Stadtforschung", *Forschungsjournal Soziale Bewegungen* 1, no. 32 (2019): 123-138; "Los espacios religiosos de los migrantes latinoamericanos y el poder político de los santos: la Virgen del Cisne en Madrid", in: Francesco Romizi (ed.): *Migrantes peregrinos. Trayectorias identitarias de la diáspora ecuatoriana en el espacio católico transnacional.* (Editorial Abya Yala 2018); (with Claudia Leifkes and Tomás León-Sicard) "Epistemic Marginality, Higher and Environmental Education in Colombia". *Gestion y Ambiente* 21, no. 2 (2018): 15-29; and (ed.), *Border Transgression: Mobility and Mobilization in Crisis* (Vandenhoeck & Ruprecht UniPress 2017).

Gianna Zipp (Dr. theol. in Church History; Johannes-Gutenberg-University of Mainz) is Research Associate in Church History at the Theological Faculty of the University of Greifswald. Her research focuses, on the one hand, on Lactantius, early Christian persecution, and the development of ecclesial history writing and, on the other hand, on post-WWII Protestantism, Gender and so-called "leftist Christianity."